CULTURES,
COMMUNITIES,
COMPETENCE,
AND
CHANGE

THE PLENUM SERIES IN SOCIAL/CLINICAL PSYCHOLOGY

Series Editor: C. R. Snyder

University of Kansas
Lawrence, Kansas

A Continuation Order Plan is available for this series. A continuation order will bring delivery of each new volume immediately upon publication. Volumes are billed only upon actual shipment. For further information please contact the publisher.

CULTURES, COMMUNITIES, COMPETENCE, AND CHANGE

FORREST B. TYLER

University of Maryland
College Park, Maryland

KLUWER ACADEMIC / PLENUM PUBLISHERS
New York   Boston   Dordrecht   London   Moscow

Library of Congress Cataloging-in-Publication Data

Tyler, Forrest B.
    Cultures, communities, competence, and change/Forrest B. Tyler.
        p.   cm — (The Plenum series in social/clinical psychology)
    Includes bibliographical references and index.
    ISBN 0-306-46497-7
        1. Psychology—Philosophy   I. Title.   II. Series.

BF38 .T95 2001
150'.1—dc21   00-047987

ISBN: 0-306-46497-7

©2001 Kluwer Academic / Plenum Publishers, New York
233 Spring Street, New York, N.Y. 10013

http://www.wkap.nl/

10 9 8 7 6 5 4 3 2 1

A C.I.P. record for this book is available from the Library of Congress

Printed in the United States of America

Oliver-Smith pointed out the lessons for all of us in the dramatic efforts of survivors in Yungay, a small town in the mountains of Peru, who struggled to rebuild their lives and their community, which had been wiped out by an avalanche in May, 1970:

> We are not merely the passive pawns of powerful forces, whether they are natural or historical, submitting unquestioningly to conditions beyond our control. While we may not be able to control those forces, we adapt, we alter, struggle, and, often, to use Faulkner's word, prevail. The lessons of this little Peruvian town [Yungay] are then, ultimately, not only how to survive materially and socially, but also how to restore meaning and significance to one's self and one's fellows. This is much more than surviving; it is prevailing (Oliver-Smith, 1986, p. ix).

PREFACE

I was born, socialized, and educated as a psychologist in the United States in the second quarter of the twentieth century. It is my view that all of these factors have contributed to the continuing development of my psychological beliefs and my ways of thinking and functioning throughout my life. As a person and as a psychologist, I believe it could not have been otherwise. In my view, our lives and our psychologies are enriched when we directly address the implications of being involved in our own conceptual systems and acknowledge that we do not just survive—we prevail. In this book, I have outlined why I think the way I do about our current psychological approaches and have proposed some changes which I believe will improve them.

It seems evident to me that my personal culturally based socializing factors have contributed to how I understand my own and other cultures, as they do for everyone. Thus, it seems ethnocentric to presume that the evolution and forms of psychology in the United States have any relevance to other countries and cultures or vice versa. Yet, psychology crafted in the United States, for the most part, dominates psychological thinking throughout the world. Further, there appears to be considerable evidence that this psychological domination is based on a widely shared assumption that human interactions are one-way transmissions of theories, facts, methods, and values from the more powerful or enlightened to the less so.

I question the psychology that I was taught; even its present day assumptions provide an inadequate basis for understanding myself or others either as individuals or as members of communities and societies. Further, I am not certain that this psychology can account for the processes of individual and social change within or between contexts. Whatever our relative social positions, we are constantly interacting as individuals, communities, and societies, and our interactions reciprocally influence us at all of these levels. All people have much to give and gain from any exchanges. I doubt that my conclusions rest entirely on my roots in the United States of the twentieth century. Rather, like the people of Yungay, I believe that I have prevailed over and transcended my limited circumstances. It is from this position that I seek to understand the interrelations between the lives of people and their societies.

Some of the seminal lessons I have taken from my experiences in life and psychology differ substantially from psychology's conventional wisdom. Central among these discrepancies is my belief that we are each involved in formulating a meaningful conception of our life out of our experiences and social contexts. Similarly, the nature of each society is shaped by the many individuals within it and by other social and ecological forces. However, individuals and social forces or systems are not completely intertwined; they can be studied and changed independently of each other, and frequently are. On the other hand, there are limits to how much either a society or individuals within it can change without the other also changing. Without some commonalities or compatibilities, some shared characteristics among and between people and the systems they have created, neither individual nor societal survival is possible.

Another conclusion I have reached is that there is inherently a *reciprocal* relation between each of us and our biopsychosocial context. It is evident in the relations between helpers and those who are to be helped, between specialists and nonspecialists. It is also apparent in the relationships between specialized knowledge, such as that of science and the conventional wisdom in which it is nested. That reciprocity has often been denied or ignored. However, until we acknowledge and understand such reciprocity, we cannot understand our own roles and our relation to society and the nonsocial world. The role of reciprocity must be considered in any effort to understand, undertake, or evaluate individual or social change.

One of my goals for this book is to provide a conceptual framework and guidelines for psychologists to relate their personal and professional activities and orientations to broader networks. Such a framework can enable psychologists to see that their personal and professional activities are interrelated and mutually supportive rather than separate or incompatible. Such synthesizing provides psychologists with new ways of thinking about being psychologists. It enables us to reconcile our personal, humanistic, and scientific perspectives in ways not currently available or acceptable.

Helped by developments in science and the philosophy of science, values and ethics, humanities, and psychology, I have obtained new findings from traditional research as well as from empirical evaluations of psychological and social programs. My explorations into the domains of cross-cultural, social, organizational, clinical, and community psychology have also familiarized me with a range of approaches to psychology, its relationships to other fields, and its uses. The distinctive new knowledge that has been generated in these fields and across cultures has provided a number of bases for challenging, interacting with, and incorporating these diverse approaches, particularly since this work is directed at overlapping areas of human conduct.

My interest in using psychology as a foundation for constructing an integrated basis for understanding people's lives and solving human problems led me to emphasize the potential contributions of the unidentified overlaps among these fields. I also spell out ways that these concepts and approaches can be used to enhance the quality of people's lives, their communities, and their societies. I do not wish to imply that we can free ourselves from the pain and suffering that are part of the human condition, but I do want to emphasize that we have far more substantial resources than we currently use to reduce suffering and increase the satisfaction in our lives. For example, an important contributing factor to my beliefs has been my participation in cultures other than my own. Integrating what I have learned from those experiences with the psychology I have been taught in the United States has provided me a richer framework for understanding and improving the quality of individual and social lives in any context.

My experiences have also led me to become acutely aware of the imperialistic approach and impact of Western psychology. Although its paradigms and perspectives are assumed to be universally applicable, they have been developed and standardized almost entirely in Western cultures. For psychological paradigms and perspectives to be generalizable beyond the context of their origin, a three-stage approach is required. First, we need psychological paradigms and perspectives that balance our emphasis on deficits and pathologies with an emphasis on strengths, resources, and our capacities to prevail. Second, as a basis for interrelating the separate paradigms that all people construct, it is necessary to acknowledge that these paradigms are embedded in our cultural, ethnic, and individual lives. Finally, we thereby identify the underlying role of participatory involvement in the collaborative processes of developing and maintaining any paradigm. In my judgment, the broader cultural, community, and individual approaches that have integrated these ideas have made a major contribution to the well-being of individuals and our societies. The purpose of this book is to convey the power of these ideas and approaches. I hope that you find them as compelling as they have been to me.

ACKNOWLEDGMENTS

There have been far more contributors to this book than I can ever acknowledge. My most important source of institutional support has been
the Department of Psychology at the University of Maryland, where I have
spent more than thirty years. A number of universities in other countries
have welcomed me graciously and have been more than helpful in accommodating my efforts to understand their worlds. My hosts have also been
unfailingly gracious and patient in their efforts to explain to me how my
world appears to them. Included have been the Universities of Allahabad,
India, and Waikato, Hamilton, New Zealand. In Bogotá, Colombia, there
were the Universities of Javeriana, Los Andes, and the National University. Also in Colombia, there were the Universidad del Valle, Cali, and
Universidad del Norte, Barranquilla. In addition, the National Institute of
Mental Health, National Science Foundation, Agency on Aging, Office of
Substance Abuse Research, Fulbright Commission, and Indio-American
Fellowship Program have provided institutional and financial support
without which most of my journeys and much of my work would not have
been possible.

Equally vital to my understanding have been the people in many
walks of life and countries with whom I have had an opportunity to
interact. Their vitality and commitment to the joy of living even under the
harshest of circumstances never cease to amaze me or rejuvenate my own
spirits. Their generosity and trust in sharing their lives and experiences
with me have been truly remarkable and greatly appreciated. They have
given me far more in the way of insights and wisdom than I have been able
to provide in return.

Finally, there are the people who read this manuscript many times and
contributed much to making it intelligible and coherent. Among them
have been several psychology students to whom I am particularly grateful;

they are Ragnhild Aukland, Sarah Blumenthal, Sarah Hiller, Anne Priftis, and Stephanie Weiss.

Most important, my wife Sandy has been a relentless and unforgiving editor in forcing me to organize my often wayward thoughts. She has also been a wonderfully supportive and caring wife and companion. I am in far greater debt to her than I will ever be able to repay.

My editors at Kluwer Academic / Plenum have been more than patient and understanding with my tardiness in completing this work. I am deeply grateful to them. It is my hope that the response of readers will make them feel that their investment has been worthwhile.

CONTENTS

INTRODUCTION
A Transcultural Ethnic Validity Perspective

We can justify thinking about ourselves as individuals whose conduct is based in our biogenetic heritage and shaped by our ecology and our psychosocial history. We are also capable of creating new possibilities and transcending our pasts. To support those beliefs, we have to take account of the complexity of our lives and societies. We must conceptualize our sciences and professions, cultures, communities, other social organizations, and individuals in ways that embody their internestedness. Part I provides a conceptual framework that is consistent with this view and the reasoning and empirical evidence that support it. I call this integrated formulation a transcultural ethnic validity model (TEVM). To provide a framework for understanding the concepts in the model, this section summarizes relevant background considerations, describes nested frameworks, and provides a paradigmatic historical perspective.

CHAPTER 1

BACKGROUND

INTRODUCTION

One of the most striking aspects of arriving in a new culture, community, or relationship is that it seems simultaneously fascinating and chaotic. We are confused by our mixed reactions and discover that we must reorganize our understanding of ourselves and find new ways to conceptualize and manage these unfamiliar experiences and situations. That kind or reorganizing is an ongoing part of all of our lives, and our capacity to do so is a particularly important aspect of what makes us distinctive as a species. In this process, we rely on our previous experiences, skills for coping with and prevailing over circumstances, and capabilities for learning.

I believe that, although all of us have these skills and capabilities, we have not fully incorporated them into our psychological theories and approaches. I will argue that to understand these characteristics and build on the possibilities they offer we need a comprehensive paradigmatic formulation that I call a transcultural ethnic validity model (TEVM). This paradigmatic formulation is based on the assumption that we guide our lives by creating diverse conceptions of ourselves and our collective realities within the limits of our natures and our social and physical contexts.

At its broadest, the work of psychologists is directed toward organizing their observations into coherent frameworks in order to understand, predict, and guide human conduct. These frameworks must meet scientific standards and serve as guides so that we can use that information. Further, it is important to realize that the particular framework (or paradigm) we use determines in important ways the aspects of human conduct that will be studied, how they will be studied, and what will be done with the knowledge produced from those studies.

For a variety of reasons, there has been and continues to be controversy about the most appropriate way to structure psychological knowledge. The structural form or paradigm on which modern psychology was originally built was that of the physical sciences. There is considerable debate as to whether that model is adequate for the study of human conduct. For example, unlike inanimate matter, people have capacities for abstraction, develop senses of self-awareness, and have long social histories.

Regardless of the resolution of that controversy, the formulations that guide psychologists in their work are paradigm-like in their characteristics and serve the same functions as those used in the physical science paradigms they have emulated. In order to understand psychology's characteristics, as well as the people who produce and use it, information is first needed about the defining characteristics of the general paradigms used by the sciences. Knowing what is involved internally and externally in order to change paradigms can help make that process more manageable. We also need to know what psychology's paradigms are and the purposes they serve. Therefore, background material about the nature of paradigms is presented in this chapter in three sections.

In the first section, the historically dominant conception of scientific paradigms is described. The sciences have been developed not only because of their problem-solving capabilities, but also because they have organized their approaches into the coherent conceptual frameworks we call paradigms. These paradigms add substantial efficiency in solving a large class of problems, or at least in improving our capability for manipulating and managing them. One of the basic assumptions of these paradigms is that subjective factors limit the accuracy of all human observations but do not have any further systematic effect on human conduct. It is also assumed that the subject matter under study is not influenced by being studied and does not actively participate in that process. Most Western-oriented universities teach that psychology is a relatively straightforward search for truth, much in the manner of the physical sciences. Many psychologists approach their subject matter in this way. That is, they assume that people can be studied like inanimate objects because human conduct is determined by people's components and the processes by which they combine. Consequently, no special problems are expected to arise in the scientific study of human conduct. The first section of this chapter explores both the general nature of these deterministic paradigmatic approaches and the implications of how they have been applied in psychology. In this section, the nature of such paradigms is outlined and attention is called to the implications of how they have been applied in psychology.

Constructivist paradigms are described in the chapter's second section. People using them assume that human conduct and its meaning are determined by the people involved in that conduct. From this view, it is meaningless to consider the nature of people's reality apart from their construction of it. Both the data and the paradigmatic framework used to understand it are thought of as subjectively constructed and part of the ongoing dialogue of people's lives.

Described in the third section is a *transcultural ethnic validity* paradigmatic framework that encompasses both of these other perspectives. It approaches the study of human conduct by including both how people create and use distinctive conceptions of their own individual and collective realities and how the possibilities and limits of their natures and their social and physical contexts influence their range of possibilities. This paradigmatic framework is the only one that incorporates all of the earlier-listed assumptions about the nature of human conduct. One of the objectives of this book is to present arguments that a TEV paradigm is best able to account for the complexities of human conduct that we encounter in individuals and across the range of diversity found in the world's cultures.

TRADITIONAL PARADIGMATIC FRAMEWORKS AND HOW THEY HAVE SHAPED PSYCHOLOGY

It is somewhat confusing, but the term *paradigm* refers both to a field of study in general and to any content oriented framework within a field of study. In either case, a paradigm's range of applicability is limited by the nature of the phenomena to which it is applied. Consequently, paradigms developed for one field of study, such as physics, may need to be modified to be applied in another field, such as psychology. Also, a paradigm developed to study one aspect of human conduct, such as cognition, may need to be modified to study another area, such as emotion.

PARADIGMATIC COMMUNITIES

Paradigms do not exist apart from the people who use them. They are embodied in, identified with, and perpetuated by groups of scientists who share much in common. These scientists communicate well among themselves because they have adopted the same biases and make similar professional judgments. They form communities in relation to their formal and informal exchanges about their shared approaches and areas of work. Their shared sense of commonality is based on their similar educations in the same academic disciplines, memberships in professional societies, external certifications, and related activities. These closely knit communities exist because their members identify themselves with each other and use the terms central to their common paradigm as the basis for working with the phenomena of their common concern. In that sense, they organize their world much in the same way that devotees of sports or music do, using the metaphors of their particular focus to communicate about an extensive range of issues and interactions.

CONCEPTUAL MATRICES

A community of scholars working on a common set of problems needs a shared way of organizing activities and a shared language for communicating with each other, the broader scientific community, and the public. Their paradigm serves these purposes by providing a conceptual matrix that includes symbolic generalizations, laws, models, exemplars, and values. These aspects of each paradigm and their functions are described in the following paragraphs.

Symbolic Generalizations

The names given to formally designate the observable (e.g., person) and hypothetical (e.g., trait) objects of study of a particular scientific community are called symbolic generalizations. In Western medicine, common symbolic generalizations include terms such as organism, host, transmission, and disease process. In psychology, common symbolic generalizations are person, environment, behavior, superego, self, unconscious, and trait. The phenomena that we designate as symbolic generalizations indicate what we consider to be the significant aspects of our subject matter. For example, *superego* is defined as the storehouse of feelings about right and wrong. In ordinary conversation in AngloEuropean cultures we use the term "conscience" to refer to these phenomena.

Laws

The nature of the relationships among symbolic generalizations is specified by the laws within the paradigm. Laws are the rules that govern the development, occurrence, maintenance, transformation, and elimination of the content of the symbolic generalizations. In psychology, symbolic generalizations such as motives, stimuli, reinforcement, and extinction refer to elements and process effects that are linked in causal sequences. These sequences are called laws when empirical verification determines that they have predicted effects on people's conduct.

Models

Models outline the nature of the subject matter being studied and the relationships among its components (symbolic generalizations) as expressed by the laws within the paradigm. A well-known paradigmatic psychological model is Freud's hydraulic model. In it, he proposed that psychic pressures act like those of water and other liquids to force the expression of behavior. In contrast, stimulus–response models view human conduct as developing in a mechanical, deterministic way so that a given conditioned stimulus (e.g., a light) automatically produces a particular conditioned response (e.g., an eye blink). Such models are used by their adherents to identify the nature of the relationships among the factors that influence a phenomenon under study. For example, the model of intelligence that we endorse determines how we will study differences in ability and what we well recommend as ways to deal with those differences. In psychology, we have nothing even approaching a comprehensive model that accounts for human psychological characteristics. The field is fractionated in many ways, and the adequacy of communication between different groups of psychologists (paradigmatic communities) is often quite poor.

Exemplars

The basic links to "common sense reality" on which paradigms are built are called exemplars. They indicate what is being studied and how the job of studying is to be done. They provide the information that allows everyone, from laity to professionals, to understand and deal with a given situation. As Kuhn (1970) noted, the paradigm's exemplars provide:

> the concrete problem solutions that students encounter from the start of their scientific education whether in laboratories, on examinations, or at the ends of chapters in science texts,... [plus] at least some of the technical problem solutions found in the periodical literature that scientists encounter during their post educational research [or professional] careers and that also show them by example how their job is to be done. (p. 187)

Kuhn's assertion has constituted a major challenge to the traditional assumption that problems are just examples and the basic content of science is in the theories and rules for applying them. He argued that the content within a scientific paradigm lies in the implicit aspects of learning to see the world in a particular way. To him, these tested and shared perceptions constitute the basis of the shared world of the members of a successful group of scientists. Through these exemplars, the novice acquires the shared perception that is essential for successful group membership. Polanyi (1964) provided a similar argument and even stressed that maintaining a scientific community requires intense and sustained efforts on the part of that community.

Psychology's exemplars provide concrete illustrations of what to look for as evidence of, for example, psychological disorder. In that vein, the psychiatrist–revolutionary, Pinel, created "mental illness" at the time of the French revolution by declaring that his patients' inappropriate behaviors were exemplars of illness, not exemplars of demonic possession or a criminal nature (Reisman, 1966). Thereby, he expanded the medical paradigm of illness to include mental illness as a generally accepted symbolic generalization. Since then, scientists, practitioners, and lay people have been faced with defining mental illness, determining its measurement, understanding it, and using this paradigm to diagnose and treat themselves and others.

Values

Built-in values provide the largely procedural guidelines that ensure the empirical power of scientific findings. Many of these procedural values are quite explicit, are widely shared, and are considered to be the distinguishing characteristics of scientific approaches to knowledge. They include empirical testability as a basic criterion for confirming the validity (truth) of any hypothesized fact or relationship in science and predictability as the most basic criterion for confirming that truth or validity. Accuracy is valued in empirical measurements, and quantitative accuracy is more highly regarded than qualitative.

In the traditions of science in the Western world, it is considered better to have knowledge than not to have it. This position is regarded as self-evident, not involving any value judgments, although to outside observers it may seem to be a value judgment. Mannheim (1936) documented that this position is a consequence of the historical development of science in the Western world. Differentiating the realms of facts and values served to shield the pursuit of empirically oriented knowledge studies from royal and religiously based criticism and sanction. Commitment to the approach that publicly verifiable knowledge is superior to the lack of knowledge or to other forms of knowledge, including distinctive individual unverifiable judgments, has served society well with regard to learning about the nonliving and many aspects of the living components of our world. However, another consequence of that decision with a less salutary effect has been to exclude value issues from explicit consideration and scrutiny within the realm of science.

Value-based subjective judgments are involved at all stages of scientific activity. Questions concerning what areas to investigate, what questions to ask, what information to seek as answers, and what judgments to make about the obtained results permeate scientific activities on a daily basis. Within the domains of the biological, social, and psychological sciences, there are additional judgments that center around issues such as the particular worth or survival of an individual or a species and how to take account of competing value claims on behalf of individuals and society at large. Further, the particular values of scientists influence their particular activities. Studying and using psychology becomes an interactive process that is influenced by values and is subject to the intrusion of unacknowledged values.

PARADIGMATIC CHANGE

Paradigms are not permanent. One of their functions is to facilitate the process of identifying their own limits and providing empirical grounds for their own replacement. The information outlined in the preceding paragraphs has, to a considerable extent, stressed the structural framework of the paradigms which characterize science. The science–knowledge enterprise also has a characteristic functional framework, a major component of which is called *normal science*. The process of normal science is similar to that of working on a puzzle designed so that it can be solved. It contributes to the systematic accumulation of knowledge and support for the larger paradigm. Examples of normal science endeavors in psychology include Skinner (1973) calling attention to operant conditioning, Rotter (1966) to locus of control, and Barker (1964) to the study of environments.

As investigators such as these demonstrated the salience of their discoveries, they attracted others to use the normal science puzzle-solving approach to explore particular aspects of human nature or of other species. For example, Rotter hypothesized in his social learning theory (1966) that peoples' beliefs in whether they can control the reinforcements they receive (their subjective expectancies) are important determinants of their conduct. That hypothesis led to the introduction of new measures into the field of personality assessment, to thousands of studies, to changes in therapeutic approaches, and to people focusing on their own subjective expectancies (Lefcourt, 1984). As with other hypotheses, investigators eventually found that there are numerous significant problems that cannot be solved using this specific puzzle format. At that point, they began to question the paradigmatic model, concentrate on its limitations and contradictions, and seek alternative frameworks.

Periods of paradigm change are inherently contentious, but they eventually produce a new set of discoveries around which a new consensual paradigmatic model is built. The involved fields then accommodate their older *truths* or *realities* to this newer paradigm which, in turn, is explored and utilized until its limits become more important than its contributions. It is worth noting that all of psychology's conventionally accepted paradigms have changed radically over the past century, differ somewhat in contemporary cultures, and are currently in states of flux.

Scientific Revolutions

Scientific discoveries provide the bridge for the noncontinuous transitions in scientific fields between normal science and scientific revolutions. Scientific revolutions are "noncumulative developmental episode[s] in which an older paradigm is replaced in whole or in part by an *incompatible* new one" (Kuhn, 1970, p. 91). They are precipitated by a sense of *system malfunction* and involve a choice between incompatible modes of proceeding. Since each new theory must be logically incompatible with the old (in some points only, of course), revolutions are, of necessity, changes in world-views. For example, the shift from Newtonian physics to Einsteinian physics is not completely reversible; neither is the shift from a Freudian focus on sexuality and the unconscious to a behaviorist focus on conditioning of stimulus–response connections. That is because what occurs in such a revolution cannot be reduced to a reinterpretation of individual and stable data. The data are based on interpretations, so they are not completely stable and will be different when viewed from another perspective.

The decision to adopt a new paradigm is one of persuasion, as there is no standard higher than assent of the scientific community. That can, and does, occur because our data are not unequivocally stable. Reality involves interpretation; our findings are not "given," but collected with difficulty. The embeddedness of paradigmatic perspectives in both the internal and external realities of the adherents is what makes paradigmatic shifts necessarily occur to some extent beyond the conscious rational control that scientists so highly value in themselves and believe is guaranteed by their approach.

One of the strengths of scientific paradigms is that they are structured so that the expected outcomes of procedures and courses of events can be specified. Consequently, paradigms are judged to be deficient when unexpected outcomes occur (a) that cannot be accounted for within the paradigm, and (b) whose significance would not even be evident unless investigators had known what to expect. Anomalies may also be found by accident and facilitate paradigmatic change. For example, following a tragic nightclub fire in the United States during World War II, psychiatrists

Gerald Caplan and Eric Lindemann assisted in the care of the survivors as well as the families and friends of its victims. Their observations about people's responses to crises led them to formulate a new understanding of how people grieve and heal from such traumas. That new understanding, in turn, became the basis for their development of a crisis intervention paradigm (Lindemann, 1944) and contributed to the creation of a community mental health paradigm.

Theory-induced pressures and improvements in scientific instruments can also contribute to new discoveries and provide a stimulus for paradigm changes. For example, comprehensive statistical analyses made possible by the advent of computers demonstrated that theory-based psychotherapies are so limited that we can never train enough psychotherapists to provide needed therapeutic services. The pressure to seek other approaches to ameliorate people's psychological difficulties gave substantial impetus to the development of a community psychology paradigm.

Science and Progress

As of this point, scientific approaches have been characterized as having two main components, *normal science* and *revolutionary science*. The first emphasizes the systematic accumulation of knowledge within a paradigm. The second emphasizes that the paradigmatic framework is deficient in ways that limit progress. However, Kuhn argued that science cannot be said to progress to reality, to "some one full, objective, true account of nature" (1970, p. 171). We are left to question whether there is scientific progress and, if so, what form it takes. Kuhn's answer is that, within a paradigm, steps toward solving problems is progress. Further, even in paradigm shifts there is "evolution from the community's state of knowledge at any given time" (1970, p. 171) because the scientific community moves to a new state of knowledge based on new discoveries.

A new paradigm is considerably less fleshed out in its earlier stages. It provides an impetus and context for shaping new personal, scientific, and social identities and priorities, and new approaches to identifying questions, procedures, criteria, answers, and inferences. Eventually, people accept these new identities, priorities, and methods. They begin using them to guide their efforts to expand their understandings, solve their problems, and enrich their lives. While the forms of new states of knowledge are not totally predictable, they do incorporate important aspects of their predecessors and provide a basis for addressing previously intractable problems. Progress in science parallels the history of changing views of the world as scientific discoveries have challenged successive paradigmatic systems. Each paradigm was accepted as a true picture of reality while it was dominant. It has lost favor as it has been found deficient in addressing questions considered important by the scientific community supporting it.

A number of arguments have been advanced as to the adequacy of Kuhn's formulations for describing, understanding, or directing scientific enterprises. Criticisms have focused on his emphasis on (a) the predominance of a single paradigm; (b) the nature and degree of incompatibility of succeeding paradigms; (c) the relative role of conceptual, empirical and political (persuasion) factors in the birth and demise of paradigms; and (d) the question of continuous progress. While the answers to these questions are indeed important and interested individuals may wish to pursue them (see Gholson & Barker, 1985), they do not materially affect the Kuhn-based arguments.

This process of paradigm development and overturn has largely characterized the history of psychology and psychologists' commitments to their successive deterministic paradigms of individuals and societies. The historically dominant paradigm in psychology has assumed that we can be understood only if we are conceptualized as objects whose nature changes in deterministic ways independently of any discretionary capacities to respond selectively to events. However, paradigms that were designed to study the nature of nonliving phenomena may need reformulation before they can be used to study living phenomena. Even further modifications may be needed for adequate understanding of human conduct and for solving, or at least ameliorating, human psychological problems. Polanyi (1968) pointed out that a hypothetically complete molecular or atomic description of an organism would not provide a basis for judging whether it was dead or alive. Atoms, molecules, or chemicals have the same properties whether they are part of a lifeless rock or of a living or nonliving human. From this perspective, in order to understand living systems, it is essential to introduce what Polanyi called the "principles of right functioning" among an organism's components and then study it from that perspective to determine whether or not it is alive.

In studies of the organic or psychological nature of living beings, particularly humans, we become focused on specific outcomes with particular implications. Which atoms make up an individual is irrelevant; the kinds of relationships the individual is involved in are significant. Accounting for these complex discretionary aspects of human relationships and the principles of right functioning are the major challenges to the adequacy of the physical general paradigmatic form for studying human conduct. These major ongoing challenges are addressed in the next two sections.

CONSTRUCTIVIST PARADIGMS

There has been a long-standing controversy in psychology over the existence and role of mind, consciousness, and choice in people's lives. The behaviorist position has been that the "mind" can be reduced to biological functioning and that symbolic generalizations such as "mind" add nothing to scientific understanding of human conduct. In contrast, some psychologists have insisted that symbolic generalizations such as mind, consciousness, and choice refer to emergent properties of human conduct that are not directly reducible to less holistic patterns of functioning. These incompatible assumptions between the two paradigms have far reaching consequences.

Concepts such as mind, consciousness, and choice provide a basis for understanding how people contribute to the construction of their own lives and use their capabilities to define and redefine their interests in relation to those of others. The constructivist argument is that psychology's existing paradigms need revision before they can attend to the omitted study of people's roles in creating their own realities. This questioning of the adequacy of mainstream determinist psychological approaches has been their major contribution. By arguing that these problems are legitimate to study, they have turned the scientific community to considering some important questions for psychology which cannot be stated in the conceptual terms of the traditional community or measured with its instrumental tools.

CONSTRUCTIVIST CONTRIBUTION

Constructivist paradigmatic frameworks emphasize the importance of symbolic generalizations such as self-efficacy and self-awareness and the possibility that people create, monitor, evaluate, and even change their paradigms. In this framework, at any given time, people both guide their lives with their previously developed understandings of events and incorporate their ongoing experiences into their established paradigms or into new ones as they construct them. Gergen (1985) summarized core aspects of this perspective, emphasizing that it does not offer a basis for obtaining *objective* knowledge. However, he noted that science's traditional approaches have not proven that they can meet that criterion either. A constructivist paradigm does introduce a criterion that knowledge and the rules that regulate it be, of necessity, culturally and historically embedded. It does take a step toward identifying the nature of knowledge as constructed.

Adoption of a constructivist perspective also requires that moral (value) criteria be explicitly acknowledged as part of scientific practice. This stance also makes it clear that scientists are constructing their scientific knowledge and can no longer justify a position of detachment and moral neutrality. They no longer have grounds for saying that knowledge exclusively reflects external states of affairs with its nature in no way determined by those studying or using it.

At least one consequence of a constructivist theory perspective is that it changes our conception of the nature and purpose of science. The traditional view says that the purpose of science is to identify reality, to establish a nondiscourse-based (detached, value-free, culture free, etc.) description and explanation of events. In that view, science is about establishing and describing truths (facts) that are independent of the implicit and explicit communication limitations of the participating scientists. Discourse theory, a contrasting constructivist point of view, argues that the purpose of science is to establish the prevailing views of the scientists, their communication basis, and how these views are being used (e.g., what actions they prescribe and proscribe).

According to the discourse theorists, mainstream psychology is a social and psychological world view constructed by its adherents. It gives its adherents differential power over nondominant groups and their members. That is, it defines the nature of dominant group members (e.g., men, heterosexual, Caucasians, Anglo Americans) and nondominant group members (e.g., women, gays, African Americans, persons from the third world) as being possessed of particular inherent natures rather than as being from socially constituted statuses. In that same sense, mainstream science does not question the legitimacy or purpose of the category "race." It is committed, for example, to demonstrating that the reality of African race as defined by Caucasians is embodied in African Americans and functions causally in their lives. Since that racial status is defined and evaluated in relation to the nature of Anglo Americans (whose nature and merit are not subject to review), African Americans are "defined" as deviant and inferior. The view of African Americans is considered a *point of view* while the view of the mainstream Anglo scientists is considered to be the *unbiased truth.*

Sampson (1993) focused on common features of challenges by specific nondominant societal groups in the United States, as mentioned above, to the presumed right of dominant groups to assign devaluing psychological identities to them. The nondominant groups considered any attempt on their part to accommodate their interests to those of the dominant group as destined to be unsatisfactory. That is, the dominant group sets the terms for being a "full" human in ways that advance its own interests. In other words, mainstream scholars view all individuals from their own culturally normative perspective and, therefore, classify nonmainstream individuals inaccurately and to the latter's disadvantage. Unless all individuals and groups are allowed to participate in defining their own identities, those definitions will inevitably put them at a disadvantage.

Sampson (1993) emphasized that discourse theorists argue that talk constitutes the realities of our lives; it does not express a reality that existed before language nor is it independent of language. They assume that there is no reality more primary than our own constructions of it. This second assumption fundamentally challenges conventional wisdom. It raises the question of whether there is a reality other than that constructed by discourse, including the status of what others have considered to be reality. According to Sampson, discursive theorists do not deny reality; rather, as Wetherell and Potter (1992, p. 65) noted,

> New Zealand is no less real for being constituted discursively—you still die if your plane crashes into a hill whether you think that the hill is the product of a volcanic eruption or the solidified form of a mythical whale. However, material reality is no less discursive for being able to get into the way of planes. How those deaths are understood … and what caused them is constituted through our systems of discourses.

In other words, they argue that the ways we define events take on a reality that is as significant in its own right as is what we are defining.

From this constructivist view, words are not *just* representations of deeds, etc., which exist apart from discourse. They are the acts which define those deeds, and in that sense they are deeds themselves. They define what we consider (and can consider) to be real. For example, the belief of Hindus that they will live many different times on this earth makes their reality very different from those who believe they live only once.

Sampson (1993) stressed that there is a final consequence concerning the possibility of dialogue between individuals with a discursive perspective and mainstream psychologists. His point is that these two groups can have a dialogue among their variously positioned standpoints only if they don't abandon their perspectives and don't presume that their perspectives have primacy. That is, mainstream psychologists must abandon their belief that they possess unbiased truths and methods before they can participate in such a dialogue. In addition, the nondominant groups have to abandon the view that they are the only experts qualified to define their own reality and the realities of others. Only then can proponents of the two groups begin to formulate a shared position which would not give either an unquestionable advantage. That position would still be socially constructed, but would incorporate the perspectives of the different participants in a new way, giving neither side the insurmountable advantage of being able to preemptively exclude the other's personal, social, theoretical, or empirical referents.

What that new way would be is less clear. The basic question that constructivists need to answer is how they link the reality of our ongoing experiencing selves with influences from our past experiences and with our social and biological natures. Partial answers to this question can be found in representative approaches to conceptualizing the nature of the self. Schlenker (1985) provided a historical review of major themes and changes in our self-conceptions and noted that *self* has proven to be a somewhat elusive term. However, he also cited how attempts to define the nature of the experiencing self have consistently included acknowledgment that there is more to people than just that self. For example, in modern Western thought, Descartes most fully developed the idea of a separate mind and body. The Scottish moral philosophers introduced the concept of the social self, asserting that a science about people had to consider the relations between a person and society. Early in American psychology, the distinction between self as knower and self as known appeared in the writings of William James. Sociological approaches assumed that society and individuals do not exist independently of each other but individuals are active agents (*knowers*, with judgmental and decision-making capabilities) in the interaction. Psychological approaches assumed that individuals and societies are separate, with individuals considered passive (*known products* of life processes).

For several decades, experimental social psychologists have demonstrated that there are circumstances under which individuals function as knowers. They even choose to misrepresent themselves in order to obtain unwarranted favorable outcomes. These findings resulted from explorations of the dynamics of ingratiating behavior in humans and showed that we create impressions that have an *egocentric bias* and include a public persona (Jones, 1964). Further studies indicated that these misrepresentations subsequently influence public perceptions and, in turn, private perceptions people have of themselves (Jones, Rhodewalt, Berglas, & Skelton, 1981). Such findings suggest that over time our conduct involves sequential patterns of self–self and self–world interactions, some of which may be directed by the self as knower and some of which may be a product of the self as known. These studies support that we do contribute to the construction of our personal and social realities, to misrepresentation of them in order to accomplish desired effects, and to being influenced by people's responses to our presentations.

In brief, the contructivist critique of mainstream psychology is limited as a paradigm in that it does not provide an adequate formulation of how to account for empirical evidence that is consistent with an externally oriented, reductionist account of humans. Further, its adherents have not addressed how traditional and constructivist paradigmatic approaches might complement or supplement each other and, therefore, how they can be integrated. However, there is support for its basic argument that any psychological paradigm must include attention to our roles in constructing our own realities and further, that unless individuals or groups are allowed to participate in defining their own identities, any definition will put them at a disadvantage.

A TRANSCULTURAL ETHNIC VALIDITY FRAMEWORK

unless we ask others!

Although we cannot directly know how we function as knowers, we need to specify how we can approach psychological inquiries in ways that will allow us to identify the processes of everyday living. To do so requires bridging the gap between deterministic and constructivist views of people to incorporate these different, psychologically based approaches to mind, body, history, and society with those used by all of us in everyday living. The TEV approach I have proposed rests on a number of basic assumptions about our functioning as knowers. They are summarized here to make their nature and role explicit.

1. *People are active, creative beings* who live by organizing their lives and societies.
2. *People create organization in their lives by a core psychological process of abstracting*, of assigning *meaning* to the events they experience.
3. *People's abstracting occurs progressively in relation to the time-embedded, ongoing course of their lives.* These abstractions combine to provide the basis for an emergent property of discretionary choice as a central aspect of our lives.
4. *Living is an open-ended process requiring choices across a wide range of situations and with differing consequences.* We are inextricably involved in influencing our own fate and the fates of others around us.
5. *We bear a responsibility for our well-being and destruction.* Specifically, we have the potential to construct psychosocially benign and supportive patterns of living as well as psychosocially destructive patterns for ourselves, individually and collectively.
6. *The sciences directed at studying humans are humanly constructed enterprises in which both scientists and their subjects are involved.*
7. *The value systems developed for guiding humans are humanly constructed enterprises in which we are all participants.*

8. *Our sciences and value systems serve us best when we are most aware of and responsive to their limits as well as their possibilities.*

These assumptions provide a basis for incorporating knower characteristics and their implications into our approaches to human conduct as outlined in the following sections.

THE NATURE OF A COMPREHENSIVE INTEGRATED PARADIGM

A psychological paradigm is needed that provides scholars and lay people with a basis for understanding, for instance, the trauma faced by the survivors in Yungay (see the Preface) and how some of the survivors prevailed over that tragedy while others succumbed to it. Such a task requires that we: (a) define the nature of science as more than a detached, value-free pursuit of truth, (b) build our science on people's subjective decision making in ways that enable us to integrate our studies of our conduct with those of our subjective processes, and (c) interrelate psychologists' disparate approaches in ways that enrich all of us along with our understanding of science and people. These topics are addressed in the following sections.

Define Science as More than a Detached, Value Free Pursuit of Truth

A declaration that science is not a detached search for truth need not lead to the conclusion that it is simply and completely subjective. Most of us who are psychologists acknowledge our inability to establish absolute truth as opposed to statistical and probability-labeled truth. For example, we have rules for working with the trade-offs involved when choosing a balance between the rejection of hypotheses on statistical grounds when they are valid and not rejecting them when they are non-valid. We use our scientific approaches as a somewhat self-correcting mechanism to reduce bias and error in untested observations and continue to check on those which have been tested.

As already discussed, values enter into science. We need further consideration for how they enter, how we can understand their role, the differences that values make, and what we can do about their impact. Historically, the goal to reduce the role of subjective bias, including values, was a major factor that led to the development of the scientific method with its decision rules and serial checking of observations. At this point, we need to reexamine how well that method has served us, seek to improve our procedures, and make more informed uses of the value elements in our scientific knowledge.

A colleague and I (McClure & F. Tyler, 1967) argued in considerable detail thirty years ago that values have been part of science all along and have not completely undermined the scientific endeavor. They underlie all claims about facts, but in ways that can be subject to criticism and reform. For example, to establish that an individual can discriminate colors, we have to identify something the individual desires or wishes to avoid (values) and make getting or avoiding it dependent on discriminating colors. If the individual cannot discriminate colors, he or she cannot obtain the desired outcome or avoid the undesired one. Someone may choose not to use their capability for discriminating for other reasons, but using this strategy in empirical studies is necessary to determine whether a respondent can make the discrimination being studied.

Values also are an essential part of *procedural controls*, the shared rules that guide scientific endeavors. They provide the criteria for judging the extent to which we can rely on our findings; however, they can also be counterproductive. By acknowledging their presence, we can use other procedural controls to assess their potential biasing effects. For example, investigators may use outcomes they value but that students do not in order to test academic performance capabilities of the students. That approach is likely to lead to underestimates and negative interpretations of the students' capabilities. Only by recognizing such value differences and establishing procedural controls to offset their effects can such biases be minimized.

Values can also be used to regulate sciences in relation to societal norms. They can be used to prohibit the use of procedures that harm or otherwise exploit participants in the pursuit of scientific information. On the other hand, they can be used to restrict research approaches that challenge people's beliefs. In either case, only if we acknowledge that science exists within societies' broader values contexts and can potentially challenge the bases of those contexts will we be able to address the role of values in science.

Building Our Science on People's Subjective Decision Making in Ways that Integrate Our Studies of Our Own Subjective Processes

We build sciences with uncertainty, in part because irreducible subjective processes enter into judgments about procedural controls and the nature of the data. The power of scientific approaches has rested on their built-in mechanisms for controlling explicit sources of bias. To extend that power, we need to identify and adjust for subjective biases.

Historically, examinations of the implicit subjective (tacit) elements of any paradigm have identified the socialization of the involved scientists. That socialization has usually been embedded in a formal educational process which encourages students to train themselves to exclude personal, cultural, ethnic, or other value-based considerations to be entering into their scientific world views. That process led to students succeeding by internalizing the field's paradigmatic framework as their version of reality. For example, in both basic and applied science-oriented fields, students are provided exemplars: characteristic problems and ways to investigate and understand them. This crucial part of our educational processes functions to teach neophytes how to conceptualize learnings, insights, and discoveries in a way that is highly congruent with those of their teachers and mentors. These conceptualizations are labeled and presented as *truths* and *direct representations of reality*.

Presumably then, a potentially powerful way to incorporate attention to the subjective and uncertain elements of any paradigm is to change the educational process for neophytes into a more complex socialization process. It would include increasing students' awareness of the cultural context, knowledge context, and values/preferences context in which they and the field are embedded. This approach would introduce possibilities for students to contribute more actively to their own education and the ongoing education of their mentors. It would better enable them to evaluate their own questions about the field, as well as the field's substantive, procedural, and value bases, and to do so with some understanding of the contextual framework in which the field is embedded. It would not only provide students an enriched self-awareness for entering into a chosen scientific field, but also contribute to the process of developing, critiquing, and using the science. Scientists and students would begin to accept that scientific facts and theories are shared representations which have been agreed upon as useful working models of reality in the chosen area of study. Further, they would be seen as having been organized from personal, social, and cultural experiences, as well as systematic empirical study by the members of that scientific community.

This type of paradigmatic conception is potentially of considerable value in providing a more comprehensive and defensible psychology. It provides a basis for including in our paradigm of psychology that we are capable of insights that transcend our current individual and collective personal and paradigmatic limits. We can incorporate the idea that we are somewhat free and detached from our situations and can contribute informed judgements about them. Yet, at the same time, we can acknowledge our own involvement in those systems and their outcomes. Maslow (1962) described such a stance as descriptive of the individuals he identified in his studies as healthy. As Schenkler (1985) documented, these ideas have a long history.

Interrelate Psychologists' Disparate Approaches in Ways That Enrich All of Them Along with Our Understanding of Science and People

Given that scientists are constructing their individual sciences out of their somewhat idiosyncratic existences and their shared experiences and educations, obtaining an objective unified science of psychology and psychologists is not possible. However, we have plentiful evidence that disparate approaches do come together, and we have an internal sense of unity in and among our knowledge fields. We need to think differently about the nature of these different paradigms and how to use them.

Mainstream deterministic psychologists study us as knowable objects in the manner of nonhuman species; constructivist psychologists study us as knowing beings. Perhaps these disparate positions supplement rather than contradict each other, and all along we have been switching back and forth without acknowledging it or examining how we were doing it. Since we have not been considering this interaction as part of our scientific endeavors, we now are required to create a new approach for doing so.

Hyland (1985) took such a step by proposing new theory construction rules that he saw as necessary for psychology "to progress as a single, theoretically based science" (p. 1003). His focus was on *person variables*, i.e., variables referring to individuals based on "the premise that they have some form of existence and are not just a convenient summary of data" (p. 1003). He differentiated between three kinds of psychological person variables, *physiological, mentalistic, and mechanistic,* saying that each grows out of a different assumption about the nature of human existence. *Physiological* variables come from the belief that human existence *is* physiological, and individual conduct is a product of physiological states. *Mentalistic* variables are based on the belief that human existence *is* mental and individual conduct is an expression of mental states. *Mechanistic* variables are founded on the belief that our existence *is* physical (mechanistic) in nature, and individual behavior is a product of mechanistic states analogous to the output of programs that are run by computers.

Hyland's proposal challenged the belief that any of these person variables is primary and adequate by itself to account for human conduct. He appealed to the concept of *complementarity*, defined as "a feature of any scientific discipline in which events can be fully described only by employing mutually incompatible forms of description" (Hyland, p. 1005). To work with complementarities, we must distinguish between *causal* relations and *identity* relations. "*Causal* relations can occur between person variables having the same nature, but not between person variables of different natures" (Hyland, p. 1006). *Identity* relations can be found between person variables of different natures when they are measured simultaneously, since no form of description can encompass the entirety of the meaning discernible in a phenomenon under study. These kinds of person variables are *not* separate realities, and none of them is *the* reality. Whether we are running, enjoying a sunset, or studying, physiological, mechanistic, and mentalistic processes are involved together; they are not separately causing each other.

TASKS IN DEVELOPING AN INTEGRATED PARADIGM

It follows from Hyland's argument that reliance on only one paradigm limits our capacity to describe a phenomenon and understand its fullest possible meaning. Rather, psychological theory, psychologists, and the public are better served if we construct overarching approaches that incorporate the meanings that different systems contribute. Such paradigmatic frameworks must integrate the complementarities of (1) people as knowers and as known; (2) concerns with facts and with values as well as with the personal subjectivity and the generality of scientific laws; (3) differing research/theory and basic and applied paradigms; and (4) universalism, particularism, and transcendism.

People as Knowers and as Known

Sperry (1992) added conceptual arguments to those of Hyland, proposing that cognition is an emergent property of human functioning, not a property of a mind separate from the body. He argued further that cognitive properties of a complex organism cannot be predicted from a knowledge of that organism's separate parts. Rather, these holistic properties must be studied at the level of their functioning.

Sperry included the idea of *reciprocal causation* between people's knower (cognitive) and known (e.g., behaviorist) properties, using the example of a wheel rolling down a hill. While the atoms function in the same way at any point on the hill, the overall functioning of the wheel determines their location in the world. This point also applies to the example of people moving from one culture to another; our atoms and cognitive processes function in the same way, but that knowledge is of little value in understanding why we decided to move or experienced culture shock when we arrived. Hyland (1985) added that the more levels of analysis we exclude, the more we restrict the meaning that we obtain, ending up with less complete truths. Describing any phenomenon from the perspective of only one system limits our knowledge and understanding of the meaning of that phenomenon.

Specifying the nature of the relationships between levels of analysis presents a more complex problem. Reciprocal causation between these levels suggests that what Sperry (1992) called reciprocal causation corresponds to what Hyland called *identity relations,* the simultaneously occurring relations between levels of functioning within a complex organism. Causality is customarily used to identify sequential relationships between phenomena as observed over time at any given level. Causality carries with it an implication of if–then relationships, not now–together relationships. For example, any of us may choose to learn another language. Doing so will depend in part on the commitment we make (as *knowers*) to that task, the general approaches we have acquired to learning, and our biological status (including how old we are) at the time of our decision. These knower and known factors operate simultaneously to influence our success at learning the language, but they do not cause each other.

Conceptualizing and studying the person as a knower in a way which cannot be accounted for by a reductionist analysis presents a major challenge to psychology's historically reductionist approach. This new approach provides evidence that there may be a more complete truth about people than we have been able to learn with the earlier one. If people can use acquired meanings to influence their future choices in nondeterministic ways, then the concepts of science and free will are not mutually exclusive. Smith (1972) argued as follows:

> The indeterminate is *not* what people have meant by freedom. It certainly provides no basis for a conception of ethical responsibility. What we mean by freedom, rather, is *personal causation* or *self-determination,* causal processes with ascertainable antecedents in which the *self* figures as an agent. The antonym of freedom is not determination but constraint. Freedom is limited by causal processes that bypass the self or constrain its options of choice; it is enhanced by processes that increase one's range of choice and one's resources for attaining what one has chosen. (p. 18)

These ideas tell us that we can think of ourselves as having choice as knowers with differing capacities for self-determination and also as constrained by other causal processes that are part of us as known individuals.

Reasoning similarly, Sperry (1992) provided a definition of free will (as not contradicting determinism) because "freedom of will is defined to mean, not freedom from *all* causation but degrees of freedom to do whatever one's subjective inclinations may lead to" (p. 275). That is, free will refers to the extent to which individuals can utilize their *knower capabilities* (their minds) to guide themselves in ways that are not predictable from a deterministic analysis of their history and condition as *known subjects.* Rather, it includes people's capacity to function consciously—to be self-

aware and self-reflexive and thus able to analyze and reanalyze the significance of events and construct and evaluate alternative meanings and
possibilities as bases for future actions.

Integrating Subjectivity, Facts and Values, and the Generality of Scientific Laws

Building a psychological conception of people as complex, intertwined, knower–known, voluntaristic–deterministic organisms is a complex task. However, it is something most of us understand at a common
sense level. We believe that we are influenced by our natures, our pasts,
and our imperfect capabilities; but we also believe that we show judgment
and decision-making capabilities. We think of these characteristics, including how we form and destroy relationships and societies, as reflected in
parallel ways in the internal and external aspects of our lives. We rely on
them to provide the basis for building powerful systems such as the
sciences to aid in understanding and guiding our lives. Sciences cannot
tell us what to value; they can only tell us reasons why we value what we
do, the consequences of acting on those values, and how to change them if
we choose to do so. They can also help us control the ways our values may
mislead us when we are trying to understand ourselves and others.

We use these knower components of ourselves to guide our lives
within the possibilities and limits of our known characteristics and our
external contexts. Our task as scientists is to understand how we link our
constructions (meanings) from our past experiences to our current interpretations (the meanings we assign to events) to formulate a basis for
action and to construct the meaning of our actions. To accomplish that
linking successfully requires taking account of the imprecision and uncertainty of knowledge, the inherent diversity in people's experiences and
perspectives, and the above mentioned capabilities of people to find
shared commonalities and differences.

Because of our subjective differences, it seems impossible for a person
to make exactly the same judgment twice, for two people to make exactly
the same judgment, or for two people to have exactly the same scientific
paradigm. Neither does it seem possible for any people to have identical
belief systems, whether they concern science, religion, politics, culture, or
more individual matters. Since we all contribute to the construction of
these larger explanatory systems, it also does not seem possible for us to
construct an overall, unified explanatory system. However, we do find
coherence in our individual lives and experiences, and we identify and act
on shared meanings about the nature of experiences and events. Since we
have lived for centuries with these apparent contradictions, it seems evi-

dent that we are able to build on combinations of beliefs and selected empirical input.

By elaborating on this central model of ongoing human conduct, a paradigmatic framework can be constructed that can incorporate both complementary and contradictory relationships among distinctive approaches to psychology and other general academic and historical systems. For example, Sperry (1992) proposed that, in the interest of our individual and species survival, we need religions which can be linked to science and sciences that acknowledge and support people's constructions of their belief systems. He emphasized that "what we value depends on what we believe, and what we believe about ourselves and the universe has come to depend very much on science" (Sperry, 1992, p. 277).

The shift to a reliance on the empirically verifiable for making life decisions has brought a changed sense of the role of ultimate values in our definitions of reality and evolving nature. Sperry (1993) argued that science and religion need to reconcile, noting:

> A new sense of the sacred holds our greatest hope for redirecting human priorities in a manner that now seems imperative to avert disaster.... Accordingly, and in conjunction with hierarchic value theory, it is important to note that our described paradigm shift logically retains human spirituality, conceived to be the highest peak or growth tip of evolution. As the most critically powerful determining factor shaping world events, our evolving human spirituality is preserved, but, it is interpreted in terms that *do not conflict with modern science* [italics added].... In another approach, morality is viewed in terms of a supreme plan for *existence on planet earth* [italics added]. (p. 12)

Sperry's suggestion may provide an important pathway to an increased likelihood of human survival. However, he did not address the problems that arise from differences between the values imposed by some belief systems and those of scientific perspectives. For example, the highest value of some religions is survival beyond this life and world with the destruction of this world being the route to eternal spiritual survival. In contrast, some sciences see the destruction of religious belief systems as essential to human survival. The need to address such conflicts reflects the point just made that decision rules are required as a basis for any shared endeavors. Decision rules are needed for resolving disputes, for establishing what range of disagreement is acceptable, and for how to proceed when there is agreement among the parties involved.

Sperry (1993) acknowledged that a deterministic scientific perspective is inadequate as a basis for guiding our lives and we need to include the role of individuals as knowers. However, he did not discuss the idea that science may also function as a kind of religion because it can be used as what the sociologist of science, Mannheim (1936), called a *general paradigm*. That is, scientists often consider that their science provides a perspective which cannot be questioned and serves as a basis for critiquing all other positions. Such a paradigm provides a justification for rejecting the values and truths of other systems such as the humanities and historically and culturally based value systems such as the religions. Neither does Sperry consider that religion may function as a *general paradigm* for people. Those people may reject other systems, including science. Thus, both scientists and religionists, as well as others who views their own system as *the general paradigm*, reject the possibility of developing an interrelated complementarity with other explanatory systems.

As noted earlier, integration of incompatible perspectives requires that the proponents of each arrive at some shared agreement as to how their beliefs can be legitimately scrutinized from the perspective of alternative systems. Psychology can contribute to the establishment of such shared agreements by making a commitment to use its methods to question even its own biases and hidden assumptions. One objective of this text is to use psychological methods to identify such biases and assumptions while also identifying our substantive and procedural contributions to people's individual and collective well-being.

Scientific Models and Methods

Using scientifically based models and methods is a powerful way of figuring out the generality of psychological laws and of individual and cultural beliefs, and the significance of historical events. It can also identify the value bases and empirical strengths and limitations of alternative approaches to human endeavors. For example, psychology's development has been influenced by efforts to establish its legitimacy as a *general paradigm* of a physical sciences form. Consequently, models preferred by psychologists have been those of experimental science and statistical probability survey analyses. Further, psychology has been divided into basic and applied areas (F. Tyler, 1970). In basic areas, phenomena have been studied apart from their history or context, or both, in controlled laboratory settings. This approach has been considered to provide unbiased value free, and therefore more legitimate, truths. In contrast, psychologists in applied areas have explicitly and directly been concerned with the value (however measured) of specific effects and, even more directly, with accepting responsibility for producing those effects. Until recently, both frameworks assumed that people's lives developed within a universal, homogeneous context and an evolutionary perspective with regard to sociocultural and individual differences. Psychologists also assumed, often implicitly, that their own cultural and social context is the legitimate one on which to base their value judgments.

However, all psychologists live in and are products of their own individual and sociocultural contexts, and the psychologies they produce are based in those contexts. Each of these contexts and psychologies can be shown to have empirically verifiable strengths and limitations. To include consideration of contextual factors requires the development of a different kind of paradigmatic perspective for psychology. Psychology needs a historically embedded, multicultural perspective with a focus on the changing nature of knowledge and values and the irreversible nature of human lives.

The perspective within psychology that has most embodied such an approach is applied, oriented, life-span developmental psychology. Its focus has been understanding and informing the public about many of the psychological processes that become cumulative over the extended lives of individuals. Despite often being ethnocentrically based in just one culture and one historical era, these more comprehensive developmental studies more closely approximate the diversity of our lives, our contexts, and our roles as knowers than do ahistorical acontextual studies. Incorporating concepts such as "knower" provides a basis for considering the exercise of choice as an understandable aspect of holistic human behavior. Such changes provide a basis for including material from current, limited, and disconnected paradigms and contribute to efforts to construct an overarching paradigm for transcending their limited foci.

Universalism, Particularism, and Transcendism

As my colleagues and I (F. Tyler, Brome & Williams, 1991) emphasized, there are paradigmatic differences as to who within psychology is considered qualified to study, understand, and provide expert services to whom. These paradigms also impact on the possibilities for constructing more comprehensive psychological paradigms with the new information being generated and new challenges raised to existing ones. We classified the advocates of these different views into the following three groups. The *particularists* argue that only those with similar characteristics such as race, gender, ethnicity, culture, or psychological persuasion can study, understand, or provide services to each other. The *universalists* argue that none of these factors are relevant to understand and work with psychological principles and processes because they are the same for everyone. Both of these positions are characteristic of determinist-oriented psychologists.

The third group, *transcendists*, incorporate the views of the universalists and particularists. They argue that people with different characteristics and backgrounds can understand and work with each other and that each has something unique to offer the other. They suggest that any group has blind spots about itself that can be informed by the perspectives of others with different backgrounds. The transcendist position includes the belief that each person's approach to living is a product of her or his culture, history, destiny (both from inborn characteristics, such as gender, and from accidents of birth, such as time and place of birth), and autonomy (range of discretionary choices). This kind of position is central to the possibilities of building the more comprehensive paradigm outlined in this book.

SUMMARY

This chapter emphasized that all of us contribute to our own lives as self-aware knowers by developing systems for understanding and influencing ourselves and our external living and nonliving worlds. We learned, consequently, that it is important for us to include attention to these diverse influences in our psychological theories and interventions if we are to enhance the quality of our lives and societies. An overview was provided of how academic and professional psychology has been developed as a scientific endeavor with a paradigmatic form like that of the physical sciences. That approach was evaluated, and the costs and benefits of studying ourselves in the same way we study inanimate objects and nonhuman animals was summarized. Particular attention was paid to the inability of this approach to address the role of subjective factors in people's perceptions and of people as sentient beings who influence and are influenced by their life experiences. Finally, the issues basic to the development of a paradigm that encompasses the complexities of our natures were identified. The chapter was concluded with a description of the nature of a psychological paradigm that can integrate these considerations. That paradigm, called here a transcultural ethnic validity paradigm, provides the organizing framework of this book.

THE STRUCTURE OF A NESTED FRAMEWORK

INTRODUCTION

It is impossible for any framework to be completely objective. Consequently, any paradigmatic framework needs to be addressed, understood, evaluated, and used with reference to the context of its origin, current situation, and the perspective of its supporters. A paradigmatic framework which attends explicitly to the nested nature of human creations may offset some of the major limitations imposed by existing paradigms because it includes attention to that nestedness. The term *nested framework* can refer to the way the overall system or paradigm relates to its broader context, to the paradigm and its embedded components, or to the way the components in the system relate to each other and to the system itself. These differentiations are arbitrary because a framework and it components are all interlinked, but at times it is useful to focus on these aspects in relation to each other. In this book, whether the term *nested framework* is used to refer to the overall configuration or one of these embedded frameworks is indicated in each specific instance.

Constructing, using, or evaluating a framework to understand human conduct requires choosing a starting point. There is no logical starting place; consequently, an arbitrary choice has to be made on the basis of the intended purpose. I have chosen the individual in context as a particularly appropriate beginning point for my framework because my goal is to provide a psychological understanding of ordinary human living. My approach is based on the following assumptions. First, we as individuals are active agents who form our realities, seek to advance our individual and collective understanding of them, and then use that understanding to enhance the quality of our lives. Second, we would not want or try to understand ourselves unless we had a capability for self-reflection; that capability must be included in any understanding of ourselves. Third, we, individually and collectively, are the ones who benefit from knowing what we contribute to the process of guiding our own futures.

THE ROLE OF THE INDIVIDUAL

It is commonly accepted that at birth, human infants do not have a functioning self-awareness capability and so cannot make and be accountable for informed decisions. Instead, they are expected to evolve that capability as a function of their physical growth, psychological development, and socialization experiences. Philosophies, religions, and other collective approaches to societal ordering establish an age or developmental stage considered to define a status of autonomy, accountability, or reason. With the advent or attainment of this autonomous status, we humans are considered to have some capacity for making and being responsible for our choices and actions. Understanding this two-faceted nature of our selves, i.e., our independence from our context and our embeddedness in it, is the core issue in understanding human conduct.

As emphasized earlier, even as scientists we have not been able to transcend our human natures to become totally independent or objective observers. In other words, it has not been possible to eliminate or transcend the subjective factor in human observations, the so-called *personal equation*. At a minimum, it is important to identify the limitations that this personal equation factor places on our efforts to understand and manage ourselves and our worlds.

The term *personal equation* was initially introduced into the domain of experimental psychology through a series of events in astronomy (Boring, 1929). In 1796, Kinnebrook, the astronomer royal at the Greenwich Observatory, realized that his assistant, Maskelyne, was not recording star positions accurately. Rather, his observations were deviating from Kinnebrook's in a consistent manner. Kinnebrook dismissed his assistant, but also reported this discrepancy to other astronomers. They began to investigate the possibility of this occurrence in their own observatories and by 1815 had arrived at the consensus that it was not possible to eliminate the *personal equation*. This insight led to the realization that they were studying their own observations, not the stars.

The evidence has continued to build that we cannot completely transcend the inherent limits to a framework in which we are its instrument of our knowledge (e.g., Churchman, 1948; Polanyi, 1968; Kuhn, 1970). That evidence has further indicated that the personal equation exerts an influence at all levels of our human observations and judgments. Scholars such as Polanyi and Kuhn have identified and emphasized its presence in our most basic knowledge, the most elemental sensory perception that Polanyi called *tacit* knowing.

It may not be possible to eliminate personal equation factors in human judgments or identify them directly, but they are not completely unidentifiable. We identify them indirectly by making inferences such as the following: (a) people are responding to some reality beyond themselves because there are commonalities between the observations of different observers, (b) people differ because their observations are not identical, (c) we can learn something about people as *known* (knowable) sentient beings by studying their patterns of conduct. In these ways, we can learn about their distinctive inlying and acquired characteristics as well as their external circumstances.

The personal equation is also a component of the functioning of people as *knowers*. Lefcourt (1973) highlighted this point in a challenge to Skinner who had asserted that concepts such as choice and freedom are prescientific illusions that do not serve people well. Lefcourt rebutted this argument by agreeing that such beliefs are illusions, but so are beliefs of control by external events. He marshaled substantial empirical evidence in support of his point that the illusions which we choose have important consequences for our survival and well-being (Lefcourt, 1973, 1976). That is, people make judgments about the extent to which they can control situations, and they act on those judgments when deciding how to deal with their lives in those situations. When people judge that they control their lives, they learn more from experiences and, for example, actively take better care of their health. In effect, our judgments about the nature of the world serve to change our realities. We act for good or ill on the basis of those judgments.

Lefcourt's (1973, 1976) evidence provided scientific confirmation that each person's role as knower has a causal effect on his or her life. That effect is also progressive, and, as we come to know that we influence our futures by making choices, we potentially become self-reflexive. That is, we become capable of thinking about ourselves as choosing to influence our lives. This capability not only adds another level of complexity to our potential self-input as knowers, it can be repeated infinitely. Similarly, to the extent that we assign properties (e.g., intelligence, rationality, etc.) to others, we also influence the lives of those individuals. Discourse analysis and identity oriented groups refer to these levels of influence in their arguments that we must change our conceptions of people to create more equitable discourses among dominant and nondominant groups (Sampson, 1993).

Incorporating the idea of *person-as-knower* into a nested framework paradigm of human conduct provides a mechanism for considering the role we each have in the construction of our realities. It provides a basis for exploring the question of whether as *knowers* we influence only our explicit choices or also contribute to our *tacit* knowing. For example, when we are socialized to make distinctions among people on the basis of pigmentation or gender, do those learned concepts influence our implicit frameworks for making future judgments about all people? If our knower-based constructions about our psychosocial worlds influence our patterns of perceiving the world, then it would follow that our personal equation characteristics are also influenced by our broader socialization in addition to our personal experiences. That possibility is quite important as a basis for understanding and interacting with people from differing ecologies and with differing histories and identities. It suggests that we can identify at least some of the collective, as well as individual, implicit personal equation factors in humans. Even so, we can never consider human activities as being fully determinable; we must consider them as inherently open and not entirely predictable.

The question of where to start in seeking to understand human behavior has an added component; we must include the factor that human functioning is itself an imprecise process. Consequently, we begin by arbitrarily picking a starting place with the realization that there is at least a degree of uncertainty involved. We begin by accepting that all beginnings start with a leap of faith, resting on some "facts" (ordered experience) as well as some "values" (desires, wishes, senses of good and bad). Each beginning empowers us in the sense that it provides a basis for and a direction to our activity; that activity forms a psychosocial spiral as we accumulate internal and external consequences. However, each beginning also restricts us, as it closes off the possibilities inherent in other psychosocial leaps we could have made. At some point, continuing to build on any particular psychosocial leap may no longer seem worthwhile, so we abandon it, make a leap to another starting point, and build on it.

SOCIOCULTURAL KNOWLEDGE SYSTEMS

The role of these paradigms in our lives can also be analyzed from the perspective of the field of sociology of knowledge. Mannheim (1960) founded the field and defined its basic structure and functions as including theoretical and research studies of the social origins and nature of human knowledge. Its goal is to analyze the relationship between knowledge and existence; its research aim is to trace the various forms which that relationship has taken in the intellectual development of mankind.

Mannheim (1936) insisted that human knowledge must be understood in relation to two concepts: (a) the significance of the nontheoretical conditioning factors in knowledge, and (b) our means of knowing how the symbolizing capacities of humans relate to their actions, particularly to directing their actions. These two factors are the same as those from the psychological perspective referred to earlier as contributing to the nature of humans as *known* beings. However, Mannheim, at least implicitly, also assumed that people function as *knowers*, as individuals and collectives who are capable of making self-aware, knowledge-based decisions. Further, his primary concerns were directed toward the social factors that contribute to people's acquisition and use of knowledge and to the social consequences of how they use it, once acquired.

Consistent with his sociological orientation, Mannheim's (1936) first concern was to identify how our social circumstances contribute to our learning about the relationship between our existence and our knowledge. Specifically, it is exposure to different social circumstances that forces us to become aware that our previously acquired knowledge may not apply to all situations. It also informs us that at least some of the conditions of our existence have a social nature.

He cited how different kinds of changes in our individual or group social circumstances have the effect of showing us that our knowledge is based in our experience and our social circumstances. For example, on an individual level, when we leave our family to set up our own home, our individual and social positions change and we are forced to change our understanding of both. At a group level, the members of a community may be forced to become refugees and relocate because of their identity. They face the same kinds of pressures because their basis of existence is shifted away from its traditional norms and institutions and they must establish new ones. In addition, when two or more socially determined modes of interpretation within a society come into conflict, they are forced to confront a third type of change. The many conflicts in recent history between entrenched dominant social groups and nondominant groups seeking to improve their positions by obtaining more equitable access to education and employment exemplify these struggles. The proponents of the conflicting views reveal the flaws in each other's arguments by criticizing each other. In doing so, they establish conflicting perspectives that require all of them to confront the social basis of their situations and the social implications of the competing positions. Everyone involved is required to formulate a new perspective that is detached from their already entrenched ones.

The new perspectives may later become the recognized mode of thinking. These outcomes suggest that both a sociology of knowledge and a psychological approach must consider the impact of events on the formation of the self and self-reflectiveness and on the constructivist possibilities detailed earlier as indicators of the *knower* characteristics of people.

With these ideas as our basis, we can now hypothesize that people may form three interlinked knower perspectives to protect and enhance the quality of their lives: detachment, relationism, and particularization. Possibly the most basic of the three is *detachment*, our ability to consider any relation or situation as only one of many possibilities. For example, we may come to see that the traditional division of household labor between husbands and wives is only one of many perspectives. From an analysis of how our views were formed, we can conclude that their origins lie, at least in part, in social customs.

The second knower perspective is the concept of *relationism*. That is, all knowledge, without exception, has arisen from some social structure. Its validity cannot be asserted absolutely but must be considered in relation to that structure. For example, the truth of any concept, such as the definition of intelligence, is a function of the social contexts in which is was formed and to which it is being applied.

Particularization is the third knower concept. The scope and extent of the validity of any knowledge is limited to the social structure of its origin. For example, any people's "knowledge" that it is human nature to be competitive arises out of their limited social context; we cannot assume that it is natural in other people's particular circumstances. Rather, the meaning of human nature and other such concepts differs from group to group, and each such definition is valid in its context.

IMPLICATIONS FOR UNDERSTANDING SCIENCE

Mannheim (1936) reasoned that, of necessity, any knowledge and the system which spawned it arise in a particular historical social context and can be analyzed to determine their underlying social contextual origins. He applied this approach to Western science, particularly political science, in order to understand it as a knowledge system, and provided us with a distinctive perspective for answering the critical questions raised earlier. These questions include: How do people become aware of their knowledge systems or change them, or do both to develop a scientific approach? How do knowledge systems function politically, and what difference has a scientific approach made? What does an analysis of the origins of science tell us about science and its implications for humanity's current situation? Answers to these questions, particularly for psychology, are addressed below.

Mannheim (1936) constructed a historically based, sociology of knowledge approach for critiquing science. According to him, the context of the western world's emergence from the Middle Ages was marked by the rise of craftsmen as a growing middle class. They began to gain worldly power by acquiring empirically grounded knowledge through the development of their crafts. However, they lacked political power and control over their individual and collective lives. Political power was vested in the clergy and the royalty by virtue of, respectively, divine right by revelation and birth, resulting in their unique, previously unchallengeable, position. As the craftsmen began demanding a share of political power and control of their lives and circumstances, a contest arose between them and the entrenched clergy and royalty. Mannheim argued that this emerging middle class achieved its very practical goal of gaining some power and control by gaining acceptance for the core ideas of western science. Those ideas are that rationalist style of thought is to be used to establish logical truths and that explicit measures and observer agreement are to be used to establish the validity of empirical knowledge. However, it was agreed that the scientific approach and its criteria applied only to phenomena accessible to observation by everyone.

There have been far reaching consequences from the decision to consider only observable phenomena for study and empirically demonstrable relationships as universal and necessary (factually valid) phenomena. It has excluded qualitative (nonquantitative in a mathematical sense) and unique phenomena from scientific study or as bases for challenging scientific truths. On the other hand, this approach has provided a protection against knowledge systems being assaulted by privilege, whether that privilege be the special claims of the royalty, the clergy, or representatives of any other "special" group. However, this scientific approach has costs which bear examination from the point of view of sociology of knowledge and with regard to its impact on our individual lives and the human condition in general.

One of these costs has been that the connection between people as members of their societies and as thinking and knowledge-accumulating individuals has been broken. For example, because of this distinction a controversy has arisen about whether there is any relationship between facts and values, general and specific knowledge, and basic and applied science. These controversies have generally been characterized in science by a polarization which pits advocates of so-called basic general factual knowledge against those of applied, specific, value-based knowledge. The former have considered themselves the *true* scientists representing an unbiased, value-free perspective. The latter have asserted that the values or interest-related concerns of individuals or groups are legitimate aspects of the processes for arriving at scientific understandings and applications to improve the quality of people's lives and circumstances.

As discussed in Chapter 1, the structure, content, and overall nature of science contains properties which are an outgrowth of its origins and are, in some sense, particular to its context. It cannot be assumed to be universal or value free. Although scientific knowledge can and does have empirical validity, that validity is necessarily embedded in its social origins and is, in some sense, limited by the context in which it was established.

Polanyi (1968) and Kuhn (1970) provided in-depth analyses of the basic physical sciences and set forth arguments as to why even those sciences must look to their social origins. From their reasoning, sciences labeled basic, as well as those labeled applied, can justifiably be considered relationally embedded, knowledge–value systems. Both areas of science are subject to scrutiny and include perspectives from which to scrutinize other knowledge systems. This characterization leads to a position in which all knowledge and primacy claims are subject to scrutiny both from without and within the system in which they are embedded. So-called basic sciences, value-related sciences, and sciences of action-oriented endeavors (for example, political sciences and clinical or community psychologies) have claims to validity within their defined scopes. Their validity is considered a basis from which to scrutinize other systems, and they are also subject to outside challenge and scrutiny (Mannheim, 1936).

From this broader perspective, Mannheim (1936) challenged the universalist claims made by experimental scientists of the Western determinist tradition. His challenge still provides powerful arguments for disputing the present, largely unassailable positivist approach to psychology. First, he protested what he called their excessive methodological zeal in rejecting any but a narrow range of methodologies. Instead, he insisted that the appropriateness of any methodological approach rests in part on the context and the phenomena under study. Second, he emphasized that the scope of our knowledge extends beyond the boundaries of present-day science. Where existing conceptions are not adequate, they need to be questioned; that is how we obtain new knowledge. Third, he fought the practice of preserving scientific purity by labeling as "prescientific" or "intuitive" any knowledge discovered outside of science's defined limits at any given time. He emphasized that science proceeds by questioning its own paradigms and exploring the nature of new knowledge rather than by automatically rejecting information that does not fit into existing frameworks. Fourth, Mannheim stressed that science's definition has been too narrow. For historical reasons, only mathematically based sciences have been considered models of what a science should be. This definition is a historical product of people's efforts to understand and master a particular relatively homogeneous range of phenomena.

Finally, Mannheim (1936) pointed out that, in particular, the subject matter of cultural sciences includes a range of phenomena which differs from the physical sciences. The cultural sciences are concerned "with the wealth of unique, concrete phenomena and structures which are familiar to practical men of affairs but which are not attainable through the axioms of positivistic science" (p. 164f). We need a model that will encompass both these ongoing life-in-context phenomena and phenomena that must be understood quantitatively.

The task of creating a nested scientific framework that encompasses general principles as well as individual and sociocultural differences may be better understood by examining an effort to compare two systems in psychology. Paranjpe (1984) undertook a comparison of Eastern and Western psychologies as represented in the traditions of India, his native land, and North America, his adopted one. He noted that "most of the psychology in India today is another edition of Western psychology" (p. 3), because most departments have been staffed by individuals educated in the West.

Paranjpe (1984) emphasized that this state of affairs has continued in spite of the many possibilities inherent in India's own traditions. India has a historical record of several thousand years' attention to the phenomena of psychology. It antedated Western contemporary scientific approaches. It also (a) is empirically (observationally) based, (b) includes an elaborate conceptual framework comprising a world-view and encompassing humanity, (c) provides a theoretical analysis of the structures and processes that underlie human personality, and (d) includes a normative account of the nature of higher and lower levels of the functioning of personality. Techniques designed to help the not-so-well-developed individual reach more desirable levels are available, along with a set of socializing institutions to facilitate personality growth. In short, Indian psychological traditions include attention to most of the concerns which are addressed in Western psychology. Important differences include the far more extensive focus by Indian psychologists on observational and introspective approaches to understanding and enriching people's holistic functioning. Unfortunately, neither Western-influenced contemporary Indian psychology nor contemporary Western psychology has provided a paradigmatic framework which can readily incorporate the contributions from India's historical psychological tradition.

An example of a perhaps more marked area of cultural contrast has been the difference in Indian and Western approaches to fact–value and science–religion issues. Paranjpe pointed out that "whether the fields of psychology and religion should encroach upon one another is a matter of opinion; that the two overlap is a matter of fact" (p. 9). Indian and Western differences are clearly reflected in the contrasts between their secular and religious views of the nature of humans, of deities, and of the relationships between religious and scientific activities. Specifically, the Western tradition teaches that one god created man in his own image and expects obedience. Issues of disobedience are settled from time-to-time or will be settled once and for all at some future judgment day. In either case, judgment will be made by the deity on the basis of the extent to which humans live in accordance with the god's standards and may be tempered by their belief in the deity and appeals for forgiveness. In the Eastern (Hindu) tradition, the many gods and people are part and parcel of creation as well as the ebb and flow of daily life. People carry their fates with them (Karma) and resolve those fates by attaining self-knowledge. That task may or may not involve attention to the fates of others. However, each person's fate is a result of their merits; the gods do not intercede.

The roles of deities and the activities of people in relation to the laws of nature thus assume quite different positions within these two traditions. In the Indian tradition, scientific investigations or other human activities are not a challenge to divine matters. Consequently, there have been no religious sanctions or persecutions for raising or investigating scientific questions. In contrast, in the West there have been major religion-based efforts to constrain and punish scientific and other human actions that might be considered a challenge to theological pronouncements. Examples from the past include the Inquisition and the punishment of Galileo; more contemporary struggles include those surrounding the public study and teaching of theories of evolution or human sexuality.

Other differences which present problems for the development of an overarching paradigm of psychology are embodied in an essay by Ho (1985). He wrote that conflicts in cultural values and professional issues arose from his efforts to establish a clinical psychology training program in Hong Kong and deliver clinical services. As Ho described it, "there is a basic contradiction between the traditional moralistic–authoritarian orientation and the psychological–therapeutic orientation of clinical psychology.... To follow the psychological–therapeutic orientation would lead, sooner or later, to a head-on collision with entrenched traditional values; to yield to these values would necessitate making uncomfortable compromises" (p. 1214). The limit to which he believed he could compromise the psychological–therapeutic orientation led to the conclusion that he could ally himself only with "those forces in the culture that point to directions congenial to, or at least compatible with, clinical psychology" (p. 1214). He thus became an acknowledged agent of sociocultural change.

Ho and Paranjpe have been particularly clear about the irreconcilability of some aspects of their culture's paradigmatic framework with the comparable frameworks of other cultures. What science is and how it relates to religious belief systems differ in noncompatible ways between the West and India. Paranjpe responded by focusing on a search for commonalities, such as a common interest in self-identity and self-realization. Concepts of what personality is and how dysfunctional personalities can be changed through professional intervention differ in irreconcilable ways between the West and China. Ho focused on the need to choose one of the perspectives and become either an agent of social status preservation or of social change. To him, consideration of broader, nested framework issues cannot be avoided since individual personalities are psychosocially embedded, even in the limiting situation of individual therapy. These exemplars illustrate how both theoretical and applied components of psychological science are nested in the cultural contexts of their origin. They also raise questions about whether and how those differences can be reconciled.

An even casual consideration of these cultural differences suggests that people and, in particular, scientists from diverse traditions have much to learn from each other. It suggests that each culture's scientific approaches are subject to ethnocentric cultural blinders as long as the professionals who perpetuate them believe their approaches are self-contained or culture free. In order to transcend these limitations, it is necessary to consider that an exchange is worthwhile and some sort of nested framework within which to pursue that endeavor is needed. One further requirement of a transcultural nested framework is provision of a definition of the nature of and criteria for general versus culturally specific knowledge and the relationship between them.

GENERAL AND CULTURALLY SPECIFIC KNOWLEDGE

From both a logical and an empirical perspective, we must conclude that limiting the scope of the psychological sciences to phenomena that are culture free and universal is not possible. Knowledge that we form in a cultural context includes who we are and how we know ourselves and our worlds; these aspects of ourselves are psychosocially and culturally embedded in us. Further, we function in an emergent holistic fashion as knowers with regard to ourselves and our conduct. The result is that any scientific observation or explanation rests on both general truths and truths particular to the person(s) making the observation or advancing the explanation. Science and scientific knowledge are not culture free.

However, a number of psychologists with cross-cultural interests have attempted the construction of a framework to differentiate what they consider to be universal (culture free) and particular (culturally limited) truths. For the most part, their approach has been grounded in Western positivism with their primary objective being to identify universal principles of human conduct. They advanced a taxonomy for identifying and classifying information into universals and particulars. Identifying two kinds of scientific knowledge and studying them separately created important problems for building a nested framework to interrelate them. Because this approach has been widely accepted, we need to understand it and its limitations.

Berry (1969, 1980, 1989) is a major architect and proponent of this widely used category system that dichotomizes universal and particular truths. The system is derived from the linguistic approaches for distinguishing between phonetics (general or universal aspects of language) and phonemics (sounds employed in a single linguistic system). In Berry's system, conduct which meets the criteria for universality, or at least generality to more than one culture, is referred to as *etics*. Conduct with more limited generality is classified as *emics*. He constructed a table that provides rules for making these distinctions (Berry, 1980, pp. 11–12) (see Table 2.1).

Berry's central point about emics is that they are internal to a particular cultural system. However, *internal* may have two definitions with important distinguishing characteristics. Emic can refer to behavior occurring only within a particular cultural system, however measured. It can

TABLE 2.1.   Rules for Identifying Universals (Etics) and Particulars (Emics)

Emic approach	Etic approach
Studies behavior from within the system	Studies behavior from a position outside the system
Examines only one culture	Examines many cultures, comparing them
Structure discovered by the analyst	Structure created by the analyst
Criteria are relative to internal characteristics	Criteria are considered absolute or universal

Note. The entries in the table are quoted directly from "Introduction to Methodology," by J. W. Berry, 1980, in H. Triandis & J. W. Berry (Eds.), *Handbook of Cross-Cultural Psychology: Methodology* (Vol. 2, pp. 11–12). Boston: Allyn & Bacon. They are not italicized as they were in the original.

also mean behavior identified and used by members of a culture who are acting as *knowers* about their reality. In relation to the first meaning, Berry's table states that the "structure is discovered by the analyst" using criteria internal to the culture. That statement indicates that Berry does not view indigenous individuals as knowers creating their own psychological reality; rather, their psychological reality is discovered by the analyst. The second meaning of *internal* is emphasized in a quote of Malinowski's to which Berry referred. Specifically, "the final goal ... is, briefly, to grasp the native's point of view ... to realize his vision of his world" (Malinowski, 1922, p. 25). Berry added that Malinowski was attempting to "produce internal descriptions of behaviour, and correspond(s) to the emic type of analysis" (Berry, 1980, p. 12). However, Berry does not indicate that the criteria of verification necessarily include asking whether members of that culture consider the discovered emics to be internal to them. Thus Berry's approach seems to fall short of requiring that "grasping the native's point of view" rests on the natives' confirmation as knowers that their point of view is accurately represented.

Berry (1980) required a different approach to establish etics. The investigator starts with extant hypotheses about behavior, even openly acknowledging that the approach is culturally specific to the investigator, to establish whether an *imposed etic* (a hypothesized concept from outside the culture) can be modified until it matches the emic point of view of a culture under study. If some of the original etic remains in that modification, then a valid *derived etic* for these two cultures has been established. If the process is repeated so that its *conceptual equivalence* is established in all cultural systems and meets two other criteria, the derived etic can be considered to be a universal. It must also have the same measurement properties (*metric equivalence*) and *functional equivalence* properties in the cultures examined. Berry does not mention that these universal criteria are defined by the investigator, an approach which allows for inclusion of ethnocentric biases from the investigator's background. Further, his approach to identifying etics does not in any of its phases require that members of a culture report or agree that the characteristics assigned to them actually represent their view of the world, that is, their understanding as knowers of their psychological reality.

This ethnocentric possibility also appeared in an essay by Kelley (1992) in which he discussed scientific versus common sense psychologies. In his view, indigenous psychologies fall in the common sense grouping and only Western psychology meets the criterion of "scientific." He rejected that individual or cultural personal equation factors necessarily bias both the science and scientists of the Western tradition, although he assumed they inevitably do so for their indigenous counterparts. Finally, Kelley also rejected the legitimacy of the internal–external knowledge perspectives which Berry at least acknowledged.

A salient critique of Berry's, and presumably Kelley's, approaches has been advanced by Eckensberger (1992). He, too, endorsed the idea that social processes are present in theory building and epistemology and that, consequently, the cross-cultural psychological approach is an especially apt one to contribute to a transcultural psychology. Unfortunately in his view, this field has more or less imperialistically imposed Western ideas on other cultures throughout its history. In that regard, the

> proposed "emic–imposed etics–derived etics"-strategy (which in fact presents the problem of comparability, but is unable to resolve it) [needs to] be replaced by a more deductive approach: In a first step, to reflect upon and explicate the "hidden assumptions" contained in the various indigenous psychologies; next, to construct consensual knowledge of those aspects, which are common to all of humanity by means of communication processes; these processes will also enable us to define consensual truth criteria against which psychological concepts can be tested; and only then, in a final step, to construct psychological theories which can be applied transculturally in empirical research. (Eckensberger, 1992, p. 4.)

As indicated in the above quote, Eckensberger outlined an alternative approach that addresses some of the limitations of Berry's position. A central point is that it is essential that we communicate across cultures about the models of humankind that underlie the psychologies of the West and the rest of the world. However, it is not possible to identify any universal characteristics within the diversity of human perspectives by using an inductive approach based on the unexamined standards of one culture. Further, differentiating observed phenomena into universals and particulars may identify at least some knowledge that is culturally embedded, but it provides no way of dealing with that information. Rather, he argued, it is essential that psychologists look at themselves first to identify the "hidden assumptions" (tacit elements) in respective indigenous psychologies and, presumably, in the cultures in which they are embedded.

If Eckensberger's approach is interpreted to mean that Western psychology is also an indigenous psychology, then it provides a way to establish comparability of meaning across cultures (etics) in a nonethnocentric way. Specifically, all psychologies become equally subject to scrutiny, rather than relying on Western psychology as the general paradigm against which the others are evaluated. However, Eckensberger does not present a means of transcending the limits of an etic–emic distinction. We need a framework in which differences in meanings across cultures can be incorporated into an overarching paradigm for understanding both transcultural commonalities and differences in human conduct and communication. A framework is required that will take into account enduring cultural discrepancies and conflicts in psychological meanings that stem from dissimilar histories, life circumstances, and events. To provide a nested framework that can address these issues, additional considerations must be included.

INTEGRATIVE FRAMEWORKS

A framework which can support a more broadly based approach to the core issues of psychology must transcend existing cultural, historical, and scientific limitations. Constructing such a network involves the disjunctive tasks that are part of shifting paradigmatic perspectives. This section highlights the nature and implications of those tasks from two different perspectives, a predominantly psychological one and a broader psychosociocultural one.

PSYCHOLOGICALLY BASED INTEGRATIVE FRAMEWORKS

We begin our search for a transcendent framework by considering how scientists generate, verify, and use knowledge, particularly within psychology and from inside and outside the people and cultures involved. Recent scientific references to the experiential component in paradigm shifts highlight the importance of considering that factor in our formulations of our psychological paradigms as well as our individual ones. For example, Kuhn (1970) described the outcome of paradigm shifts, even in the physical sciences, using sentences such as "the scientist with a new paradigm sees differently from the way he had seen before" (p. 114), and "the data had changed" (p. 135). That is, the phenomenal world of the scientists changed in ways they could not anticipate, and after that change, their measurements of established phenomena provided different results.

Klineberg (1980), one of the pioneers of social psychology, spoke of a paradigmatic shift in himself. "The major impulse came from contact with ... anthropologists (who were my friends as well as my teachers or colleagues) accompanied by an exposure to the relevant literature; the consequence for me might almost be described as a "religious" conversion (Klineberg, 1980, p. 40). He suddenly realized that some knowledge of the behavior of societies and cultures different from our own was needed prior to being able to discuss human instincts successfully. He responded by writing the first social psychology text by a psychologist that incorporated ethnological materials and was based primarily on a comparative, cross-cultural approach.

This disjunctive experiential transformation seems to be a common feature of the process of identifying any new meaning. However, it is not the only direction in which such dramatic shifts can occur. Scientific fields can also potentially be combined into a new, more encompassing paradigm through a similar process of dramatic changes in the internal and external realities of those involved. These accounts provide us an acknowledgment of the personal equation and constructivist properties of any formation of meaning. A similar process is presumably also involved in making judgments such as Malinowski's hypothetical grasping of the native's point of view and, also hypothetically, the native's grasping that the anthropologist finally understands (Malinowski, 1922). In fact, when that process of checking back and forth is codified, it provides our most basic scientific tool for advancing our understanding of each other individually or socioculturally as knowers, not just as objects of each other's analysis.

The checking process must be guided by a structure. A number of years ago, I used such a structure as a basis for describing how psychologists used different ways to combine three interrelated aspects of their work to generate and apply distinctive aspects of their scientific knowledge (F. Tyler, 1970). Specifically, I analyzed the assumptions psychologists have made about (a) the source of psychology's knowledge and authority, (b) what the nature of that knowledge was considered to be, and (c) how psychology's service to society was defined. That structure provided a basis for gaining a fuller understanding of psychology's evolution and status at that time.

Separating today's current and emerging ways of organizing psychology into four distinct approaches provides a fuller understanding of psychology's evolution and current status. Paranjpe (1984) described and critiqued two of these disparate approaches and called them, respectively, *Hellenic* and *Hebraic*. I have added what I consider to be successive outgrowths of these two somewhat polarized positions. They are, respectively, the *scientist–professional* and the *resource collaborator* approaches (F. Tyler & Speisman, 1967; F. Tyler, 1970; F. Tyler, Pargament & Gatz, 1983). These four approaches provide anchors for understanding the field's internal and external structures and its justification within the broader society. They are presented and critiqued here because they shape any existing paradigm-type enterprise in psychology. The critique leads progressively toward the final *resource collaborator* approach as the most comprehensive and defensible of the four. Table 2.2 indicates how each system is organized and the issues that must be addressed in order to build the more comprehensive resource collaborator framework that integrates them.

TABLE 2.2. Knowledge Frameworks

Name	Source of knowledge and authority	Nature of knowledge	Service to society
Hellenic	Reason; experiment	Closed set of general principles	Policy and facts detached
Hebraic	Faith; special access	Closed set of general values and truths	Commitment and involvement that validate self and society
Scientist–Professional	Faith, reason, empirical investigation, experience	General and particular principles, facts, values—open for elite, closed for others	Policy and particular responsibility for well-being of others
Resource collaborator	Faith, reason, empirical investigation, experience	Nested facts and values, convergence/divergence/conflict, open-endedness for self and others	Nested individual and collective values, policy, facts, action, personal and social responsibilities and constraints for self and others

Hellenic Frameworks

The Hellenic perspective is based on the assumption that the experimental approach as defined in the positivist science model is an unbiased, value-free approach to objective empirical knowledge. It is considered to reveal the nature of reality. Further, adherence to formal logic guidelines provides a necessary and adequate basis for establishing the validity of statements about the nonempirical relationships among the elements of the knowledge system. It is believed that the Hellenic approach contributes basic empirical knowledge that is superior to the common sense knowledge otherwise available to guide human decisions.

This approach has provided for amazing human progress in understanding and manipulating physical and biological aspects of the world. However, it has significant limitations for understanding people's individual and collective psychological worlds. Its commitment to limit empirical knowledge to only experimentally demonstrated, replicable findings excludes a substantial range of human experience, including people's private experiences and their individual self and world views.

The Hellenic approach has been thought to function as detached and value-free in relation to the ongoing conduct of individuals and societies.

Analysis of that position raises a number of questions that illustrate its paradoxical nature. Scientists using the Hellenic approach make discretionary decisions about which problems to investigate, how to investigate them, what to consider as evidence, what conclusions to draw from their findings, how their findings can be put to use, and the potential benefits and costs of different uses. These same scientists are, in many instances, the most, if not the only, qualified individuals available to make such decisions.

As indicated in Table 2.2, the question of whether and how scientists can or should assume any responsibility for the knowledge they construct beyond that of doing their work with integrity remains open. It is part of the "service to society" aspect of their societally supported work. Possibly the most widely known issue in modern history in which the validity of the Hellenic position of detachment was challenged was with regard to the development of the atomic bomb. The scientists involved and the general public questioned the social responsibility role that these scientists had with regard to the real and potential uses of atomic bombs.

Similar controversial issues in the social and behavioral sciences have not been resolved. For example, psychologists continue to debate whether they have any ethical or social responsibility to investigate controversial issues such as whether there are racially linked differences in intelligence. Another example is whether psychologists need to consider the ethical justification for, and efficacy of, different approaches to controlling violent and other antisocial behavior or becoming involved in ameliorating the causes or consequences of such behavior.

The paradoxical consequences of assuming a position of detachment are readily evident with regard to psychological issues. When scientists decide not to assume responsibility for the consequences of the knowledge they generate, at a minimum their findings can be misunderstood. Who, then, is qualified to assume responsibility for knowledge if the scientists themselves do not? On the other hand, if scientists assume social responsibility for their work, others may question whether their personal biases have influenced their findings and whether they are involved in special pleading in ways not supported by their work. Such important issues cannot be debated or resolved from the detached perspective of the Hellenic framework.

Hebraic Frameworks

Paranjpe (1984) represented the Hebraic perspective as being in stark contrast to the Hellenic one. The Hebraic position is that knowledge is based on faith and attendant, specialized access to ultimate sources of knowledge or morality or both. Using this approach is assumed to produce a closed, universal set of facts and values (truths). In turn, its adherents serve society by providing this absolute basis for commitment to its truth and by acting on that truth.

The Hebraic approach confers legitimacy on at least some people's individual experiences, even though the experiences cannot be directly verbified by others. In that way, tolerance for human differences and a range of possibilities within which people can think and behave independently of control by majority consensus becomes possible. However, the presumptive stance of the individuals identified by themselves or others as having special access to new and accumulated knowledge (factual and evaluative) is often one of an elite status and a right to power unchallengeable by others in society. Unfortunately, as history has shown, for example, by the fate which has befallen many women accused of being witches, there is a major limitation to this framework. It not only produces little basis for challenging the validity of its designated elite or their methods, truths, and practices, but it may also justify destroying challenges and challengers.

Scientist–Professional Frameworks

The evolution of a psychological framework that combines scientific and professional endeavors has involved aspects of the Hellenic and the Hebraic approaches. A basic assumption of this approach is that individual, nonreplicable and nonverifiable human experience are legitimate sources of information about human conduct, but they are not *the* primary or only source of knowledge. They must be incorporated within a science-based, psychological approach to the study of people along with publicly observable and experimentally verifiable knowledge. That is, people's dreams and fantasies, hallucinations, expert scientific judgments, professional sensitivities and insights, and culturally distinctive experiences cannot be directly verified in the ways overt actions can, but they can be reported as experiences which are related to overt actions.

From the scientist–professional perspective, observed external actions and reported internal experiences are considered equally legitimate and necessary; they have different but complementary and supplementary functions in the generation and utilization of scientific knowledge. The personal equation component of such verifications can be studied by means of repeated experiments and by the use of different and differently oriented experimenters to identify idiosyncratic contributions. Just such a process is regularly involved in making judgments about psychopathological experiences as well as in identifying cultural differences found in the nature and meaning of experience. Similarly, psychologists' stances of detachment and involvement also have different but complementary and supplementary functions in the generation and utilization of scientific knowledge.

However, the scientist–professional approach is not without troubling limitations. It includes the assumption that expertly qualified scientist–professionals have a command over their limitations that is not available to lay people. Proponents believe that their professional training provides them ways to question and challenge accepted "realities" or "truths" as knowers in ways that the untrained cannot. Without professional assistance, untrained individuals are considered more limited by their "known" attributes. In other words, proponents argue that the systems that scientist–professionals construct and advocate yield somewhat different sets of principles, facts, and values than those produced by others. By virtue of their specialized educations, professionals are assumed to be more capable of producing active, creative ways to transcend their histories and acquire special insights into their own conduct and that of others. In contrast, the conduct of lay people is considered to be more subject to their histories as "known" and lay people are treated as objects of study, not active participants in their subjective worlds.

In the realm of service to society, the scientist–professional approach fuses the Hellenic responsibility to guide humanity in general and the Hebraic public policy responsibility to care for the well-being of individuals. Within this framework, the dichotomies between facts and values and between science and practice have been rejected in favor of the position that each dichotomy represents contrasting end points on a continuum. As a consequence, within the scientist–professional framework, the tasks of identifying fact–value and science–practice interrelationships are incorporated as legitimate and necessary both in principle and in practice.

Resource Collaborator Frameworks

The resource collaborator framework was initially presented as a model to guide interactions between change agents and community members (F. Tyler, Gatz, & Pargament, 1983). It is built on several assumptions about the nature and sources of knowledge that differ from the preceding, less comprehensive frameworks. These assumptions provide a basis for integrating the earlier approaches.

The resource collaborator framework's first assumption is that sources of knowledge and knowledge itself have a limited scope and range of legitimacy. The second related assumption is that all knowledge (facts) and preferences (values) are in part subjective and in part consensually based or otherwise verifiable. For example, possibly the most widely known controversy in modern day psychology is over how much of Freud's theories were a function of his personal circumstances and his cultural context rather than representative of transcultural human experiences. Both Jahoda and Bettelheim, who lived in the same cultural milieu as Freud, provided insightful accounts about those possibilities. By comparing Freud's account of his life circumstances and the accounts of other contemporary professionals with similar circumstances, Jahoda (1977) identified elements of Freud's views that were probably a product of his personal life history. In contrast, Bettelheim (1990) focused on the unique historical and cultural circumstances that shaped the lives of Freud and his clients, arguing that they provided a distinctive cast to his clinical data, general cultural milieu, and subsequently to his theories. Thus, these two scientists found information that supports the first two assumptions of the resource collaborator approach.

The resource collaborator framework's third assumption is that the knowledge and value/preference base of all parties and approaches is assumed open to new subjective insights and interpretations, although every individual is also constrained by her or his own limits. People can create new knowledge and preferences, although their current ways of functioning facilitate or place limits on doing so, or do both. As people create new forms of factual and preferential knowledge, they also create different limits and possibilities. Thus, while it is assumed that all individuals may differ in the degree to which they function as knowers and may also differ across domains, their capabilities do not differ in kind. The assumption that there is a distinct gap between the knower functioning of its experts and the *known* functioning of others is rejected within the scientist–professional framework.

In a resource collaborator framework, a fourth assumption is that everyone has both personal and social responsibilities. The service of a discipline and its members to society involves a resource exchange and collaborative process. Everyone has strengths and limitations. Each party contributes from its strengths and relies on resource contributions from others to offset its limitations. Responsibility is allocated in relation to resource relevance. For example, although all contribute to decisions about their own well-being, to the well-being of other parties, and their collective well-being, people's roles differ. Questions which require special knowledge are allocated to individuals or groups with appropriate expertise, but their conduct and answers are subject to group oversight and review. Questions about each person's well-being are allocated primarily to that person, but also with some oversight and review.

Within a resource collaborative/exchange framework, the fifth assumption is that there will be areas of convergence as well as areas of divergence and conflict. Identifying, maintaining, and building on areas of convergence, accepting divergences, and resolving conflicts are both collective and individual responsibilities. In order to achieve that objective, my colleagues and I (F. Tyler et al., 1991) have proposed an extension and modification of these cross-cultural approaches that provides not only a taxonomic framework for attending to the range of human conduct in all contexts, but also a structure for understanding how people address their differences as well as their commonalities. All of us are defined by, define ourselves within, and live in social contexts. We also have unique and highly developed capacities for defining ourselves as autonomous, asserting our individual identities, and guiding ourselves as though we were independent of the contexts in which we are embedded. Nevertheless, our internal and external processes of searching for meaning involve, in part, defining those meanings in relation to our social contexts, whether these contexts be intracultural or intercultural.

Although it is impossible to achieve a complete taxonomy of these interrelationships, it is possible to outline a broad schema for classifying them. I have proposed a three-category structure as a way of dealing with what are undoubtedly very complex patterns, possibly of a continuous rather than a discrete nature. Specifically, even to carry on a conversation we have to find some *convergence* of meanings between ourselves and others. As we converse, we also find that we view events somewhat differently. That is, we find *divergence* in the meanings that we assign even to words. We also find that the meanings we assign and those which others assign *conflict*, and we may argue about who is right. Both divergence and conflict present us with tasks of expanding our own frameworks or limiting our understanding and interactions with others. Particularly in the instance of conflict, any effort to proceed faces differences that require the parties to change in ways which are initially unacceptable to them.

The advantage of this framework is that it begins with the assumption that we are all involved in searches for meaning in a psychosocial context and that we are involved in communication with others, whether they are from the same or different cultures, as part of that search. Thus, convergence is as much a constructed area of meaning as are divergence and conflict, and the process of finding convergences, divergences, or conflicts is interactive on the part of all involved. Consequently, it is important to approach psychological research and interventions from a paradigmatic perspective that emphasizes not only procedural controls but also the psychosocial, contextual, and interactive aspects of the conduct being studied.

To summarize, a resource collaborator paradigm is built on the assumption that there are facts, values, priorities, and people with differing needs and qualifications. No one is free of his or her nature and limitations, and no one is without qualifications and resources to contribute to his or her own and society's ongoing life. None of these positions and no one person can be considered totally and absolutely correct in any circumstances, but must always be subject to scrutiny. Further, it is also assumed that humans can derive or imagine individual or collective *general paradigms* to guide their lives and relationships. However, such paradigms are time and context limited; they are subject to review and revision as time passes, circumstances and people change, and new information and experiences are added. In short, universals as well as eternal truths and verities may indeed represent broad-based convergences and legitimately enduring anchors for people to rely on, but they are not free of their human origins. In a parallel manner, cultural and ethnic patterns of diversity may indicate distinctive socialization patterns as a function of differing historical and ecological circumstances, but they, too, are rooted in their human origins. Much the same can be said for patterns of cultural and ethnic conflict. They are outgrowths of conflicting historical and ecological circumstances, but their distinctive character rests also in their human origins.

A Psychosocioculturally Based Integrative Structure

The above analyses and formulations have been characterized by their predominantly psychological orientation and by their underlying assumption that psychological characteristics are individual and internal, while sociocultural characteristics are collective and external. That approach provided people an initial scientific basis for accounting for human biopsychological, and even individual psychosocial, characteristics. It did not account for the shared *knower* choices involved in decisions such as those that enable a generational cohort of people with a common heritage to arrive at a convergent view of how to maintain their ethnic paradigm under changing external circumstances. An individual's psychological paradigmatic framework and a culture's or ethnic group's paradigmatic societal form are not the same, but they are inseparably intertwined in an ongoing process–structure dynamic. Only by embedding an understanding of both in a comprehensive nested framework can the nature of either or of their interrelatedness be fully represented.

To address the uses of knowledge in coping with social changes, Brown (1980) advanced a view of the human condition which provides a basis for integrating sociocultural and individual facets of human conduct into a comprehensive nested framework. He deplored the inadequacy of modern approaches to social change with the "privatization of values" (p. 47) as a substitute for concern with "the polity—the arena for the institutional enactment of moral choices" (p. 46). In his view, to understand how people organize meaning, it is necessary to attend to the presence of experiential and rational characteristics along with interactive and autonomous ones.

Brown (1980) stressed a humanistic approach as essential to understanding how people function and cope with change because that approach embodies the notion that people are active participants in the formation of their lives and societies. That is, "the most fundamental cultural forms, the collective representations, are not the product of isolated reflective intelligence, but are born out of the intensive atmosphere of collective effervescence" (p. 59). Finally, he stressed that "the humanistic change agent wishes not to 'capture the imaginations' of clients, but to help them recapture their imaginations for themselves" (p. 62). In other words, Brown argued that a cognitive, individualistic, people-as-known orientation by detached or ethnocentric experts, or by both, simply overlooks the holistic, collective, active agent, knower aspects of human lives.

Brown's (1980) emphasis that people derive meaning from active individual and collective involvement in the contexts where they live is similar to that of Sperry's view described in Chapter 1. Both emphasize the primacy of emergent *knower* attributes over reductionist *known* characteristics in human conduct and in the collective survival of human civilizations. As indicated in the preceding chapter, these and other findings are value and fact based. Verification of their origins, as well as validation of their effects, requires confirmation from cultural, community, and individual foci. Further, since the grounds for any decision to choose or use any basis of judgment cannot be specified, consensually agreed upon arbitrary guidelines are used. However, an additional factor is that, in the process of living, we change our psychological realities and we are being changed constantly so we must continue to update our bases of knowing and obtaining consensual agreement. Understanding these processes is essential to becoming aware of the necessity of grounding our psychological paradigms in cultural as well as individual contexts. However, we often become clearly aware of such changes only in the course of systematic research and efforts to understand, create, or reduce social and individual commonalities and differences.

Our lack of awareness of these processes and the effects they have on us has been abundantly documented in the history of the United States as well as in the contribution of psychology to that history. For example, in the area of intelligence testing, there has been a progression from the work of Binet, who developed a scale for determining individual children's capabilities for academic progress. His scale consisted of a series of tests appropriate for children of different ages, with children's scores referred to as their "mental ages." In his view, it measured a child's sound judgment, general knowledge, and performance characteristics, but was not a measure of the inherent nature of the child (Reisman, 1966). Binet's successors used his work as a basis for proposing an intelligence quotient (IQ) concept involving a ratio of mental age to chronological age (MA/CA). That ratio subsequently was considered to indicate an inherent quality of the child, her or his "intellectual ability." Since that early era, public education policy in the United States has incorporated widespread intelligence testing, and students' test scores are placed in their school files. At times, the students' scores become more "real" than the students. That is, students may get labeled as "overachievers" or "underachievers" so that this test score becomes an external criterion of the child's "true" capabilities, an estimate that is not modified by the child's later performance. Rather, the subsequent performance is interpreted as an aberration relative to the individual's presumably *real* ability as measured earlier. The gradual progressive change in the inferences drawn from this testing approach received little attention until recently. It is currently under serious challenge because of its individual and social consequences.

Another dramatic example of progressive changes in meaning of a concept, with even greater psychosocial consequences, stems from the way slavery was practiced in the United States. Slave owners faced the task of reconciling slavery with their Christianity-based belief in the equality of all souls before their God. Further, slave owners also sought to maintain political and social control. In framing the political compromise that enabled both antislavery supporters and the slave owners to support the United States Constitution, they agreed to accept that slavery was a matter of state, not national, jurisdiction. They also agreed to count slaves as worth three fifths the value of a white man for purposes of voting. Each slave holder had the right to cast his own vote in public elections as well as votes equivalent to three-fifths of the number of slaves she or he held (Kelly, Harbison, & Belz, 1983; United States, 1995). Their solution came more broadly to justify slavery in part by defining slaves from Africa as only three-fifths human, so less than equal. The slave holders thus held political power over other voters with different political values or economic resources. Slaves were also controlled by recourse to the law making it a crime for a slave to run away or for anyone to assist a runaway slave. A further justification for control of slaves invoked the science of medicine. It was reasoned that since slaves were not fully human, they were not capable of living as free individuals who could manage their own affairs. As a result, a psychiatrist established and employed a diagnostic category which described slaves' efforts at escape as a pathological tendency to run away (Cartwright, as cited in Franklin & Schweninger, 1999).

Slavery was a longstanding practice prior to the American experience, but those slaves were considered to be people whose lot was unfortunate. The new definition in the United States justified the low status of slaves on the grounds that they were "deficient." In short, a "meaning," a "reality," was changed by turning it upside down, and a psychosocial leap that fit the needs of the dominant members of society was made to create a different reality. This different reality has not yet been totally erased in the United States although there are ongoing public, psychological, and other scientific debates about which "reality" to endorse. To accord the descendants of African slaves full status as humans is a psychosocial leap that many citizens of the United States have chosen not to make.

More specific examples of the ways in which people change their realities and are changed by them can be found in studies of the relationships between people's psychosocial characteristics and their circumstances. In his studies of violent behavior patterns of criminals in the United States, Toch (1992) identified a pattern of spirals of development in violence and extremism. The spiral develops as follows: When people feel threatened, they act to reduce that threat in ways which force others to act protectively. These reactions, in turn, confirm an initiator's distrust and feeling that his or her self and efficacy are threatened. The initiator acts accordingly and escalates the cycle. Unchecked, this cycle continues, escalating the level of violence through reciprocal interactions. It also changes the participants' reality. They progressively begin to see the world as a more threatening place and act accordingly.

There is considerable documentary and empirical basis for concluding that the historical, geographical, and social contexts of people's lives contribute to shaping their limits as well as their possibilities. People's psychological realities are products of both the direct impact of their experiences and their self-aware involvement in organizing and interpreting the meaning of those experiences. However, the factors of context and people choosing their "reality" make a more important difference in people's lives than psychological accounts have allowed. Further, a full representation of how human attributes are organized requires that concepts of community and society also need more systematic inclusion than they have received.

SUMMARY

This chapter emphasized that people must make psychosocial leaps to develop any sense of individual or shared meaning and that the bases of those leaps can never be fully specified. Psychological paradigms as much as individual judgments are based in such leaps. It was emphasized that the power of scientific approaches is that they provide ways of identifying the nature and locus of these *leaps* and of constructing new paradigms that eliminate some of the limitations of existing ones. They also provide the most powerful way developed to date for identifying the bases underlying these leaps, as well as their natures and consequences. That is, whether a paradigmatic framework contributes to advancing human knowledge and well-being or to reducing both can be assessed using scientific approaches. Consequently, when people and societies find that the paradigms from which they are operating reduce their control of their lives and circumstances, they can utilize the tools of science to seek other perspectives, make a set of leaps to adopt a different set of assumptions, and proceed to use them and evaluate their consequences. To illustrate these points, selected existing psychological paradigms were examined to highlight their strengths and limitations as well as identify the requirements for a more comprehensive paradigm which will offset those limitations.

This scientific approach was then used to construct a *nested framework* model by attending to the following considerations. Any knowledge includes an indeterminate component of constructed human meaning; consequently, our knowledge and beliefs cannot, in some ultimate sense, transcend our creation of them. Because of this human limitation, we must begin constructing our meaning-based frameworks by making leaps of understanding/belief. We then proceed by building spirals of conceptualization, practice, and inquiry which serve to use, extend, and test that framework. That process, in turn, can lead to identification of the limits of the original leaps, modifying them, and then repeating the process. Making this repeatable process explicit is an essential part of making all relevant participants aware of their own involvement in and contribution to the frameworks they are constructing and using. They are part of the nested framework.

A nested framework also incorporates a model of human interactions with resource exchange and resource collaborator characteristics. That is, to be consistent with the overarching pattern of nestedness, actions by humans—whether directed toward the self, others, or the nonliving world—need to be characterized as interactions or exchanges. They involve receiving as well as giving, characteristics that must be incorporated for the network's paradigmatic structure to be complete. As a final point, this nested framework model provides the basic conceptual structure underlying the organization of this book. It is particularly basic to the ethnic validity framework outlined in detail in Chapter 4.

CHAPTER 3

PSYCHOLOGY'S NESTED FRAMEWORKS

INTRODUCTION

Chapter 2 explored how people actively create their own meanings using their knower capabilities. However, other factors also contribute to human meaning. The physical environment, historical and current events, and personal circumstances are the contexts which people must interpret and respond to in their creation-of-meaning-processes. To understand this aspect of the production of human meaning requires that we shift our attention away from people and on to their contexts. That shift is difficult for psychologists because their core focus is people, and the language of psychology is constructed to express its understanding of people rather than their contexts.

People assign meaning to whatever impact their environments have on them. They organize those discrete meanings into patterns and, in turn, organize their lives in relationship to these interlinked patterns. These patterns of meaning that people form about their contexts are called *nested frameworks*. People simultaneously create patterns of meaning called *ethnic validity* paradigms. Ethnic validity paradigms are about themselves and their relationships to their contexts.

People rely on their nested frameworks, ethnic validity patterns, and the interrelations between the two to guide their lives. Traditionally, ethnic validity paradigms have been central to psychologists' efforts to understand people's conduct, while nested frameworks have been of secondary importance. For example, psychologists use a person's contact with reality as a basis for judging that individual's level of psychological adjustment or psychopathology. However, the same psychologists ordinarily give little attention to the socially constructed nature of their own "reality" which they are using to make these judgments.

Although as knowers, we have discretionary capabilities to choose and interpret the nested frameworks and ethnic validity paradigms in our lives, we cannot change them at will for a number of reasons. We can never completely untangle them from the tacit assumptions on which they rest. We rely on them to assign meanings to ourselves (identities), our contexts (nested frameworks), and our relationships to these contexts (ethnically valid understandings). These meanings continue to exist and influence us, including our judgments about their validity, at least somewhat independently of our momentary wishes.

Throughout recorded history, shifts in societal views of the nature of the world and the creatures in it (nested framework conceptions) have been accompanied by changes in people's psychological (ethnic validity) paradigms. For example, if a society assumes that human nature is determined exclusively by the evolutionary maxim "survival of the fittest," people in that society will be inclined to accept that they are naturally competitive and act accordingly. These societies will tend to build systems of education and therapy to influence their people to accept this view of themselves and the events in their lives. Their psychology will account for how people behave in terms of their natural competitiveness.

This chapter uses psychology's nested frameworks to illustrate how contexts impact on psychologists' constructed meanings and conduct, which in turn influence the meanings and conduct of others. As communication and travel have improved, cross-cultural exchanges have yielded increasing amounts of evidence about how people's different nested frameworks influence their lives and their interactions. Identifying additional nested framework dimensions and their costs and benefits makes it possible to learn how to change them and improve the quality of people's lives.

FRAMEWORKS OF AMERICAN PSYCHOLOGY

As histories of psychology have documented (Boring, 1929), psychologists in the Western world evolved an ahistorical perspective of their field reflecting the rationally oriented empiricism of the late seventeenth to twentieth centuries. They believed that humans are rational and that general knowledge is directly applicable to particular instances. Little distinction was made between developing knowledge and applying it, although not all psychologists were interested in the latter task. By the end of World War II, psychologists' roles were extended to studying such topics as individual differences and even to providing psychological expertise in clinical settings.

In response to these expanded roles, the central guild organization of psychologists in the United States, the American Psychological Association (APA), extended its stated purpose from that of advancing psychology as a science to its currently stated goal, "to advance psychology as a science, as a profession, and as a means of promoting human welfare" (*American Psychologist*, 1997, p. 684). Thus, psychologists in the United States defined their field as being concerned with many domains of human conduct within a complex and multilayered nested framework.

By turning to these newer outgrowths of the field, alternative views can be found which challenge the field's dominant paradigm. In particular, cross-cultural and community approaches have led to the inclusion of contexts and social configurations as integral components of human lives. These shifts do not automatically negate insights and facts that have come from earlier efforts to understand human conduct. They do require reconceptualizing those ideas in light of more recent findings derived from newer nested frameworks.

THREE MENTAL HEALTH REVOLUTIONS

In the Euro-American world, there have been significant shifts over the past two centuries in society's conventional wisdom about peoples' individual and social natures. Hobbs (1964) characterized the impact of these shifts on psychology as a sequence of three mental health revolutions. A brief review of these revolutions provides important background information for understanding Western psychology's current nested frameworks and ethnic validity paradigms and their relevance to current issues of individual and social change.

The First Mental Health Revolution

The French Revolution at the end of the eighteenth century precipitated a societal paradigm shift that installed an egalitarian view of the nature of a just society and of the worth of people. The associated first mental health revolution was institutionalized on the basis of a contrasting Hebraic viewpoint (see Chapter 2), i.e., the superior wisdom derived from special education. Pinel, a French physician, initiated the shift from a societal paradigm in which individuals were understood to be "mad" because they were criminal or demoniacally possessed to one in which they were considered ill and in need of humane treatment. That shift spread rapidly as part of a general transition in the Western world toward according a sense of dignity and worth to all individuals (Reisman, 1966).

Eli Todd, an eminent U.S. psychiatrist and campaigner for humane treatment of the mentally ill, advanced a community approach to human distress. He argued that in a democracy the public bears a special responsibility to the unfortunate because it engenders unrealistic expectations for a better life. Consequently, it bears some responsibility when individuals fail to realize their expectations (Reissman, 1976).

The Second Mental Health Revolution

Neither a community orientation nor the humane treatment it advocated survived the growth of U.S. cities, the influx of immigrants, and the impact of Darwinian thought applied to cultural rather than species evolution. By the end of the nineteenth century, Social Darwinism and a strong cultural doctrine of individualism replaced the doctrine of humane treatment for the mentally ill and others who were socially or economically disadvantaged, or both. In that climate, psychologists began to institutionalize their discipline as an acultural, ahistorical pursuit of general laws about individual "minds."

By that time, the second mental health revolution was taking shape in Europe. It involved a blending of Hellenic (empirical science) and Hebraic (privileged knowledge of professionals) perspectives, and its articulation was most directly expressed in the work of Freud. He declared that mental illnesses, or at least neuroses, are individual intrapsychic maladies and, because of that they are not of social origin or concern so there is no justification for society's involvement. Further, he felt that the root causes of neuroses were irrational. They could be treated *only* by a professional who, through a specialized socialization process, had acquired a unique understanding of irrational psychological processes. Consequently, professionals and the public turned even further away from consideration of community or social factors in the etiology and treatment of mental disorder, and lay people were discouraged from becoming involved with the remediation of mental disorder.

Some psychologists in the United States endorsed the Freudian paradigm while others believed that acultural principles of human functioning are directly applicable to ongoing behavior. They rejected the need for distinctions between the scientist and the professional therapist and between the expert and the recipient of psychological services. William James, perhaps still the foremost U.S. psychologist, was deeply committed to the belief that "positive mental habits" can be taught, and he participated in the formation of the Mental Hygiene movement (Reisman, 1966). Witmer, who developed the first psychological clinic, used experimental psychology approaches to diagnose people's behavior difficulties and to teach them new behaviors. He did not draw distinct lines about who could serve as psychological change agents (Levine & Levine, 1992).

Psychologists' allegiances to these different nested frameworks led to conflicting social policies. Those with a Social Darwinist orientation saw intelligence testing as a tool for establishing the social policies of selective sterilization and immigration control to prevent the intellectual deterioration of the citizenry. For others, the tests were valuable tools for developing more equitable social policies and for working with low-scoring people and otherwise troubled children and adults.

The advent of World War I and its demands for classification and training of military personnel confronted psychologists with a vastly changed societal context. The effectiveness of their response led to a reconceptualization of the ways individuals are viewed by society. It created what might be called "psychometric man" (F. Tyler & Speisman, 1967), a nested framework conception that individuals are merely collections of measurable psychological attributes such as intelligence and aptitude. Two decades later with the advent of World War II, U.S. psychologists were asked to contribute to the individual diagnosis and therapy of the war's psychological casualties, a purview of the field of medicine. At the end of the war, official status was accorded to psychology, psychiatric social work, psychiatric nursing, and psychiatry as being core mental health disciplines. This status committed psychology, and clinical psychology in particular, even more strongly to the nested framework conception that psychological disorders are individual, intrapsychic, medical diseases.

Even during World War II there were challenges to conventional views about the nature of healthy and pathological responses to human stress. From dealing with war-related crises, psychiatrists Lindemann and Caplan came to believe that there is a characteristic response to crisis that is natural and healthy, not pathological nor a sign of weakness. They developed an active, psychologically oriented concept of and approach to crisis intervention (Lindemann, 1944). Others discovered that it perpetuated the disorders of military personnel to remove them from combat zones. Nearby treatment with quick returns to their units proved to be far more therapeutically effective since it built on the men's commitment to their comrades and the primary support provided by that group (Reisman, 1966).

After the war, in the United States there was a swing back to a conservative, individual pathology and treatment model plus a strong, publicly supported campaign to train enough therapists to serve the needs of returning veterans. While psychologists contributed as diagnosticians and therapists, they also brought their research tradition to their work. That combined approach led to the creation of a scientist–professional model for the education of clinical psychologists. The science base was general psychology and the professional base was training in individual diagnosis and therapy plus a medical-setting internship (Raimy, 1950).

In Sarason's (1981a) opinion, the result of psychology joining the mental health establishment was that "clinical psychology became part of a medically dominated mental health movement that was narrow in terms of theory and settings, blind to the nature of the social order, and as imperialistic as it was vigorous" (p. 833). Psychology abandoned its research tradition and intellectual sophistication and bought access to money and power by accepting an individualistic "illness" model along with permanent second class status and professional isolation.

Not until the mid-1950s did a different nested framework and broader role for psychologists as "creative generalists" get spelled out as part of a national effort to define and work toward mental health for the citizenry (Strother, 1956). That proposal began as part of a dialogue challenging the orthodox view that mental illness was a direct product of individual deficiencies and did not involve the social order. It anticipated an even more extended exploration of the country's mental health needs which, in turn, led to a massive national study under the direction of the interdisciplinary Joint Commission on Mental Illness and Health.

The Joint Commission (1961) documented that more resources were needed to treat mental illness and there could never be enough therapists to meet that need on an individual basis. It also stated that people needed to be treated in their communities and that the concept of positive mental health should be considered. However, the report declined to recommend any radical changes in public policies except that vastly increased research on mental illness was needed.

The Third Mental Health Revolution

The U.S. social upheavals of the 1960s stemmed from a public consensus that radical social changes were needed to improve the life situation of the poor, the disabled, and those who were the objects of discrimination. All individuals were to be provided access to society's opportunities, supports, and benefits. This shift laid the groundwork for the third mental health revolution, authorized legislatively by the Community Mental Health Centers (CMHC) Act of 1963 (Hobbs, 1964; Korchin, 1976). This act formalized a societal commitment to provide, if not psychological well-being, at least relief from the most debilitating ravages of psychological disorders by building CMHCs throughout the country to prevent the occurrence of mental illness and reduce its effects when it did occur.

In conception, structure, and function, the centers mixed the conservative and the innovative. They were to be under medical control (conservative), but to involve community members in their planning and implementation activities (innovative). They were required to provide inpatient and outpatient care (conservative). However, they were also required to provide a number of innovative services, including partial hospitalization, twenty-four hour emergency services, mental health consultation, and education to community agencies as well as non-mental health professionals. It was recommended, though not required, that they provide diagnostic services (conservative) plus rehabilitative and aftercare services, training, research, and evaluation (innovative). The implementation of this Act moved the nation's mental health patients out of isolated, custodial mental hospitals back into the community and involved society in their lives (innovative). However, understanding and control of the plight and fate of the patients was kept within the framework of the medical pathology model and under the control of the medical profession (conservative).

COMMUNITY PSYCHOLOGY

Although psychologists contributed substantially to the Joint Commission and the forming of the CMHCs, some of them were not content with the continued dominance of medical thinking and medical control. They fought to broaden the centers' frameworks and began to forge alternatives, an effort marked by a number of national conferences. The conveners and supporters of the conferences, including the American Psychological Association and the National Institute of Mental Health, sought to shape public policy, but were, in turn, influenced by the participants and underlying public forces.

A Defining Conference

Most of the psychologists at the first of these conferences, the Swampscott Conference, were involved in community mental health, but their interest was in community psychology (Bennett et al., 1966). They spelled out a new paradigmatic formulation as an alternative, multidisciplinary model that used psychology's methods to create new concepts for attacking new problems and building healthy communities to develop and sustain healthy people. They wanted psychology to change its approach from being a psychology of people independent of their contexts to a psychology of people within their communities. This new role required

psychologists to function as participant-conceptualizers, that is, as involved members of the community as well as functioning psychologists.

Community psychologists' education was to retain its conceptual
skills training, emphasize community involvement, be interdisciplinary,
and include content about and approaches to social, political, and psychological activism. Research training and research projects were to focus on
the new community psychology issues. Topics to be emphasized included:
(a) the impact of the physical and social environment on people as individuals and as members of social organizations; (b) people's reactions to
planned change, and the effects of alternative social organizations on
individuals and their value for reducing stress, particularly in high risk
populations; (c) the modification of motivational and personality factors in
individuals to facilitate social and organizational change; and (d) evaluation research on social change processes.

Acceptance of this new nested framework as a legitimate perspective
within mainstream psychology was evidenced by the APA's endorsement
shortly thereafter (Smith & Hobbs, 1966). The core of the official endorsement was Hobbs's assertion that "mental illness is not the private organic
misery of an individual, but a social, ethical, and moral problem, a responsibility of the total community" (1964, p. 824). The endorsement stressed
that the centers should focus on preventing emotional problems by early
detection and treatment and by helping the community's social system to
function more effectively. In preparation for these activities, psychologists
were to be educated as social change agents and participate in the training
of subdoctoral mental health workers in psychologically related activities.
Finally, the endorsement stressed that the community should control each
CMHC's goals and policies so that the centers would serve the community
rather than its professionals (Smith & Hobbs, 1966).

Consolidation and Isolation

Paradigm changes never occur easily, without controversy, or independent of the social context. During the 1960s, the United States was
embroiled in a changing political and social climate dominated by struggles about civil rights, poverty programs, and the Vietnam war. Psychologists were divided about these issues and the directions their field should
take. By the end of the decade, there was a shift to a more conservative
social climate and political administration. Community and other activist
and social-change-oriented psychologists and colleagues found their support eroding rapidly and their legitimacy questioned.

Another psychology-based and NIMH funded conference was held in
1973 to consider patterns of professional training (Korman, 1974). It

brought together advocates for two incompatible streams of development in psychology, each seeking to challenge the status quo. Community oriented participants were concerned with social responsibility, social equity issues, and democratizing psychological education and practice. Its advocates included most of the representatives from previously nonrepresented constituencies—students, minority group representatives, subdoctorally trained personnel, and their teachers. The other participants advocated further professionalizing psychology training by establishing professional schools modeled after medical schools in order to produce large numbers of professional practitioners with a status comparable to that of psychiatrists. Their motivation stemmed from two major factors. Their numbers had grown large enough to challenge the academic research orientation and antiprofessional bias in university psychology departments. There were employment opportunities because the public was increasingly supportive of psychologists as psychotherapy practitioners.

The conference became a battleground; the result was the affirmation of a professional elitist position for psychology. Professional schools and professional degrees, as well as an exclusive career entry point at the doctoral level, were endorsed. The effort to advance a community and social equity oriented nested framework was largely defeated; however, all was not lost for community psychology. The conference emphasized: (a) inclusion of more minority members in all aspects of the discipline, (b) more attention to social and psychological issues confronting minorities and poor people, (c) collaboration between universities and field agencies in training, (d) education of all professionally trained psychologists to prepare them to work with the full range of human diversity, and (e) establishment of a dialogue between mental health professionals and the recipients of their services.

In 1975, the APA's Division of Community Psychology held a conference to consolidate and ratify the work begun ten years earlier (Iscoe et al., 1977). The conferees included a generation of young people educated as community psychologists and involved in developing paradigms which differed sharply from experimental and clinical models. They conceptualized human activities as psychosocial in nature and considered their approach applicable not only to psychological problems but also to a much broader set of human activities. Finally, the conferees identified a range of community-psychology-oriented approaches (exemplars) which were guiding their work.

Conceptual and Contextual Perspectives. Community programs required psychologists to shift from using only their own professional judgment to including the community in the process of defining its needs and determining when those needs are met (Coursey, 1977). For example, the principle of community participation was incorporated in the nationwide Head Start program whose purpose was to provide underpriviledged children a "head start" in educational, social, and intellectual development in order to break out of the circle of poverty. Numerous evaluations of this program using traditional educational and psychological models yielded mixed results. However, community leadership and citizen support prevented unsympathetic national administrations from eliminating Head Start because they considered it an important and successful program. In at least this instance, the nested framework for evaluating the worth of community programs was changed by the community members' judgment.

Having acknowledged that community members are participants in community issues, these community psychologists created nested frameworks for including them in mental health plans and interventions. One such framework involved the adoption of an ecological perspective requiring attention to the environment, the individual, and the interaction between the two as essential to describing any community and its citizens. They modified the biological ecology paradigm further by introducing a value-based standard which gave preeminence to human survival and well-being. This approach led to the development and exploration of the costs and benefits of person–environment fit models, the relative desirability of environments, and ways to create more desirable ones.

Community psychologists were also faced with the likelihood that there could be a variety of ways of being human, each of which has strengths and limitations but is more suitable than others for a particular person, community, or situation. Those patterns might converge, diverge, and conflict in various respects. For example, in residential housing planning, they found that it was of tremendous value to know the relative advantages and disadvantages of homogeneity versus heterogeneity in relation to age, income, or status.

Community psychologists developed criteria and made choices about when to use a single standard of evaluation for everyone in a community versus when to use a multidimensional nested framework for judging both people and their relationships to their social context. They explored the possibility of improving human well-being, not just reducing and remedying psychological dysfunction. Their focus on preventive approaches also included the enhancement of human resistance to stress. Even more radically, they built on the assumption that individuals are, to some extent, active agents in forming their own lives and societies. Programs were designed to generate more psychologically fulfilling communities and societies and to orient people toward becoming mature, psychosocially competent persons. Further, these psychologists worked to assist individuals or groups (including entire communities) to confront the consequences of their traumas and resolve their crises. Their approach was to help people reestablish or even strengthen their resource capabilities and their capacities for self-management.

Collaborative Patterns of Social Intervention. The conferees subscribed to diversity and participative involvement as basic to their community psychology paradigm, then spelled out a variety of patterns of collaborative social intervention for accomplishing these objectives. In consultation and education, they did not take on operational responsibility but informed other professionals and the public about relevant psychological perspectives and approaches to issues of community concern, such as delinquency and care of the isolated and disturbed. Resource exchange networks required direct collaborative intervention based on a different set of interrelated nested framework assumptions. Those assumptions included that everyone has resources and resourcefulness and that it is possible to form active, open-ended exchange networks in which members offer their resources in return for psychological or material support to meet their other needs. This approach assures the realization of optimum use of the available resources. Another pattern described by the conferees was engagement in social and political activism through established societal channels to create the changes they judged to be more humane, socially benign, and socially constructive. These activities were another step in redefining psychology's and society's nested frameworks in order to link societal change activities to psychological data.

Targeted Populations. The conference participants pointed out that community psychologists had developed a distinctive focus on underserved and nonserved groups they considered to be at risk for psychological stress. Included were the aged, children, young mothers, the poor, and ethnic or racial minorities. They also identified individuals caught up or abandoned in institutions or other components of society which might be psychologically disturbing, e.g., mental hospitals and the criminal justice system.

Institutionalization of Community Psychology with Limited Horizons

Institutionalization of community psychology faced formidable obstacles. Relevant social and community interventions were controlled politically by the field of medicine and conceptually by the medical illness model. However, as Cowen (1973) emphasized, most psychologically disordered behavior

> differs quantitatively from the modal, short-term instance of physical dysfunction because it has deeper roots, longer germination periods, broader impact on many aspects of the person's functioning, and is shaped to a greater extent by significant people, experiences, and social institutions in the individual's history. (p. 430)

Cowen further described the medical illness diagnostic approach as narrowly focused on preventing only *diagnosable* illnesses and its approach to intervention with psychologically disordered behavior as having only limited effectiveness and primarily with less severe manifestations.

A community psychology prevention approach with its individual-in-context nested framework offered an attractive alternative possibility. It combined the reduction of risk factors in people's lives and the building of strengths and resources of people and communities to promote more constructive prosocial approaches to life. However, it challenged mainstream psychology and the broader society by requiring abandonment of their individually oriented nested framework. Fairweather, a pioneer in developing therapeutic communities, emphasized that social, rather than technological, changes are more difficult precisely because they require the social organization and people's roles within society to change (1972). Whether changing to an individual-in-context nested framework is more likely to be accomplished by evolving new nested framework conceptions within the rubric of prevention or by breaking completely with the medical model continues as a matter of ongoing debate.

Redefining Psychopathology. Albee simultaneously criticized the medical model and advanced the cause of prevention. He and his colleague stressed that "mental and emotional problems are not 'diseases' but learned patterns of social maladjustment and emotional distress" (Albee & Joffe, 1977, p. xiii). They refused to limit themselves to "the conventional categories included in the American Psychiatric Association's *Diagnostic Statistical Manual* … [since] we believe that sexism and racism are as psychopathological as the more conventional diagnostic categories" (p. xiv). Thus, while they retained the category, "psychopathological," they substituted "learned patterns" for "diseases" and emphasized societal patterns (e.g., sexism and racism) as network factors in producing dysfunction.

Social Ecology and Environments. Environmental and social ecology-oriented community psychologists have advanced alternative conceptions about the interactions of people's conduct, value systems, and various environments. Barker (1964) contributed studies of organism/environment interrelations in the naturally occurring contexts and units of behavior that occur in public environments such as towns. His seminal findings included that communities have different numbers and kinds of *behavioral settings* which, in turn, produce different *habitat claims* on the people in them. Otherwise stated, the nested framework of a community places direct demands on the way the people in them can live out their lives.

Moos and Insel (1974) described the environment as the major determinant of human behavior. They defined social ecology as the study of the impact that physical and social environments have on people and the development of optimum human milieus. Moos (1974, 1979) studied environmental climates, such as classrooms and military camps, demonstrating their impact on the "human aggregate" who serve as transmitters of the social and cultural aspects (the "content") of the environment. From this perspective, by identifying and installing an optimum environment, it is possible to attain a desired behavioral objective, e.g., increasing learning or reducing psychological dysfunction.

New Values. Community psychologists proposed moving beyond the traditional concepts of physical and mental illness and health. Consequently, they had to define an optimum human environment and the optimum community values necessary to establish and maintain it. Efforts to define those values have been addressed in a number of ways, two of which are cited here as examples.

Rappaport (1977) forcefully articulated his definition of the core, paradigmatic values of community psychology.

> What is proposed ... is a paradigm of cultural relativity, ecology, and diversity as a value system on which to base social interventions aimed at equitable distribution of material and psychological resources, rather than on improved socialization of all to a single standard which then serves as a means for selective distribution of society's resources. (p. 116)

As with any value criteria, Rappaport's are controversial. However, cultural relativism most clearly highlights the difficulty of reconciling conflicting value systems. Endorsing it involves asserting that there are independent, encapsulated nested frameworks of a cultural sort that are self-justifying and not subject to external scrutiny. That position immediately raises a question. What is the justification for asserting relativism for cultures but not for other societal units such as ethnic groups and families? Thus, cultural relativism leaves that issue as unresolvable, thereby making it inadequate for resolving the conflicts between individuals and their societies as well as between societies. That failure means that in this system each can appeal to being right and above challenge because of a different history, tradition, and context.

More recently, Trickett, Watts, and Birman (1994) broadened and advanced the case for including the roles of contexts and human differences when considering diversity factors. Their approach was to include attention to physical characteristics (i.e., racial/ethnic, gender, and physical handicap). In their report, they emphasized that the relevance of many such differences is primarily socially constructed and that understanding those differences requires that we attend to the nature of their social embeddedness. They focused on the importance of creating nested frameworks that incorporate mutually acceptable patterns of divergence and convergence for accommodating human diversities. They did not provide an adequate nested framework for resolving conflicts.

The proposed solution by Trickett, Watts, and Birman was based on tolerance, a willingness to assign tasks on the basis of areas of particular expertise, and a commitment to the greater good in completing undertakings. They did not provide a comprehensive approach for addressing the fact that sometimes people's nested frameworks are incompatible. Neither absolute cultural relativism nor absolute control of all interrelations by any involved party provide a defensible solution in such situations.

Research Frameworks. A fundamental aspect of any nested framework is its research paradigms. Distressingly, Ryan (1971) found that most social and behavioral science approaches necessarily blame victims of societal inequities for their own misfortunes. Caplan and Nelson (1973) documented that United States research studies characteristically assign responsibility for the difficulties of African Americans to their personal qualities. In spite of these biases, Vance (1973) identified a substantial body of evidence supporting the alternate conclusion that social disability in the United States is a result of the environmental correlates of urban poverty. Its "extreme conditions (ultimately individually defined) ... preclude individual mastery and, thus, the development of human potential and competence by both psychological and social standards" (p. 508). Vance's findings thereby highlighted that we can develop paradigmatic approaches which permit that possibility only when we use research approaches that identify contextual characteristics as causal.

Evaluation of Community Psychology's Efforts

In the long run, community-oriented psychologists must test the validity of their community paradigms by using them to produce desired community changes. They must then evaluate those efforts including whether they functioned according to their community principles. For example, a colleague and I (F. Tyler & Gatz, 1976) reported an effort to use community principles as the guidelines for a Ph.D. training program in clinical/community psychology. Evaluation of that program over a five-year period confirmed that it generated syntonic educational outcomes and functioned according to its participant–conceptualizer principles. Evaluation reports such as this one are necessary for establishing the validity of any paradigm.

In 1987, there was an organized evaluation of the state of community psychology at the end of its first 25 years. Snowden's (1987) conclusion was that it had done very little to meet its promises to focus on community systems, increase the cultural diversity of its membership, and emphasize improvement in the lives and conditions of minority individuals and communities. In his view, community psychologists were applying a universalist clinical approach, particularly with regard to minorities. However, he tempered his overall negative judgment by noting that community psychologists' conceptualizations and studies of stress, social support, and competence were being incorporated into mainstream psychology.

Elias (1987) emphasized another structural inconsistency in that numerous community projects had been started, developed, and evaluated as successful by community psychologists. However, the projects had not been integrated into the community contexts in which they were located. Rather, after evaluating their projects, psychologists abandoned them to start new projects or go on to other endeavors. Community psychologists had not incorporated the participant aspect of the participant–conceptualizer role to include their participation in communities beyond the need to meet their own, short term career objectives.

Schneider (1987), Shinn (1987), and Iscoe (1987) highlighted the failure to broaden the field's work beyond the traditional clinical mental health orientation. Glidewell (1987) emphasized that the vision of community psychology was of "a psychologist who studied, understood, conceptualized, and carefully intervened in the processes by which communities enhance or deplete the psychological well-being of the people who live in the communities" (p. 603). That vision had not been realized because it depended on psychologists making a shift from a personal style approach oriented to "cures" to one oriented to "a profession of validated knowledge and practice" (p. 603).

In summary, efforts to introduce a community perspective into the individual-oriented discipline of psychology have had implications for the success of community psychology, for the discipline of psychology, and for their relationship to society. Involvement in communities has challenged community psychologists to identify values that are consistent with and supportive of a community psychology orientation and assess when psychological findings (in contrast to personal or cultural values) are substantial enough to support or justify particular courses of action. Adopting a network stance would have required community psychologists to become team members focused on generating data for use in formulating public policies or becoming community change agents, or both, rather than independent, professional practitioners.

Community psychologists are still reluctant to make those changes although these issues will continue to confront them and other psychologists in any context. However, community psychologists have made important contributions. Their data base, although limited, includes empirically substantiated demonstrations of the efficacy of community-based approaches and a variety of increasingly sophisticated and tested problem-analysis and problem-solving approaches. These are being adopted in other areas of psychology as well as in societies more broadly. The community psychology nested framework orientation, although only imperfectly implemented, has demonstrated its importance for understanding individual and collective human conduct and improving the quality of both (F. Tyler, 1996).

PSYCHOLOGY AND CULTURAL CONSIDERATIONS

Argyris (1969) documented that, if research is confined to naturally occurring situations, evidence to challenge or transcend those naturally occurring limits can never be generated. Only by exploring environments beyond those of one particular culture can we provide the richer array of information and possibilities needed to mount such a challenge. Psychological findings from different cultures can help us to reexamine the roots and biases in each culture's paradigms and traditions and the culturally limited regularities established in each culture. Introducing such a cultural/ historical perspective can be of particular value with reference to the relatively unchallenged dominant framework of Western psychology.

CROSS-CULTURAL PSYCHOLOGY

Within cross-cultural psychology, the traditional assumption has been that there are universal psychological principles underlying all human behavior. Psychologists who challenge that tradition have argued that people, including psychologists, from different cultures live in different psychosocial worlds, form different, culturally based identities, and, therefore, formulate psychological phenomena in somewhat unique configural ways (Paranjpe, 1984). Blowers and Turtle (1987), reporting on the developments of psychology in Asia and the Western Pacific, concluded that there are distinctive indigenous psychological characteristics in that region of the world. They also noted that Euro-American dominance has made it difficult to identify unique perspectives and contributions surviving from pre-Western historical and cultural traditions. Those barriers make it imperative to identify, in particular, how cultural factors impact people's nested frameworks.

Examining the common sense definition of culture in a Western dictionary and comparing that definition with those developed by cross-cultural psychologists gives a way to identify the paradigmatic biases in each definition. A dictionary's definition of culture is the collective product of people's capability for acquiring and transmitting symbolic language and overt behavior (*Miriam–Webster's Collegiate Dictionary*, 1997). In this definition, culture refers to the nested framework characteristics of a group or to the ethnic validity attributes of its members, or to both. It does not address whether cultures form people or people form cultures, whether people are the creative agents of their own lives or societies, and what the "social glue" is which impels or sustains a culture. Without this information, we cannot determine whether there is a culture-free, universal psychology of individuals, or whether and in what ways the people from different cultures live in different psychosocial milieus or have distinctive psychosocial characteristics, or both. How cross-cultural psychologists define culture and address these issues is described in the following section.

A Universalist Cross-Cultural Psychology

Triandis (1980) provided a definition of culture that served as a guide for contributors to the first handbook of cross-cultural psychology. In his view, a culture is a group of people defined by a period in time, by either interpersonal contact or political organization, and by a language that provides for mutual intelligibility. He excluded historical factors, hierarchical factors such as status, and considerations of belonging or continuity, or both, ranging from nationality and race to family. He did acknowledge that the interactions of such characteristics with those of culture are of interest. He did not specify whether such a collection of people forms a cultural group as individuals or as a collective, or whether people are considered the creative agents of their own lives or societies or the products of external forces. Finally, his definition did not address whether culture is a descriptive category or an explanatory construct, although the definition suggests the former.

Consistently with that definition, Triandis and Lambert (1980) wrote that the goal of cross-cultural psychology is to establish similarities and differences that advance our understanding of humanity by comparing people across cultures. In their approach, the work of cross-cultural psychologists is to develop universal dimensions (etics) and measures using culture-specific items (emics) and then validate their universality in multiple ways. The first priority is to establish the generality of psychological laws in order to identify a framework of transcultural similarities as a basis for interpreting cultural differences. Simultaneously, procedures are to be developed for the measurement of those differences. Lonner elaborated on the underlying paradigmatic model that this search for psychological universals entails. He stressed that the field's task was to identify the "basic, passionate motives [that at an earlier time] had clear survival value for the species" (Lonner, 1980, p. 195) and are now obscured by cultural overlays.

These three writers delineated the core elements in the dominant Western cross-cultural psychology paradigm. Their work had an important homogenizing impact on the development of this field and the form of the nested framework within which cross-cultural studies have been conducted. The nested framework in which they located human behavior within and across cultures is primarily positivistic, reductionistic, essentially behaviorist, and not phenomenological. They viewed the nested framework in which human conduct occurs as a static milieu within which human "universals" evidence themselves in observed human conduct. Consequently, their cross-cultural approach did not create any basic change from that of Western mainstream psychology.

Berry (1985) expanded this paradigm to include indigenous perspectives by focusing on the "identity" of dominant and nondominant cultural or subcultural groups as they interact. His assumption was that the nondominant group inevitably acculturates to the dominant and frequently becomes assimilated. For example, in the United States some Native Americans abandon their heritage and accept a Euro-American identity. In New Zealand, some Maori reject their heritage to assume a Pakeha [Anglo] identity. However, Berry contradicted his main thesis by acknowledging that some immigrants reject acculturation and assimilation and revert to the "traditional" characteristics of their nondominant group.

None of these psychologists considered the possibility that members of a dominant culture also acculturate and assimilate to a nondominant culture. Perhaps most importantly, these cross-cultural psychologists did not allow the possibility that two groups could develop new or hybrid forms of identity, autonomy, and relatedness as they interact with each other. Their proposed paradigmatic frameworks marginalize nondominant groups and view distinctive cultural characteristics as irrelevant to a universalist perspective.

A Context-Based Cross-Cultural Psychology

One alternative to the extremes of universals and particulars is to assume that cross-cultural interactions are at a minimum two-way (like Newton's principle of gravity) and that the parties involved are active participants. Then, for example, we can use a variety of approaches to study participants' perspectives and contributions to the creation of meaning in those interactions. Each culture's people have a conception of their own nested framework including rules about how strangers are expected to conduct themselves and how they expect to conduct themselves as a stranger outside their own culture.

The two-faceted definition of culture that I use in this text is designed to incorporate those possibilities. As a categorizing term, it refers to a group of people who meet requirements such as language, location, social organization, and continuity characteristics. As a nested framework, it integrates these characteristics to provide a meaningful way of life for its members. That is, a culture involves specific people in a particular context and their characteristic behaviors and common forms of interaction. It also includes the shared activities and social forms that maintain their individual and group identities and their relationships to each other and to outsiders. Using this definition of cultures requires explanations that go beyond description and involve demonstrating whether the concept of culture is useful for understanding human conduct.

One of the conceptual matrix terms I have identified is *nested framework*. A second is *ethnic validity* paradigm, and a third is the *active agent* nature of individuals. These concepts (symbolic generalizations) can be interrelated to meet the requirements of an integrated conceptual matrix for cross-cultural psychology.

Nested framework, as discussed in detail in Chapter 2, refers to the understandings shared by a culture's people of the possibilities and limits of their life circumstances. Those circumstances include: (a) their physical ecology, ranging from their artifacts to the characteristics of their "natural" world; (b) their means of interaction (e.g., physical proximity or means of transportation and indirect contact) and communication (e.g., language, writing, etc.); and (c) the controlling beliefs that define and maintain their culture's coherence. *Ethnic validity* is the integrated factual and value bases that individuals who have been socialized and identified with homogeneous groups in a culture believe constitute the appropriate guiding framework for organizing their lives. Individuals conceptualized as *active agents* capable of making and acting on choices that involve judgments are the third element in this conceptual matrix.

Defining nested frameworks, ethnic validity paradigms, and individuals independently and in relation to each other provides a basis for empirically identifying their properties, interrelationships, and values for generating a better understanding of all three. Doing so also supplies a framework for determining whether culture, as defined here, is a concept with any substantive content. Finally, it furnishes a basis for applying that information to enrich the quality of lives of people and the societies in which they live.

This framework can also serve as a basis for exploring how cultures change in relation to possibilities and pressures for so-called programs of development or modernization. It may be that so-called underdeveloped indigenous people do not move in a unidirectional, cumulative, and linear fashion to adopt the characteristics of the people or the cultural forms of a dominant, more (or differently) developed culture. It may even be difficult to decide what constitutes development, progress, or even civilization. From a humanistic perspective, human progress (civilization) took a very negative turn when the early Christians became powerful enough to destroy earlier Roman, Greek, and Egyptian knowledge and conceptions of life. From an ecological perspective, human progress took another very negative turn when the early Spanish colonists in Colombia destroyed a vast ecologically self-sustaining irrigation-based agricultural system and the indigenous cultures were forced to flee in order to survive. Some, such as the Tairona, retreated to the high elevations of the Sierra Nevada de Santa Marta where they are still confined.

Cultural changes in so-called developed societies do not occur in unidirectional, cumulative, and linear fashions, nor do these societies readily adopt each other's characteristics. Immigration patterns do not always involve movement of "less developed" people to "more developed" people and circumstances. For example, were the many European refugees from Nazism who immigrated to North and South America in the 1930s immigrating to more, less, or similarly developed cultures? Was their course one of linear assimilation to their new cultures? It would seem that both they and their host cultures were changed in a wide variety of ways.

Unilateral ethnocentric actions to change cultures may have deleterious effects, as was evident from the results of one widely publicized debacle. Behavioral and social scientists participated in a United States government funded effort in South America, Project Camelot, to study how to undermine unfriendly governments (Vallance, 1966). As knowledge about that project became public, its culturally imperialistic values were challenged, and the legitimacy of cross-cultural research was undermined throughout much of the world. Elements in the public and the scientific community challenged scientists' presumed right to study any society's reality (nested framework) with the purpose of controlling that reality to the investigators' benefit.

These examples illustrate the impact of cultural, social, and individual network factors on research endeavors and on individual and collective behavior. Even more importantly, they identify interactions between cultures and ethnic groups as an important source of information about how different people's nested frameworks are constructed and influence the groups and individuals in them and others whom they encounter. They also underscore that, by beginning with a context-based multicultural nested framework, these interactions can be identified and their meanings interpreted in ways that reduce the influence of ethnocentric biases.

EMERGING PERSPECTIVES

Moghaddam (1987) examined differences in social psychology on the basis of the relative resources and power among what he classified as the first (United States), second (other industrialized nations), and third (developing countries) worlds. Comparing them provided an excellent starting point to explore the impact of culturally based, nested frameworks on psychological orientations. Emphasis in the first world was on how social factors impact individual behavior; in the second, on intergroup relations; in the third, on social/economic development, often modernization. The interchanges among these worlds were predominantly, but need not be, a one-way flow to the third world. The third and second worlds have significant contributions to make to each other and the first world, especially from their distinctive approaches to studying their physical and cultural ecologies.

Further, psychologists do not often look at what can be learned from other fields, such as anthropology and literature, or how psychology can build on their scholarship. An anthropologist, Cohn (1983), provided a striking example in his analysis of the British reorganization of their control of India after the so-called "Indian mutiny" in the 1850s. The British had misinterpreted the ritual offering of gifts by India's Mughal rulers as signifying a pattern of hierarchical economic exchange; to the Mughals, it was only a pledge of personal fealty. Consequently, the British created a linked hierarchical economic and power-based system for ruling India. Both the British and the Indians assumed the Indians were unable to rule themselves. They jointly created a republican tradition to provide for the diverse elements in India to function together and to educate a competent civil service which would support British control. When India declared its independence, it retained these predominantly British traditions. Britain had not just ruled India, it had changed the nested framework of its culture in a fundamental way.

Today, when the psychosocial characteristics of people in India are studied, little or no thought is given to the impact that this foreign nested framework still has on the lives of Indians. Those imposed nested frameworks and ethnic validity based rituals must be untangled from India's indigenous ones and be understood before it can work out its future. That untangling is equally essential to a better understanding of India's psychosocial data and why its psychologists function and formulate their theories as they do.

Other examples of the interaction of nested frameworks and events can be found in the humanities. Fussell (1977), a U.S. veteran of World War II and subsequently a professor of English, provided a literary, historical analysis of the impact of World War I on Great Britain and the British. At that time, British society was so homogeneous in a literary cultural sense that enlisted men and officers of all ranks read the same literature and used the same literary metaphors to describe their experiences. The application of industrial technology in that war destroyed that shared cultural sense of meaning, the sense of the participants about themselves and their society as humanistic, and the meaning of service to their country and ideals. Different nested frameworks and ethnic validity paradigms had to be constructed.

Examples such as these have relevance for the work of psychologists, whether or not they have a cross-cultural focus. People's cultures incorporate their historical traditions; consequently, historical material is relevant to the questions psychologists ask in any culture and the answers they get. However, psychology today shows little evidence that historical material is considered in formulating research questions or interpreting answers to them.

Most psychologists, like most lay people, accept their own society and its perspectives as being the appropriate stances on which to organize their lives and from which to study others. Yet, when participating in other cultures and interacting with psychologists from those cultures, all involved gain new insights about both their own and each other's perspectives. It seems vital that we step back from developing universal and indigenous psychologies to take into account not only our personal equation biases, but also the cultural factors embedded in them.

Kelley (1992) differentiated between scientific psychology and common sense psychologies, among which he included indigenous psychologies. He argued that western-based experimental approaches tran-scended their cultural embeddedness to provide a basis for an objective, general scientific paradigm. Argyris challenged that possibility when he differentiated espoused theories of action and theories-in-use. The former are accounts people provide of theoretical principles that guide their be-havior; the latter are principles derived from observing their behavior. In his experiments with college students in the United States, Argyris dem-onstrated (1969, 1975) that, even when they wanted to behave in a collab-orative way and were instructed in how to do so (Model II behavior), they quickly reverted to behaving in the manipulative, individualistic, competi-tive fashion characteristic of their culture (Model I). Argyris' research and arguments provide a solid basis for the conclusion that no psychologist from any culture is going to create a universal, culture-free psychology.

To develop multicultural, multidisciplinary psychological paradigms, we need to answer how and why Moghaddam's (1987) "three worlds" differ and how we can interrelate them. To some extent, psychologies are different because psychologists are products of and participants in differ-ent cultures and because the psychologies they create reflect those cul-tures. Reconciling the discrepancies between these different perspectives rests, in part, on our understanding of the role of psychologists. If psychol-ogists (as individuals as well as scientists) simply reflect society, the only scientific model needed is that of the natural sciences with its assumption that all consequences are determined and laws can be established by prediction and control approaches. On the other hand, if psychologists inform society, then we are creative agents contributing new insights and perspectives in only somewhat predictable ways to the available human record and to people's experiences, including our own. Our task as psy-chologists is and will continue to be one of checking and revising our many culturally embedded paradigms because, among other reasons, we are changing them and they are changing us as we form them and use them.

At times, we psychologists assume we are creative agents with free choice and objectivity, while those with whom we interact are predictable products of their natures and experiences. Scheibe (1985) referred to this stance as the "psychologist's advantage—his or her maintenance of a superior and invulnerable role vis-a-vis his or her patient or subject" (p. 52). However, as Robinson (1991) stressed, the human record suggests that all people are creative agents and that factor must be included in our psychological formulations. Specifically, "for there to be morality at all ... it must be possible for the actor to have done otherwise.... Thus, 'morality necessarily presupposes freedom.' But what is it that possesses this free-dom?" (p. 7) His answer was that "a developed theory of human nature takes the historical record seriously and is prepared to find in it ... a record of agents seeking ends which, whatever else they might bring ... are pursued for the sake of autonomy itself" (pp. 7–9).

Examples of the role of choice in people's lives are illustrative. The neurologist Sacks (1985) argued that we need a concept of agency, of choice. He cited the cases of two elderly women who chose different approaches to deal with the consequences of similar neurological accidents. Their cerebral strokes produced a rapid and unstoppable flow of songs with attendant memories from early childhood. One of the women, who had a wonderful early childhood but a miserable subsequent life, loved the songs and memories and wanted to retain them. The other woman had a less happy childhood but a more pleasant later life and pleaded to be rid of the songs and memories. Sacks also cited the case of the composer, Shostakovich, who had a shell fragment in his brain as a result of his military service. If he leaned to the left, he heard song fragments. They stimulated his creativity, and he resisted having the splinter removed.

The social psychologist Smith (1966) postulated such dispositions from his studies of styles of competence in the Peace Corps. The competent participants chose from an array of personal and task oriented styles, including a warm nurturing style and a nine-to-five task-oriented style. Less competent participants were characterized by dependent-anxiety, but the usual measures of pathology did not predict the level of effectiveness for any of the volunteers.

Construction of a serviceable transcultural paradigm must begin with a representative number of psychologies and cultures, each with its own nested framework. From that sample, we can obtain a first approximation of the role of cultural factors in our scientific paradigms. The necessity of including these considerations becomes evident from examining some current examples in which the role of parochial cultural embeddedness is still unresolved.

Bettelheim (1990) challenged the view that Freud's theories constitute a culture-free general paradigm. He argued that at the end of the nineteenth century the Austro-Hungarian Empire was in decline and the people in the capital, Vienna, had turned their thoughts in on themselves, on sex, and death. These historical and cultural considerations were uniquely necessary to create the patients Freud had and enabled him to develop his psychoanalytic theories with their emphases on sex and death. Jahoda's (1977) work strengthened this argument. She analyzed the discrepancies and concurrences between Freud's perceptions of the life of a Jewish professional in Austria and those which would have been normative, judging from the perceptions of his contemporary Jewish professionals. By differentiating between his idiosyncratic experiences and more typical ones, she identified interpretations that were more likely based on his unique experiences than on presumably universal human characteristics.

Other psychologists have explored presumably universal locus of control attributes and found that they are subject to quite different cultural interpretations. Primary (internal) control is defined in the United States as power to shape the world; in Japan, it is power to adapt to the world (Azuma, 1984; Kojima, 1984); and among Hindus and Buddhists, it is power to renounce desire. According to Diaz-Guerrero, a Mexican family's domestic world is affiliative, their outside world is one to be mastered. "The optimal way out in the Mexican society [is] one that permits the child to be affiliative-obedient when adjustive, and actively self-assertive when necessary for achievement" (1977, p. 941). In each context, internal control was defined as a particular kind of control in relation to the framework within which people in that culture considered human life to be nested.

To reiterate briefly, the nested frameworks and life paradigms within any culture are context based; they are not universal. Creating a transcultural psychology requires starting from a multicultural data base and involving psychologists from a diverse group of cultures to be actively involved in that task. It also requires attending to the role of people's individual decision-making capabilities and even to possible culture differences among them.

PSYCHOLOGISTS AND CULTURES: ACTIVE AGENTS AND INTERNESTED PRODUCTS

People manage their lives, in part, by creating or using available individual, ecological, and social network resources in a discretionary manner. The ways we live are neither totally a matter of free choice nor totally determined. They are bath. In principle, human conduct is not totally predictable. To the extent that people are agents in their own lives, we may be able to predict how they will approach issues and even a range of possible outcomes, but not their exact courses or outcomes.

To incorporate this perspective into our science, it is necessary to identify the free aspect and the determined aspect, and then establish how they interrelate. I consider four classes of inputs essential for that task: destiny, history, continuity, and autonomy (choice) (F. Tyler, Brome & Williams, 1991). Each of us can be characterized as having a *destiny* which, in part, shapes our lives. We are born male or female, tall or short, with a particular skin color, in a given location, and at a given time in history. We cannot change much of that unique configuration of characteristics and circumstances. We also have a unique personal *history* which has become part of us. It includes the sense of *continuity* we each have with our family, ancestors, real or anticipated offspring, and the human species in general. It may also involve the possibility of continuity for ourselves before and beyond our current existence, our spiritual nature, the traditions of our country, etc. Finally, we have a sense of *autonomy*, of choice or agency.

Communities and cultures also have a destiny, history, continuity, and autonomy, although their characteristics may be less clearly denoted as such. Each of us organizes the structure and content of those contextual inputs in a nested hierarchical way. Generally accepted psychosocial context groupings include culture, race, ethnicity, community, family, and individual. We cannot find all meaning embodied in any one perspective or at any one of these groupings because meaning is derived not only from each, but also from their interactions, their relationships, and the contexts in which they are embedded.

To complete our framework for encompassing an understanding of how people organize their own experiences, we need to take into account how they interact with others. Our framework must include a basis for understanding how people arrive at and build on convergences of experience, knowledge, and beliefs, how they handle divergences (acceptable areas of difference), and how they manage conflict (F. Tyler, Brome, & Williams, 1991). Further, that convergence/divergence/conflict perspective must include attention to people's levels of social embeddedness. One illustrative approach to social embeddedness currently being addressed is that of *cultural identity*. Embodying it requires attending to three core notions, namely: (a) One aspect of each person's nature and reality is her or his culture, (b) each person has some choice about her or his identity, and (c) identity influences behavior.

I described in more detail the reasoning and implications of this position in an earlier paper (F. Tyler, 1989). Major points included that psychology is not acultural, but rather psychologies are based on tacit cultural perspectives embedded in people's cultural identities. They contribute to the irreducible personal equations which shape our individual and collective questions and observations.

Acceptance of these new views drastically changes how we think about what have been traditionally accepted as legitimate activities and how we will proceed to develop and use our science. For example, we may still search for universal principles, but we will understand them differently once we think of them as built on a convergence–divergence–conflict foundation and on the active participation of individuals in forming them. Further, we will approach that task from a new paradigmatic basis and draw conclusions that will be different from what we draw using current approaches.

SUMMARY

This chapter provided an approach to psychology that brings together considerations of cultures, contexts, and individuals. It incorporates considerations of people as creative agents (because we are knowers), people as natural products (because we are known), and people as embedded in particular contexts (we are creative in the way we are, in part because we are Chinese, Belgian, etc.). This chapter introduced choice and meaning as part of the diversity we see in human conduct. An embedded nested framework paradigm that indicates the impossibility of constructing a transcultural psychology from any one cultural/scientific base was presented.

To build an integrative paradigm of psychology that transcends any particular cultural bias will require that we depart from our current dominant paradigm to (a) accept that human conduct is partially open-ended, not totally predictable; (b) incorporate the concepts of freedom and morality into psychology; (c) formulate ways of dealing with freedom's and morality's empirical roots and limitations, as well as their possibilities; (d) change our definitions of cultures, communities, and other social groupings to include the active agent role of people in forming them; (e) incorporate cultural, community, and other nested framework factors and cultural and community identity factors into our psychological theories and formulations; (f) consider that basing our endeavors exclusively on the dichotomies of basic/applied and etic/emic may not only be arbitrary, but counterproductive; and (g) incorporate resource collaboration as a primary prototype of scientific endeavors along with existing individual, autonomous, even adversarial, efforts.

If we are to develop a multiculturally useful integrative paradigm, it must come from an acceptance that all psychology paradigms are indigenous, even the dominant indigenous paradigm of the first world. Attention must be paid to contexts, cultures, and individuals separately and in relation to each other. Building on such an approach will yield a different set of transcultural psychological convergences, divergences, and conflicts than those that we get from any one perspective. It can lead to important psychological and social benefits, including increased individual and societal effectiveness, more prosocially constructive conflict management, and broader participation in creating and sustaining a better quality of life for people.

CHAPTER 4

THE ETHNIC VALIDITY
OF PEOPLE'S LIVES

INTRODUCTION

This chapter outlines how ethnic validity conceptions help all of us understand the ways individuals find meaning, significance, and direction in our lives as we organize our individual experiences within the nested frameworks of our societies. For this purpose, it is necessary to use the words ethnic and ethnicity in a broader way than has been customary. Specifically, the primary definition of the words *ethnic* and *ethnicity* refers to less powerful individuals or population subgroups with a common cultural heritage as designated by customs, characteristics, language, common history, etc. (*Webster's Unabridged Dictionary*, 1972, p. 628). That definition has served to sustain and justify hierarchical and inequitable patterns of human relationships. There is an overlooked, secondary meaning given to these terms. It designates as ethnic any group having a common heritage. This broader definition is necessary to understand how ethnic validity paradigms, nested frameworks, and people's ethnicity influence the way everyone manages their lives. Ethnic validity models for psychology framed in this broader way do not tacitly or explicitly support a power-oriented normative bias in our approaches to individuals or groups.

In a presentation supporting the use of an ethnic validity model approach to psychotherapy, my colleagues and I made several points about the core difficulties raised by the ethnocentric use of ethnicity designations. Those points included the culturally normal assumptions that: (a) issues of race and ethnicity are relevant only for such groups (called here *nonculture-defining*, NCD); (b) dominant (called here *culture-defining*, CD) groups of individuals within a particular context whose values, rules, style of life, and criteria for competence set the standard for that society are deculturized in this regard; and (c) ethnocentricity is spawned and nurtured by the CDG's assumed preeminence and by NCDG's deferring out of powerlessness, hopelessness, or acceptance (F. Tyler, Brome & Williams, 1991). In contrast to these assumptions, the ethnic validity model (EVM) emphasizes that sensitivity to one's own and others' race and ethnicity is important for everyone. Each of us forms a perspective—not ultimate truth, but a point of view—on the basis of the ecology in which we are embedded. That perspective is characterized by a distinct value system and way of life and by criteria for competence and dysfunction. People develop a CD perspective because of historical, social, and political events, but that perspective is intrinsically of no more or no less value than a NCDG one.

The EVM provides a comprehensive framework that allows for application of the ethnic validity concept to everyone's life. The core meaning in the concept of ethnicity is that each of us lives out our life embedded in a nested framework, a culture, and an ecology which offer a complex range of possibilities and limitations. To some extent, we are defined by our context, irrespective of our wishes. Each of us lives within that ethnic-individual nestedness and relies on it as we are shaped by and contribute to our own lives, our societies, and the lives of others. We may accept or reject the efforts of others and the ways our societies define us in their terms; however, as we choose how to identify ourselves and organize our lives we must inevitably begin to do so from our perspective within our nested frameworks.

Neither identities nor life pathways are ever frozen beyond the possibility of change, nor are they totally determined by either internal or external factors. As individuals, our active choice or passive acquiescence to any particular identity or life path contributes to maintaining its influence on each of us. We, in turn, influence its nature. However, some characteristics may be more constraining than others. For example, attributions based on or associated with immutable physical characteristics create identities that are more resistant to being changed than those which are not so linked.

There are significant differences between being a member of a CDG and of a NCDG. The two groups have an asymmetrical relationship, with the benefits of their society ordinarily favoring those with CDG identities. However, there are costs to that more favored position, including the potential loss of any sense of a cultural identity or heritage. This asymmetry highlights the point that for people to transcend their nested frameworks they must also redefine themselves and their relation to the world. That task may be somewhat different for CDG than for NCDG individuals. CDG individuals may have a nonexistent or poorly developed sense of themselves and their way of life as nested in a socially constructed context. NCDG individuals more often have a sense of living within a nested context that defines them as inferior or otherwise not suitable and therefore limits their life opportunities.

These transcendist possibilities are being presented as a valid basis from which to understand and implement approaches to individual and social change. The particulars of the change process may differ for individuals in different life situations because people's identifications with collective entities is, in part, a function of their choices and their circumstances. That is, people may actively agree with or reject, rather than just passively accept, external suggestions about who they are and to what ethnic categories they belong. They also may challenge or change any or all of these alternatives. The necessity of attending to the interactive nature of these processes becomes evident when considering that others are also accepting or rejecting efforts to be included or excluded, or are trying to redefine the group. For example, Sabnani, Ponterotto, and Borodovsky (1991) analyzed the cross-cultural counselor education training process in psychology in the United States. They emphasized that this process is largely monocultural and dominated by psychologists with a CDG European American heritage; changing that orientation will require developing a "transcendent world view that affirms multicultural diversity" (p. 89). Highlen (1994), in a subsequent and more extensive review, argued that this dominant monoculturalism permeates psychology more broadly, including its research strategies, and will require structural changes from the top down to offset it. This chapter emphasizes that individuals are active agents in creating, maintaining, and changing their individualities, their ethnicities, and their nested frameworks. Further, change must involve all of these facets of people's lives, plus their contexts if it is to have a significant impact on their futures, their ethnicities, and their nested frameworks.

ETHNIC VALIDITY FRAMEWORK

HYPOTHESES AND ASSUMPTIONS

The general hypothesis of the ethnic validity model is that each of us is nested in a culture and an ecology and we define ourselves as individuals having a particular cultural/racial/ethnic/gender nature, set of experiences, and identity. We use that ethnic/individual nestedness to shape ourselves and contribute to our own lives, to others, and to our societies. Support for that hypothesis requires evidence of interactions among the ecological, cultural, and individual patterns within people's frameworks and contexts. It also requires confirmation of several related hypotheses. First, there are differences in self, self–world, and coping patterns between NCDG and CDG individuals in specific contexts. Next, individuals can transcend, blend, or otherwise shape unique life patterns in their society's contexts and not be totally controlled by their own ethnicity. Finally, in any relevant context, people are agents who contribute some portion of the variance. The material corroborating these hypotheses must fit conceptually within the nested context format advanced in the previous chapter. A substantial amount of research whose findings are consistent with these hypotheses has been conducted, and representative examplars are cited throughout this chapter.

ECOLOGICAL PERSPECTIVES

Community psychologists interested in social change and human betterment seek an alternative conceptual framework for organizing their innovative thoughts and efforts. Models of individual treatment are hopelessly inadequate for improving the quality of the lives of people in communities or other large population groups. The disease prevention model offers advantages over individual treatment models, but it, too, limits the possibilities for conceptualizing and developing constructive prosocial communities and societies.

A model with the potential of being more useful to society must meet several requirements. It must encompass the full range of life conditions and life capabilities, including people's possibilities, not just their pathogenic vulnerabilities. It must also incorporate attention to both the supportive and destructive effects of systems and environmental variables because only by changing their composition is it possible to generate large-scale societal and community changes. If we add that such a model must also incorporate the possibility of each person acting as an agent in his or her own behalf, we find that all of these requirements are met in an ethnic validity model.

Ecology

A number of community-oriented psychologists have turned to an ecology model as potentially useful for guiding social intervention. However, it does not fully meet the requirements of a socio-behavioral science model because it is not concerned with identifying or creating more and less desirable ecological balances. As a biological science, ecology is concerned with the mutual relatedness of species in their physical and biological environments. Relatively autonomous environments are referred to as *ecosystems*, and the nature of their functioning can be readily grasped by considering the example of an aquarium. For the plants and animals to survive in an aquarium, there must be biological equilibrium. A balanced exchange of carbon dioxide and oxygen must exist between the animals and plants. With too many or too few fish, snails, other animals, or plants, the balance is destroyed, and nothing survives. This also occurs with the presence of incompatible animals or plants. The survival of the ecosystem also requires that the physical environment's characteristics are sustained. If there is too little or too much light, heat, chemical concentration, or food, the ecosystem is disrupted, reproduction and growth are impeded, and the system is eventually destroyed.

The methodological emphasis in ecology is on studies in natural (rather than laboratory) settings of identifiable self-sustaining ecosystem characteristics such as adaptation, interdependence, and system change. *Adaptation* is defined as the capacity of organisms to cope, survive, and grow in their environments. *Interdependence* refers to the relationships among living and nonliving elements which together define an ecosystem. *System change* refers to the observable differences over time in mode of organization, the thriving of some species, and the changing or dying-out of others in an ecosystem.

Social Ecology

When an ecological perspective is applied to human societies, additional factors must be given consideration because our emphasis is on optimizing human survival. In addition, we have highly developed capabilities as agents acting in our own behalf to anticipate, choose, plan, and change our environments and then evaluate the impact of those changes. However, those choices also often have unintended consequences. Our choice patterns have sustained not only creative, prosocially oriented individuals and communities (ecosystems), they have also sustained highly destructive ones. For example, we developed agriculture and provided reliable food supplies for billions of people. In doing so, we contributed to deforesting the world and are now confronting negative consequences such as erosion, environmental pollution, and climate changes. Similarly, we have controlled many life-threatening diseases with considerable effectiveness and now face problems of overpopulation.

We have developed complex and intricate patterns of relationship to ourselves, other people, and the rest of the world. Many of these patterns are nonverbalized, others often cannot be expressed verbally because of social taboos or legal constraints, or both, and still others are common subjects of communication. Our relationships to ourselves and others are often expressed in forms of dress, including which parts of the body to cover and which to expose. These rules are primarily meaningful to our own ethnic groups and convey a sense of ethnic otherness to outsiders. Similar patterns are reflected in our relationships to the physical environment. Some treat nature with reverence; some treat it as available for exploitation but as of no intrinsic value. We use these patterns to identify our own ethnicity to each other as well as to outsiders. They also serve to define, facilitate, or delimit areas of cross-ethnic convergence, divergence, and conflict. Review of two ecological models used in community psychology will serve to highlight some of the basic value considerations involved in adopting such a model.

Person–Environment Fit Models. Barker (1964), Holahan (1978), Kelly (1978), and Rappaport (1977) were early advocates of person–environment fit models. Holahan identified three basic postulates of these models: (a) The environmental context is a major determinant of events in human communities, (b) environments are conceptualized in social-system terms, and (c) people's psychological adjustment is determined by their transactional relationships with their environments. Optimal adjustment is defined as a close correspondence (or fit) between the person's qualities and the environment's requirements. Whether more desirable or less costly person–environment correspondences might be developed does not enter into consideration, nor do questions about whether people carry patterns of adaptation, once developed, into other situations. For example, questions do not arise about whether people organize patterns of living which provide them an ethnically valid identity that they carry with them and expect others to adapt to and honor.

Barker (1964) viewed ecology as a descriptive science. The psychologist is a *transducer*, a docile receiver, coder, and transmitter of psychological phenomena, not a manipulator, evaluator, and controller of events. The psychologist simply describes patterns of person–environment fit in the naturally occurring behavior units of a total population, not individuals. These *behavior settings* are the basic *natural units* of study because they provide the concrete contexts of purposive behavior. Behavior settings are the specific place–thing–time constellations of people's behavior en masse which occur within particular parts of their milieu so that their behavior and the setting fit together, regardless of which individuals are involved. Examples include characteristic games, such as cricket or basketball, formal gatherings, such as community meetings or religious pilgrimages, and informal gatherings, such as those in a coffee shop or outside a theater.

Behavior settings are described in terms of *habitat qualities* and *habitat claims*. Habitat qualities are the typical demographic and behavioral characteristics and behaviors (e.g., playing or watching a game) of the inhabitants who frequent the setting and the psychosocial functions it provides them. Habitat claims are the number of positions of responsibility which must be filled for the normal occurrence or functioning of that behavior setting (games require players and referees).

This approach yields information such as that reported by Barker and Schoggen (1973) after studying the behavioral settings in a small midwestern town in the United States and a somewhat comparable town in England. The smaller, U.S. town, with only 830 inhabitants, had 884 behavior settings and 10,224 habitat claims. In contrast, the English town had 1,310 inhabitants but only 758 behavioral settings and 7,764 habitat claims. The U.S. town had 117% as many behavioral settings and 132% as many positions of responsibility (habitat claims) that needed to be filled for the town to function in its characteristic manner.

These findings made it possible to introduce another dimension for describing the characteristics of communities, namely, a bipolar one with the extremes being *overmanning* and *undermanning*. Overmanning refers to the person–environment relationship when there are many people with few habitat claims; undermanning to when there are few people and many roles to be performed. Using relative degree of manning produced information that could not have been obtained by simply studying the individuals involved. For example, the inhabitants of the relatively undermanned U.S. town spent, on the average, more time in public settings and more frequently assumed positions of responsibility in those behavior settings. In short, they were more involved in town life than were the inhabitants of the relatively overmanned English town.

Barker and Gump (1964) studied other environments, such as schools. They found that smaller schools also tended to be relatively undermanned and involved their students in more activities. Because these schools had relatively more habitat claims to be met, marginal members were provided with more opportunities and pressures to participate in school activities and, thereby, gain in competencies. They were less likely to create a group of outcasts or to support student specialization.

An important contribution of this work is that we are confronted with questions about the overall advantages and disadvantages of encouraging specialization or more broadly based homogenized participation. Also, how do we create environments which combine the advantages of both specialization and broad based participation? However, Barker's approach does not give us a framework for deciding what constitutes a prosocial setting, which settings are more prosocially useful, or what kinds of intervention roles or strategies can create more desirable milieus.

Kelly and his colleagues (1978) tested a different person–environment relationship hypothesis. They tested whether people's levels of adaptation were directly related to their degree of fit with their environment by comparing two U.S. high school systems that were selected as representative of quite different ecosystems. One, considered to be a *fluid* ecosystem, was characterized by a 42% change in the student body each year; the other, with a change rate of less than 10% each year, a *constant* ecosystem. To compare the two schools as ecosystems, student coping styles, extent of anticipation of the future, preference for exploration or novelty, sense of personal control of the outcomes in one's life activities, and social effectiveness were measured in each. Student behavior was also observed in a number of representative school settings, including the office of the principal, hallways, cafeterias, and lavatories.

The study's major findings were consistent with its central hypothesis. For example, students who scored high in "preference to explore" improved more on competence measures in a fluid school environment; those low on that measure improved more in a constant school environment. Life in the constant school revolved around fixed status and group membership. Newcomers were treated cautiously and accepted only if they fit into the established structure and behavior styles. In the fluid school, the nature of the psychosocial environment and the patterns of interaction were more free flowing and varied. It provided more ways of fitting in and more openness for new students to fit in. To summarize, students in the constant environment who were rated high on adaptation were passive, responsive, well-behaved citizens, and those who were rated low on adaptation were innovative and exploratory. In the fluid environment, students who rated high on adaptation were creative, adventuresome, and exploratory, and those who rated low on adaptation were passive, receptive, and rule oriented.

These findings support the hypothesis that good adaptation is related to close person–environment fit if adaptation is measured exclusively in terms of a person's current environment. They also provide us with additional valuable information about the influence of a current nested framework in determining which behaviors will work and, consequently, how adequately adjusted certain types of people will be in that context. They do not indicate whether environments, in part, influence how successful people will be in other situations and how they are likely to feel about themselves in other situations. That is, for person–environment fit models to provide a full account of individual behavior, they must demonstrate that people are predominantly creatures of their current environments. They must also establish that there is a "fit" which is devoid of disadvantages or, at the least, possesses a combination of advantages and disadvantages that provides an outcome superior to other possibilities. These models do not yield that information because person–environment fit models are, by their nature, situation specific.

In summary, the major limitations of person–environment fit models include their inability to account for the interaction effects on people of the many environments in which they live at any one time and over the course of their lives. Neither do they give consideration to an additional issue that is basic to an ethnic validity conception of how people lead their lives. They do not provide information about people as *knowers* who may identify with and internalize a particular identity and ecology as being a desirable reference context.

Optimum Environment Models. The quality of environments in relation to the quality of human lives and, ultimately, human survival is another social-ecological issue needing attention. Moos and Insel (1974, p. ix) pointed out that "social ecology may be viewed as the multidisciplinary study of the impact that physical and social environments have on human beings. It is concerned with the assessment and development of optimum human milieus." Their approach directly confronted some of the issues not addressed by person–environment fit models because they acknowledged that environmental effects may vary from benign and supportive to malignant and destructive. They also assumed that the merits of those environments could be studied and the findings used as guides for social and community planning and action.

Moos (1979) focused on the study of *environmental climates* because he assumed that environments play the major role in the interaction between people and their environments. Consequently, he emphasized the necessity of investigating the impact of people's environments on them. In his view, people's efforts to adapt to their environments influence such characteristics as their personal interests and values, self-concepts, aspirations, achievements, and health. In turn, their characteristics effect the outcomes of their coping efforts and those outcomes influence the environment and the environmental climate. That process continues to repeat itself.

Moos (1979) constructed a detailed schema of the nature of environmental systems as a basis for studying and understanding their structures and impacts. According to his schema, an environment is defined by the normative properties of its elements: a physical system, organizational factors, a human aggregate, and a social climate. Consequently, while the people in any environment contribute in a small way to its nature, they remain separate from it as individuals.

An environment's *physical system* is made up of characteristics such as physical design and architecture. Its impact can be seen in research findings about the greater cohesiveness in schools which are concentrated in one building. That design facilitates interaction, informal and otherwise, and thus enhances the likelihood that students, faculty, and staff will form a sense of shared belonging and togetherness. In contrast, a school that consists of many buildings is more socially isolating. Everyone's opportunities for interpersonal contacts in any part of the school are reduced and they spend more time moving around within the system.

The *organizational factors* in environmental systems refer to the formal and informal forms and processes which guide its functioning. The characteristics considered relevant under this heading are similar to those that Barker and Gump (1964) identified in relation to overmanning and undermanning. For example, universities with a large number of students are usually overmanned. The students are relatively less likely to interact with faculty, be involved with school government, or to achieve leadership skills or positions. They are also more likely to be dissatisfied with the faculty and with classroom instruction. These patterns tend to be reversed in undermanned, small universities.

The *human aggregate* consists of the people in the environmental system. They transmit most of the cultural and social environment to each other and over time. Characteristics such as their ages, socioeconomic levels, educational attainments, and beliefs influence the system and define much of its content. For example, an elementary school, high school, college, and university are all educational environmental systems, but are composed of quite different human aggregates. The same is true of science-oriented and humanities-oriented universities and of universities in different cultures.

Moos (1979) placed primary emphasis on the fourth environmental system factor, the *social climate*, as the mediator of the other factors. He defined social climate as the characteristic environmental *press* (pressure) that can be inferred to be providing consistency and continuity to otherwise discrete events in that situation. For example, if students' seats are in rows and are assigned, if faculty see students only by appointment, and if there is a prescribed form for most activities, the *press* or *social climate* of that school emphasizes the orderly conduct and responses characteristic of students in the school. In military schools, the climate emphasizes the aggression as well as orderliness that are typical of their students. In contrast, in slums and impoverished communities, the climate emphasizes the moment-to-moment-survival focus of their residents.

Because of his conviction that the social climate dimension is the most significant contributing factor to environmental climates, Moos further analyzed this factor. He described social climates as having three major dimensions, each of which is measured separately by assessing how it is perceived by the aggregate of people in each environment. He was not concerned with individual perceptions and relied on group scores rather than computing or analyzing individual scores.

The first of Moos' (1979) social climate dimensions is the *relationship* dimension. In its measurement, attention is directed to the extent to which people are involved in a milieu, support and help one another, and express themselves freely and openly. For example, hierarchically organized and authoritatively conducted schools with clearly specified goals and standards, plus strict rules and codes of conduct, generate characteristic patterns of relationships. They have low student involvement, little peer support and help, and little openness or freedom of expression.

The specific nature and content of the second dimension, *personal growth* or *goal orientation*, varies from setting to setting in relation to the nature and purposes of that setting (Moos, 1979). Attention is directed toward identifying and measuring the areas in which personal growth and self-enhancement tend to occur. Among student groups, emphasis is often placed on growth in independence, achievement, and intellectuality. In family groups, emphasis is more often placed on self-enhancement through mutual caring, sharing, and respect.

Lastly, in the *system maintenance and change* dimension, measurement is directed toward characteristics such as the orderliness of the environment, the clarity of expectations, the maintenance of control, and the response to change or innovation (Moos, 1979). Schools vary in the degree to which they emphasize an open environment or one which stresses structure and obedience. Communities differ in emphasizing authoritarian control or citizen participation. Mental hospitals, clinics, and community centers vary in their emphasis on professional control, community participation, openness, support, and other related factors.

Results of a number of Moos's (1979) studies of educational environments provide guidelines for constructing social environments to achieve desired prosocial outcomes. For example, student satisfaction, interest in the subject matter, and social and personal growth in a classroom can be enhanced by emphasizing the social climate dimensions of relationships and system change. However, facilitation of academic achievement, including gains on standard achievement tests, is most likely to occur in a class with warm and supportive relationships, an emphasis on specific tasks and goals, and a clear, orderly, and well-structured milieu. Classroom settings which have a high expectation and demand for academic performance can also enhance creativity and personal growth. Large achievement gains may occur in classes that stress that aim along with organization and clarity. These classes are lower in warmth and are not as effective in raising student interest, morale, creativity, or personal growth. These results suggest that basic skills programs would have more positive effects if they were supportive as well as task oriented and that open program classes should benefit from an emphasis on task orientation, though not if affiliation and support are de-emphasized.

Moos' studies indicate that a combination of tasks and relationships can produce gains in achievement as well as personal growth and fulfillment. In fact, gains in each of these dimensions can enhance the gains in others. Another implication of such findings is pointed out by Walberg, Rasher, and Singh (1977), who found similar results from their school studies in Rajastan, India. In addition, they noted that only a quarter of the teachers in India are trained and more teacher training programs are needed. As Moos (1979) suggested, those teachers are more likely to be effective if their training programs stress the creation of more optimal learning environments for the students. Even with limited resources, programs can introduce changes in learning environments which will potentially improve the effectiveness of existing educational units. The alternatives, construction of buildings and other facilities and increased academic achievement levels among the teachers, are environmental improvement approaches that are more costly and more time consuming than the creation of more optimal learning environments.

Thus, environments can be designed to accomplish certain objectives, such as maximizing learning and shaping interpersonal relationship patterns more efficiently. However, this approach does not deal with the *knower* role of people. Participants have been considered knowers in these studies only in the investigators' implicit acceptance of their own roles in the formation of their theories, the setting up of the environments they design, and the making of decisions about the nature of desirable social circumstances and individual characteristics. In effect, whether by intent or otherwise, these experts' approaches are based on their creation of two types of psychosocial validity: that of professionals, or *knowers* acting as change agents who create nested frameworks, and that of workers, students, or clients/patients as *known* individuals who are directed by nested framework structures.

Summary of Ecological Perspectives

Ecologically oriented psychologists and other investigators have made significant contributions to our understanding of the psychological aspects of human communities and other sociocultural systems. Their study of environments and the measures they developed for that purpose provide important tools for planning, implementing, and evaluating system changes. They have also constructed more adequately informed bases for developing prosocially constructive environments and assessing their effectiveness. Their work demonstrates that environments are important in a number of crucial ways because they substantially influence the behavior that takes place in them.

As valuable and as important as environmental approaches are, those which have been developed are seriously limited. They do not provide (a) a means of conceptualizing, studying, or approaching the task of balancing individual values and concerns with those of groups or systems in ways that contribute to improved lives of the people in them; (b) a basis for addressing the issues which arise for individuals who are different from the norm in any given context; (c) aid in considering the issues faced by individuals who find themselves in an environmental context where they otherwise fit but have nonnormative goals; (d) a way to address transituational issues, such as those embodied in life styles, psychosocial or ethnic identities, or ethnic validity; and (e) a basis for considering people's capabilities for making choices, such as active agent decisions to oppose situational expectations or to exhibit transituational consistency.

To give attention to these additional individual-systems relationships first requires inclusion of the idea that individuals are active agents on their own behalf and in the pursuit of broader human and societal issues. Further, given the validity of ecological findings such as those outlined here, consideration must be given to the role and influence of ecological factors in people's choices of psychosocial identities and ethnic validity perspectives. In our theories, our research, and our interventions, we must address the impact of ecologies on the people living in them. Our approaches as individuals and in our work as professionals must take account of how experiencing an environment or ecology and accepting or rejecting it as *ours* contributes to (a) the ways we form our psychosocial identities and make choices based on our ethnic validities for guiding our ways of living and (b) the ways we organize the possibilities and constraints of our relevant nested frameworks.

CHOOSING AN ETHNIC VALIDITY PARADIGM IN A HETEROGENEOUS CONTEXT

A central aspect of a social ecology approach is its holistic nature, its assumption that the components of an ecological unit must be mutually self-sustaining for its survival. Its tolerance for flexibility is limited by the consequence following any changes that disrupt its balance. Those changes must be counterbalanced by others to restore the unit's integrity. This formulation implies that, as factors change in human communities, other factors must, individually or collectively, adapt or perish.

While these effects seem self-evidently valid, they provide little basis for understanding the well-springs of the individuality or creativity, human or otherwise, that appear in any ongoing ecology. Further, they provide no understanding or evaluation of the sources or consequences of diversity. Thus, person–environment fit models have no basis for the predominant focus in the study of such models on the negative consequences for individuals who do not adapt to the normative characteristics of their milieu. To understand the nature and consequences of atypical conduct as agentic and as potentially of benefic requires an extension of social ecology models to include individual–system interaction possibilities.

The concept of ethnic validity assumes that, to some extent, we choose how to function and what to use as reference perspectives while trying to retain our identity, sense of continuity, and sense of belonging. Ethnic validity refers to the organized guidelines that we use for directing our *knower* capabilities and resources to manage our circumstances, negotiate changing circumstances, or change ourselves. The concept of ethnic validity rests on evidence that our conduct is not totally accounted for by the ecological context; we make choices and take responsibility, moral and otherwise. These ideas are the core of Sperry's (1992, 1993) argument that human cognition is an emergent, holistic property of human functioning. To provide illustrative empirical support for this reasoning and extend it to human behavior more generally, several examples are presented here.

Differences in people's psychosocial circumstances occur in any CDG–NCDG social context. Society's CDG members often define and maintain nested framework differences which support their sense of greater merit and justified privilege. In response, NCDG individuals often form nested framework conceptions of their context and ethnic validity patterns that differ from those of its CDG individuals. Although individuals from the two groups adopt characteristically different optimal and poor ethnic validity styles of psychosocial functioning, there is enough variability in their styles to suggest that everyone is also influenced by their individual preferences.

Findings from several conceptually interrelated studies illustrate these points. They were conducted by my colleagues and me in a racially heterogeneous white–black suburban county along the mid-Atlantic seaboard in the United States. One series of these studies involved an analysis of the psychosocial competence characteristics of selected elderly and adolescent, black and white women (Gatz, Gease, F. Tyler, & Moran, 1982). Some of the 58 elderly women were identified by community members as exemplary community leaders (17 black, 17 white), and by those leaders as marginally functioning individuals (14 black, 10 white). The 56 adolescent women were senior-high-school students nominated by high school counselors as exemplary (15 black, 15 white) or marginal (13 black, 13 white). All of the participants were from lower-middle to middle income families, with no socioeconomic differences between the groups. Given the area's history of racial discrimination, it was assumed that (a) the environments of the white women (CDG) were generally more benign and supportive than those of the black women (NCDG) and (b) the younger women, due to social changes providing more support and opportunities for women, lived in more benign and supportive environments than their elders.

The study's basic hypothesis was that individuals who were more psychosocially competent would be more internally oriented and interpersonally trusting and would exhibit a more active, planful orientation to negotiating life events. However, that hypothesis was qualified by the prediction that it would hold most directly for individuals living in a benign and supportive environment. It was also hypothesized that, in comparison to those who had done less well, the women who had done well in their life circumstances would form characteristically different psychosocial competence configurations in relation to their differential race and age statuses. Consequently, it was predicted that the women's characteristic psychosocial competence configurations would vary in relation to the supporting and constraining effects in their lives, their common status as women, their differential race and age statuses, and the individual differences in the effectiveness with which they had managed their lives (exemplary versus marginal status).

Findings indicated that, as expected, the white participants lived in communities that provided their residents more services than was the case for the black participants. Individual differences were also found, including the expected one that, overall, the more competent women tended to be more internally oriented, trusting, and active planners. The hypothesized pattern associated with benign support was found, as exemplary white adolescents were found to be more internal, more trusting, and more active planners than were their marginal white cohort. Finally, subgroup differences included a three-way interaction involving age, race, and competence level.

Jackson (1972) characterized elderly black women as being in "triple jeopardy" because they were black, female, and old. Indeed, the psychosocial competence configurations of differently competent elderly black women were quite different from those of the white women. Correlates of these distinctive patterns were also reflected in a measure of social desirability and a measure of system blame/individual blame for the treatment of blacks. The competent older black women scored highest of all groups on Tyler's Behavioral Attributes of Psychosocial Competence (BAPC), suggesting that their successful adaptation required particularly strong, actively planful coping skills. They also showed a low level of concern with social approval. As Jackson emphasized subsequently,

> it makes sense that a group who are more negatively valued by the social structure might respond by becoming strong believers in self-reliance—be initiating, show persistent effort, and learn from one's successes and failures without blaming oneself or becoming too concerned about others' judgment. (Jackson, 1972, p. 11)

The impact of circumstances on these women's adaptation patterns were further highlighted by the finding that both the *more* competent black women and the *less* competent white women had low social desirability scores. In other words, a concern for social approval served white women well; ignoring it served black women well. On the individual/systems blame measure, black women scored higher in blaming the system for inequities, but here, too, there were age-by-race effects. the older white women were the least system blaming; the adolescent black women were the most. The black women were more active planners than the white women. Overall, the older women and the more competent women were more internally oriented; that is, they assumed more responsibility for their lives. Differences such as these are consistent with the idea that ethnic validity is an active, constructivist part of people's lives.

There is further evidence in these studies that ethnic factors influence people's choice patterns and that, in turn, individuals construct their choice patterns with an eye to ethnic considerations. Patterns of problem solving, resource utilization, and community involvement within a black and a white community were found to reflect both ethnic and individual choice factors (Barbarin, F. Tyler, & Gatz, 1979; Mitchell, Barbarin, & Hurley, 1981). Representative service providers and residents who were high or low in civic activities were interviewed about community strengths, deficits, problem-solving alternatives, and satisfaction with life in the community. Results indicated that satisfaction with community life for black respondents was related to how active they were in using influential people to solve their problems. In contrast, community life satisfaction for whites was related to the number of ways they knew for handling problems themselves and their perception of the adequacy of formal resources in the community. In both towns, service providers and active citizens (in contrast to non-service providers and inactive citizens) reported more strengths, deficits, and alternative possibilities in their communities and more satisfaction with them. For all respondents, more information about the community and the possibilities it provided led to a more positive sense of community. This finding was especially strong for people who were more internal.

The results of this research support several relevant points: (a) Community context makes a difference in what people can do, what they actually do, and how they come to be the individuals they are. (b) There are differences in any context in how individuals interact with their living conditions. (c) For example, in both the white and the black communities, people who were more involved knew more about their community, more actively used its resources, and were more satisfied with it. (d) The ethnic/racial-based differences support the conclusion that the ways people come to have an ethnic validity quality about them contribute to shaping their futures, although their sense of autonomy also plays a role in what they can and, individually and collectively, choose to do. (e) Finally, people's personal approaches reflected their ethnicity. The members of the white community more often used formal channels; the members of the black community more often used informal ones.

Choosing Tradeoffs in Patterns of Fitting

From a person–environment fit perspective, individuals will be advantaged by conforming to societal (ecological) expectations and disadvantaged when they do not. However, there are no situations that have patterns of fitting which advantage everyone; perhaps there cannot be. All patterns of adaptation yield mixed benefits and costs. Further, empirically identified fit patterns reflect that individuals choose among those tradeoffs.

Pargament, F. Tyler, and Steele (1979a) studied the psychosocial correlates of the ways religious congregants in the United States fit their religious beliefs and activities and the norms of their church or synagogue into their lives. Members of 12 congregations (4 Jewish, 4 Protestant, 4 Roman Catholic) participated. Central ($n = 79$) and peripheral ($n = 56$) members of the congregations were identified by their respective clergy as representing different patterns of fit in the congregation. The adaptive value of each chosen pattern was assessed in relation to F. Tyler's psychosocial competence configuration measures adapted to be responsive to the life styles and situations of religious congregants.

Central and peripheral groups were significantly different on a number of dimensions. Central group members had greater satisfaction with their congregation, a greater sense that their lives were controlled by God, a lesser sense that their lives were controlled personally or by chance, and they were less active planners. Peripheral group members exhibited the contrasting pattern of greater personal control, more active planning in managing their lives, less satisfaction with the congregation, a greater sense of control by chance, and a lower sense of control by God. Neither of the ways of fitting yielded unequivocally better psychological outcomes. Instead, across substantially disparate congregations (nested frameworks), they yielded different tradeoffs with contrasting patterns of psychological benefits and costs.

In a quite different area, Shedler and Block (1990) employed a longitudinal methodology to study a U.S. urban adolescent population's involvement in a legally prohibited activity (drug use). They studied 101 (49 boys, 52 girls) eighteen-year-old adolescents who had been followed since their preschool years. These youth were heterogeneous with respect to race, social class, and their parents' education. Extensive interviews were used to classify them into categories of *abstainers, experimenters,* and *frequent users.* Comparisons were then made of their personality characteristics and the antecedents of those attributes in order to explore the relationship between drug use and psychological health. The findings provide strong support for the view that *fit* is not everything that makes for a meaningful life. They illustrate how cultural expectations and individual experiences can influence the development of different ethnic validity perspectives and influence choices about adaptation patterns with different benefits and costs.

Compared with the experimenters, frequent users were alienated, deficient in impulse control, and manifestly distressed; abstainers were anxious, emotionally constricted, and lacking in social skills. The authors pointed out that, in contrast, the experimenters seemed to be

> the psychologically healthiest subjects, healthier than either abstainers or frequent users.
> Psychological health is meant here in a global and nonspecific sense, consistent with ordinary conversational usage, and consistent also with empirical recognitions by mental health researchers that a general psychological health/psychological distress factor underlies diverse clinical syndromes. (Shedler & Block, 1990, p. 625)

There had also been differences between the groups during childhood. When compared with experimenters, the frequent users had a history of being relatively insecure, unable to form healthy relationships, and emotionally distressed; the abstainers were relatively anxious, inhibited, and morose during childhood. Further, both frequent users and abstainers had received poorer maternal parenting than experimenters.

Shedler and Block (1990) pointed out that other investigators have found that frequent users are relatively maladjusted, but their finding that abstainers also show some signs of relative maladjustment is also note-worthy. They specifically rejected the conclusion that using marijuana makes adolescents psychologically healthier. Instead, their view was that in the current societal context of the United States (nested framework), when marijuana is widely used and acceptable among adolescents, it is a form of protest (ethnically valid pattern) that is likely to have been experimented with in part as a way of differentiating from parents and forming independent identities.

These findings seem particularly consistent with what would be expected from an ethnic validity perspective. The youths' different reasoning and choices about using drugs represented alternative types of fit with cultural expectations—expectations that are not totally consistent. Conformity to explicit legal and adult social prohibitions constituted a *fit* through abstention. It involved a legally safe choice but was associated with less than optimal corollary psychosocial characteristics. Conformity to the adolescent tasks of making transitions through experimentation required a more active stance of self-searching and choice-making with its consequent benefits and costs. It required a willingness to take risks, even to challenge and disobey social, medical, and legal constraints. Thus, it also had short-term and long-term positive and negative consequences. Turning to the escape offered by frequent use was a fit which had the least to offer for the benefit of the individual youths and their relationships or society. However, in their own ways all three choices about drug use seemed to have developmental antecedents that required the adolescents involved to assume a pattern of responsibility and choice (an ethnic validity) in relation to past and present life contexts, rather than just fitting passively into a prescribed mold.

Changing to a New Culture

One of the increasingly frequent and most demanding tasks that individuals face in the contemporary world is that of adaptation to life in a new culture. Few adaptations so challenge the very roots of our identity and our capability for sustaining, let alone enriching, our lives. Even so, the process of adaptation is predictable if we are merely products of our past, merely consequences of our biopsychological characteristics. If, however, we are active participants in constructing our identities and directing our lives, reorganizing our frames of reference about who we are, what our circumstances are, and what we need to survive and manage our new circumstances takes on a more varied character. The studies summarized in the following paragraphs support that this latter possibility is, at least to some extent, the case.

Birman and F. Tyler (1994) studied the relationship between the sense of alienation of 49 Soviet Jewish emigres and their behavioral and identity acculturation to the United States. The patterns were substantially different between men and women. Those differences may reflect the divergent cultural expectations for men and women (nested frameworks) of the Soviet and United States cultures and the disparate ethnic validity patterns acceptable for women. For the women, retaining their Russian identity and behavior and adopting American identities and behaviors were inversely related. They made their choice as a unilevel one of adopting the identity and behaviors of one culture or the other, and they were more assimilated into U.S. culture. Those who had lived longer in the United States had come to identify with U.S. values, and they had adopted U.S. behaviors without becoming more alienated. Those who retained their Russian identity and behaviors were more alienated from their relationships and society.

For men, the process of reconciling their Russian and U.S. identities and behaviors was a more complex process, and, in part, a bilevel one. That is, they could behave in both a U.S. way and a Russian way and not experience a sense of alienation. Retaining a Russian identity was related to a sense of alienation; adopting an American identity was not. Further, the longer these men had lived in the United States, the more alienated they were from their lives.

In both men and women, age was negatively related to U.S. behavioral acculturation, a not surprising finding given the general preference of aging people for stability. The most striking aspect of Birman and Tyler's (1994) findings was the gender contrasts. Of those who had resided in the United States longer, the men were more identified with and engaged in Russian behaviors and they were more alienated; the women were more identified with and engaged in U.S. behaviors and not more alienated. Out of the contexts of their lives and in relation to their histories and their futures, these men and women had chosen different patterns of adaptation with different benefits and costs.

Celano and F. Tyler (1991) studied the behavioral acculturation, values acculturation, and level of depression of 64 Vietnamese immigrants to the United States. The findings highlighted the complexities of these processes as well as their relationships to past circumstances and ongoing events. Behavioral acculturation scores were increasingly high for up to six months in residence; after that, they varied in relation to a number of factors. Those who came with more education and a higher Vietnamese socioeconomic status and were employed scored higher on adoption of U.S. behaviors. Those who were unemployed, less educated, and had lived longer in the United States retained or returned to using higher levels of Vietnamese behaviors. These findings suggest that those with more choice possibilities (higher socioeconomic status in Vietnam, more education, and jobs in their new home) acculturated more to American behavioral patterns. Those with fewer possibilities in the United States reverted to a stronger commitment to the behaviors of Vietnam, their culture of origin. There were no clear findings about any relationship between immigration circumstances and values acculturation or level of depression. However, the different behavioral acculturation patterns indicated that these immigrants were making different choices about how to reorganize their lives in relation to their pasts and their futures in their new environment.

Ways in which people construct life patterns which integrate their ethnicity (their ethnic validity) and their desires for new and better lives, can also be seen in generational changes that occur in relation to external pressures. Such changes are reflected in a variety of forms, including the ways people deal with the unknown, with change itself, and with conflicting generational perspectives. A good example is Jahoda's research in Ghana (1970). He explored whether people facing social pressure to become modernized like the people in the industrialized Western world all change psychologically in the same way and in a direct linear fashion. He developed an index of supernatural beliefs (e.g., "twins are different from ordinary children", "fortune tellers really know the future") and administered it to 280 university students in Ghana.

Despite a decade of exposure to modern Western culture, the acceptance of supernatural beliefs was still high. About two-thirds of his respondents indicated total or qualified belief in fortune tellers and witchcraft. However, their beliefs were related to other aspects of their lives and their environments. Entry into the university had been delayed for students over 25 years of age, and their earlier education had occurred during a period when the modernizing elite were negative about anything traditional. Among them, students who were freer from conformist pressures (more field independent) had retained more traditional beliefs. Students in the younger group had been educated more recently when there was a societal (ethnic validity) backlash involving a recommitment to indigenous values and a rejection of foreign ones. They had retained more supernatural beliefs than their older fellows; among them, there was no relationship between field independence and choice of beliefs. These findings suggest that people form and internalize capacities to construct their own patterns of self, self–world, and coping, and they choose among various versions of external reality in doing so. The two generations and students within them chose divergent patterns of *fit* with disparate benefits and costs for their relationships to their cultural heritages and their futures.

The studies in this section have demonstrated that theories and findings about the direction and nature of acculturation vary in their complexity; in the number of dimensions considered, from two dimensions (Szapocznik et al., 1978) to six (Berry, 1986); in their nature, from linear unidirectionality to a back-and-forth pattern (Triandis, Kashima, Shimada, and Villareal, 1986); and across change dimensions. All of the theorists have included a behavioral acculturation dimension, presumably because people must behave in at least nondestructive and minimally productive ways to survive. We have a range of choices about how we may interpret and justify our behaviors (values acculturation), but they too must involve a coherent sense of ethnic validity to sustain us psychosocially as a member of significant reference groups, including family, community, and culture.

This active agentic, psychosocial integration of concepts of acculturation is illustrated in the graphic, humane, and at times poignant account by Cigdem Kagitcibasi (1996) of her life-long personal and professional adventure as a native of Turkey. She transcended her childhood ethnic validity to become an internationally distinguished social/developmental/cross-cultural psychologist. Her journey has involved a multifaceted process ranging across many aspects of her life, including how "an important part of my self-induced preparation/orientation to life in the United States was to restrain myself from showing physical affection" (p. xv). Her reading of psychology was influenced by her cultural filter with her initial reaction emerging out of her realization that "some of the characteristics of the so-called authoritarian *personality* were in fact *social norms* in Turkey" (p. xiv). This observation led her to examine "the assumed inherent dynamic of personality attributes and attitudinal variables underlying 'authoritarianism' in light of a cross-cultural comparison" (Kagitcibasi, 1970, p. 444). She added that she has been an active agent in intertwining these aspects of her life and creating her unique sense of ethnic-validity-based individuality. She described different perspectives about interpersonal connectedness as the most salient dimension in the cross-cultural interpersonal misunderstandings and readjustments involved in her personal and professional experiences. These differences and processes have become the central focus of her cross-cultural research.

Choosing Communication Styles

Languages and written records serve as significant tools in helping us to define ourselves and communicate with others. Cross-cultural scholarship on communication has contributed to our understanding and evaluation of people. Unfortunately, that scholarship has been primarily focused on the languages or dialects of people in NCDGs, limiting our ability to generalize the findings. However, they are particularly instructive about the role of choice in how we use language.

A particularly important example concerning language studies in the United States is the substantial attention that has been paid to the nature of so-called Black English and its significance as an indicator of the intellectual adequacy of those who speak it. The research of communication scholars suggests that Black English may be used for reasons of individual and ethnic validity, not because its users lack the ability to grasp the dominant mainstream forms of English. Weber (1994) emphasized that the uniqueness of black language is related to the uniqueness of black experience and that it binds black community members together across barriers of education and social position. It also makes the political statement that black people have not totally given up their African cultural heritage and identity. In closing her discussion, Weber raised the question of how to respond to Black English and then supplied an answer.

> What one should do about the language is be open-minded and not judge the speaker by European standards of expression.... The use of black language does not represent any pathology in blacks.... The beginning of racial understanding is the acceptance that difference is just what it is: different, not inferior. And equality does not mean sameness. (Weber, 1944, p. 225)

Weber's remarks are supported by the research of Ribeau, Baldwin, and Hecht (1994), who studied African American communication. They interviewed African Americans, Mexican Americans, and European Americans to identify issues of intragroup and intergroup communication and strategies for improving it. They found that members within these groups used different ways to define a satisfying conversation within their own groups. To Mexican Americans, the relationship was important. To African Americans, a goal orientation and a sense that ideas and feelings were exchanged were important. European Americans were not concerned about or interested in their conversational partner, but considered it important that the other person might say something that could help them in the future.

Ribeau et al. (1994) also explored black–white interethnic conversations and identified issues important to the African Americans. Those issues included concern with maintaining their identity as individuals against negative stereotyping, creating an acceptable self-image in the face of demeaning images, handling different levels of personal expressiveness, choosing how to manage what was seen as standoffishness or racism, and managing the different patterns of power dynamics they faced in these interactions. They found, for example, that many African Americans switch to being less directly assertive when talking with European Americans than they are with each other.

Ribeau et al. (1994) also examined how their African American respondents thought they could improve interethnic communication with European Americans. The twelve strategies that they suggested ranged from ways to assert one's view to ways to treat others as individuals and how to manage language (talk the same language) for effective communication. There was agreement that in the face of stereotypes or lack of acceptance, no strategies are likely to be effective and indicators of those kinds of attitudes and responses can usually be detected early in a conversation.

There were substantial differences among African Americans about which of these factors were salient and how to respond to them. Thus, while Ribeau et al. (1994) found characteristic ethnic validity patterns, they also emphasized that their respondents were behaving as active agents in their own behalf. The respondents' senses of who they are and how they relate to and communicate with others were chosen and constructed ways of conveying both their individuality and their ethnicity; that is, their distinctive psychosocial ethnic validities.

IMPLICATIONS FOR BROADER INTERACTIONS OR UNDERSTANDINGS

An ethnic validity perspective provides a coherent basis for understanding (a) the nature of cross-cultural/racial/ethnic/gender similarities, differences, interactions, and relationships and (b) how prosocial as well as conflicted patterns of cross-group interaction, unity, and diversity are developed and managed. Each person's culture can be seen as her or his ecology, the framework within which her or his identity and sense of validity is formed. Cross-cultural and cross-ethnic interactions are encounters with people who do not fit into our own ecologies. One of our life tasks becomes that of accounting for these strangers, and some of our difficulties with doing so are related to each society's historic approach to them. For example, the concept of ethnocentrism as essential to the cohesiveness of any society was embedded in the writing of the early U.S. social scientist Sumner:

> *Ethnocentrism* is the technical name for this view of things in which one's own group is the center of everything, and all others are scaled and rated with reference to it.... Each group nourishes its own pride and vanity, boasts itself superior, exalts its own divinities, and looks

with contempt on outsiders. Each group thinks its own folkways [customs] the only right ones, and if it observes that other groups have other folkways, these excite its scorn. (Sumner, 1906, pp. 12–13, as cited in Segall, Dasen, Berry, & Poortinga, 1990, p. 316)

Sumner acknowledged the social nature of human life in appealing to what he considered a universal group survival imperative (an etic), the sense of superiority of one's own group linked to a sense of the inferiority of others and the consequent fear of their hostility and of war with them. Further, he advanced an ethnocentric justification for the desirability of ethnocentrism, emphasizing that these fears of others sustain the comradeship and peace within one's own group and make government and laws acceptable as a means of containing internal discord so as not to weaken the group's discipline for war with outsiders.

In contrast, an ethnic validity position leads us to ask whether this view represents necessity or history. That is, there is substantial empirical evidence that we can be less ethnocentric and that experience and circumstance affect our views and our actions. These questions were explored in depth in Africa during the emergence of the postcolonial era after World War II. Examples of relevant studies are noted here, but more extensive reports can be found in Segall et al. (1990).

Segall, Doornbos, and Davis (1976) studied ethnocentrism in Uganda by asking whether people would come to think of themselves as Ugandans rather than as members of their ancestral tribes. They asked Banyankore tribe members who in Uganda they considered similar to themselves and to whom they were attracted. Their findings showed that the only people who mattered were the ones they knew, and they liked the ones they perceived as being like themselves. However, the Banyankore who had dissimilar kinds of past interactions with individuals from other tribes viewed outsiders differently. For example, the British had employed Baganda tribesmen as chiefs. The older and less educated Banyankore still liked the Baganda; the younger and more educated Banyankore disliked them. In other words, their presumed "natural ethnocentrism" was tempered by individual experiences with the outgroup.

Brewer and Campbell (1976) studied social distance in 30 tribes in East Africa. They asked people to name others with whom they would be willing to share a meal, work, have as a neighbor, and become related to by marriage. Respondents tended to regard their own group most highly; their regard for others diminished with less perceived similarity. However, intergroup attraction and social distance varied with circumstances. Opportunities for equal-status contact enhanced them; authoritarianism and dogmatism decreased them. Further, institutionalized norms and other forms of social control and influence mattered; if prejudice was accepted in a person's culture, then that person did not have to be authoritarian to be prejudiced.

These studies support that people identify with *in-groups*, that is, small, personally meaningful, reference groups. They also indicate that transcendent patterns of relationship and harmony can be developed. People's relationships to their reference groups (ethnic validity) and their personal patterns of interaction (their choices) also contribute to their choices of psychosocial stances within and across ecologies, ranging from local ones to cross-cultural ones.

Although the classic work of the Sherifs (Sherif, 1958; Sherif & Sherif, 1953, 1956) focused on how to resolve differences between contending groups in the United States, it also provided parallels to cross-cultural situations. When they placed competing groups in a win–lose situation, neither contacts between leaders of contending groups nor efforts at preaching and coercion reduced intergroup tensions. When two such groups were joined together to defeat a third group, tensions were reduced between them, and the level of conflict with the third was increased. The presence or development of outside group hostility served to both exacerbate and reduce intergroup tension.

In additional studies, Sherif and Sherif (1953) established that the most effective ways to reduce intergroup tension included combining individual actions and group cohesion. For example, contending groups in a summer camp were faced with a loss of their water supply and the need to work together to obtain water. Approaches to the common effort reduced intergroup tension when both groups desired a solution, developed a single shared definition of how to solve the problem, and found a way for representatives of the groups to work together without being seen as having betrayed their own group. The individuals who elected to work together became motivated to transcend the limits of their ethnic validity in order to understand and work with each other.

SUMMARY

Research findings such as those cited in this chapter support the conclusion that the ways in which we respond to and, at times, prevail over our circumstances are consistent with the idea that we construct an *ethnic validity* as a framework for guiding our lives. We are not totally at the mercy of what the world imposes on us; rather, we are involved as active agents in creating our own lives by taking some responsibility for the choices we make. Each of us uses our contexts, our nested frameworks, to form an ethnic validity-based conception of our identity and our individual and social reality.

As emphasized in Chapter 3, we create our life contexts out of our own natures and the situations in which we live. Each of us abstracts meanings about the world and ourselves from our direct, vicarious, and symbolic life experiences to form and reform our nested frameworks. However, while this framework provides the background and context for our lives, it cannot in and of itself compel any particular thought, belief, feeling, or action. We face the necessity of taking some responsibility for managing our lives as we necessarily choose among a range of person–environment fits yielding different costs and benefits.

Complex settings such as cultures do not provide the same nested frameworks or ethnic validity possibilities for everyone in them. They include CD and NCD statuses and group memberships with different choices. Also, people who immigrate into new cultural contexts approach that experience with different ethnic validity perspectives. They are confronted by different aspects of the heterogeneous nested frameworks of their new context, and succumb to, adapt to, or prevail over their new circumstances in ways that reflect both their differences and their commonalities.

In summary, there is no single adaptation/acculturation process or outcome that is optimal for any one person or for everyone. Rather, each of us forms and reforms ethnic validity perspectives out of the meanings we assign to our actual and vicarious experiences. We rely on these meanings to make choices about how we are going to live within the broad nested frameworks of our ecologies.

Part II

A BIOPSYCHOSOCIAL FRAMEWORK OF COMPETENCE

Part I described an ethnic validity perspective and the enriched understanding that it brings to psychology. However, its influence is limited by psychology's acontextual individualistic focus. In order to understand ourselves and others as individuals with reasoning and choosing capabilities, we need a paradigm that includes attention to how and how well we make our choices and address their consequences. That is, a comprehensive psychological framework must be able to account for how we make decisions and take actions to fulfill our desires and minimize the negative aspects of our lives. Of necessity, that framework must include consideration for the narrative course of our lives, our relationships to others, and how we interact.

All of these requirements are attended to in an individual psychosocial competence (PSC) model. This model has been formulated from research and projects in socialization, positive mental health, community, transcultural, and clinical domains. Because the course of human life is progressive, it includes patterns of continuity, disruption, and reconstitution. In the PSC model, these patterns are formulated as being composed of psychosocial spirals. In the process of living our lives as psychosocial beings, we form a sense of ourselves as being both autonomous and related to others. Our autonomy and relatedness provide the basis for our interactions, the most comprehensive form of which is resource generation and exchange networks. The roles that these conceptions play in our individual and interrelated lives rest on a number of underlying assumptions. They are summarized here to make them explicit and highlight their central role. The chapters in this part are based on these assumptions and build on them to clarify the value of a PSC model for psychological undertakings.

1. People's lives, communities, and societies are shaped by a combination of individual factors, social factors, and the interactions between the two.
2. The possibilities as well as the limitations within which people live out their lives are to some extent a function of not only their present circumstances but also their cultural/historical heritage and their imagined futures.
3. Individual and social change facilitate or inhibit each other. It is essential to study ourselves and our environment in relation to each other in a context in which the individuals doing the studies and those studied are involved and have an investment in the studies and their outcomes.

INDIVIDUAL PSYCHOSOCIAL COMPETENCE

INTRODUCTION

People display patterns of coherence and continuity with respect to who they are and how they organize their lives. The belief that we have a capability to form and change these patterns rests on an assumption that we function as *knowers* and, consequently, that we contribute to defining and guiding ourselves and others. Such a belief has been part of human society for as long as history has been recorded. Western psychologists refer to the Greeks for psychological concepts that differentiated between the cause-and-effect nature of the inorganic world and the motivation and purpose characteristics of the organic world. Psychologists from other traditions refer to their own histories and traditions for comparable concepts. Linking the study of human psychology to empirical science is a more recent endeavor.

This chapter focuses on the ways in which we reveal patterns of both causality and choice in our psychological characteristics. As already noted, the linkage of psychological characteristics to people's empirical histories raises questions about how behaviors can be both orderly in the causal sense assumed by the sciences and, at the same time, free in that they are somewhat unpredictable and subject to human judgments and choices. The conceptual formulation that I have developed to describe and understand this capability is *individual psychosocial competence*. This conception can also refer to collective behavior patterns, ranging from those between couples to those between societies. These patterns are addressed here primarily in references to their ethnic validity nature.

A METACONCEPTION

Individual psychosocial competence is a paradigmatic metaconception about an empirically identifiable, meaningful, and measurable aspect of individuals. That is, it can be established only indirectly by determining the empirical validity of predictions based on it. Its underlying postulates include:

1. We are part of the natural world and as such are products of our natures, circumstances, and experiences.
2. We function in part as self-aware *knowers* who have some discretionary control over their own lives.
3. We use our individual experiences to construct our lives, identities, and relationships to our contexts. However, our private experiences occur in a context whose meaning is somewhat socially constituted, so they also have a social as well as an individual character. Thus, our experiences are psychosocial.
4. We also construct the meanings of our contexts out of our individual experiences with our world, so our contextual meanings have both a social and an individual character. While these contexts and our private experiences of them are also psychosocial, they are different from our experiences about ourselves.
5. Accounts of our individual experiences and their social contexts cannot be given without reference to each other, but the two are not the same.
6. Over time, each of us and our individual social contexts change in different ways. Each is influenced by the other, but neither is completely predictable from the other.
7. Our personal functioning is somewhat open-ended. It is not completely determined; therefore, it is not completely predictable.

These seven postulates integrate deterministic and discretionary considerations (our natures) and contextual as well as personal ones (our circumstances), and Postulate 1 makes these considerations explicit. The other postulates build on Postulate 1 to enumerate the discretionary aspects of our functioning, including our capacities for self-aware knowing, interpreting, and acting. They also specify that our capacities for self-awareness are part of our psychosocial natures.

The postulates provide us with the underpinnings for an *individual psychosocial competence* model of how we conduct our lives. The model, in turn, provides a basis for describing and organizing our hypotheses concerning how we construct our life strategies with their incredible range of psychosocial individuality and complexity. It builds on the assumption that both our individuality and our social embeddedness are reflected in the ways we initiate individual actions and interactions, judgments and self-corrections, and responsiveness to resources, limits, and constraints. To assess the utility of these assumptions requires that we delimit our task to studying particular instances, contexts, and their interrelationships.

ETHNIC VALIDITY FRAMEWORKS

With our perceptual, affective, cognitive, and manipulative capacities, we become proficient at adapting to and shaping ourselves and our physical and psychosocial environments, our ecosystems. If we are to effectively use these capacities to structure frameworks for guiding our lives, they must have at least minimal ethnic validity. These frameworks must meet the criteria of others and ourselves as legitimate understandings of reality and the social order: its nested frameworks. The particular ways in which we integrate these nested frameworks with our own experiences make up the ethnic validity frameworks within which we construct our individual psychosocial competencies.

Understanding these ethnic validity frameworks is necessary because they influence how our life contexts and experiences become an integral part of the ways we conduct our lives. Chapter 4 provided a discussion of *destiny, history, continuity,* and *autonomy* as dimensions underlying the structure of who we are. They are briefly reviewed here because they also impact on our ethnic validity.

Destiny: Each of us has a nature composed from attributes such as life cycle stages, unique psychological characteristics and talents, the era to which we are born, gender-specific characteristics, other characteristics used to classify us into socioracial groups, and socially imposed realities such as citizenship by birth. Even though these characteristics are considered a part of each person's nature and self-definition, they are also socially defined.

History: The events of our personal and collective pasts are incorporated into the lives of our families, communities, cultures, and humanity, and they may also affect the nonhuman world. They contribute to who we are, what we dream, fear, and believe, how we see and understand ourselves and others, and the ways we negotiate the events in our lives.

Continuity: There are ongoing consequences resulting from being part of particular social units from families to culture-defining (CD)/nonculture-defining (NCD) groups and cultures. They are the basis for our relationships to something outside ourselves: our sense of belonging and nonbelonging and of past and future ties.

Autonomy: Autonomy refers to the aspects of our functioning that enable us to make personal choices about our lives. For example, we can change our present and future characteristics and situations, and we can change the meaning of our past, if not our past itself.

NESTED FRAMEWORKS

Before we can focus on the *individual psychosocial competence configurations* that everyone forms, we need to identify and consider the underlying shared and unshared senses of reality that we use to organize our societies and our lives. They range from our broad conceptions about the world and its people to family and individual factors that comprise our sustaining fabrics, our nested frameworks. Individual nested frameworks and those of any social grouping have particular strengths and limitations which have been formed in relation to differing life contexts. We must transcend the belief that any particular one of them is the true view of reality if we are to gain a less ethnocentric basis for forming a comprehensive picture of our societies, our lives, and ourselves.

The structure of nested frameworks was discussed in Chapter 2. The following paragraphs highlight the major nested framework categories that need our attention because the contemporary developed world uses them to describe and understand people and their experiences.

Culture. At birth, each of us becomes to some extent a member and carrier of a particular culture. We embody and display our culture in all that we feel, value, think, know, and do. Unless otherwise indicated, the word culture implies all of these characteristics. It represents the most encompassing and self-contained way we have of expressing the common characteristics of and differences between people from various human societies.

Culture-Defining Group/Nonculture-Defining Group (CDG/NCDG) Status: Acknowledging that CDG/NCDG status is a factor in societies' nested frameworks gives us an important way to address the idea that heterogeneous cultures include at least one, but more often several, subgroups (NCDGs) with their own nested frameworks and ethnic validities. Individuals within these groups have to negotiate their lives and identities with the dominant CDG. They know that the CDG defines the terms of their existence and that they are often relatively powerless to change those terms.

Ascribed Race: Helms (1996) emphasized that the concept of race has no legitimate scientific basis, but continues to be ascribed to people and used to define them. To make the societal basis for the term *race* more explicit, she proposed dividing the concept into two parts, namely, *Sociorace* to designate references to groups of people, and *Psychorace* to refer to particular individuals. Even though we may personally choose not to define ourselves in terms of our ascribed sociorace, the ascription is usually based on largely unchangeable aspects of ourselves, such as our physical characteristics. Because others either explicitly or implicitly define us on such bases and then treat us accordingly, ascribed race inevitably becomes a defining part of our psychosocial reality.

Ethnic Status: Ethnicity also affects the psychosocial status of individuals and groups within CDGs and NCDGs. It refers to characteristics that identify an individual as being a member of a group with its own organizing coherence and sustaining cultural traditions. As indicated in Chapter 4, the word *ethnic* usually refers to minority and other NCDGs in heterogeneous societies which must sustain their ethnicity and themselves within the larger CDG framework. CDGs also have an ethnicity that is an aspect of their reality and provides them a coherent way of life, but it is usually unchallenged and not recognized as ethnic.

An important distinguishing characteristic between ethnicity and socioracial status is that ethnic status is usually based on an individual's shared cultural or subcultural coherence with others while socioracial status need not and often does not involve any such commonality. Further, individuals may conceal their ethnicity or change their relationship to it far more readily than they can change their ascribed socioracial categorization which is usually based on their ancestral physical characteristics.

Belief Systems: Belief systems are a particularly distinctive, codified aspect of how we define ourselves and conduct our lives. Any system of understanding rests on at least some untestable assumptions. For example, an important aspect of many people's lives is a spiritual, perhaps religious, belief system. The validity of spiritual systems is not subject to empirical testing if they include convictions about the absolute meaning of life, nonverifiable assumptions about people's natures (such as their possession of a spirit which either preceded their current lives, will continue after their deaths, or both), and the presence of beings (such as deities) whose nature is unknowable and whose acts transcend empirically verifiable challenge or verification. Believers may consider their spiritual belief systems as providing more basic truths about the nature of people and reality than other belief systems such as the sciences. For instance, spiritual belief systems rest on an approach that Paranjpe (1984) called Hebraic; that is, on faith and presumed special access to insights about their beliefs.

In Mannheim's terms (1936), belief systems serve as general paradigms that provide explanations which are not subject to critique from other perspectives. In that regard, they differ from scientific belief systems which acknowledge that scientific truths are constantly subject to question and that there are limits to the questions that science can answer. The distinction between scientific and similarly constructed belief systems, which are subject to empirical confirmation or disconfirmation, and spiritual belief systems, which are not, is vital in developing psychologically based understandings of human conduct.

We sustain our allegiances to our various belief systems for many reasons. We incorporate them as part of ourselves by virtue of the circumstances of our birth and early socialization. We rely on them to help us define the nature of life and morality. They provide justification for our expressed values, attitudes, and ways of behaving. However, if these systems are internally contradictory or contradict each other and other empirically linked belief systems such as the sciences, they create a distinctive kind of problem for us.

Accepting particular beliefs or belief systems can often be shown to have empirical consequences, including those that believers themselves consider undesirable. However, the undesirable consequences may not lead to a change in the belief. For example, parents' religious beliefs may lead them to refuse medical treatment for their children even when the parents are informed that the treatment can prevent death or severe infection. As believers, they dismiss the relevance of the empirical scientific evidence or the appropriateness of acting on it, rather than allow that evidence to challenge their belief.

We may choose, as scientists often do, to simply ignore or discount the commitment that many people have to base their life decisions on nonscientific belief systems. However, we cannot fully understand humanness without a comprehension of the nature and role of beliefs. This knowledge is also vital to a fuller understanding of the limits of science and the contributions that it can make to improve the quality of people's lives.

Community: Our local community, however organized, is the major socializing crucible in which most of us confront a complex and diverse world. It is there that we define our internal and external realities in relation to our interactions with those like and different from ourselves. The sense of community and of self-in-community serve as important components of the nested framework background within which we manage our lives throughout our life spans.

Family: The unit within our community that cradles most of us is our family. Even people without families are likely to create a substitute family (F. Tyler & S. Tyler, 1996; F. Tyler, S. Tyler, Tommasello, & Connolly, 1992) for a sense of belonging, context, and continuity. In that broader sense, for most people, family is the central nested framework of their lives.

Individual: Our individuality is nested in the broader frameworks described above. Each of us may interact with others in regard to only one aspect of ourselves. Even so, we are always composed of all of these frameworks, and each, in part, shapes our responses to and from other aspects of ourselves.

INDIVIDUAL PSYCHOSOCIAL COMPETENCE CONFIGURATION

Over the decades between 1960 and 1980, there was a flurry of activity as a number of social and behavioral science professionals sought to identify and understand what constitutes the positive side of people. Their work highlighted the notion that we all have strengths and resources which are as basic to who we are as are our weaknesses, frailties, and defenses against threats. Table 5.1 lists a number of the contributors to that effort and the focus of their work. Their paradigmatic conceptions of the nature of human conduct illustrate that human behavior can be framed in positive psychological terms.

More than two decades ago, I (F. Tyler, 1978) advanced a somewhat unique conception of individual competence which supplements that work. I defined individual psychosocial competence as being based on an

TABLE 5.1. Representative Investigators and Their Conceptions of Positive Human Psychological Attributes

Author[a]	Date	Positive attribute
M. Jahoda	1958	Positive mental health
Seeman	1959, 1966	Personality integration
White	1959, 1974	Coping, mastery
Grinker	1962	Nonself-reflective, nonidentity-actualizing competence
Barron	1963	Personal soundness
Erikson	1963	Initiative, industry, generativity, integrity
D. Heath	1965, 1977	Psychological maturity
Klein	1972	Pleasure motivation separate from anxiety reduction
Smith	1966, 1968	Competent self
Poe	1973	Psychological effectiveness
Coelho, Hamburg, and Adams	1974	Masterful, directed, self-responsible, optimistic problem-solving approach
Spivak and Shure	1974	Means–end thinking
Loevinger	1976	Integrated ego
Antonovsky	1981	Sense of coherence

[a]Listed in chronological and alphabetical order.

identifiable configuration of psychosocial characteristics which are related to the way individuals interact with life's events for problem-solving and fulfillment. It includes three personal components and two environmental components that function in concert. Separating the nature and functioning of our personal characteristics from those of our environmental milieus is necessary for a discussion of them, even though in reality they are inseparably intertwined.

In this model, competence is considered to be a psychosocial phenomenon. Each of us has characteristic personal patterns of competence and noncompetence which are formed and maintained or changed in relation to ongoing external circumstances, i.e., the supports and threats of the nested frameworks in which we function. Any adequate conceptualization of how we organize our lives must incorporate the nested framework structures that shape the cultural or social factors which impinge on us. To understand anyone requires an explicit formulation of their individual psychosocial competence configuration, their environment, and the interrelationships of the two. It also requires research strategies and approaches to individual and social change that provide separate information about all three facets and their interrelationships.

This chapter includes representative findings from my work and that of my colleagues. That work provides a broad-based account of the nature of these personal and environmental factors and their interrelationships, along with empirical support for their validity and psychosocial nature. The studies also indicate how people are influenced by cultural or social factors, along with their individual experiences. Finally, it documents how these characteristics function independently and together to provide greater or lesser effectiveness or fulfillment in the ways we live.

PERSONAL COMPONENTS

The personal components of psychosocial competence are the aspects of a person that psychologists usually focus on in their studies of personality and adaptation. In my configuration, there are three major categories of personal components. They include self attributes, self–world attributes, and behavioral attributes. Table 5.2 provides a brief summary of these attributes in relation to benign and predictable versus malign and unpredictable circumstances. They are discussed in detail below.

Self Attributes

Self-efficacy, or internal locus of control, is the component about which there has been the most extensive theorizing and research. It is a

TABLE 5.2. The Personal Components
of a Psychosocial Competence Configuration

Personal component	Environmental expectations	
	Benign, predictable	Malign, unpredictable
Self attributes	Sense of self-efficacy; of effectiveness in the world; of being responsible for outcomes Somewhat favorable self-evaluation	Sense of self-impotence; of ineffectiveness; of outcomes being out of own control Somewhat unfavorable self-evaluation
Self–world attributes	Optimism and hope; expectancy oriented to positive outcomes Interpersonal trust	Pessimism and dread; expectancy oriented to negative outcomes Interpersonal distrust
Behavioral attributes	Planning, forbearance, effort Realistic goal setting Active, high initiative, mastery oriented, coping orientation	Fatalism, passivity Unrealistic goal setting Passive, low initiative, or defensive coping orientation

core concept of the individual as *knower* because it focuses on the extent to which people believe that they have some choice and responsibility for how they conduct their lives. Rotter (1966) was the first psychologist to provide an empirical approach for measuring at least one aspect of this broader domain. To improve the accuracy with which predictions could be made about people's responses to the consequences of their actions, he developed a scale that measured respondents' expectancies about their ability to control the outcomes (reinforcements) of their actions. These scale scores provided predictive validity. Even more importantly, this approach bridged the gap between viewing people as *known* subjects and as individuals who function as *knowers* who interpret the meanings of the outcomes of their actions and then act accordingly.

Perceived control was viewed as a normally distributed variable ranging from high internal to high external control, not as a dichotomy. However, the scale gives the impression that locus of control is a dichotomy because it presents respondents with a forced choice between an internal and an external possibility. For example, respondents are asked to indicate whether they believe the results they obtain in school or at work are a consequence of their actions (internal control) or of other factors (external controls).

Irrespective of such measurement limitations, Rotter (1975) reported that over 600 research papers on this topic were published in about 15 years; since then, many more studies and reviews have been produced.

Lefcourt (1976, 1982, 1984) summarized hundreds of studies that used Rotter's scale and scales derived from it. Results of those studies that are particularly relevant to the role of self-efficacy attributions in psychosocial competence include the following:

1. People with more of an internal sense of control learn more from their experiences and from training than those who are less internally oriented, particularly when they think the activity in which they are engaged is based on skill.
2. Therapy tends to lead people to become more internally oriented, particularly in the case of the more action-oriented therapies. Further, the people who improve more in therapy are more internally oriented when they enter therapy.
3. People's levels of internal orientation reflect their circumstances and change accordingly. For example:
   a. Parental behavior providing an attentive, responsive, critical, and contingent environment tends to lead to the development of an internal locus of control in children.
   b. People in a deprived social position and punishing external circumstances are more externally oriented. As an illustration, Jessor and his colleagues (1968) measured objective access to social and economic opportunity and locus of control among Anglo, Hispanic, and Native American residents in a southwestern U.S. town. Within each group and across the groups, people with greater access to opportunity were more internal. Interest in self-efficacy spawned other formulations of the internal–external dimension.

DeCharms (1976) defined self-efficacy as an origin/pawn distinction. "Origins" are people who believe that they cause events to happen in their lives; "pawns" are people who believe that events happen to them. He taught inner city, African American school students in St. Louis, Missouri, to think of themselves as origins and act accordingly. These children became less disruptive, more organized, and planful in their school work, and their academic performance improved.

Other self-efficacy differentiations have focused on the nature and complexity of people's attributions about the course of life events. Levenson (1974) developed a measure that enabled respondents to rate separately the extent to which they felt personal control, chance, and powerful others were controlling factors in the course of their life events. Kopplin (1976) developed a similar scale to measure people's belief that God controlled the events in their lives.

My colleagues and I (F. Tyler, Gatz, & Keenan, 1979) used structural and factor analysis to identify the assumptions underlying the forced choices in the Rotter scale. We found that the scale incorporated a complex set of factors influencing locus of control attribution patterns. They included *focus* (personal, impersonal), *area* (personal, task, and general areas at individual and systems levels), *self-world attributions* (internal control, collective control, powerful others, and no control), and *self-attributions* (active agent, passive agent, victim). Identifying these control attribution factors enabled us to isolate and study their complex effects.

Gurin and his colleagues (1969) identified another type of differentiation, *personal control* and *control ideology*, in studies with African American populations. Personal control items tended to be in the first person and concerned with people's senses of control over personal events. Control ideology items tended to be in the third person and referred to whether the actions of individual people influence events in the world generally (e.g., political affairs, wars). Although African Americans reported views that were similar to CDG European Americans about how much they could control broad events, far fewer of them believed that they had control over their personal lives. These authors argued that researchers should be sensitive to this differential pattern of response when studying African Americans because of the general discrimination against them in U.S. society. This item distinction has not only proven to be relevant at a practical level, it also supports the concept that each person's optimal psychosocial competence configuration is a function of environmental circumstances.

The conclusion that environmental conditions influence locus of control patterns was supported further by U.S. studies that modified Rotter's locus of control measure so that respondents rated separately the extent to which they control the outcomes in their lives and the extent to which those outcomes are not in their control. For European Americans, a negative correlation was found between those choices, and internality was correlated with their level of active planfulness. It may seem logical to reason that the more individuals believe they control events in their lives, the more they should go about their lives in an actively planful way, and, as these findings indicated, that reasoning held for the CDG respondents. However, that logic did not fit for the NCDG African American respondents. For them, the correlation between internal and external control was positive, and internal control and active planfulness were marginally negatively correlated (Gatz & Good, 1978).

It is possible to argue that there is something wrong, strange, or deficient about African Americans because they respond differently from their CDG counterparts. On the other hand, it is equally possible to question and investigate whether the patterns they exhibit are a product of living with a historical and current climate of oppression. If people live in a hostile and oppressive environment, it makes sense for them to understand that while they do not control their fates, they must be actively planful in order to survive. Moreover, they probably need to embody a sense that they both may and may not control events because they have little basis for knowing which will be the case in any given instance.

Another facet of the self-efficacy or locus or control issue is reflected in cultural differences about what it means to control one's environments. As documented in Chapter 3, the normative notion of primary control is culturally dependent. It ranges from establishing control by manipulating the environment, to adapting to it, to denying desire. These varied control orientations would, indeed, lead to quite different behavioral manifestations at both an individual and a broader systems level, yet no one can say which orientation, if any, is better for everyone in all situations. The accuracy of these orientations as perceptions of reality and as strategies for effective functioning are contingent on the contexts themselves.

My colleagues and I (F. Tyler, Dhawan, & Sinha, 1989) found that gender and cultural factors influenced both cross-cultural control attribution differences and commonalities. We compared the structure-factor patterns of attribution among U.S. students and a comparable sample in India. In both cultures, the men believed that external events controlled outcomes of personal and general activities more than they controlled task-related activities. In contrast, the women felt that external events controlled task related issues more than they controlled personal and general issues. They also differed in that men placed greater emphasis on the role of chance as an external source of control, while women placed greater emphasis on their belief that they were controlled by powerful others. There were also differences between the response patterns of Indian and U.S. women. The Indian women had no expectations that the world would provide them a fair share of opportunities; the U.S. women did. Overall, the data reflected observable cultural and gender differences and similarities.

Self–World Attributes

The second personal component of the psychosocial competence configuration is a self–world relationship. Our estimates of the extent to which we control events incorporates an often implicit calculation that our lives are somewhat shaped by people or circumstances outside of ourselves. To take account of these external influences, we must make judgments about their nature and our relationships to them. In particular, we must answer core questions about whether we can trust people and whether they are positively or negatively disposed toward us. That is, we must establish some level of trust and of hope as a basis for gauging how to approach our interactions with the world.

Rotter and his students made an initial important contribution to exploring these considerations by investigating specific subjective expectancies—the probability estimate by each of us that a given response in a given situation will lead to a specific reinforcement (Rotter, 1954; Rotter, Chance, & Phares, 1972). Their work confirmed that the level of subjective expectancy predicts the level of constructiveness of behavior in a variety of situations. Rotter pursued this line of investigation by developing a scale focused on measuring interpersonal trust as a generalized expectancy. During this same period, Smith (1968) suggested that assuming a modicum of trust, optimism or hope may be a more significant determinant of behavior patterns than is trust itself. Thus, both conceptually and empirically, trust and hope, or positive expectancy, were being linked. Rotter summarized a decade of subsequent work using the Trust scale, emphasizing that

> we have determined that it is indeed possible to speak of a generalized expectancy for trust defined as belief in the truthfulness of communications. An individual difference measure of such trust is able to predict behavior in a wide variety of circumstances in a logical or construct valid fashion and evidence of discriminant validity is present. (Rotter, 1970, p. 22)

He stressed that "perhaps most important, we have demonstrated that a personality variable closely related to our social problems can be reliably investigated" (Rotter, 1970, p. 23). His point is particularly pertinent because previous research in the area of self–world attributes had not addressed the relationships between social conditions and individual personality characteristics. Within another decade, research using Rotter's (1980) trust scale had also made important contributions, including the following points, to our understanding of human competence.

1. People who are otherwise more competent in handling their lives are optimistically trusting to a moderate degree.
2. More trusting people are more trustworthy, but they are not more easily deceived.
3. Trust scores reflect people's perception of trustworthiness in their public institutions and leadership. For example, the level of trust scores dropped each year among college students in the United States during the social upheavals of the late 1960s and early 1970s (Rotter, 1980).

That is, a critical element in the development of any constructive basis for interacting with the world is our ability to establish the nature of the regularities in our world (e.g., positive reinforcement for skilled performance) and respond appropriately to them. For example, if the CDG world typically responds negatively toward NCDG individuals whether their behavior is constructive, destructive, or inept, then, in fact, much of the world of NCDG people is hostile. Faced with a hostile world, their effectiveness rests to some extent on behaving in ways that take those negative external factors into account. This pattern is illustrated in the next two examples.

Gurin and his colleagues (1969) hypothesized that an internal orientation may represent intrapunitiveness rather than efficacy for people exposed to systematic oppression. They subsequently found that African Americans who blamed themselves rather than external factors ("the system") for racial discrimination reported lower levels of self-efficacy. Their sense of internality was correlated with lower aspirations.

Ridley (1984) suggested that African Americans' low levels of trust of European American psychotherapists in the United States indicated a pattern of "adaptive paranoia." He argued that what the therapists called "unwarranted lack of trust" was, from the African American point of view, an experientially justified low level of trust. However, Ridley's term "adaptive paranoia" creates a contradiction. Warranted distrust is not paranoia, but reality-based. The inability of therapists to understand confirms the clients' beliefs. Unfortunately, it also has other costs for both.

Wood (1979) tested the role of socioracial differences in interpersonal trust among African American (AA) and EuroAmerican (EA) college males in the United States. Each respondent was placed in a situation in which he was to close his eyes and fall backward into the arms of a catcher. Respondents were paired in a random fashion with AA and EA catchers. On the basis of measured time to fall, EAs were found to be more trusting. However, when the psychosocial factors contributing to speed of fall were considered, a more complex picture became evident. EA respondents seemed to fall quickly to the extent that they felt they controlled their lives, were in a nonthreatening situation, and tended to be relatively passive or acquiescent. In contrast, AAs fell more quickly if they felt they had little control over their lives, were in a threatening situation, and tended to deal with events—even threat—in an active fashion. To them, the situation of apparent "trust" seemed potentially threatening and had to be confronted and resolved actively and directly. Wood's findings support two conclusions: (a) trust is an important individual psychosocial competence variable and (b) a respondent's ethnic validity perspective influences his or her assigned trust-related meaning to an environmental context and how to deal with it.

Trust can also be influenced by, for example, religious belief system structures. We (Pargament, F. Tyler, & Steele, 1979a, 1979b) included trust as part of a battery of psychosocial competence measures used to analyze adaptation patterns of religious congregants in the United States. The congregations were grouped as hierarchical (high authoritarian, high social control) or horizontal (low authoritarian, low social control) structures; the members were classified as central or peripheral participants. Hierarchical-congregation members were significantly less trusting than their counterparts, but there were no significant trust differences between central and peripheral members of either type of congregation. It was the nature of the congregation, not the relationship of the members to it, that influenced the members' trust orientations.

Cultural differences in hierarchically nested, societal frameworks also influence the role of trust in our ethnic-validity-based patterns of competence. Comparisons of adolescent students in the United States (CDG European American and NCDG African American) and India (CDG youth from educated families and NCDG youth from noneducated families) on a range of psychosocial competence characteristics underscored the importance of trust and its culturally embedded role in shaping these students' approaches to education. Its role was different for the CDG and NCDG students in each society. It was also different for comparable groups between the societies. Most striking were the differences between the NCDG students of the two cultures. Specifically, the NCDG students in India were generally *more* trusting than their CDG counterparts. For them, trust was positively related to their commitment to their education. The NCDG students in the United States tended to be *less* trusting than their CDG counterparts, and those who were less trusting did better in school.

Syntonic patterns between trust and cultural circumstances were also identified in a set of studies focused on the psychosocial competence patterns of street youth. One set (F. Tyler, S. Tyler, Echeverry, & Zea, 1991) involved street youth in Bogotá, Colombia. They were differentiated by whether the respondents had ever been in institutions (charity-based homes, runaway shelters, detention centers, jails). The other studies (F. Tyler, S. Tyler, Tommasello, & Connolly, 1992; F. Tyler, S. Tyler, Tommasello, & Zhang, 1992) focused on street youth from the Washington, D.C. area. One group was Latino immigrants, some of whom had left their countries to escape being engulfed in a war; the comparison group was institutionalized non-Latino street youth.

Although the youths from both studies valued whatever support and caring there had been in their families, many had left home because there was also abuse, exploitation, and betrayal. These youth were often responsible for someone else and had positive interpersonal ties with other youth. Their child–adult status was reflected in their leisure activities which ranged from playing childhood games to having sex, drinking alcohol, and using drugs.

The psychosocial competence configurations of these street youth yielded commonalities and differences related in expected ways to their life circumstances and experiences. The U.S. Latino immigrant youth and the Bogotá youth without institutional experiences were most similar. Both groups had left their homes or home situations (e.g., war torn countries) because those environments were intolerable. While they knew the survival requirements of their new situations were different, they had not fully accepted that reality. They reported being more trusting at home, less so on the streets and in institutions. To them, home was the most desirable and supportive of the settings in which they had lived, and they were less competently adapted to their other settings where they felt less in control of their lives and were less actively planful.

In contrast, the Bogotá youth who had been in institutions were much more like the United States comparison group of non-Latino homeless youth. Both groups were more alienated from their homes and felt more trusting in institutions. They differed in that the non-Latino youth in the United States were more trusting on the streets; the Bogotá youth were least trusting there. Both groups had responded to negative home situations by making an active commitment to build a life and ethnic identity on the streets and saw themselves as more psychosocially competent there.

These studies of street youth indicated that children can and do differentiate between their various environments and respond in ways they see as meaningful. For example, common across these groups were their ways of responding to supports and threats. Their perceived levels of psychological, and to a lesser degree, physical supports served as major contributors to their reported levels of self-efficacy, trust, and active planfulness. Conversely, they reported that they were largely unaffected by threats as they had already learned that their worlds were dangerous.

These youth were also forming a sense of ethnic validity that defined the socially sanctioned adult world as threatening. They had created prosocial relationships among themselves and, when asked about their wishes, voiced their desires for prosocial families and careers of their own (F. Tyler & S. Tyler, 1996). That is, they differentiated among their various situations on the basis of trustworthiness and other characteristics. They then developed approaches (competence configurations) that seemed most oriented to survival and to as good a quality of life as possible in and across their current situations and their future lives.

Behavioral Attributes

We may have a view of our own causal efficacy and the trustworthiness of the world and the people in it, but that is not enough. We have to act and react toward the events in our lives by trying to ignore, defend against, manage, or prevail over them. In doing so, we each acquire a characteristic style of acting toward those events. That style can be described as an organized set of behavioral attributes that includes an orientation to contending with ongoing external and internal events and a strategy for managing their phases across the many aspects of our lives. These behavioral attributes are the ways we translate plans and expectations into behavior. We use them to focus our feelings about ourselves and the world and apply our specific skills and knowledge to sustain us and accomplish our desires.

These patterns of behavioral attributes are summarized in Table 5.2. In a benign and predictable environment, we develop competent patterns of behavioral attributes which are characterized by an active orientation, realistic goal setting, and substantial planning, forbearance, and effort in the service of attaining goals. Although the specific activities and skills that are involved may differ as circumstances vary, the broad outlines of this pattern of behavioral attributes has been found to hold up across a range of cultures. The same is true of the less competent patterns that are developed in malign and unpredictable environments. They are characterized by passive or defensive orientations and unrealistically low or high goals implemented in ways that are erratic and planless, uneven, and lacking in effort or persistence.

This third area of personal characteristics has received the least systematic attention from behavioral and social science investigators. There have been a number of descriptive conceptions of mastery-oriented activities and related findings about them from studies such as those of Grinker (1962), Smith (1966, 1968, 1972), Ezekiel (1968), and Coelho, Hamburg, and Adams (1974). However, none of these investigators provided an explicit conception of competence in their research design or measures of competence itself.

On the basis of that previous body of work and my conviction that a conceptually based operational measure of the behavioral characteristics of competence was needed, I developed the Behavioral Attributes of Psychosocial Competence (BAPC) scale (F. Tyler, 1978). This scale provides an overall estimate of an individual's level of active, mastery-oriented planfulness in engaging with life events. Its use in a battery of related measures enabled us to investigate these behavioral attribute components of respondents' psychosocial competence configurations.

BAPC scale items are designed to indicate different styles of addressing the challenges and opportunities in our lives across a representative set of situations. They are presented in a forced-choice format whose alternatives describe different levels of active engagement in pursuing desired outcomes in the indicated situation. Respondents select which of two alternatives more accurately depicts how they would deal with the indicated situation. The situations are representative of three major *areas* of life functioning—personal, interpersonal, and task—that each of us must address. The response alternatives focus on the *activities* that are involved in responding and the *phases* that are part of any activity's sequential nature. Three sample BAPC items are presented in Table 5.3 with the competent response alternative indicated for each. Each item focuses on an area, activity, and phase; together, they provide an overall indication of how each of the life area, activity, and phase categories is incorporated in the scale. The components of the behavioral attributes matrix are described in more detail in the following paragraphs.

Life Areas: Measuring how individuals approach the personal, interpersonal, and task areas of their lives is necessary to obtain two important pieces of information: (1) a broad estimate of their level of behavioral competence and (2) a way to identify whether they form different patterns of coping with the events in different areas of their lives. For example, people who are quite competent in their personal and task activities may function incompetently in interpersonal relations. Similarly, people may handle interpersonal relationships and task-oriented activities and yet not manage their personal lives well.

TABLE 5.3. Behavioral Attributes of Psychosocial Competence Scale
(Form AR)

Sample items	Item characteristics
9. a. I generally rely on events and other people to direct my course. b. I generally follow my own course as a person. (Competent response)	Personal area; autonomy activity, implement phase
12. a. In new situations, I usually look for the kinds of personal relationships that I want. (Competent response) b. In new situations, I usually let other people indicate what kinds of personal relationships they would like with me.	Interpersonal area; coping stance activity; search and organize phase
35. a. When I don't do as well as I expect at something, I usually turn to some other job without getting too upset. (Competent response) b. When I don't do as well as I expect at something, my disappointment makes it more difficult to figure out what else to do.	Task area; self-maintenance activity; culminate, conclude, and redefine phase

Note. Column 1 lists three BAPC items with the more and less competent alternative choices. Column 2 identifies the life area and sequential phase in which this choice of activity is characteristically made.

Activity Focus: Measuring the activities involved in coping with events creates a particular kind of problem. It requires attending to the ongoing nature of life and, at the same time, to some specific actions. Unfortunately, focusing on any specific involvement obscures some aspects of life's ongoing flow. For example, behavioral activities can include massive and long-term overt sequences, such as moving halfway around the world or building a factory. Alternatively, they can be focused on getting through the day. Behavioral activities can also legitimately include meditating on the meaning of life or the beauty of a flower, or for that matter, working out plans in one's head to get married or write a book. We are behaviorally engaged when deciding on the appropriate level of active involvement with external events (*coping stance*), managing our internal states (*self-maintenance*), maintaining an ongoing sense of *autonomy*, or coordinating all three to formulate an organized response. To address this range of concerns, the BAPC scale samples the structure and process of behavioral engagement in a range of ongoing activities over time.

Behavioral Phases: Assigning a point as the starting or ending point of a given life sequence is somewhat arbitrary. Nevertheless, the assumption that there are beginnings and endings facilitates our understanding of life's nature. To capture that ongoing flow, the situations and response alternatives presented in the BAPC are focused on different aspects of the phases of any ongoing activity. Those phases are characterized as *search and organize; implement*; and *culminate, conclude, and refine*.

As can be seen in Table 5.3, these activity phase labels are somewhat self-explanatory. They represent an abstracted conception of the apparently sequential features of functioning. However, they are not meant to imply that these activities are mutually exclusive or that each occurs only once over the period of engagement with any ongoing event. Such an event may vary from attending a party to completing a college degree. As such, these phases provide an operational approach to measuring the internal and external nature, process, and meaning of any behavioral engagement.

Any new situation or interaction requires an entry-type pattern of activity called *search and organize*. When first encountered, situations and interactions are not yet meaningful; they require that we search for and impose meaning in order to function effectively. Once the characteristics of the context have been defined and the possibilities it offers established to our individual satisfaction, it becomes feasible to undertake whatever course seems most appropriate in view of our present situation, condition, history, and expected future.

Implementation of chosen activities to obtain what we wish from a situation becomes the second of the phases involved in moving through life's events. It, too, is broadly conceived and may range, for example, from cooking dinner to listening to music to building a highway. In all cases, nothing is going to happen without some implementation, whether short-term and simple or long-term and complex. For example, the judgment by middle and upper class individuals that the poor and unemployed are not planful may rest on an expectation by the former that being planful involves long-term goal commitments and discipline. The poor and unemployed may think primarily in terms of short-term survival and implement their plans on a day-by-day basis. It is not that they are less planful or that their plans are less complex. They may even be more planful, but their history and circumstances orient them to a different time frame of implementation. However long this implementation period may take, it is undertaken in a particular way, and measuring the quality of that way is part of the BAPC scale.

Culminate, conclude, and redefine are activities that identify the multifaceted nature of this phase which begins with the completion of implementation activities. That completion leaves us facing success or failure, termination of our efforts, and reevaluation. These activities can be described separately, but they encompass this phase as an integrated sequence. For example, as I stated elsewhere, one facet of a healthy style of negotiating events is the "capacity for enjoying success, suffering failure, and building on both" (F. Tyler, 1978, p. 313).

Culminate refers to enjoying success and suffering failure. It may involve grieving for the loss of a loved one, celebrating a newly formed relationship as in the ritualized postwedding honeymoon, or a short term outburst of rage or laughter. These activities, public or private, overt or symbolic, constitute a shift from seeking an outcome to realizing the fulfillment of attainment or the failure and loss of being unsuccessful.

In turn, this act of culmination permits and facilitates our *concluding* that activity by disengaging from it. Without the culmination, the implementation is unresolved and we cannot turn our full attention to other activities or to determining what the past sequence has meant to us. Concluding may be a short-lived activity, or may involve a myriad of other activities, as in disconnecting all of the ties formed in a long-term relationship.

Coming to terms with the meaning for and about ourselves in relation to any sequence is the final step. With this step, we complete resolution of the activity sequence by *redefining* ourselves in relation to the nature of the experience and its impact. Redefinition repeats the aspects of the entire configuration; namely, redefining our sense of self-efficacy, of self–world relationships, and of the nature of our behavioral attributes. It also includes assimilating the differences in knowledge, skills, etc. that have been acquired through the activity. Redefinition is more than just a last step. It also signals our readiness to begin new sequences.

A substantial number of studies have used the BAPC scale to measure the empirical correlates of behavioral attributes. They have involved a range of ethnic, socioracial, and cultural groups and have extended over the life span from adolescence to old age (see F. Tyler, 1992, 1991, 1978; F. Tyler, Brome, & Williams, 1991). These studies support the conclusion that people's levels of active planfulness contribute significantly to their overall effectiveness.

ENVIRONMENTAL COMPONENTS

In earlier conceptualizations of competence or maturity, attention was paid almost exclusively to the psychosocial attributes of individuals. People's histories or current environmental conditions were largely ignored. Over the past twenty years, studies have produced increasingly compelling evidence of important, though complex, relationships between people's psychosocial and environmental characteristics.

To know me is not to know my environments, though it may provide some clues about them. Conversely, to know my environments is not to know me, though they may yield some clues as to who I am. My environments and I are not mirror images of each other. These discrepancies occur to some extent because as *knowers* we make choices about what we attend to in our environments, how to interpret what we attend to, and how we are going to use that information to manage our lives and interact with our environments. They also arise because accounts of our environments are external accounts and, therefore, limited. No matter how much an external account is tailored to fit me as an individual and how much detail is provided, such an account unavoidably remains incomplete without knowledge of my internal environment.

Two people located in proximity, i.e., in what others define as the same environment, may view themselves as being in quite different environments because of the differences in *meanings* they each assign to that setting. In the United States, many CDG people of European descent consider people of African descent to be different from themselves; consequently, they treat these NCDG African Americans differently from how they treat CDG people. The impact is that individuals in the two groups approach their lives in characteristically different ways. As noted earlier, it may indeed be more competent for African Americans to feel less efficacious and less trusting than their CDG counterparts in spite of whatever other effects that orientation may yield. Thus it is important that in our work and our personal lives we be aware that everyone has a unique subjective personal, psychosocial, and social environment. Further, each environment has a unique combination of costs and benefits associated with it.

Such factors can be given full consideration only if we incorporate independent consideration and measurement of the environment into our models of human functioning. Environmental characteristics that need consideration include their evaluative natures (supports versus threats), their predictability, and their location in the nested context of each individual's or group's life. While efforts to include psychosocial environments in my psychosocial competence model are in their beginning stages, findings from relevant research illustrate the complexity and necessity of attending to them. For example, as noted earlier, internal and external expectations of control were positively correlated among African American students. Among European Americans, they were negatively correlated (Gatz & Good, 1978). In other words, the same college environments were defined differently by individuals from different groups, presumably in relation to the different nested frameworks associated with their CDG and NCDG statuses.

Examples of the impact of nested framework differences in psychosocial environments can also be found in gender differences. Societies seem generally to be more accepting and supportive of boys using direct, active confrontation of issues, but emphasize more indirect and passive styles as being preferable approaches for girls (see F. Tyler, Gatz, & Keenan, 1979; F. Tyler, Dhawan, & Sinha, 1989). A colleague and I found another difference in behavior attributes related to gender differences in socialization (F. Tyler & Varma, 1988). In a study of helping and help-seeking behavior among middle class boys and girls in India, we found that the helping behavior of high competent (high self-efficacy, trust, and active coping) boys was rated by observers as equally constructive in response to high and low competent help-seeking boys. In contrast, high competent girls were influenced by the context and behaved less constructively in helping low competence (in contrast to high competence) help-seeking girls.

The importance of environmental factors in interpersonal relationships, as well as in social policy, were identified by Warner (1990). She studied the social and individual psychosocial competence factors that contributed to the support that young unwed fathers in the United States Job Corps were giving to their children and the children's mothers. On the average, these fathers were 19 years old and had dropped out of school after completing the eleventh grade. Most of them reported that they tried to provide emotional and financial support to their children and the children's mothers. The three factors that contributed to the level of support they gave were distance from the mothers (the less distance, the more support), the father's active planfulness, and the closeness of the relationship between the father and the mother. The physical environment, as well as psychosocial factors, influenced their behavior.

Unfortunately, U.S. policies based on social condemnation of these youth serve to distance them from the mothers and their children by stigmatizing them and assigning them to geographically distant job placements. With such policies, society contributes to the creation of an environment destructive of prosocial competence patterns in the father, mother, and their children. It interferes with the family's maintenance of interpersonal closeness and the youths' sense of ethnic validity being built around family coherence.

In the studies described earlier of street youth in Bogotá and the United States, analyses indicated that the youths' perceived levels of psychological or, to a lesser degree, physical supports almost exclusively influenced their reported levels of self-efficacy, trust, and active planfulness. That is, these youth could and did assess the nature of their environments and responded to them by forming a sense of ethnic validity in which the socially sanctioned adult world was seen as threatening. They ignored its threats and responded to supports in developing psychosocial competence configurations that were oriented to surviving outside of the context of the CDG world (F. Tyler, S. Tyler, Tommasello, & Connolly, 1992).

These examples of environmental impacts on the formation and functioning of people's psychosocial competence configurations illustrate the environment's pervasive effects. They underscore the conclusion that it is difficult, perhaps impossible, to understand the perspectives or behavior of people without reference to their past, present, and anticipated environments. Consequently, throughout the remainder of this text emphasis is placed on separately measuring the environment, the person, and their interactions, and then taking all three into account in our efforts to understand conduct and use that knowledge to enhance the quality of people's lives and societies.

CONFIGURALLY EMBEDDED PSYCHOSOCIAL COMPETENCE STUDIES

The integrated nature of human conduct cannot be documented by conducting separate studies, each focused on a particular aspect of that conduct. We need studies that examine how the various dimensions relate to each other and to overall outcomes. The following two studies were designed accordingly, and their findings support the validity of the competence configuration as a generalizable concept.

Otero (1982) tested whether psychosocially competent individuals respond to psychological stress in a constructive growth-oriented fashion while less psychosocially competent individuals respond in a stress enhancing way. More and less psychosocially competent college students were differentiated on the basis of scores on the Rotter I-E, Rotter Trust, and BAPC scales, and then were randomly assigned to experimental and control groups. Participants completed a questionnaire (LEQ) identifying positive and negative events in their lives over the past two years. They also rated their degree of positive or negative feeling and amount of preoccupation with each event. After a three-week interval, the experimental group members were shown a psychologically stressful movie depicting a family confronting the deterioration of the beloved family matriarch. All participants then completed the LEQ again.

The experimental–control differences confirmed that the movie had a significant effect on the experimental group participants. Further, the more and less competent students responded as predicted to the stress, confirming the study's hypotheses. Specifically, the positive nature of the post-stress (in contrast to prestress) LEQ memories of the competent students was more closely related to their competence scores. In addition, they shifted to remembering more positive events, feeling more positive about them, more involved with them, and overall more preoccupied with past positive events. Their response to stress was to attend more selectively to the positive events in their own past lives and to do so in a more focused way. In contrast, the less competent students remembered more negative events in their past lives, were less focused, and had more overall negative involvement and preoccupation with their negative memories.

Jin's (1992) cross-cultural study compared the psychosocial configurations of college students from the People's Republic of China which has a closed, totalitarian social system and configurations of U.S. students in their more open, democratic social system. He used a causal model to explore the general hypotheses that (a) the more controlling Chinese socio-cultural environment would have a greater impact on affect (level of depression) and behavior (BAPC) than would traditional versus modern values and locus of control; (b) in the Chinese socio-cultural setting, modern values and internality would be inversely related to social self-efficacy and, consequently, directly related to more depression and less active behavioral coping; (c) in the U.S. socio-cultural setting, modern values and internality would be directly related to social self-efficacy and active behavioral coping and inversely related to level of depression; and (d) the effects in China (b) and the United States (c) would consequently differ.

The study included 223 participants. There were 61 male and 81 female students from the University of Beijing in the spring of 1990 (one year after the Tiananmen Square conflict), and 81 male and 100 female students from the University of Maryland in the winter of 1991 (during the Gulf War). The U.S. sample included 119 CDG European Americans and 59 NCDG other sociorace/ethnicity students.

Overall results yielded cultural, gender, and CDG/NCDG differences. The Chinese students had significantly lower self-efficacy scores, were more depressed, less oriented to active planning, and less internal. They also rated their sociocultural environment as being significantly more negative. In cross-gender, cross-cultural comparisons, men were more internal than women. In China, the men were more actively planful than the women. In the United States, the men were more self-efficacious and perceived the sociocultural environment as being more positive than did the women. In the United States, there were expected CDG/NCDG psychosocial competence differences. The CDG students were more self-efficacious, less depressed, more actively planful, less traditionally oriented, and perceived the sociocultural environment more positively.

The proposed model was supported only in a modified form. Jin summarized its overall pattern as a "big loop from behavior to environment, from environment to cognition, from cognition to affect, and from affect back to behavior" (1992, p. 106). These findings suggest that the sociocultural environment is a major determinant of psychosocial attributes across cultures. For example, the psychosocial responses of these students differed depending on their power status and the extent to which they could have an impact on their environment. The U.S. students' more positive perceptions (relative to the Chinese students) of their environment were reflected in more competent senses of self-efficacy (ability to effect changes in their life), internal control, positive affect, and levels of active planning. Yet women in both samples and NCDG members in the United States sample perceived their status as disadvantaged compared to their male counterparts. Also, more traditional value orientations were more efficacious for women and minority group members, more modern ones were for males.

Jin considered the finding that U.S. students were as affected by their overall environment as the Chinese students to possibly be a function of the two crisis situations at the respective times of data collection, i.e., post-Tiananmen Square and the Gulf War. Without further evidence, the possibility that such national crises may overwhelm otherwise evident cultural differences remains viable. In any case, the study's other findings about the environment's overall impact are relevant.

These two studies support the conclusions that (a) there are common personal and environmental underpinnings to constructive psychosocial approaches to life; (b) the patterns people form are influenced by their sociocultural contexts, their status, and their own experiences; and (c) all of these aspects must be taken into account in relation to each other to improve our understanding of individuals and our undertakings to promote prosocial individual or social change, or both.

SUMMARY

This chapter demonstrated how individuals incorporate the diverse aspects of themselves as *knowers* who display patterns of choice, and as *known* causal products whose patterns of conduct reflect their natures and their pasts. I advanced the individual psychosocial competence model as a conceptual framework which can reconcile and integrate empirical information about a broad range of individuals who conduct their lives across a variety of circumstances. This model incorporates attention to each individual's interrelated destiny, history, continuity, and autonomy. It nests individual psychological functioning within environmental supports and threats and outlines how we guide our lives by forming an interrelated sense of self-efficacy, optimistic trust or its opposite, and a passive-to-active style of planning. It also provides for understanding how we can use our knowledge of these possibilities to move beyond being completely constrained by our histories and circumstances. Understanding these considerations within and between interpersonal and societal groupings is central to identifying patterns of communication, interaction, conflict resolution, adaption, and the consequences of using these patterns in various contexts.

The individual psychosocial competence model provides a guide for understanding and contributing in a variety of ways to the well-being of individuals, communities, and their interactions. The studies cited in this chapter provide clues about the impact of life experiences and life situations. They suggest that there may be ways that psychosocial attributes can be developed as particularly facilitative of our psychological well-being and there may also be a range beyond which psychosocial attributes cannot vary without producing detrimental personal and social effects. Identification of these limits and possibilities can benefit our socialization practices and our efforts to establish socially supportive environments. Although findings reported here have been drawn primarily from the culture of the United States, they are relevant to other cultures in that they support the value of viewing individuals and cultures from a psychosocial competence perspective. However, their relevance is limited because the details and processes of forming individual and collective identities, inter-relationships, and styles of interacting differ in significant ways from culture to culture. The major contribution of these findings is that they provide a broader framework which people in separate cultures can use to identify the unique aspects of their own realities. These insights and strengths can be used by other cultures to construct more enriching and productive, individual and collective, ethnically valid characteristics.

There is substantial diversity in all cultural and ethnic populations. We need to be sensitive to such differences as well as to the commonalities that define our different heritages. Several focal areas to which we must attend for success in our work with NCDG individuals and families have been highlighted here. Individuals and families need support, encouragement, and guidance in maintaining their historical ethnic identity while overcoming the barriers they face and building on their possibilities. NCDG members, whether immigrants or from within the host culture, need to work out how to adapt to the CDG culture while remaining true to their history and the values of their past heritage. At the same time, CDG organizations and individuals need to learn how to accommodate to and value the diversity in their societies.

Theories and programs designed to produce individual and social change require accurate and detailed information about what can be expected from groups or individuals, especially oppressed ones. Until change agents and programs learn to base their approaches on realistic expectations, they are likely to remain ineffective and frustrated. In the long run, ill-informed efforts and lack of attention to ethnically valid diversity may set back our understanding of the environmental, personal, and societal changes needed and the rate at which they can be accomplished.

As professionals or as concerned individuals, we may choose to invest our energies in improving human societies in a variety of ways. We may focus on contributing to the development of more constructive interrelations between people in different societies, on developing societies oriented to providing equitable possibilities for both CDG and NCDG members, or on working with groups or individuals within such societies. When we are able to approach these activities from a multicultural ethnic-validity-based psychosocial competence perspective, we will be more informed about how to be helpful. Working solely from a pathology or uniculturally oriented perspective is as frustrating for us as it is counterproductive for those with whom we work. Attending to how people construct and build on their own approaches to personally fulfilling and societally constructive activities provides an important alternative to currently prevalent individual and social change efforts.

CHAPTER 6

PSYCHOSOCIAL LEAPS AND SPIRALS
Their Role in Our Lives

INTRODUCTION

More than a decade ago, I introduced "psychosocial leaps and spirals" as a model for how the social realities of individuals and their societies are formed, maintained, and changed with time and circumstances (F. Tyler, 1987). I emphasized that any individual or collective pattern of human functioning, whether psychosocially competent or destructive, is based in part on discretionary choices made by the person or persons involved. I have called those choices "psychosocial leaps." Once we make such a leap, we have a basis for constructing spirals of development.

We use three points of reference to guide our lives: our *individual and collective senses of self* (personal attributes), *our senses of the world* (self-world attributes), and our *behavioral approaches to events* (behavioral attributes). We anchor, maintain, and change the relationships of these reference points with each other in ongoing interactive patterns as we encounter and respond to the supports and threats in our lives. These interaction patterns approximate the form of a spiral whether they cumulatively augment increasing psychosocial competence, decrease current levels of it, augment destructive spirals, or yield some combination of these possibilities. These interactions and changes are ongoing at all levels, from individual to cultural, as our judgments and choices converge, diverge, and conflict with other choices and judgments that we and others are making.

However, the incoming data from these ongoing processes never forces a decision about whether something observed is a fact or whether an experience is good. Those judgments require a "leap of faith." In the realm of science, it is accepted that all judgments eventually rest on "soft" criteria and involve the individual's personal equation. Judgments of preference or value also rest on such criteria. The use of any explicit criteria as a basis for judgment rests on some other criteria that by nature cannot by specified—otherwise we would get into an infinite regress and confront the impossibility of eliminating the personal equation (Kuhn, 1970; Polanyi, 1968). Although there have been many arguments that science is value free, it has been demonstrated that judgments of fact and of value inevitably rest on each other (McClure & F. Tyler, 1967).

CHOICE BASES OF PSYCHOSOCIAL LEAPS AND SPIRALS

To illustrate that these judgments rest on tacit criteria requires specific examples and empirical evidence for support. I have included four categories of psychosocial research and theories to illustrate these points and show how it is our choices that lead to our psychosocial spiral patterns of development. These categories are (a) Hope, Excuses, and the Self, (b) Violence, (c) Belief Systems, and (d) The Coherence and Continuity of Spirals.

HOPE, EXCUSES, AND THE SELF

Snyder (1994) and his colleagues (Snyder, Higgins, & Stucky, 1983) documented that people's formations of meaning (interpretations of life's events) are consistent with the conclusion that *personal equations* are not neutral, but are psychosocial in nature. Their studies of hope and of excuse-making also support the leaps and spirals theme. They confirmed that once individuals make leaps to form particular self-images or develop expectations such as hope, they are subsequently influenced in a spiral fashion toward behaving in ways that build on these leaps, use them, and seek to maintain or enhance them.

Snyder (1994) noted that hope has often been viewed as a dangerous and self-defeating characteristic. He advanced the contrasting position that when hope is tied to a goal and becomes part of the perception that one's goals can be met, it is a powerful, positive characteristic. He defined hope as consisting of *mental willpower* or *agency* and of *waypower for goals* or *pathways*. Mental willpower seems comparable to what I have called self-efficacy. Waypower for goals is similar to behavioral attributes. It includes our capabilities for planful thought, and is based on a previous history of successfully finding one or more avenues to one's goals.

Snyder (1994) documented that among equally intelligent individuals, those with higher levels of hope made better grades, and college athletes with higher hope scores outperformed coaches' ratings of their physical abilities more than did their otherwise comparable teammates. High hope individuals also managed failure and frustration more constructively. Snyder also hypothesized, but did not test, that people adjust their goals to fit with their understanding of their external realities. He suggested that such adjustments explain why women and minorities in the United States (NCDGs) report equally high hope scores in comparison with white males (CDGs).

Snyder and colleagues (1983) also suggested that using excuses may be both psychosocially constructive and limiting, citing the widespread prevalence of excuse-making and its relationship to people's efforts to maintain a positive self-image. They identified different kinds of excuse-making and their correlates, including those which lessen responsibility, reframe performance, or derogate a negative evaluation source. Individuals used excuses when it would influence their internally regulated and externally mediated self-image. Further, individual differences influenced excuse-making. People with a more internal locus of control orientation used excuses less than did others. Deciding to offer an excuse involved an effort to reduce external and internal disapproval and maintain a positive self-image.

Once self-images are formed, we respond to events by offering excuses which we choose as consistent with our own hope images; we may adjust our goals to maintain our levels of hope. Such behaviors are consistent with a psychosocial spirals perspective in that they embody a social cushion for societal and individual limitations, yet retain human responsibility and standards of social justice. In contrast, indiscriminate or exploitive use of excuse making or goal setting can be destructive because it reduces prosocial learning and results in negative social and self-images.

Violence and Psychosocial Spirals

Violence is a topic of enormous significance for individuals and societies and will be addressed in depth in Chapter 11. It is mentioned here because patterns of violence are particularly revealing of the nature of psychosocial leaps and spirals. To behave aggressively and destructively rests on the belief, the leap, that it is justifiable to do so under the circumstances. Acting on that belief is particularly likely to generate an "in-kind" response from a recipient as a defense against the violence and as a preventive measure against further violence. That defensive response tends to confirm the originator's belief that she or he is in danger and requires further protective action, usually more violence. Thus begins an often-seen escalating spiral of threat-oriented psychosocial perceptions and violent acts.

Toch (1992, 1979) spent his career documenting the characteristics of escalating cycles of violence and ways to reduce them among imprisoned violent men. His summary of these cycles is similar to the description above. He added that such cycles, repeated and widespread, can, in turn, lead to broader beliefs that the world is violent and threatening. Involved individuals then invest more time and resources into being sensitive to the possibilities of violence, to confirming their beliefs that the world is violent, and to preparing to cope with that violence.

A relevant and particularly enlightening area of research is focused on the relationship between people's propensities for violence, i.e., watching it on television and subsequent violent behaviors. Groebel (1986) summarized the major conclusions from the results of a longitudinal, seven-nation, cross-cultural field study: (a) television violence has the power across cultural contexts to spawn and facilitate children's aggression; (b) norms powerfully influence the development of prosocial and anti-social behavior; (c) the mechanisms that facilitate or inhibit violence vary from country to country and between genders and groups in hetero-geneous societies; and (d) low levels of societal and television violence are the best overall predictors of low levels of aggression.

The United States is the most heterogeneous and violent of the countries studied. Further, it is in the United States that the separate and combined contribution of these mechanisms to a psychosocial-spirals effect in generating violence is most evident. Huesmann and Eron (1986) concluded from their U.S. data that a multiprocess, reciprocal action model is the most plausible model for explaining their findings. Aggression and viewing violence facilitate each other and also contribute to academic and social failure. They are, in turn, further stimulated by such failure. Other contributing factors include the resulting social isolation, attitude changes, cues for aggression, information gained about how to be aggressive, and imitation of specific, aggressive acts seen on television.

The findings from these studies support the psychosocial spirals model. Once a leap is made, whether by being aggressive or by watching violence on television, individuals involve themselves in a process that is likely to function in a reciprocally confirming way. Eron and Slaby (1994) noted that patterns, once acquired, can become self-sustaining and self-enlarging, and they can establish aggressive patterns which are used over a lifelong period.

None of these findings mean that such spirals cannot be reversed. We live in environments with many sources of input and are consistently barraged with conflicting as well as supportive feedback. Therefore, we can develop systematic approaches to changing undesirable behaviors. They do mean, however, that we must take into account the role of psychosocial spiral effects in the process of sustaining or changing our conduct or that of others.

BELIEF SYSTEMS AND PSYCHOSOCIAL SPIRALS

Empirical studies of adults' belief systems reflect the strategies people have followed in forming their adult psychosocial natures and also reflect the cumulative impact of their past experiences. Further, because we are usually unaware of our belief systems and their relationship to the psychosocial configurations that we have formed, empirical studies are particularly instructive about these leaps of faith and the consequent psychosocial spirals that shape our lives. For example, a central aspect of many religious orientations is the belief that we are responsible for our conduct; the companion belief is that our deity or deities influence or control at least some aspects of our lives. These two beliefs are associated with still others about the nature of the world and each individual's relation to it. Altogether they support further leaps concerning appropriate and inappropriate patterns of conduct.

Antonovsky (1979) described how belief requirements are reflected in people's psychosocial spirals when he introduced the concept of a "sense of coherence," defined as

> a global orientation that expresses the extent to which one has a pervasive, enduring though dynamic feeling of confidence that one's internal and external environments are predictable and that there is a high probability that things will work out as well as can be reasonably expected. (p. 123)

This formulation includes the elements of a sense of self, a self–world orientation including hope (as well as can be expected), and an orientation to things working out (through someone's efforts). Antonovsky (1979) explicitly challenged the presumption that internal control is necessarily good and external control necessarily bad. He argued that central to a sense of coherence is a belief that power rests where it should, whether that is in the self, a god, the family, the state, or some other legitimate source. In other words, a constructive, supportive sense of coherence includes a psychosocial leap that satisfies our tacit and explicit criteria as to what constitutes our relationship to ourselves and the world.

The point was illustrated in a study cited in Chapter 4 (Pargament, Sullivan, F. Tyler, & Steele, 1982) that the role and impact of power (or control) depends on whether there is adequate power and whether it is in the right place. We studied psychosocial relationships among Protestant and Roman Catholic churches and Jewish synagogues in the United States. The relationships among the organization of the congregations, the role of the clergy, the functions of belief systems for congregants, and the congregants' psychosocial competence characteristics were examined. Participants rated the degree to which they viewed four loci of control (personal, powerful others, chance, and God) as influential in their lives. They also rated their self–world and active planfulness orientations. Analyses of these findings yielded five significantly different control clusters with meaningful psychosocial competence correlates. They are described in Table 6.1.

The relationships found were complex. The two psychosocial competence characteristics that were most strongly related to the control clusters were trust level and self-efficacy (favorableness of self-evaluation). The

TABLE 6.1.   Control Clusters and Psychosocial Competence Characteristics[a]

Cluster description	Control score characteristics	Other psychosocial competence score characteristics
1. Secularly oriented, moderately uncertain	Low on God control; medium on personal, powerful others, and chance control	High on active planfulness and intrinsic motivation; low of trust and self-efficacy
2. God oriented, moderately uncertain	Low on personal control; medium on God, powerful others, and chance control	Medium on self-efficacy and trust; low on active playfulness and intrinsic motivation
3. Traditionally internally controlled	High on personal control; medium on powerful others and God control; low on chance control	High on trust, self-efficacy, active planfulness, intrinsic motivation
4. Undifferntiated externally control	Low on personal control; high on God, powerful others, and chance control	Low on trust, self-efficacy, active planfulness
5. God controlled	High on God control; medium on control by chance and powerful others; low on personal control	High on trust, self-efficacy, active planfulness

[a]Each cluster description is inferred from the combination of the control score characteristics and the other psychosocial competence characteristics.

Note. From Patterns of attribution of control and individual psychosocial competence, K. I. Pargament, M. S. Sullivan, F. B. Tyler, & R. E. Steele, 1982. *Psychological Reports, 51*, pp. 1243–1252.

different control anchors that these respondents reported were reflected in the conceptually consistent self–world and planfulness patterns that provided them a base for managing their lives. Only the Undifferentiated Externally Controlled Group 4 respondents seemed to have neither internal nor external anchors, and they reported the least coherence and competence in their psychosocial functioning. In contrast, two groups had firm control anchors, the secularly based Personal Control Group 3, and the God Control Group 5. Both of these groups reported high levels of psychosocial competence characteristics.

It would be presumptuous to generalize too widely from this one study. Others are needed to provide a more detailed picture of how people's beliefs influence the psychosocial spirals they develop. Even so, this study challenged the belief that internal control is always good and external control is always bad. It also affirmed that believing one's life events are being managed by an appropriate source is important to a coherent positive, psychosocial pattern of life management.

The Coherence and Continuity of Spirals

Nested frameworks define people's presumed natures at various life stages and how they are to be treated and conduct themselves. A widely shared view in the helping professions and in numerous cultures is that the young are shaped by their nature and society; although they are not yet productive, they are worth investing in because they will eventually provide a return on that investment. For example, Rizzini (1997) reviewed the past two hundred years of Brazil's history of social policy toward children and found that they were defined either as the future saviors of the country or as threats to the social order. They were never considered worthy in their own right as children. In contrast, most cultures view adults as being responsible for shaping their own and other's lives and expect them to carry out those responsibilities. However, views diverge about elders. Some societies believe that decline is part of human nature and that while society is obligated to care for elders, they are not otherwise worth investing in because there is no potential for them to make any future contributions. Other societies cherish and revere the elderly as their ancestors or as having special powers, or as both.

Empirical testing of views like these has primarily been by analysis of ethnographic and survey data. Guttman (1977) provided a particularly instructive overview (as cross-cultural and worldwide as possible) of the varied cultural assumptions about human potentials and the related spirals that people develop. His account included identifiable cultural differences and widespread patterns of human psychosocial spirals patterns which were characterized by peoples' changes over their life spans in relation to cultural factors, life span changes, and individual choices. He concluded that the data indicated a gender-based pattern of changes with age as the most general of the factors organizing the spirals in the continuity of people's lives. These examples illustrate the bases for his conclusions.

Traditionally, young adult men have aggressively wrested resources from the physical or social (tribal conflict) environment. Older men have shown varied patterns in relation to life-stage status, their society, and the spiritual world. Among Sub-Saharan tribes, the older men often controlled the social order and certain social perquisites (e.g., sexual access) by sorcery. Older Comanches in the United States became "peace chiefs" who controlled aggressive young warriors.

Another potential role available for older men in many cultures has been for them to focus on the next world and relationships to the gods or spirits. Older male Chinese were expected to be relaxed, meditative, and noble. These activities were considered moral work done for the community as well as themselves, so they were rewarded with food and shelter. Expectations for the Hindu elderly men has been for them to renounce worldly attachments and shift to a passive and androgynous stance. In Germany, men over sixty spent more time in church than did women.

In other cultures, older men's gender-related roles became blurred, and they took on roles previously delegated to women such as gardening and cooking. In Fiji, not only could they turn to gardening, they could also become affectionate to the women of the household. Elderly Native American warriors in the Southwestern United States were forced to do menial housework.

Women's patterns have been quite different from men's. Young adult women have been oriented to passive agent mastery plus dependence on and deference to men. Their expected tasks included child bearing and rearing, gathering food, gardening, and domestic activities. Among older women, two major roles were prevalent. One was to exercise informal power for themselves and the family. In Japan, after age sixty, women became more extrovertive, and the men became less so. Widowed mothers also ran the family with help from the oldest sons. In Africa, elderly women allied themselves with the young men against the elderly men. Postmenopausal Native American women and Chicanas in the United States became "manly hearted," particularly in ritual and healing practices. They also were accorded more sexual freedom and had more social power in the home. CDG women in the United States and England become more extroversive, more "bouncy," more dominant, and less interpersonally oriented than men.

There were limits on the extent to which these more assertive and controlling women's roles were considered benign. When women exceeded those limits, they were seen as taking on the second role, an excessively self-centered or threatening evil role, possibly as witches. In Africa, the status of witch was ascribed to old women generally and to mothers-in-law in particular (possibly because power was centered in the family and other close relationships).

Guttman (1977) hypothesized that these gender and age patterns may have arisen because of survival imperatives. Young women must care for children, so fathers must provide for the family. Individuals, communities, and cultures adapt to these gender-related roles even though they restrict aspects of development for all. Later in life, men and women can develop other facets of themselves. These variations in age-by-sex-by-situation patterns support the conclusion that our identities and roles are influenced by the psychosocial spirals that we form in our different and changing circumstances across our life spans.

Ethnographic data support the conclusion that circumstances can also shape prototypic cultural patterns. Utilitarian cultures stress an egocentric, self-seeking spirit. The Koryak are Siberian nomads who mistreat, abuse, and exploit their young. The young also abuse their elders, leave them only scraps to eat, and generally have no use for them. Industrialized societies (the developed world) generally have low regard for the elderly, segregating and devaluing them. Altruistic, humanistic societies relate quite differently. The Yucatan Maya elderly are orderly, responsible, and quietly warm. Political power is held by the young, but the old are content because "we have good sons who maintain us in our old age" (Guttman, 1977, p. 315). These life style patterns show the effects of different psychosocial spirals on widespread cultural and individual differences in life styles.

Guttman's (1977) presentation also includes evidence of individual differences in adaptation and survivability within and across contexts. One striking example is the ability to externalize anger. Individuals in oppressive situations, such as concentration camps, prisoner of war camps, or homes for the elderly, survive longer if they maintain and express their anger towards their circumstances and oppressors. Passivity and self-blame tend to be related to lower survival rates.

In a final, pertinent statement, Guttman (1977) concluded that psychologists do not even recognize these patterns, so they cannot begin to comprehend these complex relationships. Consequently, psychologists cannot conceptualize the nature and impact of the interactions between people's psychosocial ecologies, the kinds of cognition or abstracting they sponsor, and how the resulting ways that people think shape their social lives. Until we understand these factors, we cannot measure or analyze their effects for any age cohort. More than two decades after Guttman's extensive review, our theories and interventions remain inadequate. The psychosocial spirals perspective can serve as a step toward overcoming some of these limitations.

MULTICULTURAL ETHNIC VALIDITY PATTERNS

One aspect of managing life's spirals is that events, desires, and possibilities do not always fit together. We must manage convergences, divergences, and conflicts, and how we do so influences the further course of these spirals. How complex this activity of managing multifaceted, convergent to conflicting interactions is becomes more evident when we compare cultural groups with disparate nested frameworks and conceptions of ethnic validity. Such comparisons provide external checks that highlight the tacit and explicit leaps underlying the spiral nature of our personal configurations and ethnic validity frameworks.

INDIVIDUALIST/COMPETITIVE VERSUS COOPERATIVE/PEACEFUL

Change occurs throughout people's lives, with later life changes necessarily building on patterns formed in earlier years. We begin forming our individual psychosocial configurations in infancy and early childhood. They presumably take on an ethnic validity character through culturally normative child rearing practices.

Bonta (1997) illustrated such influences in his review of cooperation and competition in peaceful and nonpeaceful societies. His goal was to identify ways that competitive societies can learn from peaceful ones to reduce their violence and aggression. He chose 25 societies identified as peaceful because "(a) they appear to be somewhat, highly, or totally peaceful; and (b) information is available about their competition, cooperation, and individualism" (p. 300). They were contrasted with the world's predominant societies which are oriented to individualism and competitiveness tempered with the cooperativeness of fair play and team play. These latter societies consider competition to be beneficial and aggression necessary. Violence is, to some extent, considered inevitable, and the designs of and responses to their psychological studies reflect that worldview.

Bonta's (1997) findings illustrate how patterns of early socialization produce internalized psychosocial spirals which perpetuate societal and individual life patterns, including contradictory ones. In the highly competitive societies of the United States and Europe, there was abundant empirical evidence that socialization in cooperative environments can have many prosocial outcomes. These outcomes include that children learn and transfer concepts and principles more effectively; have more intrinsic motivation to learn; have better attitudes toward their teachers and classmates, including across gender, ethnic/racial, and status divisions; have better mental health and higher self-esteem; have more communicative conflict resolution; and have better social and cognitive development skills. These patterns are not consonant with the broader societal ethos and attendant violence of individualism and competitiveness.

Twenty-three of the 25 peaceful societies specifically rejected competition as appropriate behavior. Socialization practices involved two distinctive approaches. In some societies, children were directly taught to be peaceful and noncompetitive. In others, children were indulged and provided almost unlimited attention, affection, and nurturance for the first years of their lives, and then were suddenly and dramatically treated as being of low status and no special significance. Tantrums or other demands for special status were ignored or rebuffed. The children quickly learned that love, closeness, and dependence are important relationships and are obtained only by fitting in. They could not dominate by challenging the social order or being self-centered.

There were differences among these 23 societies. Some linked competition to aggression, a link that has substantial support in the psychological literature. Humility and modesty were valued, apparently from fear that high individual achievement would threaten group stability and peace. They held in common a combination of beliefs in nonviolence and had established, psychological structures that encouraged and supported the continuity of the harmony in their social lives. Intergroup relations were largely cooperative and guided by symbols of peacefulness and the economics of sharing and mutual assistance. These social and psychological factors encouraged linkages such as marriage and movement across boundaries.

A few of the societies had maintained their commitment to peacefulness by giving it priority, but they had also incorporated elements of individualism, achievement, and competitiveness. For example, the Amish in the United States are peaceable rural people who reject modern technology and commercial practices. They have limited their competitiveness by stressing that their business must remain small, but they sell their produce and crafts to survive. That is, they have made some adaptations to survive in an individualistic and competitive society, but have sought to maintain their core societal values.

Bonta's (1997) summary is particularly relevant to the focus on psychosocial spirals. He concluded that the 25 peaceful societies were characterized by an interrelated pattern of beliefs, socialization practices, socio-cultural practices, and symbolic rituals that guided their members in ways that sustained them and the society. Their individual and collective behaviors could not be fully accounted for by mechanistic and deterministic formulations. They functioned as knowers and actively involved themselves in creating and managing their lives and societies. They learned the nested framework templates for constructing the ethnic validity patterns that they needed to sustain the internal and external coherence of their individual lives and societies.

Such differences in socialization and cultural priorities can also be found by comparing the early education practices of more and less competitive, individualistic societies. These comparisons show how psychosocial spirals are formally instituted and that the consequences appear in children by the time they reach elementary school. Early childhood education approaches used by the Reggio Emilia group in Italy and the main stream in the United States (Edwards, Gandini, & Forman, 1996) provide instructive examples. Their contrasts are most clearly reflected in each culture's assumption's about what is developmentally appropriate for children because of its beliefs about the nature of childhood development.

The Emilia perspective is based on the assumption that children are active participants in their lives and that they need freedom for creativity. An integrated approach to development is emphasized, so liberal arts are included with traditional early childhood education. Classrooms focus on children's aesthetic sensibilities and the products of their work, including visual arts, the narrative focus of stories, lengthy projects, and long-term relations with teachers rather than yearly changes. Emphasis is placed on a prosocial orientation by encouraging collaboration between children, children and teachers, teachers, teachers and parents, and school personnel with both community citizens and the local government. Teachers work with larger class sizes than are considered optimal in the United States, and they prefer more space to smaller class sizes.

In the United States, teachers are taught that children are not comfortable with group interaction and need to work individually, cannot handle ambiguity or waiting, and do not have long attention spans. They schedule short-term activities and emphasize compartmentalizing aesthetic, cognitive, and social development and instruction. The children's social development, including relations with peers and participation in games, is more oriented to fostering a kind of social competence that promotes the individual rather than the group. Emphasis is placed more on individual rights and following the rules than on involving children in learning how to negotiate over limited and valued objects. While stable relationships with adult figures are considered important, emphasis is given to preparing children to handle the transition from teacher to teacher each year. Subject matter expertise and knowledge of age-appropriate development tasks are given high priority in teacher preparation and in classroom design and management. Lines between parent, teacher, citizen, and governmental responsibilities are clearly drawn and there is often little collaboration between them.

These differences in approach are admittedly a matter of degree, and there are many similarities between the two systems. However, each approach is justified by the adults as being appropriate to the nature of children, rather than to the cultural expectations of the adults. The observed reality is that U.S. children have short attention spans, need structure, and do not work well in groups, while Italian children have longer attention spans and function well in ambiguous situations and in groups. These differences can hardly be attributed to anything other than learned cultural expectations. An appropriate explanation is that Italian and U.S. children are being socialized to make different psychosocial leaps to guide how they live and eventually socialize their own children.

CHANGING ETHNIC VALIDITY PATTERNS IN A RELATEDNESS CULTURE

Thus far I have reviewed the kinds of self-sustaining nested framework templates that organize the ethnic validity characteristics of societies, the lives of people in them, and the people's relationships with each other and outsiders. However, people's lives and situations change, and consequently their ethnic validity paradigms and nested frameworks are not static. My next step is to show how these paradigms change along with people's lives and circumstances.

Myers (1992) wrote a carefully documented text to justify the need for First World countries to invest in broadly conceived programs of child care and development throughout the Third World. His arguments were supported by multidisciplinary and multicultural sources and provided a number of rationales for such an investment in children. They included moral and justice based concerns, such as that children have a right to live and develop their full potential and that it is through children that society's moral values are perpetuated. Emphasis was also placed on children's economic value (increased subsequent productivity) and the economic efficacy of integrated programs (health, educational, and psychosocial development programs are more efficient when combined).

Myers (1992) stressed that such programs require strengthened beliefs that combined actions are needed and appropriate, the political will to act on those beliefs, and retraining of people to carry them out. Thus, he also emphasized that the CDGs with power and money must be persuaded that they have a vested interest in supporting such programs. In my terms, the underlying nested frameworks must be changed to provide a basis for convergences, and the existing conflicts must be resolved in order to implement changes. Accomplishments can provide for further development of different and more inclusive kinds of ethnic validity models in and between individuals, families, and their communities.

Kagitcibasi (1996) outlined a similar approach as relevant to achieving the goals of other psychological interventions. She argued that psychologists have a responsibility to get involved in their societies. To her, that responsibility also includes attending to the policy implications of any applied research. She described this change process in her Turkish culture, which she referred to (along with similar cultures) as being the more relatedness-oriented "Majority World" (p. xviii). She believes that the nature of people's orientations to themselves and others is more appropriately described as separateness–relatedness rather than as individualistic–collectivistic, the more common characterization. The former is a psychological distinction; the latter, a societal one. This more accurate characterization is important because, as she emphasized,

> interventions may be expected to work better if they take into consideration and build on the existing human connectedness, as reflected in closely knit family, kinship, and community ties, rather than counteracting them, for example, in building individualistic independence and competition. (Kagitcibasi, 1996, p. 3)

She added that to achieve a theoretical understanding of the relationships between psychological and cultural variables, it is essential to study the contextual nature of each culture and then its cross-cultural generalities. This understanding is needed as a basis for developing appropriate applications of psychological knowledge to individual and social change endeavors.

Kagitcibasi's (1996) emphasis on changing both individual and societal characteristics in intervention approaches was used to guide the development, implementation, and evaluation of an Early Childhood Care and Education (ECCE) program in Turkey. While most Turkish ECCE programs for middle class children were educationally oriented, those for working class children were custodial. Social development in Turkey was quite low in comparison to other Majority World countries, and in particular, in relation to its level of economic development. She attributed this pattern to conservative values about the family, low levels of urban women's employment, and a general lack of public support for early stimulation/learning/school readiness for later school performance.

She and her colleagues (Kagitcibasi, 1996) conducted the Turkish

Early Enrichment project in a working class district of Istanbul to test her general hypothesis and provide a model for its implementation. The project was designed to support traditional close-knit family values and relatedness while introducing the notion of autonomy in child-rearing. The program was focused on three forms of ECCE: educational, custodial, and home care. The training emphasized support for the mothers and their involvement as active participants in the group. They were encouraged to develop positive self-concepts, attend to their own and their children's needs, and empower themselves to cope with their problems and those of their children. The experimental intervention included a Cognitive Training Program which used group dynamics to sensitize randomly selected mothers in each ECCE context to the needs of growing children. Mothers were also helped to develop more effective communication skills in order to improve their verbal interactions with their children.

The project involved a first year of assessment, two years of intervention, a fourth year of reassessment and evaluation, and a follow-up evaluation six years later. Its specific hypotheses, that enriched home and day care training would enhance the children's cognitive and social development, was supported, most clearly for cognitive development. The more significant overall outcomes of changing nested frameworks and related ethnic validity patterns became apparent during the follow-up assessments, and they were associated with the effects of the contextual–interactional approach to training the mothers.

The mothers were not trained individually, but in interaction with one another or in the family context. Consequently, the children's environments were also changed, and the mothers and children were sufficiently empowered that they perpetuated their gains from the programs to start a prosocial spiral of development. Gains included enriched spousal as well as parent–child interactions, higher intrafamily status for mothers relative to their husbands, and greater well-being of mothers and children as indicated by such changes as higher self-esteem, better social adjustment, and more autonomy for children. These effects were shown on many subjective and standardized measures across a wide range of areas including educational and social competence in the children, vocabulary competence in the mothers, and overall improved family relations. Further confirmation of positive changes was evidenced in the convergence of responses of fathers, mothers, and children (who were adolescents by the time of the follow-up). Further, the children's increased levels of autonomy did not come at the expense of the traditional values of relatedness. They were incorporated as an added dimension of the family members' conception of ethnic validity.

This project successfully created particular psychosocial changes through the introduction of two ideas: autonomy into a family culture of relatedness, and cognitive emphasis into a social–relational orientation to childrearing. It also supported its theoretical hypothesis by demonstrating the value of a human/family model of emotional interdependence. This model emphasizes autonomy *within* relatedness as preferable for human development to current, contrasting models of independence and (total) interdependence. Crucial to the study's long term implications was that the entire family, the nested framework of its organization, and the ethnic validity of its members were modified. It strongly supported the inter-related psychosocial spiral nature of individual and social change. As Kagitcibasi (1996) noted, it not only modified patterns of family function-ing, it led to changes in educational policy to include more early-enrichment programs for children and to add nonformal models to adult educational services. Its success has also influenced private, governmental, local, and international agencies to develop cooperative arrangements and holistic approaches in their programs.

Kagitcibasi (1996) emphasized that this type of integrated approach is particularly valuable for improving the lives and circumstances of people in adverse socioeconomic conditions. To me, it seems equally crucial to implement this model for CDG individuals and groups since the socializa-tion patterns of all groups within a society sustain each group's ethnic validity frameworks. Unless CDG members also emphasize individual autonomy within relatedness, such enrichment programs for NCDGs may not be sufficient to change patterns of social inequities.

LIFE SPAN PERSPECTIVES AND RESILIENCE

Although the preceding examples focused on the ethnic validity na-ture of developmental psychosocial spirals, these spirals are not limited to childhood. Rather, throughout life each of us encounters circumstances that threaten our survival by not providing for necessities or because they have the potential to destroy life. To survive and prevail over them, we use our psychosocial resources in a way called *resilience*. Resilience is based on much more than our known characteristics for restoring homeostatic func-tioning. Its broader nature is evidenced in the psychosocial competence patterns that we activate in response to these threats and setbacks. The focus of this section is on how resiliency develops and changes throughout our lives and on its significance in influencing the quality of our lives.

CHILDREN AND YOUTH: THE EARLY YEARS

The nature of our early lives is particularly important because of its impact on our future possibilities. As Myers (1992) and others documented, severe malnutrition can limit a child's cognitive development. Early traumatic personal experiences can also have an impact on psychosocial and cognitive development. While these later consequences may be less easily identified than those from physiological deprivation, they may also be more responsive to corrective interventions.

Resilience and Early Deprivation or Trauma

A predominant focus in psychology has been on the understanding and alleviation of the adverse impact of the arduous and traumatic life experiences that children have faced. During the last half century, that attention has begun to turn to the resilience exhibited by survivors of such experiences. Garmezy (1983) summarized the findings from five different approaches to studying children's resilience in different cultural contexts and under different stressful circumstances. They included an epidemiological study, a literature survey, two longitudinal–developmental studies, and several studies of children exposed to war. Three major sets of congruent factors were identified as playing an important role in the children's resiliency. One set was the *positive personal and social dispositions* of the children, including a sense of self-regard and self-efficacy, as well as somewhat positive social orientations and constructive coping skills. A second was a *family milieu* which provided some stability, direction, and support for the children. Third was the presence of some *external support system* of adults who provided emotional support and caring and a societal agency or agencies to strengthen the children's coping efforts.

These factors are also evident in Myers' (1992) analyses of children's requirements for healthy cognitive and psychosocial development and in the efforts of Moffitt (1993) and Kagitcibasi (1996). Their critical nature is underscored by Myers' strong argument that Third World programs must give priority to psychosocial as well as economic development. In his view, if such programs advocate for economic development only based on the belief that the benefits will automatically be reflected in enriched psychosocial lives of citizens, including children, they will fail. He insisted that economic and psychosocial development must be pursued together. As important as these points are, neither Myers nor Kagitcibasi identified the factors which differentiate resilient and prosocial from nonresilient and antisocial children. This additional information is needed if our efforts are to be optimally effective.

Antisocial Spirals of Development

Moffitt (1993) reviewed the literature from a number of cultures on the development of antisocial violence and concluded that it is a product of two patterns. For approximately five percent of children, antisocial violence is internalized early in life, usually as a product of living with continuous violence, abuse, or neglect. Environmental correlates also contribute. They include poor and crime ridden neighborhoods, poverty, large family size, and poor parenting, including parental alcohol and drug abuse. These patterns require early intervention if there is to be much hope of modifying them.

Moffitt (1993) also found that antisocial violence begins to increase at age seven, peaks at age seventeen, and largely disappears by age twenty-seven. This wide-spread pattern is more prevalent in modern societies, particularly in urban areas, and is largely sporadic and opportunistic. It seems partly related to the discrepancy between youths' biological maturity and their dependent and restricted societal roles. Overall, it suggests that there are significant disjunctions between many cultural socialization practices and the developmental imperatives that many youth face during their transitions from childhood to adulthood.

There may be a third pattern affecting a subset of those who initially were part of the second pattern (F. Tyler, 1997). Some of these youth face difficulties because of being ostracized or incarcerated. Girls may get pregnant or boys and girls may get caught engaging in illegal activities, such as gang behavior or drug use. For these youth as well as those exposed to early dysfunctional circumstances, developing or recovering constructive, competence-oriented spirals may be possible, but doing so requires internal resilience and external support, including societal opportunities.

A particularly illustrative example of how internal and external factors combine to promote children's potential for overcoming early traumatic life experiences and circumstances is found in a project reported by O'Gorman (1981). A poet and educator, he set out to highlight the issues central to the education of oppressed children in a democracy such as the United States. He established a school in the predominantly African American Harlem slums of New York City to save at least a few children from their fate in the streets. First, he involved the children in doing something about their lives, and then he helped them to review and redefine what their past experiences had done to them. Finally, school personnel worked with these students in learning the skills needed to create a better life. His evidence of success is largely anecdotal, but instructive and largely compelling.

His was one of a number of programs reported in *Prevention through Political Action and Social Change* (Joffe & Albee, 1981) in the *University of Vermont Primary Prevention of Psychopathology* series. These programs describe how broad-based social change patterns have shaped and been shaped by the people in various societies, their relationship to their governmental/cultural system, and the governmental/cultural systems themselves. They also illustrate the spiral nature of change processes by showing that integrating the activities of helping individuals, modeling approaches, and publicizing issues is essential to create such changes.

ADULT APPROACHES TO CHANGE

Even at present, with nearly instant worldwide communication of visual and auditory messages, international exchange of goods, and relatively convenient world travel, most of us spend our lives in limited geographic and cultural spaces. Consequently, we may be unaware that we and our physical ecologies and cultures are constantly changing. We may not have noticed that as we move through our life stages and our milieus, we are continually confronted with the importance of resiliency. The capacity to rebound and redefine ourselves as we and our circumstances change is vital because our earlier acquired understandings and ways to engage the events in our lives cease to be adequate.

Earlier, I described our abilities to culminate, conclude, and redefine ourselves and our circumstances as skills that provide us ways of moving forward with our lives. Chapter 4 outlined the commonalities and differences in ethnic validity aspects of competent, in contrast to noncompetent, Anglo and African American community residents. Although these people lived in close proximity to each other, they had evolved distinctive patterns of resilience in relation to their respective situations. They were unaware of their competency characteristics and their differences, as are most of us unless we are faced with life intrusions, such as natural disasters, major societal changes, external conquest, or the need to migrate for survival. Then, we have to adapt to strangers, unfamiliar customs and concepts of human identity and relationships, and possibly to an unfamiliar geography. The fields of acculturation and modernization address such processes, and the following accounts illustrate how they may be usefully understood as being of a psychosocial spirals nature.

Uprootedness, Immigration, and Acculturation

People seeking meaningful lives for themselves, for their families, or for both, in new cultural settings, face issues of culminating, concluding, and redefining themselves and their realities. This uprootedness has been defined as change that occurs in an inappropriate time span or outside of the expected path of change in a person's life (Back, 1980). The preponderance of research has been focused on its negative aspects. Coelho and Ahmed (1980) reported on extensive studies of such transitions and theoretical formulations about their nature. They also described policy formulations and programs implemented to alleviate the stresses such transitions impose and facilitate people's effectiveness at managing them. Their collection of essays makes it clear that human lives have always been characterized by the necessity to contend with untimely, unanticipated changes in circumstances. It seems that the survival and civilizing of humans and their societies are indicative of our individual and collective capacity for not only resisting adversity, but prevailing over it.

Considering three core tasks that we face in these transitions helps us understand that we build on the required leaps by pursuing psychosocial spirals to acquire new competence patterns. These tasks are, respectively, *acculturation, development,* and *modernity.* Berry (1980) defined acculturation as including mutual cultural exchange and influence that may be imbalanced and destructive, but that may also lead to developing new and creative cultural forms. Despite his suggestion that acculturation may be a two-way process, most cross-cultural/cross-ethnic approaches have been characterized by an ethnocentric power orientation, with the dominant CDG considered more civilized and morally superior. The NCDGs were to be exploited (often enslaved), civilized (secular), "saved" (spiritual), or else eliminated. Studies by CDG investigators have also tended to focus on the benefits for NCDG individuals and groups, including all immigrants, of becoming civilized and assimilated.

A subtle form of cultural imperialism has been advanced more recently under the label of modernity. Its basic assumption is that less-developed societies would be better off if they were deliberately changed by external force. That change is to increase the complexity and integration of their cultural, social, and individual forms to those derived in part from "the forms of conduct ... likely to be inculcated by work in the factory" (Inkeles & Smith, 1974, p. 5). Those societies are also expected to adopt standardized forms of exchange in relation to goods, services, and relationships.

The task of acculturating generates stress as do other forms of change, and individuals deal with that stress in one of three ways. They become acculturated, revert to their prior cultural identity and behavior, or incorporate some combination of both. The nature of these changes is spiral, as can be seen in the interactive process between our internal states and external actions. As we face new circumstances, we not only change our external activities, we also change our internal natures so that we redefine ourselves. Simultaneously, we act in and on the environment to change those circumstances. In any of these patterns of choices there are trade-offs; no adaptive configuration provides all benefits and no costs. Further, these processes continue with each change and are reflected in our evolving personal and social spirals, as is illustrated in the following three studies.

Celano and F. Tyler (1991) investigated the behavioral acculturation of 59 Vietnamese refugees who had been in the United States between one and twenty-four months and were living in the Washington D.C. area. Some respondents acquired the skills to survive in their new culture, yet over time, turned back to their familiar, earlier skills and survival strategies. Respondents who were more educated, had higher socioeconomic status, or were unemployed were more resistant to or had less need to acquire new survival skills. In other words, these people adapted to their new context in ways that were influenced by what they brought to it and what they encountered in it.

Birman and F. Tyler (1994) addressed whether immigrants abandon the values of their culture of origin, reject the values of their new culture, or integrate both. We also explored whether the members of an immigrant family or community relate to the new culture in the same way and studied the effects of their choices on them. We found that the Russian, American, and Jewish identities and behavior acculturation patterns of Soviet Jewish refugees in an east coast city of the United States interacted in complex ways. Among the women, retention of their Russian identity and making a leap to adopt an American identity were negatively related, and those who acquired an American identity were less alienated. In contrast, among men, Russian and U.S. identity acculturation were uncorrelated. The men adopted a U.S. identity without abandoning their Russian identity, and they were alienated only if they retained their Russian identity and did not adopt a U.S. one.

There were also gender differences. Men who adopted U.S. behaviors were less alienated. Those who had been in the United States longer had higher levels of Russian identity and behavior acculturation; they had strengthened their commitment to their past. Women who retained their preference for Russian behavior were more alienated, but those who had been in the United States longer identified more with the United States and behaved in culturally appropriate ways. With men and women changing in different ways, their patterns of interpersonal relations would also presumably change. Husbands and wives might find themselves facing new and different adaptation tasks within the family, requiring them to modify their relationship in order to maintain or strengthen it in this new context. Overall, these findings tell us that alienation, a major indicator of adaptation effectiveness, was related to these respondents' gender and cultural identity, choice of behavioral acculturation, and the psychosocial spirals they built in their new milieu.

The presence of children adds another aspect to these complexities.

Birman (1991) found that acculturation of poor, Latin American immigrant school youth to an urban area of the United States had implications for their families and themselves as they often faced conflicting supports and threats. Finding a new life in a new culture was fraught with greater conflict for girls than for boys. For the girls, acculturating to the United States led to better relations with their families and peers. However, giving up their Hispanic cultural identity distanced them from their Hispanic male peers because of their changed conception of an appropriate gender role for girls. The longer the girls (but not the boys) had lived in the United States, the lower the rating they gave to the level of their family's competence, with one exception. The girls who had become identified with U.S. culture rated their families as having lost less in competence; we do not know whether the choice of American identification in these girls helped sustain their families' competence or vice versa. We need to consider how these factors interrelate because these psychosocial competence configuration changes yielded short-term and long-term outcomes for the girls and their families. Further, only some of those changes were constructive prosocial outcomes.

This brief look at the acculturation issues facing immigrants illustrates some of the ethnic validity and psychosocial competence issues they are likely to encounter. They must deal with the conflict between their historic ethnic identities and their efforts to create a meaningful life in the new context. Even when they try to adapt to the new situation, the process is not simple and direct. It depends on the supports they have and the threats they face as well as on their own unique characteristics. If their initial moves toward acculturation prove sufficiently unproductive, they may turn back to their earlier identities, values, and life styles. In any case, they have to muster some resilience to sustain themselves and construct psychosocial spirals of development to manage their new lives.

Resiliency and Involvement among Professionals

The concept of resiliency is also applicable to how professionals fulfill their roles. Konopka (1981) emphasized that a professional role is necessarily personally and socially involved. She grew up in Germany, committed herself to improving the lives of young people, and participated in the development of youth programs in the Weimar Republic and in opposing the Nazi movement. She was imprisoned in a concentration camp, but escaped and emigrated to the United States where she resumed her career. Subsequently, she was active in the 1960's U.S. youth movements, became a professor of social work at the University of Minnesota, and was director of its Center for Youth Development and Research.

Konopka's experience led her to the conviction that a concern for the well-being of individuals and a commitment to social action always go together. Accomplishing social change involves knowledge, work, compassion, and commitment plus as much willingness to be changed as to change others. There must be a willingness to accept and support the empowerment of everyone and to collaborate with them rather than remain detached, judgmental, and controlling. To Konopka, the role of the socially responsible professional is built on a self and self–world view (committed, caring, and open) plus related behavioral characteristics (involved, willing to change, collaborative) interrelated in a psychosocial spiral fashion (1981).

AGING

Social structures and individual choices also shape people's spirals during the later stages of their lives. Bengston, Kaschau, and Ragan (1977) emphasized that social differentiations are based on the way aging is defined. In turn, our sociocultural embeddedness shapes our interactions and perceptions of our past, present, and future, including the quality of our lives as elders. For example, in the United States, Mexican Americans report a big drop in perceived quality of life as they move from middle to old age; African Americans and Anglos do not.

There are also substantively important individual–contextual interactions within cultures. Datan's study (Antonovsky, 1979) of Israeli subcultures showed that women's reactions to menopause were related to their identification with the culture. Women who identified themselves as modern or as traditional responded relatively well to their biopsychosocial changes during that period. Women who had no secure identity were more troubled by midlife changes.

Urban and rural contexts have also produced psychosocial differences in how people age. Men live longer than women in rural contexts, but that pattern is reversed in urban settings. Youmans (1967) and Bernard (1981) hypothesized that the reason for this reversal is based in the urbanization effects on family life. Specifically, men live longer in rural contexts because of the psychosocial spiral that forms from their working at home. Because of their role as the head of the household, they get more emotional support than do women. In urban contexts, women live longer because men are away from home being providers, so they lose their central position in the family and a spiral is developed in which the woman becomes the emotional and functional center of the home. The urban female is socialized in affection, intimacy, and informal bonding; the man is socialized in a pattern of impersonal acquisitiveness which is further isolating. Urbanization also increases the instrumental and affectional freedom of the young and their authority. These changes weaken family ties and stimulate later male passivity and early aging. The resulting patterns suggest that societal arrangements contribute to the creation and resolution of psychosocial spirals leading to what are, to the contrary, usually considered "individual" problems.

THE POSSIBILITIES, LIMITS, AND PATHWAYS OF CHANGE

There are many additional issues in relation to change that psychologists need to explore. They include factors that inhibit or facilitate change and mechanisms for implementing and evaluating change efforts. An issue particularly needing our attention is our obligation to define our societal and personal responsibilities for the use of our specialized knowledge in individual and social change activities. Our field has interests and conflicts about the use of that knowledge because our well-being is linked to its applications and the ways we participate in society.

Cooper and Denner (1998) reviewed several theories about the relationships between culture and psychology and concluded that

> psychologists are coming to understand cultures as developing systems of individuals, relationships, material and social contexts, and institutions. By viewing theories linking culture and psychological processes as distinct yet complementary, researchers and policy makers can forge interdisciplinary, international, and intergenerational collaborations on behalf of the culturally diverse communities of which we are a part. (p. 579)

Although forming multifaceted linkages is a commendable goal, existing theories do not provide an adequate framework for accomplishing that task. A summary of the available theories, the explanations they offer, and what limitations would need to be overcome to form such linkages is summarized in Table 6.2.

While these theories all have some empirical support, overall they seem to be a modern replay of the tale of the blind men and the elephant. Cooper and Denner (1998) suggested that these approaches can be viewed as complementary and used as a basis for the collaboration of researchers and policy makers. This position is true for the theories about overall cultural patterns because they supplement those that are concerned only with children's development. However, it overlooks that a number of these theories contain contradictory elements. Those that emphasize the stability of cultures and differences between them contradict others that emphasize boundary crossings and change. Also, there are different emphases in focus between them ranging from social identity to caste status and microniches. Cooper and Denner's stated goal was the forging of collaborations to further our own communities. However, none of these formulations explicitly incorporates the view that its proponents are also part of the communities and cultures they are analyzing.

Fitting these or other theoretical perspectives into a comprehensive psychosocial spirals framework brings into focus the nature and impact of the framework's characteristics and limitations. The following examples help to illustrate this point and illustrate the value of using a psychosocial spirals approach. In 1992, the American Psychological Society created the "Human Rights Initiative: A Research Agenda." Its goal was to show how the behavioral science community can contribute to critical areas of concern in the United States by helping policy makers in federal agencies set priorities for psychology and related sciences. Emphasis was placed on the "social capital" value of humans and on how to deal with threats to the realization of that capital. Topics that were addressed included the changing nature of work, productive aging, reducing psychopathology, healthy living, and reducing violence (*Human Capital Initiative*, February, 1992).

This formulation is based on existing evidence that psychologists can contribute to a better understanding of these social issues and to constructive changes in policies and practices for the benefit of society and its citizens. However, choosing to couch human priorities in terms of "social capital" influences how people define each other, themselves, and their culture. This particular choice involves psychologists in creating the definition of a good society as one in which people are considered to be production units. The psychosocial spiral generated by using this definition is quite different from one that would be generated if human priorities were defined in terms of "the quality of people's lives."

A comparison of two approaches to the socialization of children provides another example in which psychological research is used to make policy recommendations which create individually and societally significant psychosocial spirals. Scarr (1992) proposed that our knowledge of normative human development and individual differences can be combined to "explain human development as both typically human and uniquely so" (p. 1). From her view, "ordinary differences between families have little effect on children's development, unless the family is outside of a normal developmental range. Good enough, ordinary parents probably have the same effects on their children's development as do culturally defined super parents" (p. 15). That is, Scarr considers that, given a normal range, variations between children are a product of their different genetic make-ups. Parents need not feel that they are responsible for differences in children's development or that they can do anything about those differences.

TABLE 6.2.   Theories of Cultures and Psychological Processes within Nations

Culture theories	Description[a]
Core social values (Triandis, 1996)	*Characteristics*: Groups: Individualist-Collectivist; Individuals: Allocentric-Idiocentric. *Strengths*: Challenge universality; evidence of culture-specific meanings in universal processes involving self, cognition, emotion. *Limitations*: Emphasizes differences, so portrays cultures as holding mutually exclusive, stable, uniform views.
Context (Bronfenbrenner, 1995)	*Characteristics*: Ecological systems model of development, individuals nested in immediate microsystem with links across systems. *Strengths*: Shows how perceptions and interactions in relationships and settings make a difference for children's well-being; shows relationship of performance inequalities to context. *Limitations*: Minimal attention to variations and changes within specific contexts.
Cultural–ecological adaptation in stratified societies (Ogbu, 1993)	*Characteristics*: Individual competence defined in cultural and historical context of children's development. *Strengths*: Explicitly addresses access or performance inequalities; focuses on experience of specific communities. *Limitations*: Less attention to in-community variations and changes, including upward mobility.
Social capital (Bourdieu & Passeron, 1977)	*Characteristics*: Relationships and networks from which individuals can get institutional support are cumulative. *Strengths*: If linked with roles of social organizations and individual actions (Mehan, 1992), permits integrating concepts of power and access plus individual action to cultural change. *Limitations*: Possibly overdeterministic in original form, little empirical work.
Navigating and negotiating borders (Phelan et al., 1991)	*Characteristics*: Youth in diverse societies are all challenged as they necessarily move across their multiple worlds (i.e., families, peers, schools). *Strengths*: Links individuals, contexts, and people as agentic. *Limitations*: Explains all variations in performance (school) among youth with similar worlds as due to ability to move across boundaries.
Intergroup relations (Berry, 1993)	*Characteristics*: Social identity is built in a context of attitudes toward own group; related to attitudes to others, e.g., prejudice, conflict, etc. *Strengths*: Links individual and group definitions of self and context. *Limitations*: Permits of interpreting minorities (NCDGs) within deficit context in re CDG norms.

TABLE 6.2. (*Continued*)

Culture theories	Description[a]
Universally adaptive tools (Gallimore et al., 1993)	*Characteristics*: All families try to make meaningful accommodations through routines of daily living that sustain them in their ecological niche. *Strengths*: Links individual, interpersonal, and institutional processes with culture-specific content and incorporates relativism of valued qualities in different niches. *Limitations*: Vulnerable to challenge in regard to morally specific values as well as definitions of community.

[a]The descriptions of each culture theory characterize its nature and strengths, but also indicate the limitations which render it inadequate to provide a comprehensive theory for integrating the nested frameworks and ethnic validity patterns of diverse cultures.
Note. From "Theories linking culture and psychology: Universal and community-specific processes," by C. R. Cooper & J. Denner, 1998, in J. T. Spence, J. M. Darleye, & D. J. Foss (Eds.). *Annual Review of Psychology, 49*, pp. 559–584. Palo Alto, CA: Annual Reviews.

Baumrind (1993) rebutted Scarr's argument, emphasizing that average expectable environments differ between cultures as well as within them. Further, she said that some of these environments may not be conducive to the survival or healthy development of children, and that there is evidence that better than "good enough" parenting "optimizes the development of both normal and vulnerable children" (p. 1299). Telling parents that they cannot change their children's patterns of development undermines their beliefs in their capabilities and their effectiveness as parents. I would add that telling parents that they have an influence can increase their effectiveness.

Scarr's thesis would be subject to substantial criticism in most contexts if it were addressed to human output in economic, social, or cultural arenas. For example, in a sports-obsessed culture such as the United States, it would be professional suicide to recommend that an average expectable environment is good enough for all sports facilities and average coaching is adequate for players. The resulting position is that athletes will improve or not depending on their genes. Undoubtedly, there is a potential for individual and social harm in the opposite assumption, that human capabilities are unlimited and that performance standards must be defined in competitive terms. Everyone cannot be above average and everyone cannot be average. In any case, the costs and benefits of advocating limits in psychosocial development spirals are quite different from those of emphasizing possibilities. The former provides a nested framework and psychosocial spirals that support the status quo, including historical and current societal inequities. It also endorses the formation of ethnic validity patterns that are oriented to accepting our current situations and the quality of our current performances rather than trying to improve either.

SUMMARY

Many more social change perspectives and programs than those presented here are available to concerned professionals and citizens. They range from those that involve minimal numbers of people to those that encompass entire societies and even multinational and multicultural contexts. Reconciling and coordinating different kinds of programs to improve the quality of people's lives and the prosocial character of their societies can seem overwhelming. However, the issues involved and directions for resolving them are similar, as illustrated in a relatedness oriented society such as Turkey and an individual initiative and self-reliance oriented society such as the United States. The success of such programs in the United States shows that a society that respects individual autonomy can also nourish a commitment to collective well-being. Kagitcibasi and her colleagues (1996) demonstrated that a society that honors relatedness can also nourish a commitment to individual autonomy among its people.

At any level, from individual to multicultural, a prosocially oriented, spiral pattern of interactions functions in ways that generate greater opportunities and situations for people to create more positive senses of themselves and the world. This pattern teaches people that they can formulate and implement active planful approaches to their lives. They involve the positive integration of autonomous and relational attributes and patterns. All such programs involve balancing individual and collective priorities and finding patterns of interaction that can build on convergences, honor divergences, and manage conflicts in constructive ways.

The broadest and most basic implication of the change efforts and patterns described in this chapter is that social and individual changes must occur together. The extent to which either can occur independently is severely constrained by the fact that individuals are not just psychological or social, they are psychosocial, and both our psychological and our social characteristics are formed and function in relation to each other. Each person, community, and social system is continuously involved in an ongoing process of reconciling priorities that are related to individual autonomy and diversity with those of group conformity and collective well-being. Further, constructive change does not occur without individual and collective involvement, effort, and vigilance. Nor can it occur without individual and shared knowledge, compassion, and collaboration, including that of professionals. The same is true for social, behavioral, and mental health specialists. We, too, need to build on that awareness in our work, our programs, and our involvements and bring it to the attention of others. We also need to be as willing to be changed as we are to change others.

AUTONOMY AND RELATEDNESS

INTRODUCTION

There are substantial cultural and individual differences in our patterns of living and aging. However, children and older adults were traditionally considered largely prisoners of their natures and their society. Only young and middle-aged adults were considered able to shape their own destiny, transcend their psychological past, achieve autonomy and maturity, and contribute to their communities and their cultures. Recently, behavioral and social scientists challenged these views and began to examine their basis and impact on our life spans. This chapter is concerned with how our autonomy and relatedness interact with our different circumstances and life patterns throughout our lives.

How we define our separateness from and relatedness to the world and others is psychosocial. We form our autonomy and relatedness out of our unique internal and external experiences and our relationships to the world. Since these general patterns are not universal and inevitable, we must understand what produces them, how well they serve us, what alternatives might be preferable, and how those alternatives might be instituted.

As noted in the previous chapter, the patterns found in different cultures suggest that our well-being at any age is related to having a personally and culturally acceptable identity and valued role. Consequently, we need to know how community, social, and cultural perspectives on the nature of the life span influence the quality of our lives. We also need to explore how much and in what ways we *can* shape and influence the course of our lives.

Of all species, we have the most options to modify our biological destinies and our psychosocial existence. The available information shows that individual, developmental, community, social, and cultural life style factors contribute to the nature and length of our lives. A central question is how to define the nature of our autonomy and relatedness possibilities as well as their antecedents, concomitants, and consequences. Other concerns include how we can define a good life and how we can live and help others live more fulfilling lives.

To analyze the collective impact of these factors requires naturalistic and experimental methods and attention to several classes of interacting variables. For example, psychological studies need to consider age effects, cohort effects, and time of measurement effects to acquire a comprehensive understanding of the nature and role of autonomy and relatedness over the course of our lives. Yet such considerations are often overlooked. Further, large-scale cultural patterns, such as class or caste, and historical events, such as economic conditions and war or peace, often overwhelm individual plans and efforts.

However, it seems essential in any overview of life span topics to also consider the nature and potential impact of individual factors. Existing data provide a basis for concluding that everyone forms and utilizes autonomous and relational characteristics, including members of NCD groups, such as the isolated elderly in an urban society. Cohen and Sokolovsky (1980) focused on the question of social engagement versus isolation among urban elderly people in the United States who live in residential hotels. The fact that these hotels exist was cited as conclusive proof of the social isolation and alienation assumed to be thrust upon the elderly as one of the byproducts of this highly industrialized, mobile society with its utilitarian orientation to people's worth. These authors found, in contrast to their expectations, that most of the elderly residents were not isolated, but were involved in complex interpersonal and social relations in and out of the hotel. Although their social contacts were about half the number of those of younger urban hotel dwellers and other urban populations, their level of contacts was a function of their age, not their presumed alienation. Their levels of sociability were comparable to other urban elderly in the United States.

This study, even with its limits, illustrates a basic point about the role of social and individual factors in enhancing people's quality of life. We are not objective machines. At any age, we use information and solve problems in a somewhat mixed objective and subjective context. Our lives are better if we live in a socially accepting and supportive environment. However, not everyone does. Efforts to understand how we deal with mixed circumstances or improve our circumstances and well-being will have limited success unless attention is paid to how we define and shape our identities and relations with others.

For example, our roles in creating our own beliefs and ideas is central to Taylor and J. D. Brown's theory of positive illusions (1988). On the basis of their own and others' social cognition research, they concluded that

> the mentally healthy person appears to have the enviable capacity to distort reality in a direction that enhances self-esteem, maintains beliefs in personal efficacy, and promotes an optimistic view of the future. These three illusions, as we have called them, appear to foster traditional criteria of mental health, including the ability to care about the self and others, the ability to be happy or contented, and the ability to engage in productive and creative work. (Taylor & Brown, p. 204)

Though making broad-based changes in the human condition may seem beyond the power of many of us, our hopes and self-involvement are essential to the accomplishment of such changes at a personal level and for the attainment of fulfilling lives for ourselves and future generations. Therein lies the importance of integrating individual and social perspectives about autonomy and relatedness.

AUTONOMY, OTHERS, AND RELATEDNESS

Writers have expended considerable ink describing the newborn's differentiation of itself from others (Erikson, 1963) and the opposing need to bond or relate in some way to others (Bowlby, 1969, 1973). Much has been written about the consequences of forming, not forming, or disrupting ties to the mother, the father, siblings, and others, as reflected in the research about the consequences for children of parental divorce and recommendations for how to facilitate their adjustment (Twaite, Silitsky, & Luchow, 1998). Underlying all of these formulations is the implicit assumption that there are three conceptions—the autonomous self, others, and relatedness—that we must develop to become mature individuals. Throughout the world there is an enormous range of definitions for each of these concepts, with everyone assuming that the prime causal determinant of life's events lies in the area of their own interest. My alternative view is that each component is always involved and continually affects the others. Dictionary definitions of autonomy specify that it is the capacity to be self-governing, to undertake or carry on activities without outside control, or to exist or be capable of existing independently. In the abstract, these definitions seem to convey a coherent and univocal concept. Even so, each contains a tacit context, since it more completely means *without some largely specifiable external controls, but within the limits of others*. When any of us

says that we carry on our daily activities autonomously, we imply quali-
fiers such as "while I am healthy." We also include tacit acknowledgment
that external forces, ranging from those in nature to other people, may
overwhelm our efforts to manage our lives. Considering those others and
their powers to influence us is a task that requires other conceptual frameworks. Consequently, even at a minimum, the concept of *autonomy* includes the concepts of *other* and *relationship*.

In psychology and related social science fields, there have been divergent emphases between identity as self-as-autonomous and self-as-part-
of-socius (e.g., family, couple, community, class, ethnicity). In its more
extreme forms, self-as-autonomous has been conceptualized as completely self-contained and self-determining rather than being conceptualized more moderately as having some discretion and decision-making
capability. That extreme conception has been a central theme of Western
civilization as expressed in the Age of Reason, the scientific revolution,
and the myth of the autonomous individual as conqueror of frontiers.
Western and other civilizations have also supported the alternative, self-
as-part-of-socius. This conception involves the interlinking of people in a
sense of community characterized by sharing a common identity and a
common existence as in citizenship or family and referred to in phrases
such as "we are all brothers."

In psychology, social connections have usually been treated largely as
mediators, confounding processes, or sociocultural variables external to
individuals, and not as in-lying factors. Whether separating and disconnecting self and relationship aspects of our lives provides a desirable or
defensible self-conception is subject to critique. As a basis for that critique
and for formulating a potentially more justifiable conception of how we
live with ourselves and others, material from three quite different approaches to these issues is summarized below.

The often tacit inclusion of *others* as part of the individual self was
made explicit in Kluckhohn and Strodtbeck's (1961) study of value orientations in adults from three Anglo and two Native American communities.
They treated values as

> *complex but definitely patterned (rank-ordered) principles, resulting from the*
> *transactional interplay of three analytically distinguishable elements of the*
> *evaluative process—the cognitive, the affective, and the directive elements—*
> *which give order and direction to the ever-flowing stream of human acts and*
> *thoughts as these relate to the solution of "common human" problems.* (p. 4;
> italics in original)

These authors conceptualized values as embodied in processes; not as
static attributes as had been previously believed.

Kluckhohn and Strodtbeck (1961) listed five complex principles as cultural universals, although they noted that the principles vary in patterning and explicitness from culture to culture. The five principles include: *human nature, man–nature, time, activity,* and *relational* orientation. Each principle involves a continuum about how much individuals can control or alter their thoughts, feelings, and behaviors. For example, how much can we alter our "goodness" or master nature? Is, or shall, our orientation to life be one of being, doing, or some combination? Finally, and most relevant to the present chapter, what are, or shall be, our styles of relationship to others.

Table 7.1 shows a typical problem presented to respondents as part of the Kluckhohn and Strodtbeck (1961) study of the relational dimension. From the *choices* column, it can be seen that they defined *autonomy* in relation to others, to what and whom is excluded and included. *Individualism* is an orientation in which help-asking involves forming relationships with others. However, the others must have no ties with the respondent which are based on continuity through time, family, or work. Presumably, such a relationship could be considered a completely functional utilitarian transaction, one that depersonalizes or dehumanizes the interchange.

Individuals with whom the respondent had a family relationship or work ties were considered to be part of his or her self. Self was defined as a network, not an autonomous free-standing entity. Relationships formed within that network were by definition "humanized" because they included the human relational aspect of the persons making the interchange.

TABLE 7.1. Example of Item from Study of Relational Value Orientation

Item	Choices
Help in Misfortune. A man had a crop failure, or, let us say, had lost most of his sheep or cattle. He and his family had to have help from someone if they were going to get through the winter. There are different ways of getting help. Which of these ... ways would be best?	A. *Lineal* Would it be best for him to go to a boss or to an older important relative who is used to managing things in his group, and ask him to help out until things get better? B. *Collateral* Would it be best if he depended mostly on his brothers and sisters or other relatives all to help him out as much as each one could? C. *Individualistic* Would it be best for him to try to raise the money *on his own* outside the community (his own people) from people who are neither relatives not employers?

Note. From *Variations in value orientations,* Kluckhohn, F. R., & Strodtbeck, F. L. (1961). Evanston, IL: Row Peterson, p. 83f.

There was an underlying assumption that we are *autonomous* at least in the choice of whom to turn to for help. We can seek help from relatives, work associates, strangers, or no one.

Kluckhohn and Strodtbeck (1961) found that the three Western, Caucasian groups (Anglo homesteaders, Mormons, and Spanish-Americans) more often thought that the *Individualistic* choice was best; the Navaho and Zuni Indians thought the *Collateral* choice was best. These respondents differed on the other four value principles as well. Not only were autonomy and relatedness necessarily bound together, so were the alternatives on the other value principles and dimensions.

Munroe and Munroe (1994) stressed the usefulness of analyzing research findings on human development by contrasting traditional and Western–modern societies. They found that the developmental areas which had been investigated most fully were social cognition and the social motives of competitiveness, achievement, and self-orientation. Their conclusion was that differences in these areas arose from *developmental hypertrophy* of the Western child who is exposed to "a regimen purposefully designed to maximize his development: he is trained to be smart, competitive, and achieving, and he is expected to be self-oriented" (Munroe & Munroe, 1994, p. 150). A matrix of mutually supportive rewards, controls, and special institutional arrangements, such as the cognitive development emphasis of the educational system and the competitive achievement orientation of socioeconomic institutions, help elicit the child's competitiveness and achievement.

These authors also pointed out that even if a traditional society had highlighted or adopted these narrow socialization practices, it is not certain that the outcome would have been the same. To illustrate, they cited the effects on the traditional Ibo and Manus societies which had placed some emphasis on individual achievement values and training. Only when cultural change was imposed powerfully on them and change models, resources, and social support were provided, did their cultures change from living by their traditional community perspectives to become more modernized. Munroe and Munroe (1994) concluded that any particular area of cultural emphasis in socialization and its outcome are a function of the entire cultural matrix; it cannot be isolated and transferred and expected to produce the same result. They further concluded that one of the requirements for an egoistic, individualistic orientation is a complex society. However, current evidence suggests that they should have qualified their conclusion to say "a complex society of a particular kind" because there is increasing consensus among informed scholars that all societies are complex.

Finally, Munroe and Munroe (1994) felt that an individualistic orientation may be essential for survival in a Western–modern society. They speculated that sensitivity to the self may be a prerequisite to becoming aware of and sensitive to other selves. Further, in individualistic people that sensitivity to others may only be developed and used in the service of one's own ego. This perspective fits with the notion of an individualistic orientation as being one in which others are seen in a nonhuman sense, simply as resources to be utilized in the service of one's own egoistic advancement.

Although the Munroes took a more extreme position on the relational dimension than that of Kluckhohn and Strodtbeck, they did point out that people may assign degrees of priority to these differentiable self and relatedness dimensions. The latter alternative, that any sense of autonomy is defined in relation to a sense of others, leads us out of an endless regress about individualism versus relationism. It also provides a basis for considering that these interrelations are complex and do not permit of a simple dichotomization.

To further illustrate this point it is useful to consider a description of the complex patterns of cultural change among the Ik, an African culture subjected to Western influences. Turnbull's (1972) anthropological study documented how externally introduced influences may be terribly destructive. Once cooperative hunter–gatherers, the Ik were confined to a limited arid section of northern Uganda by a combination of events. Government policies turned part of their most-valued terrain into a national park, and international conflicts restricted their access to only a portion of their yearly migratory route necessary for both hunting and gathering resources as the seasons changed. Confined and forced into an unpredictable, below-subsistence agricultural life style, their "goodness," as Turnbull called it, began to deteriorate. Their society disintegrated into one in which the core organizing life principle was self-centered, competitive, individual survival. The remaining human sentiment was a generally pervasive individual and collective enjoyment of witnessing the misfortunes of others. All relationships were reduced to unsentimental exchange relations for optimizing each participant's own survival and creating power over the other participants in order to extract resources.

Even in those contexts, Turnbull (1972) found that individuals defined their autonomous selves in relation to others. Perhaps his most compelling points concern (a) how human relationships can become antisocial and destructive as well as prosocial and (b) how the story of the Ik has implications for modern society. As he expressed it:

> There is ample evidence in their language that they (the Ik) once held values which they no longer hold.... The Ik have "progressed," one might say, since the change that has come to them has come with the advent of civilization to Africa and is therefore a part of that phenomenon we so blandly and unthinkingly refer to as progress.... And the

symptoms of change in our own society indicate that we are heading in precisely the same direction. (Turnbull, 1972, p. 287).

Turnbull (1972) emphasized further that the changes in the Ik indicate that these qualities are not a necessary part of human nature. We protest that these prosocial values are basic to humanity's survival and sanity. Although they may be basic to human society, the Ik showed us that we are not inherently social animals. We are

> capable of associating for purposes of survival without being social. The Ik have successfully abandoned ... qualities such as family, cooperative sociality, belief, love, hope and so forth, for the very good reason that in their context these militated against survival. (Turnbull, p. 289)

Turnbull's core thesis was that, as much as he decried the deterioration of a once prosocially oriented society, their new sense of who they were and what relations to others were sustainable was based on their social conditions as well as their individual lives. He never argued that people do not define themselves in relation to others.

How are we to interpret this information about how circumstances influence the ways we come to understand ourselves, our societies, and our relationships to each other? It may be, as Munroe and Munroe suggested, that universal developmental characteristics can be found only at humans' primary levels of functioning, at what I have called the level of knowns. It may also be that "the next ambitious theoretical system will also provide greater understanding of adult humans' ingeniously diverse modes of thought and behavior" (Munroe & Munroe, 1994, p. 152). That is, to develop a better understanding of our complex ways of dealing with ourselves in relation to each other, we need to look at our social and personal contributions as knowers to the ways we formulate our theories of, among other topics, autonomy and relatedness.

It is not possible to address all dimensions of these self/other relationships at one time. Consequently, I will address them somewhat separately and then present an integrative overview. The contextual matrices within which the autonomous self or individual is highlighted are *Polarities*, *Personal/Social Matrices as Interrelated*, and *Culture and Cultural Change Matrices*. Finally, attention is given to the psychosocial competence configurations, supports and threats, and spirals that serve as the pathways to create, sustain, and change these interrelated structures and perspectives.

POLARITIES

Polarities are categorical groupings in which membership is assumed to be mutually exclusive. Two categories that are considered to meet these criteria are explored here. *Gender* differentiations are included because of biological differences in sexual characteristics. *Collectivism and individualism* differences are based on choices between presumably incompatible psychosocial priorities.

Gender

Bakan (1966) asserted that two fundamental modalities, agency and communion, are characteristic of all living forms. *Agency* is our concern with ourselves, manifested in self-protective, self-assertive, and self-expansive concerns and activities. *Communion* is our concern with participation in some larger organism of which we are a part, expressed in the sense of striving to be at one with that other organism. Bakan used the historical record to support his thesis that men are genetically programmed to be more agentic, that is, externally oriented and assertive. In contrast, he theorized that women are genetically programmed to be more communion oriented, as demonstrated in their focus on maintaining the family and relationships within it.

From Bakan's (1996) point of view, our survival as individuals and that of our societies rests on the successful integration of these two modalities between and within us. Although the agentic in the male and the communal in the female is what primarily brings us together, over time these modalities are cultivated and integrated in both. For example, it is these parallel integrations of agency and communion that characterize the ideal marriage.

Bakan (1996) made the further point that this agency–communion integration can be seen in the religious emphasis on the notion of "wholeness." His explanation was that science and religion are two different approaches to understanding the individual and society, but neither offers ultimate final solutions or can afford to ignore the contributions of the other. To him, science represents primarily an expression of the agentic and has contributed much to improving the quality of human life with regard to physical want, though not to its ultimate questions of meaning which are communion concerns. In his view, this omission has led to an underemphasis on communion considerations and left us with a sense of "emptiness" in our lives. As he made explicit, balancing the agentic and communion aspects within us, in our relationships, and in our societies is essential.

Bakan's (1966) argument about male and female characteristics is abstract and controversial. He did not provide research or intervention strategies for testing his hypotheses or redressing what he saw as the current imbalance of agentic over communion concerns. Even so, he highlighted the importance of investigating the gender differences in our autonomous and relatedness characteristics and interpersonal relationships.

Gilligan (1982) found striking differences in the senses of autonomy and relatedness between men and women in the United States in her work on moral development. Consequently, she and her colleagues developed an extensive research program which led to their belief that these differences are social patterns which diminish the quality of women's lives. Illustrative aspects of their work and programs to redress these inequities are included here because they highlight the issues in a singularly important way.

Gilligan's (1982) initial studies were of preadolescents, adolescents, college women, and women coping with abortion. She used Kohlberg's (1969) framework and stories to assess moral development. Her view was that morality is traditionally defined from a male perspective with its emphasis on "separation, autonomy, individuation, and natural rights" (Gilligan, 1982, p. 23). In contrast, she hypothesized that morality from a woman's perspective actively involves "recognition of the continuing importance of caring in the human life cycle" (Gilligan, 1982, p. 23). Her findings supported her hypothesis and her belief that gender differences had not previously been seen simply because there had been an assumption of a single mode of social experience and interpretation. By positing that there are two modes, separation and attachment, in the lives of women and men, the modes and their connectedness could be identified.

> In the representation of maturity, both perspectives converge in the realization that just as inequality adversely affects both parties in an unequal relationship, so too violence is destructive for everyone involved. This dialogue between fairness and care not only provides a better understanding of relations between the sexes but also gives rise to a more comprehensive portrayal of adult work and family relationships. (Gilligan, 1982, p. 174)

Gilligan concluded that to improve these adult relations will require changes in both members of couples. Women need to integrate responsibility (relatedness) and rights (autonomy). While she was less explicit about men, they presumably need to do the same. Her thinking is consistent with the idea that our senses of self-efficacy include a psychosocial identity that integrates our autonomy and relatedness.

More recently, Gilligan and her colleagues have included men and boys in their studies to develop a more comprehensive understanding of the nature of a distinctive *woman's voice* and its consequences. The aspects of their work that seem most relevant to understanding autonomy, relatedness, and their interrelatedness for girls and women is found in reports of projects that were focused on students' transition to adolescence in two private schools for girls (see Gilligan, Lyons & Hammer, 1990; L. M. Brown & Gilligan, 1992).

Gilligan, Rogers, and L. M. Brown (1990) traced how these young women's development progressed "from an egocentric, through a normative or conventional, to an autonomous or reflective or critical position: the progression that most developmental psychologists have traced" (p. 317). However, that transition often was painful and left the girls confused and distressed in ways that mainstream conceptions of psychological development were inadequate to encompass. This finding required an alternative, developmental process model, and they turned to music, primarily vocal music:

> The shift to a musical language gives us a way out of the deadlocked paradox of self and relationship that continues to plague the fields of personality and developmental psychology: that one can only experience self in the context of relationship with others and that one can only experience relationship if one differentiates other from self. Because music is a language of movement and time—notes are heard in relation to other notes, and become part of themes, leitmotifs, melodies—a musical notation gives us a way to capture people speaking in relationship and living in a body and in a culture. (Gilligan, Rogers, & L. M. Brown, p. 328)

The male-oriented compartmentalization of autonomy and relatedness into two distinct, unrelated positions, had proven inadequate to conceptualize how the women were describing their lives. It also presented a limited view of the possible forms of relationships between self and autonomy and between justice and care. The need for a new psychosocial paradigm was elaborated further by L. M. Brown & Gilligan (1992):

> Voice, because it is embodied, connects rather than separates psyche and body; because voice is in language, it also joins psyche and culture. Voice is inherently relational—one does not require a mirror to hear one-self—yet the sounds of one's voice change in resonance depending on the relational acoustics: whether one is heard or not heard, how one is responded to (by oneself and by other people).... Following girls' voices, we listened for girls' sense of themselves.... Morality, or the voice that speaks of how one should or would like to act in relationships, became of interest to us at this point primarily insofar as moral language carries the force of institutionalized social norms and cultural values into relationships and psychic life. (pp. 20–21)

L. M. Brown and Gilligan (1992) concluded that institutionalized norms affected how these girls had conceptualized their identity in order to manage their relationships. When their individual experiences could not be accommodated for within society's framework, they had to deny either their experience or society's expectations, or struggle with that irreconcilability. In contrast, boys seemed able to differentiate their feelings about their personal experiences from society's norms and their feelings about autonomy from those about relatedness. They responded to events one at a time from a specific reference perspective without reconciling it with others at the moment or over time. In contrast, the girls felt more pressure to integrate autonomy, relatedness, fairness, and care currently and over time within a relational psychosocial context. That context in turn had to integrate their personal, societal, and cultural norms and values. L. M. Brown and Gilligan added that as adults and carriers of society's standards, women presumably perpetuate these irreconcilable issues and pass them on to future generations.

Such gender differences were also found in a more heterogeneous U.S. sample of 216 Caucasian and African American high school students (107 male and 109 female) whom my colleagues and I studied. We found no gender differences in the degree to which these adolescents felt that they controlled their own fates (locus of control scores), but striking differences in the aspects of their lives which they felt they did control. Specifically, men

> asserted strong internal control over task areas of their lives; they did not over their personal lives or over the system generally. Females seemed to reflect a view of the world as made up of situations in which, once chance or fate has "lined things up," they can behave internally and create their desired outcomes [and] ... in the long run, chance factors will even things out so that they will have their share of those opportunities. (F. Tyler, Gatz, & Keenan, 1979, p. 33f)

For both genders, self-definition was related to their external reality. That is, what seeing themselves as autonomous meant was based in part on the supports and constraints in their life possibilities. Presumably each person's decisions about how to interact with the world were made in light of these self and self–world considerations, and those considerations were different for the females and the males. For example, only women included, as part of their self and world view, an expectation that reality distributes opportunities equally and the idea that sharedness with other people is a relevant factor in life.

Subsequent studies comparing adolescents in India with these U.S. students (F. Tyler, Dhawan, & Sinha, 1988) yielded comparable gender differences as well as culturally syntonic differences. Hofstede and Vunderbink (1994) also reported similar masculinity/femininity differences across a range of cultures and culturally specific variability between them. They conclude that there are substantially different dimensions in the programming of girls' and boys' minds.

These studies on gender-related patterns have yielded information about a range of differences in the ways we organize our senses of autonomy and relatedness, including the differences between how autonomy is expressed agentically and relatedness is expressed communally. Even that distinction is not adequate to encompass the multidimensionality of the ways men and women organize their relationships to themselves and others. Gilligan and her colleagues identified the crucial point that relationships may function more in the music-type format of point–counterpoint than being a visually oriented sequence of stages, steps, and levels. This approach provides a quite different perspective for understanding the origins and interplay of agentic and communion aspects of our lives. The psychosocial leaps of these two differing perspectives initiate quite different psychosocial spirals of development, and acknowledging them may provide the basis for cross-gender convergences and also for conflicts.

COLLECTIVISM AND INDIVIDUALISM

Another social emphasis on the dichotomous nature of societal and individual orientations is that of the assumed polarity between individualistic and collectivistic societies. Hofstede (1980) studied a number of cultural differences, and in his analysis found four dimensions, one of which is individualism–collectivism. The others are *Power Distance, Masculinity–Femininity,* and *Uncertainty Avoidance.* In the four societal institutions that he studied (the family, job, community, and school), he found that these role dimensions were related across those four contexts. He subsequently identified a fifth dimension, *Long-Term Orientation,* which he saw as being of comparable significance (1991). His findings about teacher–student relationships are particularly relevant because schools influence how each generation thinks of itself and its relations to others. Hofstede's definitions of *Individualism* and *Collectivism* provide a valuable description of the psychosocial exemplars that identify these orientations.

> *Individualism* as a characteristic of a culture opposes *Collectivism* (the word is used here in an anthropological, not a political sense). Individualist cultures assume that any person looks primarily after his/her immediate family (husband, wife, and children). Collectivist cultures assume that any person through birth and possible later events belongs to one or more tight "in-groups," from which he/she cannot detach him/herself. The "in-group" (whether extended family, clan, or organization) protects the interest of its members, but in turn expects their permanent loyalty. A collectivist society is tightly integrated; an individualist society is loosely integrated. (1980, p. 9)

Hofstede emphasized that these culture dimensions do not describe individuals. They refer to dominant patterns of socialization within nations and seem similar to nested frameworks. That is, they define for individuals the nature of the psychosocial reality in which they are being socialized to live and within which they form their ethnic validity based roles. This view is consistent with Hofstede's earlier definition of the culture of a society as "the collective programming of the mind which distinguishes the members of one human group from another" (1980, p. 25). Presumably the programming of a nested framework and its related ethnic validity paradigm includes the formation of each person's sense of autonomy and relatedness to others.

Hui and Triandis (1986) investigated these differences and orientations in individuals and at a national culture level. They constructed a questionnaire about how people would respond to the autonomy–relationship aspects of representative choice situations ranging from personal/family to legal, and administered it to psychologists and anthropologists who were from a range of different cultures or were working in different countries. There was general consensus among the respondents from each culture about how they believed that members of their target cultures would answer. Hui and Triandis (1986) used these responses to define collectivism and set individualism in opposition to it as the basis for a useful cross-culturally general definition of both:

> [Collectivism involves] subordination of individual goals to the goals of a collective, and a sense of harmony, interdependence, and concern for others.... Individualism, then, is the subordination of the goals of the collectivities to individual goals, and a sense of independence and lack of concern for others. (1986, p. 244f)

Implicit in the definitions of these two terms and their survey was the assumption that choices about individual and collective concerns are (1) mutually exclusive, (2) oppositional, and (3) independent (like a throw of dice). The alternative assumption is that individualist and collectivist choices are interrelated and possibly point-counterpoint and made in a composition or thematic relationship over time. This assumption would lead to quite different definitions. It becomes clear that Hui and Triandis's approach overlooks the complexity of human relationships. Even in an individualistic orientation, individualism is defined as *in relation to* others; in a collectivist orientation, there is a differentiation among others such that the person behaves *individualistically* with regard to those *not* considered a part of her or his collective. For example, the Maori of New Zealand define their identity as including their *phanu* (their family), their *iwi* (tribe), and their *whakapapa* (all of their ancestors and potential descendants). Outside of all these people in their collective identity are people toward whom they behave in what is otherwise categorized as an autonomous manner (Durie, 1994). In short, the nature of autonomy and relatedness are of necessity defined in relation to each other.

Hofstede and Vunderink (1994) emphasized that the other four cultural differences they had been found to be of nearly comparable importance were overlooked by the Hui and Triandis approach. In Hofstede and Vunderlink's view, the emphasis on individualism–collectivism focused on the cultural factors that were evident in the particular interests of cross-cultural psychologists. It differentiates Western and Eastern cultures in a fashion reflective of the multifaceted "institutional dialogue" between these cultures. Hofstede and Vunderink pointed out that the other four dimensions raise different, also important issues. For example, the more masculine oriented cultures (Japan, some central European countries, some Latin American countries, and the Anglo group plus some of their colonies) seem reluctant to explore masculinity/femininity distinctions. Grouping cultures by whether they differentiate gender roles puts them "into clusters that are not engaged in a common institutional dialogue" (Hofstede & Vunderink, 1994, p. 330).

Cooper and Denner (1998) agreed with Hofstede and Vunderink's points. Based on their work, they also concluded that the individualism/collectivism dichotomy stems in part from a cross-cultural nested framework that underlies a dialogue between Eastern and Western cultures. It is important to add that this distinction has been conceptualized as a stable and enduring one, although there seems to be little inclination for exploring change in either orientation in relation to spirals of psychosocial development and communication across cultural divides.

Personal/Social Matrices as Interrelated

We live in a context of societal groupings ranging from our nuclear families to our societies. Each of us makes basic choices, psychosocial leaps, about whether to remain within and sustain each of our societal groupings, that is, to choose a prosocial orientation to live within and sustain each of those matrices. Alternatively, we may choose an antisocial orientation or seek to live autonomously without regard to our matrix's characteristics. These decisions are influenced by our individual and ethnic validity characteristics and by the ways others in our contexts define us. The psychosocial configurations that we develop in relation to our social contexts are based on each of these initial leaps and its consequences. Although it is not feasible to examine all of the dimensions of our personal/social interactions, the issues can be illustrated by a detailed examination of the somewhat different factors that contribute to our choices and how we understand them. The three dimensions that will be considered as examples because of their fundamental roles are *justice*, *situational factors*, and *culture and cultural change factors*.

Justice

Justice is the first example of factors that have a tremendous import on defining the nature of the interrelatedness of the personal and social matrices within which we live. Dictionary definitions of justice equate it with honesty and impartiality but provide no elaboration concerning the criteria for those judgments. Yet those tacit criteria are crucial to understanding the nature of the personal/social (psychosocial) contextual matrices that we call on to guide our lives. T. Tyler, Boeckmann, Smith, and Huo (1997) used conceptual analysis and empirical findings to clarify the concept of justice as a factor in human relationships. They identified how we form conceptions of justice, the role of our senses of autonomy and relatedness in that process, the relevance of circumstances, and the ways we interpret and respond to injustice. Most of the work they cited was conducted in the United States by psychologists, but they were able to establish several basic points about autonomy and relatedness that are quite separate from any cultural biases in the material.

Their basic point was that justice is more than a set of principles derived from objective sources; it is our subjective sense of what is right or wrong. Further, justice is an important concept to us and influences our interactions (T. Tyler et al., 1997). Rephrased in the terms being used here, a sense of justice is a product of people's capabilities as knowers. The capability for making fairness judgments is both universal and a function of subjective decision making within the limits of our natures as known, our socialization, and our circumstances. Finally, society can lose or gain from people's reactions when they feel either unfairly or fairly treated.

The concern about the consequences of individual decisions for society underscores a central theme of this text, i.e., individual and social consequences go together. As T. Tyler et al. (1997) stressed, conceptions of social justice are based on the intersection of two considerations: the moral (value) judgment that a person's state is or is not fair/just/deserved and the social comparisons which serve as the criteria for that judgment. They supported their position by investigating four major conceptions, *relative deprivation, distributive justice, procedural justice,* and *retributive justice.* Their findings about the impact of these ideas on people's judgments and behavior under different circumstances are summarized in the following paragraphs.

Relative Deprivation. There are many such standards, including socially and/or economically advantaged/disadvantaged such as CDG-NCDG status, status relative to others with whom we are identified, present status in contrast to past or anticipated future status, etc. Crucial to this formulation is the ability to demonstrate that standards of entitlement are related to standards of comparison. Research indicates that people consider justice to be a function of the relationship between what people have and what they feel they are entitled to have. Further, they act accordingly.

Distributive Justice. Justice is a function of the fairness of outcomes. The predominant criterion used to judge distribution of outcomes is *equity*, the balance between contributions and rewards. It is contrasted with *equality*, the equivalence of rewards. Equity is a more widely accepted standard in work situations than in public policy or romantic relationships. Some individuals in intimate relationships question whether equity is a concept relevant to personal relationships. People's preferences for equality and equity criteria vary with levels of deprivation and psychosocial orientation. When a U.S. study was compared with one from India with its higher levels of deprivation, more support was found in India for equality over equity as a criterion of fairness. More masculine cultures, including the United States, tend to prefer equity criteria, though women in the United States prefer equality criteria more than do men. More feminine cultures, such as the Netherlands and Sweden, favor equality.

Procedural Justice. Justice is a function of following fair procedures. Of these four conceptions, procedural justice has the widest support across individuals and societies. Efforts to empirically determine what constitutes fairness support that psychosocial leaps play a role in shaping our judgments about ourselves and our relationships with others. Our initial choices about the nature of fairness lead to widening arrays of relationships between ourselves and others, organizations, and groups. Research findings indicate that we (a) prefer to resolve interpersonal conflicts ourselves; (b) make choices involving tradeoffs between procedural criteria and other criteria, such as cost and efficiency in agencies (such as courts); (c) turn to third parties when necessary, but our willingness to do so and comply with outcomes is related to our trust in these parties as disinterested and fair mediators; (d) tend to prefer adversarial approaches to inquisitorial ones and to involve outside experts as a basis for resolving disputes; and (e) prefer to have a voice in proceedings even when that voice is time consuming, costly, and we know that having our voice will have no effect on the outcome of a dispute.

These finding challenge the predominant view within psychology that people's behavior is guided by outcomes. We also judge outcomes in terms of the fairness of the procedures. Deciding what constitutes fair procedures becomes central in guiding our relationships with each other.

Retributive Justice.   Retributive justice is a function of a group's decisions about what constitutes fair negative consequences as recompense or
a penalty for rule breaking. Currently, there is a marked heightening of
the value of retributive justice as a means of social control in the United
States and a number of other countries. The United States has seen an
increase in public support for more extreme penalties for crimes ranging
from minor infractions of drug laws to crimes of physical or social/
emotional violence. Penalties such as life without parole and capital punishment are being invoked more often and applied to a wider range of
transgressions.

Although there was only slight mention of it in the T. Tyler et al.
(1997) review, recompense is another aspect of retributive justice that
warrants consideration. McCarthy (1998) called this activity *restorative
justice*. He referred to the lack of attention to it as evidence of the U.S. legal
education system's low level of interest. There is minimal attention given
in law schools to teaching law students how to protect the relatively
powerless (social or economic NCDG individuals) from injustices or to
enable them to receive redress when they have been treated unjustly.

In summary, our judgments about ourselves as autonomous and in
relationship to others are based on our knower characteristics. Whether
we orient ourselves to improving the welfare of others and society, to
harming others, or to pursuing our own interests autonomously, we make
related psychosocial leaps to beliefs about ourselves and others as individuals and as members of groups. We then build complex spirals of conduct,
relationship, and judgmental procedures and criteria to guide our lives.
Our leaps and spirals differ among us both as individuals and as members
of families, communities, and cultures. Accordingly, we variously enrich
or diminish ourselves and encounter facilitation or inhibition in our efforts
to relate to, respond to, and influence others and our societies. While these
patterns may be most readily seen in areas such as those of social justice
and prosocial/antisocial behavior, it seems probable that they are equally
pervasive in less public and more informal areas of our lives as well.

Situational Factors

Situational factors provide our second example of the determinants of
our psychosocial characteristics and realities, including our senses of autonomy and relatedness to others. They illustrate the kinds of contextual
factors that have been emphasized throughout this book as important
determinants of the nested frameworks of our lives. The two described
here are *work* and *social/ethnic status*.

Work.   Most of us spend an inordinate amount of time in the workplace, a place of critical importance to us although we frequently treat it as if it were an isolated aspect of our lives. The ways we relate to our work and the interpersonal issues involved in our work situations are particularly instructive for understanding how all situations shape our senses of autonomy and relationships. Competence is a central determinant of our identity and relationships in the workplace, although its role may not be as clear in other aspects of our lives. Argyris's (1982) workplace analysis illustrated the relationships between situational factors, our autonomy and relatedness orientations, the psychosocial leaps we make, and the spirals we build on them. Deci and Flaste (1995) hypothesized that autonomy, competence, and relatedness are the basis of personality formation. Their research program on intrinsic motivation in the workplace demonstrated that the relationships among this triumvirate of factors is a key determinant of our functioning.

Argyris' work (1982) is particularly relevant because he consistently stressed the limitations of a Model I approach to life situations. In Model I, individuals focus on autonomous control and competitive survival (winning, with competitors losing). In the contrasting Model II, people share resources, and all qualified participants are included in working out solutions. It allows many participants to win, and success need not be at the expense of others.

Argyris (1982) demonstrated quite effectively that most individuals in Western society are socialized in a Model I approach and cannot change to behave in a Model II way without guidance and extensive practice. He emphasized that learning how to blend humanistic and performance concerns in order to see them as complementary rather than incompatible requires individual, interpersonal, and organizational changes. In organizations, the changes depend on the individuals at the top beginning to behave in a Model II manner. Only then can it become acceptable for subordinates to do so.

Development of a new pattern of labor–management relationships in the Western industrialized countries has led to elaborations of Argyris's conclusions. This new workplace pattern requires that members of both groups redefine their senses of autonomy and relationship to each other. A core issue in that process revolves around changes in decision-making roles and responsibilities in the work place as illustrated in the evolution of employee democracy. The consolidation of large industries and the closing of many factories in the United States stimulated the primarily ad hoc, patchwork development of employee owned enterprises. These enterprises were based on local, state, and federal support and centered around establishing worker control. Having worker control enhanced productivity, but instituting it was often problematic because it involved a radical shift in how the participants approached potential conflicts between their individual interests and their relationships to their coworkers and managers. Workers and companies had to shift from the traditional Model I pattern of management by owners and productivity by workers to a Model II pattern.

Zwerdling (1979) identified a number of factors crucial to the success of these enterprises. They included the patriotic commitment to saving their town and their economic survival as being crucial factors in the workers' successful shift to a new model. Their success also rested on the competence of civic leaders, local businessmen, new managers of the enterprises, and the workers' competence to do the task. Further, "most Americans have never learned how to work together and make decisions in an efficient, egalitarian, cooperative, and democratic way" (Zwerdling, 1979, p. 24). The managers had to learn that their role was one of working on behalf of the workers, not over them. The workers had to learn to have "the confidence, responsibility, and autonomy to make decisions on their own—yet they must also learn to feel responsible to the entire corporation" (Zwerdling, 1979, p. 24).

In these situations, a successful outcome required all involved to change their conceptions of their own autonomy, their relatedness to others, and their shared enterprise to function in a Model II fashion. The outcome involved changing more than just one or even a few people's belief systems (nested frameworks). It may have actually involved changing the entire community's belief systems. Without such an extensive impact, those seeking to create change would have ended up fighting the community's established sense of "belonging" or "interlinking" (ethnic validity paradigms) on a number of dimensions and at a number of levels of interrelationships. Such extreme changes influenced the psychosocial competence characteristics of the individuals involved, and they also required changing far more than individual patterns.

Rosen, Klein, and Young (1985) summarized the attitudinal factors that enter into the effectiveness of employee ownership and cooperative approaches to management in U.S. companies. Their survey of 3700 employees in 45 firms found that success for these companies was tied directly to changes in both the economic and social relationships. The relationships among the owners, managers, and workers had to be redefined so that their senses of autonomy and relatedness were interrelated in complementary ways. Their autonomy grew as they gained in relatedness. In general, such plans improved employee morale and motivation, and usually, though not always, company performance. Rosen et al. argued that employee ownership can be a much needed " 'social invention' that encourages growth while fostering equity, not one that insists that one side's gain is the other's loss" (1985, p. 188). Further, they also found that some companies were beginning to develop employee ownership plans as part of good management practices.

More recently, Quarrey and Rosen (1994) evaluated the relationship between employee ownership and corporate performance. They analyzed nine studies that included pre- and post-performance data of 641 employee-owned enterprises (ESOPs) and even more non-ESOP comparison companies in the United States. Their findings supported Rosen et al.'s (1985) earlier conclusion that the combination of ownership and participative management were the contributing factors most significant for the success and generally superior performance of ESOPs.

A newer conceptual approach to autonomy and relatedness patterns in the work world is the stakeholders concept. As Freeman (1984) defined it, "a stakeholder in an organization is (by definition) any group or individual who can affect or is affected by the achievement of the organization's objectives" (p. 46). He used this definition to develop a model for management, making it explicit that the managers' and companies' autonomy is embedded in a complex set of relationships. He also defined an individual who can serve effectively in such a role as being one who may better reflect the point–counterpoint and relational approaches to justice and caring in comparison to those who emulate Model I roles.

The shift in orientation to one which emphasizes the interplay between survival (however phrased, as efficiency, productivity, competitiveness) and relationships appears more and more frequently in management theory, research, and training. Nadler, Shaw, Walton, and associates (1994) argued that autonomy-oriented managers interested in defeating others and controlling them are counterproductive. Rather, change-oriented managers "realize that human assets erode unless nurtured and developed.... (They) seek to maintain investment in people despite business downturns" (p. 196f.).

The psychosocial leaps that both workers and managers make about the nature of their work and roles, including their senses of their autonomy and their relationships to others, have shaped work patterns, interpersonal relations, and views of organizations. There is a growing body of evidence that a Model II or point–counterpoint perspective has advantages for survival and thus for leadership in the emerging post-industrial multinational world. However, there has also been a recent reemphasis on the value of the Model I approach to work and work organizations in

Western society. Which of these currently competing perspectives will prevail is a matter of enormous importance to countless individuals and to our societies.

Social/Ethnic Status. We are not defined only by our close, personal relationships or our work relationships. All of our relationships are nested within numerous sociocultural frameworks and contribute to who we are. In some frameworks, our individual identity may not be the determinant of our relationships; to the contrary, in those frameworks our identity may stem from our existence as a member of a group, e.g., an ethnic group. Its relational networks define the unique form of our individual selves and self–world relations. Although these kinds of interactions have already been described, additional examples are included here to emphasize the contextual basis of these autonomy/relatedness patterns.

We often intertwine autonomy and relatedness in the context of our communities. Young, Giles, and Plantz (1982) surveyed patterns of help-seeking and helping behavior in rural community networks in the United States. They interviewed 213 respondents (ages 18–85) about their helping and help-seeking behavior in regard to eleven problem-of-living areas (e.g., anger, depression, injury, death). Over 80% saw themselves as active givers and receivers, especially with others such as spouses and friends in their networks. They indicated a general willingness to attack problems, a preference for help from people within their networks, a feeling that this type of help was effective, and that they thought the process was reciprocal. These patterns reflected a constructive reciprocal prosocial sense of self-in-community and community-in-self.

A somewhat different, socioracially based, interlocked sense of autonomy and relatedness emerged from Gurin, Gurin, Lao, and Beattie's (1969) work with African American students. They used a variant of the Rotter I-E, adding items about blaming the system for inequities and the value of collective action by African Americans, and they identified an aspect of self-efficacy as collective control. Students who tended to blame the system favored group rather than individual action to deal with discrimination, and their sense of personal control was unrelated to their civil rights activity. Because of their collective conception, these young people were characterized by a we-ness of self, or at least of self-efficacy in the world. They integrated autonomy and relatedness in a collective action way that is different from the interpersonal one that Gilligan identified.

Other sociorace-related configurations within the United States reflect both a distinctive sense of psychosocially based identity and of autonomy and relationships. In a high school counseling study mentioned earlier (F. Tyler & Pargament, 1981), we found that "prior to counseling, black students were more systems-blaming, more social-desirability oriented, and more active planful copers than were their white counterparts. For the black students, systems-blame correlated *negatively* with internality, trust, and social desirability; for whites it correlated *positively* with trust" (p. 711). These findings support that our individual psychosocial characteristics interrelate differently when we decide our environment is hostile rather than supportive.

Taken together, these findings about the contribution of situational factors indicate some of the myriad possibilities of how self-as-autonomous and self-as-socius may interrelate or be separate and unrelated. Men may define themselves as autonomous if their world is indifferent or individualistically oriented. Women may define themselves as passive agents if their world seems to be just and to define their role as one of being cared for. They may also define their role as a collaborative caring one in a family setting. Current differences in autonomy–relatedness patterns may be a product of our socially defined circumstances and, as these findings suggest, change as we change our circumstances.

Cultural and Cultural Change Matrices

It is evident from studies of the lives of immigrants and refugees and of efforts to introduce patterns of one culture into another that each of us is a carrier of a cultural ethos and a vehicle of cultural change. I have already cited a number of such studies and additional ones are considered here. Particular attention is focused on the cultural embeddedness of autonomy and relatedness and the issues they create when we cross cultural boundaries.

Cohen (1980) relied on her ethnographic studies to write about the psychosocial issues Latina immigrants faced in the United States. Their self-subservient orientation to sacrifice for the group's benefit did not fit well with the individualistic orientation toward jobs that they found in the United States. For these Latinas, the ideal type of relationship between employers and employees included dignity and respect (trust), a culturally syntonic pattern for them. They expected their supervisors to also consider their relationship as having a personal component that extended beyond their job connectedness. Having made that psychosocial leap, they tried to build a more extensive spiral of interactions. Supervisors who acted as helpful counselors outside of the immigrant's network of family and friends became key intermediaries through whom they learned about the host society.

Diaz-Guerrero (1977) documented that Mexicans define the sense of self and its embeddedness in relationships differently than do U.S. Anglos.

As evidence of a psychosocial *Mexicanness*, he introduced the concept of *affiliative obedience* as describing a characteristic pattern of internal control among Mexican adolescents. They chose an ethnically distinct pattern of obeying and being guided by their parents as an appropriate way of controlling their lives and being human. He argued that Mexicanness should not be judged as a deficient or inferior orientation in relation to a *self-as-autonomous* (Anglo) orientation. It is an internally coherent, relational, psychosocial orientation with its own strengths, limitations, and possibilities.

When cultural differences in autonomy/relatedness patterns are not considered and cultural change is addressed from an external source, characteristic issues arise. The people of "that" culture become the target and the "problem." An illustrative example stemmed from the hypothesis of U.S. psychologists McClelland and Winter (1969) that the reason for lack of development in India was the people's lack of a need for achievement (*n*Ach). They hypothesized that teaching *n*Ach to Indian entrepreneurs would lead to economic development. Their trained participants did become more entrepreneurial, but it is not clear whether they also started a spiral of development. McClelland and Winter did not ask what the relational patterns were between these competing, achievement-oriented entrepreneurs or between them and their communities.

Indian psychologists Sinha and his collaborator, Pandey (Sinha, 1981; Sinha and Pandey, 1968), disagreed with McClelland's hypothesis and tested the effects of high *n*Ach under controlled conditions. They confirmed their hypothesis that high *n*Ach leads to maximum output only when available resources are unlimited. When available resources were limited, subjects with a need for cooperation (*n*Coop) produced more than those with high *n*Ach. In addition, they learned that high *n*Ach subjects show greater interpersonal variations in output than do cooperating subjects. The competitiveness associated with high *n*Ach also reduced the task, group, and interpersonal likings; whereas the need for cooperation fostered more liking by the participants for each other, for the group, and for the task.

McClelland responded that their experimental analogue was inadequate. He tested his alternative hypothesis that, in a free situation, *n*Ach-oriented subjects would create resources, a possibility that Sinha and Pandey had not allowed. He found that high *n*Ach subjects created some resources and cooperated among themselves, even creating group goals. However, their cooperativeness had limited generalizability outside their group (McClelland & Winter, 1969). In turn, Sinha and Pandey tested this possibility and concluded that "probably altruism puts some constraints on the functioning of the *n*Ach, and thus altruism distracts the *n*Ach Ss from 'minding' their own interest by putting an incongruent set of demands in terms of cooperation, helping the needy, etc." (1970, p. 216).

Another Indian psychologist, Pareek (1968), contributed to this dialogue by emphasizing that achievement motivation is not enough. He noted "there seems to be enough evidence in history—at least in Indian history—that many social changes, including economic development, were in the past designed and executed by people who showed great concern for others" (p. 118f). McClelland (1966) had acknowledged this phenomenon earlier, called it concern for the common welfare, and suggested it as the most probable explanation for the correlation between countries' investments in health and education and their subsequent rates of economic growth. More generally, these studies demonstrated that people's motivational configurations are embedded in their psychosocial contexts.

The accounts of uprooting and acculturation faced by sojourners, emigrees, and refugees highlight how the rootedness of each of us in our culture of origin shapes adaptation to and acculturation in new cultures. Tiryakian (1980) wrote that our roots are the source of our "being-in-the-world," of our "intersubjective reality, one of feeling of belongingness and attachment with one's geosocial origins" (p. 134). He cited the situation of the late nineteenth and early twentieth century emigrants from southern and eastern Europe to the United States. As disadvantaged rural peasants in their cultures of origin, they did not want to reestablish similar communities or their NCDG status in the United States, and could not have even if they had wanted to because they mostly settled in cities. The point of such examples is that any uprooting inevitably confronts us with the task of making new psychosocial leaps as a basis for renegotiating new senses of our identity, including our autonomy and relatedness. As with the story of the Ik mentioned earlier, this example also raises the question of how any uprooted people and their descendants construct a sense of continuity.

Tiryakian (1980) described how social institutions such as schools which provide a secular education also uproot children in that they separate pupils from the traditional beliefs and life styles of their families and communities. In that sense, they facilitate generational and cultural change within a context of continuity. For example, in certain eras in United States history, people defined their roots as being in the future as assimilated Americans, rather than in relation to their past origins. In other eras, such as the 1960s, emphasis was placed on past ethnic or racial heritage rather than on present or future status. Thus, uprooting can have positive as well as negative values. Certainly, it is an essential component of broad social changes and how we adapt to them.

Berry (1980) also discussed change and reaffirmation to traditional values as people in traditional cultures have moved toward modernism. He challenged the overly simplistic view reflected in the apparent, even if tacit, agreement among social scientists that there is some "unitary end state, most often termed 'modernization'" (Berry, 1980, p. 220). He said that change is not unidirectional and linear, but an interactive process in which both societal orientations influence each other. Characteristics of the traditional and the modern society come to coexist in both groups within a developing society and in the society's institutions, a future somewhat similar to that faced by immigrants and their children.

In summary, changes in us necessarily involve both the autonomous and the relational aspects of our lives. As societies change, the definitions of autonomy and relatedness among individuals change, as do the supports and threats associated with those formulations. Psychological change does not occur inside of us and sociocultural change outside of us, nor is acculturation a unidimensional, unidirectional process that leads to a common outcome for all of us. These changes occur at all levels simultaneously, inside and outside of us, because we are the creators, carriers, and products of ourselves and our cultures.

Brown (1980) argued that we necessarily function as active contributors to our cultures in a holistic fashion. He advanced the thesis that we are imaginative and rational, related and autonomous, and that severing the connections between autonomy and relatedness is artificial and destructive to us and our societies. His perspective is consistent with the point–counterpoint of responsibility and caring formulated by Gilligan and her colleagues (1982). That is, how well we integrate our autonomy and our relatedness is a major determinant of the quality of functioning and change in us and our societies. In contrast, the separateness and opposition of autonomy and relatedness in Kohlberg's (1969) model has substantial built-in limitations as a framework for understanding and changing us and our societies.

Consequently, questions about the interrelations between our senses of autonomy and relatedness arise in the examination of any given topic about our approaches to life. Coelho and Stein (1980) addressed that interrelation in their analyses of how we and societies cope:

> Above all, coping means exercising the creativity of individuals and groups in a social system, maintaining a coherent view of the future, and developing the ability or power to change one's situation for oneself and others. In the last analysis, coping is a collaborative enterprise of individual personalities and social support systems. (p. 15)

Once again we find the assertion that autonomy and relationship are irrevocably intertwined and not necessarily in a winner-take-all oppositional manner.

SUMMARY

This chapter's central theme has been that our individual and collective concepts of human autonomy and relatedness are necessarily intertwined in the fabric of our individual lives, communities, and cultures. These concepts include the basic knower aspects of ourselves as feeling/ learning beings as well as analytic/rational ones. Further, our autonomy is not solely within ourselves, and our relatedness is not solely external to us; both are psychosocial and, of necessity, defined in relation to each other. The Western conception of self and its independence from the world, including people's relationships to each other, is culture specific. The self-imbedded-in-socius concept that characterizes some other societies is equally culture specific.

The separation of self and others in Western societies has yielded a distinctive psychology which is useful in describing people in these cultures. However, that view is socially constructed and culture specific, and it has substantial costs as well as benefits. One cost is that it alienates people from each other and society and creates an artificial separation of autonomy and relatedness. Another cost stems from applying this view ethnocentrically to other cultures, leading to distorted conceptions of how those cultures function and the meaning of those peoples' lives. Everyone is consequently less able to interact, understand each other, or learn from each other. Even if the others' formulations are equally ethnocentric, that does not change the underlying point that ethnocentric approaches contribute to miscommunication and other difficulties.

To move beyond such culture-bound constraints requires radical reformulation of our senses of self, self-other relationships, and conceptions about how to interact with our own and others' lives, relationships, and cultures. Accomplishing such changes involves several steps. It requires accepting that none of us is entirely free from our contexts nor entirely bound by them. It requires acknowledging that changes ranging from the individual to the cultural are interrelated. Finally, it requires an acknowledgment that we are individuals whose known and knower characteristics are feeling/learning as much as analytic/rational. Once we meet these requirements, we can then begin to use our knower capabilities to change or transcend our mutually embedded selves and the ethnic validity paradigms and nested frameworks that we have created out of our pasts and circumstances.

RESOURCE GENERATION AND INTERCHANGE

INTRODUCTION

The psychosocial model used here differs from intrapsychic and social models of personality and conduct by conceptualizing social behavior as a function of social/contextual factors and the personal factors of people as known and as active agent knowers. It assumes that much of our nature as individuals is formed by, contingent on, and of necessity linked with interchanges with others. From birth onward these interchanges influence the meanings that we assign to our activities, ranging from the most basic aspects of life, such as food and sex, to the most abstract intellectual or emotional exchanges. These interchanges are biopsychosocial in that they do not have a physical existence apart from the people involved in them, and they are psychosocially formed. Further, they are not solely guided by homeostatic need reduction principles; rather, they may increase as is suggested by Rotter's (1954) concept of need induction.

Rotter (1954) conceptualized and studied personality as a predominantly social product and argued that its social antecedents, correlates, and consequences should be investigated. He built on this idea by classifying personality behaviors as products of socially defined psychological needs (e.g., recognition–status, affection), cues, and reinforcements, thereby challenging the belief that social need levels are controlled by homeostatic biological mechanisms. His alternative proposal was that psychological needs are induced by positive reinforcement and that people's choices are based on the relative strengths of these competing psychosocial needs. He added that while these needs and reinforcements might originally have been and continue to be linked to physiologically identifiable reinforcements, that connection is not what primarily sustains them. The pressures of physiology are often overridden by social considerations, and any categorization of psychological needs is likely to change with external conditions. Finally, Rotter emphasized that the socially assigned meanings of people's behaviors differ from their subjective meanings and both must be considered during interactions.

In the last half century, other research on culture, contexts, and interactive conceptions of personality and identity has been conducted. It has identified social interaction characteristics related to these concepts in ways that had been previously unnoticed, unquestioned, or ignored. Central to these emerging perspectives is the conclusion that we possess the capability of choice and thus have responsibility for our conduct. We can and do choose and act in resource enhancement and destructive ways that create "new things under the sun."

Foa (1971) constructed a resource theory for understanding our psychosocial interchanges. He called the contents of those interchanges *resources* and the reciprocal process involved *resource interactions*. "Resources" has become a generally acceptable term for what is provided by and to individuals who are expressing their positive and negative impulses in interpersonal interactions. Where and how resources exist in people when they are not exhibiting them poses a question similar to one about electricity, i.e., "where does the electricity go when we turn out the lights?" Answers to such questions require speaking of the potentials or capabilities of dynamic systems. Thus, the way they are described is to speak of the psychosocial resources people need and the ones others can offer during interchanges.

Interactions involve an *interchange* of resources, but the content and nature of those interchanges and the nature of their outcomes requires substantial specification for them to be understood. Their nature may range from competitive to collaborative to cooperative. It is, for example, only for "cooperation" that dictionary definitions include the possibility of association for mutual benefit. Another aspect of their nature is that they may vary from being of an extrinsic nature to an intrinsic one. Their content may range from being primarily intellectual to being largely emotional. In addition, one conception of such transfers is that of *exchange*, the trading of resources according to rules or standards of equivalence or fairness so that the transaction does not leave any participants advantaged or disadvantaged. This conception also implies that there are nonequivalent reciprocal transfers of resources. An elaboration of the complexity and implications of equivalent and nonequivalent transfers involves ideas related to justice that were elaborated in Chapter 7. Interactions may generate more of the resources the participants contribute to an interaction. Resources can also be lost in interchanges, so the concepts of enhancement and loss must be included to provide for consideration of a full range of possible outcomes. To the extent that individuals are active, creating agents, they can produce additional and new kinds of resources and lose and destroy them.

As mentioned above, social interaction patterns vary in the extent to which they involve intrinsic or extrinsic aspects of our conduct. According to dictionaries, *intrinsic* is defined as being located within the activity (Webster, 1999); *extrinsic* as not part of or belonging to an activity (Webster, 1999). That is, intrinsically engaging social interactions involve a mutual attraction between individuals that is integral to the ways they interact. We are drawn to these interactions and they hold our interest because they are enjoyable, make the quality of the activity richer, and increase our attraction for each other and for engaging in the activity together. That is, they are also potentially enhancing.

Social interactions may not only enhance, diminish, or simply maintain exchanged resources, they may do so in different ways. Intrinsic resources that enhance interactions potentially increase the participants' cooperative natures and capabilities. In reciprocal expressions of love, friendship, or respect, these qualities are an inherent part of the interaction. In contrast, resource enhancing cooperation that is extrinsic involves interacting to increase the value or quality of something which lies outside the relationship and is only arbitrarily related to it, e.g., cooperating on a task or project, as, for example, building a structure or selling a product to gain a reward such as monetary recompense.

The basic form of this resource interaction nested framework is that our natures, including our continual growth, change, and destruction, are related to our interchanges of resources with each other. Relationships and their associated psychosocial interactions embody the somewhat intangible element that we call *meaning*. They have no independent physical existence apart from the parties involved, but their nature has important consequences for shaping our broader psychosocial competence oriented and ethnic validity patterns of meaning, i.e., how we create and understand the nature of our lives and societies.

RESOURCE EXCHANGE FORMULATIONS

SOCIALLY DEVELOPED COGNITIVE–
BEHAVIORAL RESOURCE EXCHANGES

The first interpersonal resource exchange based social psychology theory of people's social behavior was presented by Foa and Foa (1974) as a step toward a comprehensive framework for studying, understanding, and guiding social behavior. Their work is reviewed in this section because it provides an overview of major psychosocial and contextual questions that must be addressed in devising a comprehensive theory of our psychosocial interactions. They reasoned that "an integrated approach to the complex socio-economic problems of modern society can hardly succeed in the absence of a unified science of man, integrating emotional, social, and economic aspects of his resource seeking behavior" (Foa & Foa, 1974, p. 388).

Foa and Foa's (1974) proposed unified science was based on the assumption that all of our interactions are social cognitive–behavioral resource exchanges. That is, we assign meaning to our interactions by structuring them cognitively and relating them to our past experiences and environments and to our understanding of the present and predictions of the future. These exchanges involve a *proaction* (offer of exchange) and a *reaction* (response to the offer) among individuals, families, communities, groups, and even cultures. To facilitate these processes, there are six classes of interpersonal resources (love or status; goods or services; and information or money). Our social growth occurs as we differentiate cognitive structures to construct the framework of meaning that provides our basis for resource exchanges which are the essential ingredients of life.

As development processes proceed from more concrete to more abstract and yield adult cognitive structures, they involve differentiating between two parallel partial structures, *behavioral* and *perceptual*. Further, we order interpersonal resource classes along dimensions of *particularism* (as in giving love to or receiving love from a particular lover to people in general) and *concreteness* (as in expressing love by behaving lovingly in contrast to giving money).

The occurrence and nature of interchanges depends on (a) the motivational need to receive and capacity to give of the individuals involved; (b) the appropriateness of the personal and societal environment for an exchange of a particular type; and (c) the properties of the resources to be exchanged. The *need* for an exchange occurs when a person is below an optimal range of a resource; the *power* to exchange (get rid of this resource) occurs when a person is above that optimal range. In addition, motivational structures are based on two general classes of mechanisms: the need to (1) accumulate resources (at least up to their optimal ceiling) and (2) confirm our cognitive structures. Accumulated resources can be used to meet our needs directly and to control the behavior of others by (a) threatening to deny others a resource they need and cannot obtain elsewhere; (b) threatening to take away resources others possess; and (c) taking resources from oneself (Foa & Foa, 1994).

Foa and Foa (1974) and their colleagues (Foa, Converse, Tornblom, & Foa, 1993) reanalyzed issues which had been the focus of research by social psychologists, including aggressive interchanges, interpersonal attraction, and zero-sum interactions in which a fixed amount of a resource such as money is allocated. They also examined resource-specific (e.g., love of or from a given individual) and resource-general (e.g., money from employment or public status) interactions. Their conclusions included that (a) people regulate exchanges by conceptions of equity that vary within and between individuals, conditions, and social groups; (b) exchanges usually involve benefits and costs (but they questioned what the actual costs are in exchanges which involve giving each other resources (as in love) when the giving also gives pleasure to the giver); (c) people usually prefer open exchanges of the resources they have in above optimal amounts with others who need the resources offered and have optimal amounts of resources which they will provide in reciprocation; and (d) when exchanges are blocked, people may resort to manipulation, ingratiation, or Machiavellianism by concealing which resource they seek to obtain.

Within this theory, communication is an essential activity for exchanging resources and also for carrying structural information—for what has been called here people's nested frameworks and ethnic validity paradigms. Effective communication cannot occur unless the people involved are cognitively matched; that is, they have similar cognitive structures. Thus, provision of adaptive and appropriate structural information is an essential adult–child activity in the socialization of children, and when it is insufficient children are deprived of both structural and resource information. Consequently, they become cognitively deviant as in pathology, and in the view of Foa et al. (1974, 1993) most psychotherapeutic approaches should emphasize increases in resource accumulation and assist recipients in changing their existing cognitive structures.

In addition, cognitive structures differ within and between cultures. The basic interpersonal, behavioral, and family cognitive structures and the order among them are pancultural. However, cultural differences emerge in later life and become more distinctive, and cross-cultural adaptations become more difficult. Cultures vary in their characteristic cognitive differentiations of experiences. For example, in traditional cultures *particular* resources are also exchanged in nonfamily (e.g., work) institutions. Modern societies have shifted to a greater exchange of *universalistic* resources (e.g., money) in family contexts. Finally, programs that train people to improve cross-cultural communication and understanding indicate that participants improve when they change their cognitive structures.

In summary, although Foa et al.'s work (1974, 1993) identified important questions about the nature of our psychosocial interactions, their views are subject to major challenges. For example, a major challenge to the model is whether its central concept of exchange can account for how ongoing or potentially long-term relationships which involve substantial symbolic (love, respect, self-sacrifice) resource exchanges are maintained. It neglects whether the psychosocial symbolic aspects of the way we define our lives may contain principled commitments which are thought not to be judged in terms of expected concrete costs or returns. That is, people form and maintain relationships based on love for a particular person rather than as equity based interchanges. People also form a generalized love for their family, community, country, or humanity and guide their lives accordingly, even to the extent of self-sacrifice.

Further, it is not at all clear that the question of equity is relevant to people's intrinsically satisfying interactions, or that it can be measured, or is conducive to maintaining such interactions. Asking "Did you enjoy that as much as I did?" has the potential to destroy the satisfaction of an interaction and the relationship underlying it rather than to enhance either. This resource exchange framework doesn't effectively integrate our biological survival, conditioning, and active agent judgment characteristics. It does not provide an account of how people choose among competing needs, how capacities for needs change throughout life, and how the concrete and symbolic psychosocial components are integrated into their activities.

ALTERNATIVE SOCIAL PSYCHOLOGICAL CONCEPTIONS OF RESOURCE EXCHANGE

Over the last two decades, additional models of interpersonal interaction that use equity as the basis of social exchange have been advanced by social psychologists. The following paragraphs provide a brief summary of them.

Interdependence Theory

Kelley and Thibaut's (1978) outcome interdependence theory assumes that our actions in relationships are based on our estimates of what will yield the greatest reward at the lowest cost. They introduced an equity consideration that each participant's outcome definition and satisfaction will be revised on an ongoing basis to yield an outcome based on mutual benefit as the relationship grows. They also challenged the emphasis in resource theory that particularistic resource exchanges involve an exchange of similar kinds of resources (e.g., love for love), indicating that symmetry is not always important.

Exchange and Communal Relationships

Clark and her colleague (Clark & Mills, 1993) demonstrated that communal relationships differ from exchange relationships primarily in that each is oriented to meeting the needs of the other and feels no obligation to reciprocate for any particular benefit received. In these arrangements, offering reciprocity may diminish the relationship. On the other hand, each person may feel an obligation and a desire to help meet the other's needs, even though doing so involves providing a quite different resource from any received. Communal relationships involve a desire to maintain a relationship for its own sake and, at times, may seem to be largely one-sided, as in the attachment of a mother for her children. The mother may gain a resource (feel satisfaction), but she does not receive any benefit, that is, any return that can be used.

The model of command relationships introduces a different basis for valuing and participating in interpersonal interactions and allows for the possibility of the intrinsic satisfaction felt when an individual provides a resource to meet the needs of another or the altruistic sense of contributing to the welfare of others without return, or both. Clark and Mills (1993) suggested that most people have a general sense of a communal relationship with all people, as in a willingness to help strangers. However, they also proposed that the strength of any communal concern is tempered by the cost of acting on it. They did not address whether engaging in communal relationships leads to resource enhancement. Do those who care for others and interact accordingly have richer and more satisfying lives than those who do not?

Equity Theory

The core premise of equity theory is that people's exchange behaviors or reactions to exchange are a function of the contributions and outcomes of *both* participants. Considerable support for this hypothesis comes from studies of strangers or short term acquaintances. The question those studies leave unanswered is the applicability of equity theory to people who are close and have a communal relationship (Berg, Piner, & Frank, 1993).

Responsiveness

Responsiveness is viewed as being at one end of a continuum with exploitation at the other pole. Although it has been studied and used more frequently in areas of communication and self-disclosure, it is relevant to an understanding of all interpersonal exchanges. Its presence is indicated by participants' concern for each other rather than for the content of the message or the value of the resource offered. If our relationships are based on our concerns for each other, we would be expected to be more sensitive to each other's needs, more expecting of a close relationship, and more interested in and willing to self-disclose. Maintaining equity may not be the only goal in interchanges, although Berg et al. (1993) provided no alternative to equity theory as a motive for such interchanges. However, there is an implicit hypothesis in their formulations that such interchanges build on and generate a desire for an even closer relationship. In short, Berg and his colleagues have incorporated a conception of resource enhancement as both a motive for and a satisfying part of relationships.

Berg and Clark (1986) cited five dimensions that would be expected to differentiate close and casual exchange relationship interactions. Close relationships would (a) be more interdependent, (b) exchange a greater number of resources and exchange more particularistic resources, such as love, and do so on the basis of need rather than symmetry, (c) exchange a greater variety of resources, (d) be more likely to use mutual responsiveness rules of exchange rather than reciprocity, and (e) be more self-disclosing and disclose more intimate information. Berg, Piner, and Frank (1993) reported research support for four of the hypotheses, but for (d) they found less mutual responsiveness as relationships became closer, an unexpected finding that was possibly due to the study's short time span.

INTRINSIC MOTIVATION

Intrinsic motivation is interest or desire to engage in an activity because of its inherently pleasurable or enjoyable nature. The joy of flying may be experienced quite independently of the goal of the flight. The joy of companionship with someone we care about may be experienced quite independently of any joint goal, even working at an onerous task. Sansone and Harackiewicz (1996) called the absence of intrinsic motivation "I don't feel like it" and called the positive phenomenal experience of intrinsic interest "feeling like it." Their research demonstrated that intrinsic motivation has consequences independent of those associated with goal motivation. In a controlled experiment, it increased participants' interest in performing an activity, their level of positive feeling during the activity, and their subsequent greater interest in repeating the activity.

Sansone and Harackiewicz (1996) made the further point that purpose (intrinsic) and goal (extrinsic) motivations may oppose rather than support each other. A goal orientation may reduce the level of purpose motivation and the interest in and enjoyment of performing the activity.

Offering a resource exchange, equity-based response implies that the initial resource was judged on the basis of its value rather than on the basis of the pleasure that was part of the act of sharing or helping a cared-for companion. From an extensive research program, Deci and his colleagues (1995) provided empirical support for this point in a variety of activities. When extrinsic rewards were introduced in a manner designed to control the recipient, a negative effect was generated that reduced the intrinsic quality of the activity. Introducing such rewards seemed to change the relationship to a resource exchange one; however, rewards given as an indication of merit did not reduce the intrinsic quality of the relationship.

Sansone and Harackiewicz (1996) speculated that "feelings of interest" may sustain learning how to survive and our involvement in activities which are important to achieving outcome goals. Alternatively, the causal chain could function in the opposite direction. That is, we learn and do what we have to do to survive, and we attain outcome goals because parts of that learning are pleasurable. Further, they enable us to engage in even more interesting activities and relationships, providing even more pleasant experiences. We may exercise so that we can enjoy living, not just so we will not be unhealthy. Also, exercising can be pleasurable in and of itself, not just a necessary act to survive. We may learn to play together and love each other, psychologically and physically, because it is pleasurable, not because of individual and species survival.

PERSONALITY THEORY AND CLINICAL PSYCHOLOGY

L'Abate and Harrel (1993) extended resource exchange theory by using it as a personality theory model. They applied it in clinical psychology to construct a model of personality development in which the family was central in socialization and crucial in the development of interpersonal competence. Two distinct processes, showing and sharing love and negotiating power, were identified as essential to the development of competence. They defined the exchange of resources in status and love as the "modality of *Being*." It involves expressing love and intimacy and being emotionally available to self and significant others. Negotiating power is linked to the modalities of "doing" and "having." "*Doing*" involves exchanging resources by providing services and information and is measured by how well a person performs in various roles and tasks. *Having* refers to exchanging material resources, such as goods and money, and is measured by how much we produce.

Important questions that L'Abate (1994) introduced by using different rules for Being and Doing interactions included: Are some lives richer in quality than others? Are some interactions and interaction styles enhancement oriented rather than equity oriented? He emphasized that space and time are relevant dimensions in relationships and exchanges. We may develop interpersonal styles that lead to mutually satisfying interchanges and that include the allocation and enjoyment of time together as part of our lives. If so, we may develop qualities of enjoyment that are significantly better (or worse) than the qualities of others who live differently.

L'Abate (1994) answered these questions affirmatively by describing how people's lives and interactions may differ in quality, in richness. He defined *selffulness* as the capacity to reciprocally assign importance to intimate relationships involving those who care for us and for whom we care. When we make such assignments and behave accordingly, the outcome is usually positive and results in shared victories. "Within this possibility, joy, positive feelings, and the attainment of legitimate pleasures will immunize the individual against illegitimate, or unacceptable and ultimately destructive pleasures, such as addictions" (L'Abate, 1986, p. 125). L'Abate's approach suggests there may be enhancement-oriented life characteristics and interactions rather than just exchange oriented ones. However, its validity rests an demonstrating that pleasures serve an enhancement function separately from any immunizing function.

A Taxonomy of Interaction Structures

From analysis of ethnographic and experimental social psychology findings, Fiske (1991) proposed that we use four basic forms of social relationships to structure our interactions. These forms are communal sharing, authority ranking, equality matching, and market pricing. They enable us to plan actions, anticipate those of others, and coordinate actions so that we can act in concert.

Communal sharing is based on equivalence relationships. Participants guide themselves by assigning primary importance to their common goals, superordinate collectivity, and maintenance of separateness from real or potential outside individuals or groups. "They think of themselves as being all the same in some significant respect, not as individuals but as 'we'" (Fiske, 1991, p. 12f).

Authority ranking is an asymmetrical relationship system. Social status ranks determine people's extensions of the self by specifying the hierarchical nature of their characteristics and interactions, including identity, relative entitlements, and patterns of interrelationship and interchange. Higher ranking people control more people and assets, are presumed to possess more knowledge and mastery over events, and have related prerogatives. Inferiors are deferential and, in turn, are entitled to receive protection and support from their leaders.

Equality matching describes egalitarian relationships among people who consider themselves to be separate but coequal peers and interact accordingly. They conceive of each other and their actions as distinct and as balancing each other. Their exchanges are quid pro quo and narrowly reciprocal. In conflicts, they respond with an-eye-for-an-eye retaliatory vengeance. Business or legal partners may interact in these ways, as is at times reflected in highly publicized legal cases when such arrangements dissolve themselves.

In *Market Pricing* relationships, a single universal metric, the price (or "utility") for purposes of exchange, determines the value of individuals or groups and their characteristics, including identities, entitlements, and contributions to and expected returns from interactions. People consider themselves to be separate from one another. Consequently, they give and get, and they influence others and exert themselves in proportion to the (common) market pricing standard of the social values in their current domain. Members of a community may relate on the basis of different incomes or other measures of status; they interact when they decide that it is rational to do so on that basis.

IMPLICATIONS

These various interaction models are a fundamental challenge to the adequacy of the Foas' resource exchange theory. We may interact in ways that cannot be accounted for by equity based exchange theories. We know that caring, sharing, and concern with other's needs occur in symmetrical or asymmetrical communal relations, providing rewards for merit and in the intrinsic quality of interactions. We may also interact to maintain separateness from others and seek to establish or maintain an imbalance in exchanges. Same types of interactions may increase or enhance the resources we have and enrich or diminish the quality of our lives individually and collectively. Finally, we may also enrich the lives of others with no expectation of return and even at some cost to ourselves. It is the increasing occurrence of anomalies (phenomena that the existing model or paradigm cannot explain) that is one of the reasons that scientific formulations are periodically forced to change. That seems to be the case with regard to equity based resource exchange models.

RESOURCE INTERACTION NETWORKS

The rest of this chapter turns away from a focus on equity based exchanges, although their relevance will not be ignored. Attention will be

focused on understanding the role of multidimensional resource interaction networks. Further, particular attention will be paid to resource enhancement and enrichment in our lives. For example, resource exchange
paradigms are not adequate to account for *belongingness* relationships at
any level ranging from couples to country (patriotism). Tornblom and
Nilsson (1993) surveyed residents of Goteberg, Sweden, a society characterized by material abundance. Respondents considered that all kinds of
resources were more important when they were provided by a particularistic rather than a universalistic source. Love from a *particularistic*
source (an established relationship) was much more valued than from a
universalistic source (anyone in general). Even so, they said no one resource would fulfill their lives. These findings are consistent with resource
exchange theory predictions about the relative value of particularistic and
universalistic resource exchanges. However, they are also consistent with
the hypothesis that interactions concerning particularistic resources operate according to principles different from universalistic ones.

Deci's (1995) research also supports this second possibility. He found
that extrinsic rewards introduced into intrinsically satisfying personal
relationships may destroy those relationships. Bleisner's (1993) comprehensive study of the exchanges in close and casual relationships among
elderly women in the United States supported a psychosocial relationship
model. These women were actively involved in aiding others in their social
networks in contrast to public perceptions that they were exclusively
recipients of help. Many of their patterns of exchange were consistent with
equity-based exchange theories, but there was one important exception.
The women valued giving resources to others over receiving them and felt
that they behaved accordingly. It may be more defensible to consider a
psychosocial relationship model as the universal model for human interchanges and equity exchange models as derivative and secondary.

Other challenges to the adequacy of equity based theories can be
found at community levels. The shift in the United States to a community
orientation in the 1960s challenged the assumptions of many psychologists
in profound and unexpected ways (F. Tyler, 1995, 1970; F. Tyler & Spiesman,
1967). As they tried to create better communities and societies, they began
to realize that they had vested interests, just like everyone else. Consequently, they began to question whether their perspectives and approaches were advancing the interests of lay people and society or their
own self-serving biases. Unexpectedly, they found that their answers had
ramifications for understanding all of us and for critiquing their own
theories and practices.

Several generally accepted clinical assumptions that seemed particularly inappropriate for constructive community work were challenged

(Rappaport, 1981; Ryan, 1971; F. Tyler, Pargament, & Gatz, 1983), including: (1) problems lie in individuals and are to be solved in them; (2) the experientially derived efforts of ordinary citizens are characterized by inadequacies, deficits, inefficiencies, and even pathologies; (3) professionals are characteristically adequate, resourceful, capable, efficient, and mature; (4) the way to solve problems for the benefit of the individual and the community is by having expert professionals develop and implement solutions on the basis of their relevant knowledge. It was noted that using these assumptions as the basis for socially oriented community enterprises was contributing to unintended, undesired social consequences (Sarason et al., 1977; Sarason & Lorentz, 1979; Caplan & Nelson, 1973). Social problems seemed to be increasing along with the numbers of professionals and programs meant to solve those problems. Simultaneously, the clients and citizens in general felt more and more isolated, alienated, and helpless.

AN ENHANCEMENT ORIENTED RESOURCE EXCHANGE PARADIGM: A PROTOTYPE

Sarason and his colleagues (1977) developed and studied an alternative paradigm, the resource exchange network, for community oriented research and social action. Their focus was on mutual psychosocial and material resource enhancement and integration of intrinsic and extrinsic aspects of interactions. Sarason and Lorentz (1979) collected considerable evidence that testified to the gains for communities and groups who adopted this approach. The characteristics of these networks and their integral role in resource enhancement outcomes are summarized here, beginning with the resource exchange network's assumptions:

Assumption 1: The resources available to meet human needs are limited— and always will be. Despite the conventional belief that enough resources to meet people's needs can be obtained, there will always be a discrepancy between what people need and what is available for them. Resource exchange network approaches must be directed toward better use of limited resources.

Assumption 2: People are resourceful and have many strengths. Professionals assume that people need resources and guidance because of their deficiencies. In contrast, it is assumed that people and communities can contribute to solving their problems, no matter how deficient they seem to be.

Assumption 3: The resources available can be best utilized and multiplied by evolving programs of reciprocal exchange. The best way to enhance the well-being of each of the parties involved is to identify and establish reciprocal exchange relationships. By establishing patterns in which I offer something to you, and you, in turn, offer something to me, both of us are better served.

Assumption 4: The exchange network is an important part of the interrelated well-being and task oriented problem solving of the people in the network. Networks are not just empty service vehicles. Rather, their interchanges are the central catalyst of the resource exchange network. This assumption contrasts with the alternative that each person's autonomous involvement is for purposes of enhancing autonomous well-being.

Networking can perhaps be more clearly illustrated by considering its role in a family that functions as a resource exchange network. If the family is operating as a cohesive unit, its members exchange resources and help each other in an infinite variety of ways. They grow in feelings of self-worth and caring, in resources, in problem-solving efficacy, and in their valuing of their family as a network. Members emphasize that it is important to honor and remember the family, to keep in touch with each other, and to not forget that "we're all part of the family." Membership is enjoyable in its own right and enhances the quality of life of its members. Family membership does not imply that other needs do not compete with those being met within the family, but that family membership and interactions enhance the quality of life for the individuals and the family as a whole. Highest priority is given to the ritual activities, informal and formal, that emphasize the value of the family and facilitate networking within it. When the family network loses this central significance, it begins to lose its vitality and validity.

Assumption 5: Networking requires leadership/coordination in combination. Networks require someone to identify and match valuable reciprocal pairings. However, this leader/coordinator must not do the work of these pairs. They must evolve their own reciprocities, new exchanges, and subsequent interactions. For example, families and communities may have someone who serves as an informal matchmaker for marriageable members. The matchmaker's task is completed when a couple is brought together; it does not include conducting the courtship or going on the honeymoon. When leader/coordinators do the work, they begin to destroy the network.

Assumption 6: The focus and power of a Resource Exchange Network always remains with the individuals in the network. Everyone must be invested in the networking and its ongoing interchanges. Power does not reside in or shift to the leader as it tends to do in professional and other formal organizations. A network is somewhat analogous to the "commons," an area which historically existed in many communities for everyone's use. That space belonged to everyone and had to be sustained by everyone. Otherwise, it was eventually destroyed by individuals who exploited it for their own purposes.

Assumption 7: Resource Exchange Networks are voluntary. The essential ingredient of networking lies in the active commitment of members to participate as knowers. People cannot be forced to form or maintain relationships. This resource exchange network assumption raises a question that will continue to be explored throughout this text: How can formal systems with fixed structures be organized in ways that retain the element of voluntary involvement?

Assumption 8: Resource Exchange Networks are fluid and changing. Networks are designed to be open-ended and build on the continual forming and reinforcing of exchange patterns as the people in them and their resources and needs change. A resource exchange network that is not fluid and changing has ceased to be a resource exchange network.

Sarason and Lorentz gave a clear, concise description of the workings of one such resource exchange network in which they participated.

> The Essex Network is an instance of a loose, informal voluntary association of individuals whose interrelationships (their frequency and substance) depend on a few self-selected individuals seeking to make resource exchange a basis for existing and new interrelationships so that membership expands, interrelationships are reshuffled, new clusters are formed around new self-selected individuals who will serve a role similar to that of those who brought them into the association. There are no geographical, substantive, education, or status criteria for membership; no formal rules; and no time- or calendar-determined tasks. Members may or may not know each other, although each knows self-selected individuals and some members. They have access to each other; the most frequent way this access initially takes place is through the self-selected individuals; over time, access takes place more directly. (Sarason & Lorentz, 1979, p. 164)

Sarason and his colleagues contributed to our understanding of resource exchange networks by spelling out their requirements, modes of operation, and distinctive strengths. Unlike other formal and informal interaction patterns, they are not dependent on professionals or professional expertise. Consequently, in many fields of life people with common concerns and notably limited resources have formed such networks.

The Range of Resource Enhancement Possibilities

Resource enhancement networks may be built for many purposes and in a variety of ways. They provide examples of circumstances in which they function, of forms they take, and of activities for which they have proven valuable. Their effectiveness also highlights the limits of equity based resource exchange models of relationships. This section describes a range of such networks.

Self-Help Groups

Self-help groups are among the more common forms of resource networks and can be used by any group trying to solve common problems. They are often voluntary, cooperative associations of people who are economically or socially deprived, or both, who have been unable to improve their lives by individual efforts or appeals to official agencies. Two quite different self-help groups in the United States provide a picture of their common and unique characteristics.

The *Humphrey's County Union for Progress Farmers' Cooperative, Belzoni, Mississippi,* illustrates how an economically oppressed group formed a cooperative that evolved into a broader resource enhancement network. The patterns of life in this agricultural delta were controlled by the white population, and the financial credit, supplies, equipment, and marketing for African American farmers was controlled by white businessmen. A few of these farmers formed a cooperative to buy supplies at lower rates and used their savings to obtain a warehouse for storing supplies and harvests and marketing their harvests cooperatively. Their profits enabled them to provide better lives for themselves and their families. The cooperative also organized politically to change public policies and ensure more equitable treatment for African Americans and a more equitable distribution of public resources (Washington Consulting Group, 1974).

The *Homemakers Organized for More Employment, Orland, Maine* formed a resource network among heterogeneous groups and individuals to enhance the quality of life in their impoverished community. Roman Catholic nuns had established a hermitage there and sustained themselves doing cottage industry work for a factory. When the factory closed, they formed a cooperative so that they and their neighbors could earn a living and improve the quality of life for both by selling goods in a nearby tourist area. Their most marketable products were home crafts, and since not everyone had craft skills, they taught each other. The cooperative rejuvenated the quality of the members' lives, their community, and their sense of community (Washington Consulting Group, 1974).

Both of these networks brought a variety of benefits to their participants and their communities, including improved health care and reduced life stresses. They differed in that one involved a homogeneous, economically and socially oppressed, socioracial group; the other, a heterogenous, economically depressed community. Both built on people's resourcefulness and willingness to cooperate for their collective and individual benefit.

Health-Related Self-Help Groups

Self-help and service groups have been formed to improve the health and health care situations of their members or the people they serve. A core resource enhancement characteristic in such groups is Reissman's (1965) "helper-therapy" principle. As Gartner and Reissman (1977) documented, one of the best ways to learn is to teach, and helpers learn as much or more than those they help. The following programs embody that and other resource enhancement principles. They also show that formal and informal organizations can interact in mutually enhancing ways.

The *Boston Self-Help Center* was organized by people dissatisfied with the services available to those with chronic diseases or handicaps, such as diabetes and paraplegia. They set out to provide appropriate resources ranging from counseling to advocacy to social contacts. First, they successfully completed a workshop entitled "Living with Chronic Disease and Handicap" that was restricted to individuals, including the workshop facilitators, who had a chronic disease or a handicap. Subsequently, a trained and experienced core group formed a nonprofit cooperative center staffed with volunteers who were handicapped or had chronic diseases. The center's activities included (a) assisting individuals referred to them; (b) serving as consultants to agencies and institutions whose responsibilities and services required sensitivity to the needs of people with chronic diseases or handicaps; and (c) consultation with similar groups in other cities and encouraging them to form cooperative self-help groups. They improved their own quality of life and that of those they served, and they increased their sense of community, a sense that they passed on by encouraging others to form self-help groups (Sarason & Lorentz, 1979).

A school administrator in New York state established a program which involved students in *a community services program*. He believed that children aged 11 to 13 could learn about their community by participating in meaningful projects, and he worked out a cooperative arrangement for the students to spend one hour each week in a nursing home. The children got acquainted with the elderly residents, helped with their care, and got involved in their lives. Some of the elderly objected and were unkind, and some of the students had to face the death of residents with whom they had become friends. The students gained from learning to handle these rebuffs and sorrows, from assuming meaningful responsibilities in caring for someone else, and from reporting back to their classmates and teachers.

The teachers reported that they were learning more creative ways to teach and a surprising amount about the resourcefulness and capabilities of the students. This modest cooperative program improved the quality of life of those involved. It also spawned a complex resource enhancing community network that included a commons-type integration of the schools and social agencies (Sarason & Lorentz, 1979).

Daphne Krause (1975, 1978), a social worker, wanted to improve the services provided for the city's elderly, an effort that led to forming the *Minneapolis Age and Opportunity Center*. She tried to work out patterns of coordination among existing programs and persuade their staffs to implement them, but met unyielding resistance. Agencies insisted on protecting their integrity and programs, and she had no funds to implement coordinating activities. She shifted to a different approach, taking on the role of a leader/coordinator to establish a resource exchange network and developed an association of partners from local agencies and groups working with aging people. They analyzed the individual objectives and concerns of each agency or group and designed mutually beneficial programs.

Once this consortium was formed, Krause took steps to strengthen the network and improve the services for the aged. She formed a nonprofit agency and assigned the responsibility for its coordinating activities and service programs to its policy board composed predominantly of elderly leaders of senior citizen organizations. Program and coordinating activities were planned carefully to make efforts more cost effective and humanly effective by involving the elderly people. Federal support funds were obtained for needed services that existing agencies could not give. The consortium's primary role was to counsel agency personnel, but it also invited and encouraged the formation of self-help programs among the elderly and volunteer programs to work with them. Although it grew to employ 175 people, it retained its network format and helped other organizations develop and sustain similar networks.

In *A Collaborative Group Counseling Program*, my university colleagues and I worked with a large suburban high school system near Washington, D.C., to evaluate its group counseling program and assist in using it to expedite the court ordered socioracial integration of its high schools. We formed a resource exchange network, jointly verified the effectiveness of the counseling program, documented the psychosocial competence changes in the counselees, and provided feedback to the counselors about factors to emphasize to enhance their counseling effectiveness (F. Tyler & Gatz, 1977; F. Tyler & Pargament, 1981; F. Tyler, Pargament, & Gatz, 1983). To evaluate the resource collaborative approach, our university and school participants independently rated whether the project had operated in a resource collaborative manner. Neither group felt exploited, and members of both felt that they were treated as active agent individuals and contributors to the project. The program accomplished its goal of building on everyone's strengths and creating a collaborative network that benefitted everyone involved (F. Tyler, Pargament, & Gatz, 1983).

In sum, these programs illustrate the power that resource enhancement approaches have to generate more effective care than can be attained from formal, institutionally controlled programs. They engaged the participants as active agents in ways that enriched the care they provided as well as their own lives. The programs that involved broad community participation demonstrated their potential for generating a spread of effect.

Resource Enhancement Approaches to Other Social Issues

The major impetus in the United States to build resource enhancement approaches came from the social change and community psychology movements of the 1960s. Subsequently, there was a societal shift to a more conservative orientation, but these approaches were continued and spread to other parts of the world. The following examples illustrate the nature of their contributions to human relationships.

Wolff (1994) and his colleagues developed a model for communities to address their quality of life issues and participated in creating ten successful *community coalitions*

> in many of the poorest communities across Massachusetts. These coalitions: 1) increase local planning capacities, 2) develop specific problem solving mechanisms for addressing community-identified problems, 3) increase information available to communities, and 4) build advocacy capacities within those communities. Membership in the coalitions is open to all and in practice includes ... [a range of community organizations and influential people] and increasingly, neighborhood organizations and citizens.... Coalitions allow communities to set collective priorities, and create a unified voice. We [don't enter communities and tell them they have a problem and should build a coalition]. We say, "tell us what your issues are and our job is going to be to try and help you solve them no matter what they are." (p. 22f)

They focused on bringing together each community to function more collaboratively and its helping systems to function more competently. Their efforts required a coordinated, holistic, planned, accessible, collaborative, preventive, comprehensive, and culturally relevant approach. The coalitions varied from community to community and included efforts such as working with a community to design and establish a preventively oriented homeless program and working with a community's health care system to develop an interpreter program to reduce linguistic barriers to health care access.

Resource enhancement approaches may also prove more useful than equity oriented, mutual resource exchange gains for resolving conflicts between groups. However, mediating such interchanges can confront professionals with issues they don't always face when adopting *participant–conceptualizer* roles. In Australia, Bishop and Syme (1992) were invited to determine what a small rural community's "aims should be by the end of the century in the face of imminent social change" (p. 94). Community concerns included the environment, economy, society, arts, and culture. The community not only had a sense of cohesion and common purpose, it was also diverse and beset by social conflicts embedded in the varied perspectives and interests of its individual members and differing groups. These community psychologists expected to simply develop a data base outlining the community's resources and needs, then formulate recommendations and provide them to the community in workshops.

However, because the reports were to have an impact on the community, individuals and groups seeking to defend and advance their own positions and agendas asked about the roles and values of the consultants. These questions and interviews of a wide range of community members brought to the fore that the psychologists, too, had underlying values, including vested interests in the desirability of certain societal arrangements. They had to become involved as conceptualizers in defining the nature of conflicting views, including their own, and possible alternative outcomes. Thus, Bishop and Syme (1992) took on the role of participant–conceptualizers in shaping the future of the community and necessarily included themselves as participants.

They accepted that they were legitimately subject to challenge and attack and took several actions to ensure that their recommendations would be given consideration. They made explicit their own values and criteria regarding the characteristics of a healthy community. Those values included their belief in (a) the merits of a resilient community designed to tolerate and value diversity of opinions and conflict, (b) community participation and a commitment to informing and empowering everyone, (c) open decision of issues by agreed-upon fairness procedures, and (d) a shared sense of the fairness of the outcomes (distributive justice) such that they protected the least well-off and maximized the equal liberty of everyone (Bishop & Syme, 1992).

Bishop & Syme (1992) also acted in ways that were consistent with and exemplified these principles by being open, accepting risks including conflict and attacks on themselves, and modifying their approach as the ongoing process indicated rather than sticking to a preconceived methodology. Further, considering themselves too involved to directly measure the efficacy of their own efforts, they conceptualized and implemented a research process that was consistent with their values. It included depending to some extent on the perspectives of others and additional indirect indicators of the merits of community changes. Positive indicators included that they were asked to help structure a new, environmentally oriented group in the community, that the town council was beginning to own the project report and work with it, and that the public had begun responding to it. They had become part of the community's history and their impact could be evaluated indirectly simply by examining public records.

Bishop and Syme's overall evaluation of their efficacy was admittedly incomplete. They believed that evidence of the way the community came to manage such issues as conflict and competing demands were more appropriate criteria for judging the value of their efforts than would be defining an optimal solution for the community. For example, in their view, indications of the community's increasing resource enhancement orientation would need evidence that the community members behaved toward each other in more prosocial ways, had a more positive sense of community and community cohesion, handled conflicts and community issues more productively, and increased their proportion of resource enhancing interactions. That information could only be gathered over time.

Community psychology resource exchange models can also be used to maintain *public order* and reduce the destructiveness of predominantly violent antisocial public events by reordering them so that they become prosocial and collaborative. Veno and Veno (1992) consulted with public authorities to control the violence at an Australian Motorcycle Grand Prix, an annual event that had been characterized by violence, particularly between spectators and police. They based their approach on their belief that the development and implementation of an appropriate public order policy was essential for long-term solutions, that consensus was the most desirable form of conflict resolution, and that shaping situational factors to promote peace rather than conflict was essential.

Veno and Veno (1992) monitored several race gatherings, explored the dynamics of the event patterns, and worked out a violence prevention strategy. Its major components included enhancing the status of the event, working with the police to get them to approach the bikers, spectators, and residents as they would any socially acceptable group (not as hostile, antisocial groups), and developing a collaborative approach with the bikers' groups to self-police their members and activities. Operators of camping areas and alcohol vendors were required to take responsibility for health and public order in their facilities. Organized efforts were made to prevent media representatives from creating confrontations or sensationalizing antisocial occurrences. Follow up evaluations indicated that instead of the event being fueled by divisive antiauthoritarian and oppressive authoritarian orientations and clashes, it was fueled by and yielded positive resource enhancement exchanges. The strategy resulted in bikers, spectators, residents, and police acting better toward each other. They seemed to feel better about themselves and each other, and everyone got more enjoyment from the Grand Prix.

The relevance of collaborative resource enhancing alternatives is not limited to health care or educational endeavors. They also provide a basis for solutions to the societal problems of economic and ethnic inequities and violence. The diversity of these community projects suggests that collaborative resource enhancement projects offer productive approaches to a full range of community, ethnic, and other social problems.

PATTERNS OF INTERACTION AND THE PROCESSES OF PERSONAL AND SOCIAL CHANGE

This chapter has described a range of perspectives about our patterns of interaction with particular attention to the necessarily interrelated processes of personal and social change. These processes contribute not only to changing our personal lives, but also our relationships with each other, our communities, and our societies. The role of psychologists in studying them and using the findings to influence people is complex because these same psychologists have a critical role in defining how we understand ourselves and others and how we make individual, relational, and social changes.

The assumption that psychologists can stay detached and avoid influences from their personal backgrounds and life views has been challenged in the past half century. The position more generally held currently is that we all inevitably influence our interactions in a variety of ways, but we can use scientifically and professionally based approaches to help us identify and minimize the effects of our personal biases. Asking questions in a way that permits respondents to identify our biases is an important factor which contributes to contextual variations in research findings. Our patterns of interaction and the dynamics of change can be explored as contextually embedded processes only if we consider that possibility. Further, studying and evaluating these processes rests, in part, on the cultural embeddedness of the evaluators and their acknowledgment of that embeddness.

ETHNIC VALIDITY AND RESOURCE INTERACTIONS

The concepts of ethnic validity (F. Tyler, Brome, & Williams, 1991) and resource collaboration (F. Tyler, Pargament, & Gatz, 1983) provide a framework for incorporating and evaluating our active agent capabilities and contextual embeddedness. My colleagues and I outlined why psychologists and other professionals need to use a resource collaboration approach. We emphasized that any interaction between people is characterized by an interchange in which all participants are contributors and all are beneficiaries. That is, professionals must see themselves as necessarily participating in ways that include their personal as well as their professional natures and commitments, their ethnic validity orientation.

Only if we allow for the possibility of a variety of self–other orientations and interactions can we understand such exchanges and formulate new approaches to them. For example, psychotherapy data for the United States shows that therapists who are effective across ethnic/racial barriers are themselves more experienced, democratic, comfortable, flexible, able to use appropriate strategies, and accepting of ethnic diversity (F. Tyler, Brome, & Williams, 1991). Thus, there is empirical support for respecting diversity and valuing an ethnic validity conception of people's interactions. Valuing diversity and ethnic validity perspectives is also supported empirically by evidence cited earlier regarding the concepts of psychosocial leaps and spirals, spirals of development, and active agentry.

A significant contextual factor in shaping these differing interaction patterns is that of culture. Utilitarian societies promote patterns of interactions that enable antisocial aggressiveness to contribute to survival competence. In contrast, in humanistic societies prosocial collaboration contributes to survival competence. Western-oriented psychologists have incorporated aspects of both perspectives, but in a convoluted way as can be seen from how they have dealt with help-seeking and helping.

A review of books and book chapters identified in the American Psychological Association's Psychlit computer file for the period of January 1987 to March 1995 yielded 1197 entries for helping and only 56 for help-seeking. Helping behavior was considered a socially supported, psychosocially competent activity. In contrast, of the 56 studies that focused on help-seeking, only 20 (37%) considered it a normal or constructive behavior rather than an indicator of pathology or other deficiency. In experimental personality and social psychology, help-seeking has been studied as a threat to self-esteem. This review reveals the contradiction that is conveyed by Western psychologists about their services. They encourage people to seek help and demonstrate that their services are valuable, yet they consider help-seeking and those who seek help as being deficient rather than resourceful individuals taking a constructive approach to solving problems or gaining more mastery over their lives and situations.

Such findings show that isolating our studies from their cultural and other contexts perpetuates built in biases. They also suggest that contextually based collaborative patterns of interchange are likely to be most effective for producing constructive interactions and change among individuals or groups, including interactions between professionals and those they are serving. It is only through such openness that the possibilities of mutual resource enhancement can be realized. The characteristics of successful resource exchange networks point to important guidelines for constructive individual and group interactions and social change processes.

THE QUALITIES AND IMPLICATIONS OF SUCCESSFUL RESOURCE EXCHANGE NETWORKS

Many human relationships are characterized by voluntary participation based on a shared conviction that the relationship is important and that those involved are gaining from it mutually, want to continue to invest in it, and expect it to grow and change but still be engaging and rewarding. Even so, people in societies that are individualistic or utilitarian, or both, do not readily assume that these important characteristics may be missing in people, relationships, and communities that are beset by problems. As Ryan (1971) underscored, people in individualistic societies often blame those with problems for not being sufficiently individualistic or utilitarian, or both. Yet resource exchange and enhancement networks provide solid evidence that their ingredients contribute powerfully to the effectiveness of people's functioning. Network participants conduct themselves as resource enhancement oriented individuals who integrate personal, interpersonal, and task oriented skills along with intrinsic and extrinsic motivation considerations and who bridge the differences between formal and informal organizations. They also build patterns of activities that are self-sustaining, beneficial to the participants, and often spur the development of their relationships and their community.

Social change networks range in complexity from self-help groups to broad societal development efforts that include complex relationships among and between professionals and nonprofessionals and their respective formal and informal organizations. Whatever the scope and composition of successful groups, they share important collaborative characteristics. All are participant controlled and contain a small core of leader/initiator/coordinators who are embedded in a variety of community networks. The participants successfully redefine themselves as resourceful experts providing assistance to those who need it and as active agent resource collaborators rather than as supplicants in search of assistance to meet their needs.

Coordination and leadership are important to the success of any complex undertaking, including networking. Further, since there will never be enough resources to meet all human needs, networks emphasize mobilization of our often untapped capabilities and require us to find ways to combine and interchange those capabilities as a way to gain mutually. The leadership of networks is focused on arranging and facilitating such exchanges and developing and sustaining people's investments in the network. Control of policies and program directions remains with the people who are participating. Their uniqueness lies in the sense of involvement, well-being, and community that they engender—characteristics that are a significant part of any network's goals and an element in enriched lives and communities.

This leadership emphasis on redressing systemic imbalances and enriching everyone's quality of life is relevant to changing social systems, including communities, as some of the recent work of community oriented psychologists has shown. Wolff (1994) emphasized that healthy communities have two components, a competent helping system and an empowered citizenry. Using a somewhat larger frame of reference, Hancock, who participated in the World Health Organization's efforts to define the characteristics of healthy cities, stated that they require as prerequisites "a just, equitable society, a sustainable ecological system, peace, shelter, food, education, and income" (Wolff, 1994, p. 21). These characteristics are also requirements for creating successful resource exchange networks that will sustain healthy people, relationships, communities, and societies.

Networks continually change and evolve as do people's roles in them. Yet they cannot be directionless, planless, or poorly managed. Network participants plan, manage, and proceed with information derived on an ongoing basis from each other's active involvement. In that way, they tap into and constructively mobilize the resources of people, successfully challenging the professional assumption that resourcefulness lies only in themselves. Further, they provide evidence that the effectiveness of social change agents is related to their commitment to the people and the changes they work to promote. Socially oriented programs or changes that ignore the worth and dignity of the individuals in them are, in the long run, destructive of their own goals.

SUMMARY

This chapter has presented and evaluated resource exchange and resource enhancement as models of prosocial interaction which lead to various benefits, including individual and social change. Resource exchange conceptions have focused on the assumption that the goal in interpersonal interactions is to maintain fairness of exchange as judged by two types of criteria, equity and equality. Equity exchanges are considered fair if the parties involved receive returns of equivalent value. Equality exchanges are considered fair if parties receive returns equivalent to their needs rather than their contribution. In either case, the underlying assumption is that the interchange neither adds to nor detracts from the available resources.

Much of the research in support of equity interchanges has been produced by experimental social psychologists studying short-term interactions between strangers. This limited formulation led to the possibility that interchanges can involve more than an exchange of resources. Interactions between individuals in intimate or other long-term relationships suggested the idea that people respond to each other's needs and do not just exchange comparable resources. These studies have also found that the resources can be increased to provide mutual resource enhancement for all concerned.

Rotter (1954) introduced the idea that the psychosocial aspects of human motives can override their biological aspects. He proposed that psychosocial motives, such as affection, can function in a need induction manner. That is, need satisfaction increases the desire for that resource and satisfaction from it, though not necessarily in an equity-based fashion. Additional ideas introduced by Rotter have included that people may differ in their capabilities to experience and exchange love and intimacy and that there are several types of social exchange involving different patterns of resource interaction.

There is a tremendous range of human interrelationships and social change perspectives in any society and between societies. Societies vary in the adequacy and nature of their resources and in experience and sophistication in reconciling and coordinating different perspectives and programs to maintain the character of the society itself. Yet the issues seem remarkably similar across contexts. Approaches to change are counterproductive when experts, or powerful social agents, or both, seek to define and manage change without the involvement of the relevant people. The same is true when individual and social inequities are blamed on those who are less powerful. In contrast, participatory collaborative endeavors provide a much more productive base for improving people's life quality and even enhancing the resources available in any given context.

The most basic implication of the change efforts described in this chapter is that social and individual changes must occur together. Constructive change does not occur without both individual and collective involvement, including shared knowledge, compassion, and collaboration. Perhaps the most valuable contribution that we social, behavioral, and mental health specialists can make toward creating better societies and better lives for individuals is to base our efforts on that awareness. However, we must remember that the process of change takes different forms in different contexts. In the highly individualistic and participatory society of the United States, there are programs that have successfully respected individual autonomy and nourished a commitment to collective well-being among its people.

We have evidence that people value personal relationships (including love) over less particularistic ones, that they do not believe that all exchanges need to be balanced, and that participation in activities for intrinsic satisfaction can be enhancing. To build on this growing body of evidence requires a number of fundamental psychosocial changes. These changes include formulating a sophisticated understanding of communities that embodies their crucial elements (communality, identity, sharedness, and interlinking), all of which incorporate interpersonal relationship components. We need a comprehensive formulation of the interplay between individual and community processes, one that views them as intertwined.

We cannot justify a continued view of communities as exclusively external arenas for action and individual's internal processes as the exclusive causes of psychological processes and conduct. Continuing to believe that everyone is or wants to be like us is unsupportable and destructive. We must accept that everyone's growth begins with the possibilities that their lives, communities, and cultures have provided for them. We are all active agents with choices about constructing our lives and societies. Building on these considerations does not require rejecting our autonomy or our belongingness; it requires integrating them within a broader ethnic validity based active agent context.

A TRANSITION

At this point, there is a shift in focus. Because Parts 3 through 5 consider how psychology, psychologists, and other change agents can impact the lives of others, I want to give emphasis to a particular lesson from the earlier sections. That is, we are better served when we think of ourselves as interacting *with* others, not acting *on* them. They, too, are knowers. So, as the following quotes highlight, they see and hear what we mean as wewll as what we say.

> I am on a man's back, choking him and making him carry me, and yet assure myself and others that I am very sorry for him and wish to ease his lot by all possible means—except by getting off his back
>
> LEO TOLSTOY, as cited in *The Oxford Dictionary of Quotations* (3rd ed.) (1979)

Comments Overheard

"I have a number of occasions everyday to be reminded that I am a black man." A gentle and compassionate African American counselor at a U.S. university.

"Seems like they'd sooner t' hurt you than to he'p you." An unlettered maintenance man watching an arrogant U.S. park ranger order campers around.

"Other people only hear what I say, you hear when I mean." An inarticulate client who often felt misunderstood.

REPRESENTATIVE AREAS AND TOPICS

The arguments presented so far lead to an important conclusion about the issues of individual and social change. That is, in order *to contribute to the well-being of individuals and their societies, it is important to study significant human issues, and study them in life contexts.* Only by doing so can the complex interrelations among individual and social change patterns be identified. In Part III, four representative areas are addressed including (a) the role of *belief systems,* (b) our ways of understanding and utilizing the differentiations we make about *pathology* and *competence,* (c) *status* in its many forms, and (d) the role of *violence* and our ways of expressing and controlling it individually and societally. These areas are important for the information they convey about a few select, significant human issues; they also serve as exemplars of the significance of this approach. I include them because they are significant issues in the lives of most people. They are also particularly illustrative of the role that individuals play in large-scale social change and the role of patterns of social organization or change in the lives of individuals.

CHAPTER 9

BELIEF SYSTEMS

INTRODUCTION

Belief systems are important to study because our psychosocial being is embedded in our beliefs. They influence how we think, feel, and act in everyday life and in controlled experimental contexts. All people are psychosocial, self-aware, and busy abstracting meanings from their on-going lives, from the available records of past lives and civilizations, and from imagined alternative futures. We become knowers, continually re-constructing our understanding of our circumstances to guide us. Beliefs are starting points or first principles, are never fully specified, and are seldom scrutinized. They underlie the general paradigms which influence our thoughts, feelings, and conduct. Only as we understand them can we understand ourselves and the nature of our knowledge and use both as we intend.

This chapter considers how we form belief systems, how they influence our behavior, how they can inform each other, and how our understanding of them can serve prosocial purposes. Explorations of the nature of and interactions between common sense, scientific, and religious beliefs and the impact they have on each other and on each of us illustrate these points. A transcultural ethnic validity model is presented as a belief system which bridges these different systems to enhance our lives and societies.

FRAMING THE PROBLEM

Belief systems influence, are influenced by, and provide explanations for our conduct. They answer philosophical questions about the nature of reality, about the existence of deities, about the purpose of human existence, and about our nature as humans. The phenomena that they address and the appeals made to justify them differ greatly. Each contains conflicting premises, procedures, criteria, and judgments about topics relevant to our conduct, leaving us to manage as best we can.

We need to resolve these conflicts for three major reasons. One, holding incompatible beliefs leads to conflicts within us that may have destructive psychosocial consequences. Two, our actions influence our own and others' conduct and judgments and the nature of the communities and societies we are constructing. The conflicts that belief systems create within and between us must be understood before any psychological understanding of our internal and interpersonal conduct can be complete. Three, the information available is predominantly from studies within the United States and is focused almost exclusively on Judeo–Christian beliefs. It is not informed by and does not provide a basis for evaluating their cultural embeddedness or their strengths and limitations from other perspectives. Nor does it provide a basis for generalizing to or from other cultures or religious belief systems. Rather, these topics have been largely ignored as an area for psychologists' investigation.

THE CORE ISSUES

Our understanding and prosocial use of these belief systems rests on our knowledge about how our decisions, common sense beliefs, and specialized knowledge influence each other. That understanding begins with consideration of the nature of common sense and its relationship to specialized knowledge systems. Common sense functions in the same way an individual's first language does in relation to subsequently acquired languages. Specialized belief systems, such as those of religion, science, the professions, the humanities, and the arts, are also based on common sense, our first knowledge system. Their designated experts may possess specialized knowledge, but they and that knowledge all rely on common sense.

COMMON SENSE

WHAT COMMON SENSE IS

On its surface, common sense seems to have more self-evident and less specialized content than do formalized belief systems, but the situation is not as simple as it seems. Fletcher (1984) argued that "common sense may fruitfully be conceptualized as a form of psychological theory" (p. 212). However, he also argued that it is impossible to construct a psychological theory without relying on common sense beliefs. They are essential to cultural, philosophical, religious, and other belief systems.

To the philosopher Forguson (1989), common sense straddles philosophy and psychology and "the individual members of our species would not get along as successfully as they do on this earth if their common-sense beliefs about the world, and about why people act as they do, were not for the most part true" (p. iv). He described common sense as being a network of interconnected beliefs, or *common-sense realism*, that we create out of our commitment to the belief that we are predominantly rational beings. It is manifest in our behavior and used to justify our claims about facts and defend our actions.

Forguson (1989) based his concepts of a rational psychology and a common sense realism on psychological research. He believed that adults who rely on these beliefs are more successful in their interactions with the world than are young children who do not have them. As children grow to adulthood, they change in ways that are consistent with their having the characteristics of "rational psychologists." They become adults who assess their desires and use their knowledge of the world to behave in socially approved, organized ways.

Common Sense as Shared Self-evident Truths

In 1776, the Declaration of Independence (United States, 1995) tied the notion of common sense to that of First Principles about the nature of people and their societies, by stating "we hold these truths to be self-evident." Its authors endorsed the idea that people are capable of reason and judgment and that there are certain universal conclusions, or truths, which would inevitably be arrived at by all rational people. Such truths, they argued, require no further justification.

More recently, there has been a growing tendency to challenge the universality of the unquestioned givens of particular cultures, of Forguson's (1989) conception of "the common-sense view being true in its most fundamental features" (p. 3). That is, we increasingly find ourselves asking "what are the underlying common sense assumptions of different cultural groups?" Consequently, we are faced with addressing the relative truth statuses of different common sense beliefs and how they relate to each other. How do we decide which is more true when faced with incompatible common sense "truths" such as "everything comes out alright in the end" and "life isn't fair"?

The Pluralism of Common Sense

While cultural, scientific, philosophical, and religious belief systems may each be based on common sense, they are based on at least partially *different* common senses. We need a set of agreements to reconcile the disparities in these systems, i.e., a meta common sense system. We may use scientific or religious systems to understand the nature of common sense; however, that is, in part, a bootstraps operation because these special systems, like others, are embedded in common sense. Their critiques of common sense can make a difference only if they are consistent with people's common sense or if their adherents can provide a persuasive case for making changes to override existing common sense. To do so, advocates of the specialized knowledge systems must be persuasive that their views improve on common sense.

Common sense psychosocial truths function as true, as do physical truths, because they are not so untrue as to be destructive of their adherents or their societies. However, psychosocial truths are more subject to particular circumstances and permit of a wider range of acceptable resolutions. Ecologically, culturally, and ethnically different common senses are each true for the conditions in which they come to have consensual acceptance and contribute constructively to the functioning of the people involved. It can be just as true that parents and children eating together keep the family united as it is that parents and children eating separately keeps the family united. People of any generation and circumstances face making sense of their lives, relationships, and social conditions within the framework of these often incompatible beliefs that confront them.

COMMON SENSE AND SPECIALIZED KNOWLEDGE SYSTEMS

The relationships between everyday functioning and specialized knowledge based functioning have been scrutinized innumerable times without considering that their relationship is reciprocal and of a psychosocial nature. Specialists have not considered that common sense systems are compatible with specialized knowledge systems and contribute to them, as well as benefit from them. For centuries, people have worked out ways of selecting beliefs from many belief systems and combining them to better manage their lives. This psychosocial character of belief systems, including common sense, is a necessary consequence of their integrative and holistic natures. This point was stressed not only by Forguson (1989), but also by Kuhn (1970) and Polanyi (1968) in their analyses of how scientific knowledge is formulated. It is briefly reviewed here and integrated in a new way.

The Contexts of Discovery and Verification

As discussed in Chapter 2, philosophers of science advanced the idea that the *personal equation* is a core element in all observations, the process that occurs in the *context of discovery*. Observations are humanly constructed and limited accordingly. The same is true of the process of verification, of establishing the empirical validity of observations. At all stages, knowledge has its own personal equation; it is embedded in the psychosocial context of human activity.

Messick developed and analyzed psychologists' approaches to assessment, emphasizing that judgment underlies decisions about whether observations are valid. Validity is "an overall evaluative judgment of the degree to which empirical evidence and theoretical rationales support the adequacy and appropriateness of interpretations and actions on the basis of test scores or other modes of assessment" (1995, p. 741). Assessments are efforts to get evidence about whether a current decision is valid, that is, will accomplish its desired goal (its criterion) in an unbiased fashion. They involve a number of factors which are, to some irreducible extent, dependent on each other and incorporate values underlying the judgment that we wish to verify, disconfirm, or influence, such as a selection process. That is, as Messick stressed, assigning meanings to our observations and verifying our judgments about them rests on our individual decisions. The holistic framework that provides the background for these decisions is embedded in our ethnic validity based common sense and our psychosocially constructed natures. It cannot be otherwise.

Social Dimensions

It may seem that the *personal equation* aspects of discovery and verification may indeed be personal and not influenced by social factors. Examination makes it clear that any judgment is inherently both personal and social. Geertz (1983) argued from an anthropological perspective that *common sense* is a constructed picture of reality based on both the individual judgments of those involved and their social/historical context. Specifically, he argued that

> if common sense is as much an interpretation of the immediacies of experience, a gloss of them, as are myth, painting, epistemology, or whatever, then it is, like them, historically constructed and, like them, subjected to historically defined standards of judgment.... It is, in short, a cultural system, though not usually a very tightly integrated one, and it rests on the same basis that any other such system rests; the conviction by those whose possession it is of its value and validity. (Geertz, 1983, p. 76)

He also maintained that no common sense system accounts for all exigencies; people must also account for the phenomena that do not fit. They appeal to alternative systems or a category that might be called "that's all there is to it." Common sense is not spontaneously apprehended truth without preconceptions. It is conclusions made by a mind filled with un-acknowledged presuppositions.

Formal cultural systems can be described directly because their pre-suppositions have been made explicit. Common sense systems must be approached indirectly by calling attention to their tone and temper be-cause they are largely embedded in what scientists call "tacit knowing" and others call "intuition." Understanding the nature of common sense as tacit knowing is essential to understanding presumably specialized sys-tems such as science and religion; it also helps us understand how com-mon sense can serve as a formal knowledge system.

Each of us lives in a self-constructed cocoon built within the individu-ally and socially intertwined contexts of our lives. Our social cognitive capacities enable us to understand and interact meaningfully with others and to abstract the idea that they, too, have minds, identities, and unique perspectives. These processes are essential to making us psychosocial individuals. By accepting that the verbally and nonverbally demonstrated views of others about themselves, about us, and about the world are as valid as our own, we can know that our own knowing is unique, that we and others have within us our own personal equations. The capacity to imagine that others have the same creative powers as we do also allows us to believe that there are other kinds of creatures, such as spirits or deities, who may have created us or who manage our lives. These capacities to formulate an organized sense of our existence and its nature also enable us to move beyond a tacit, unexamined common sense to an abstracted and structured formal system of common sense.

COMMON SENSE AS A FORMAL SYSTEM

An abstracted common sense is a complex explanatory system in its own right. These systems in different cultures necessarily have distinctive internal logics and anchors to external referents. Although common sense systems may be considered mutually exclusive, they can inform and be informed by each other and by other formal systems. We can interpret them and draw conclusions to guide our understanding of our origins, natures, and processes of change.

Geertz (1983) noted that an informal common sense system is fairly loose and incomplete relative to the more specialized formal systems it underlies. However, even science has gaps, so it cannot account for all of the phenomena that people rely on to make their lives and circumstances understandable. Only religious systems assert that they are complete in and of themselves. However, before considering the commonalities and differences of these belief systems, it is helpful to provide a fuller characterization of *common sense* as a formal system.

Geertz' thesis was that common sense is

> a frame for thought, and as a species of it, common sense is as totalizing as any other: no religion is more dogmatic, no science more ambitious, no philosophy more general.... Like them ... it pretends to reach past illusion to truth, to, as we say, things as they are. (1983, p. 84)

Common sense is the cumulative "truth claims of collective reason" (Geertz, 1983, p. 77) and includes two aspects of experience which do not require or permit a further accounting: in effect, it says, *"That's all there is to it."* We commonly dismiss a topic by denying that it can be explained further. Doing so may render an imperfect life more tolerable. However, it also inhibits efforts to make phenomena more understandable and manageable by looking for explanations to improve our existing framework.

Extra-Natural Forces

Common sense, as science, also cannot account for events thought to occur outside the realm of what is considered natural. These events are made acceptable by appealing to explanations created to account for forces whose properties cannot be humanly understood. Such explanations may also prohibit or restrict attempts to use natural (empirical) means to understand these phenomena or to challenge the proposed explanation. Systems of superstitious beliefs, magical thinking, etc., fill these functions. They may also be precursors to more formally organized religious belief systems that serve the same functions and are assigned higher status in societies.

SCIENCE AS A BELIEF SYSTEM

Scientists have taken the position that science is an alternative to belief systems because its methods are publicly observable and its proposals are subject to disconfirmation by appeal to its explicit, generally accessible approaches. The position here is that the sciences are a particular kind of belief system. Because of its scientific nature and its focus on people and the contextual influences in their lives, psychology is particularly well suited to be our example for exploring the nature and role of scientific belief systems. First, we need to examine psychology's strengths and limits as a belief system.

Bishop (1996), in a discussion of the crisis of contemporary science, focused on the physical sciences. However, his reasoning has relevance for the behavioral and social sciences as can be seen in the following quotation:

> Science, of course, is not the exclusive source of knowledge about human existence. Literature, art, philosophy, history, and religion all have their insights to offer into the human condition. To deny that is scientism—the belief that the methods of the natural sciences are the only means of obtaining knowledge. And to the extent that scientists have at times indulged in that belief, they must shoulder some of the blame for the misapprehensions that some people have about science. (Bishop, 1996, p. 19)

In Bishop's view, science's approach offers "moral conflict and ambiguous choice," but "to reject science is to deny the future" (1995, p. 35). To him, science is a great adventure to learn about human existence; it must be continued if we are to understand the world because it is the best way of finding out how the world works. Consistently with the ambiguous nature of scientific information, he also argued that scientists do not even understand each other and that it is difficult to make science intelligible to nonscientists. Unfortunately, his only suggestion for solving this dilemma was for scientists to take on the task of selling science, a solution that would only address people's misunderstanding of it.

A more important task is to clarify that science's methods can resolve issues of empirical consequences; they cannot resolve hypothetical realities or free their enterprise from untestable assumptions and value choices. Science cannot resolve whether we have choice or merely have the illusion of choice, or whether we have lives before or after our current one or both; it can determine whether people's beliefs about these matters makes a difference. Acknowledgment of these strengths and limitations provides a defensible position for scientists and others to conduct a common dialogue about each other's contributions rather than rejecting them arbitrarily.

THE INTERRELATEDNESS OF SCIENCE WITH CULTURAL CONTEXTS AND RELIGIOUS BELIEF SYSTEMS

Individuals often order their lives on the basis of belief systems without examining those beliefs or their interrelationships. On the other hand, psychologists try to identify people's beliefs and their interrelationships in order to understand how personalities, interpersonal relationships, and social arrangements are formed and managed and, in turn, manage them. These psychological approaches and answers are also embedded in the cultural and scientific contexts that nurtured them; consequently, as illustrated in the following paragraphs, they too may reflect and impose underlying cultural biases. Those biases must also be identified to be challenged and modified for good or ill.

In a multicultural interdisciplinary seminar in India that examined the psychosocial relativity of identity, Kakar (1979) compared "the notions of ideal adulthood in two 'therapeutic' systems—Western psychoanalysis and the Hindu Yogic schools" (p. xiii). In his view, the psychoanalytic vision of life is tragic "insofar as it sees human experience pervaded by ambiguities, uncertainties and absurdities where man has little choice but to bear the burden of unanswerable questions, inescapable conflicts and incomprehensible afflictions of fate" (1979, p.127). This vision is also ironic in its fostering of a self-depreciating and detached perspective and a deliberative acceptance of this tragic state of affairs. The Yogic view also defines life as tragic since man is buffeted by fate's vagaries; but it is not ironic, it is romantic. Yoga emphasizes that "the seeker (*Sadhak*), if he withstands all the perils of the road, will be rewarded by an exaltation beyond his normal human experience" (Kakar, 1979, p. 127), presumably in this lifetime.

Kakar stressed that the aim of these formulations is to impose a meaning on human experience, *not* to discover absolute reality. Belief systems achieve that goal by combining the subjective and the objective. None of them answers whether life is tragic, ironic, or romantic without appealing to subjective beliefs. Further, these versions of ideal adulthood are, in part, incompatible. Introducing Yogic romanticism into Western culture or psychoanalytic resignation into Hindu culture would require changing the individuals involved and their respective social contexts. All that can be done empirically is to determine the consequences of organizing our lives and societies according to any particular beliefs.

Paranjpe (1984) built on his bicultural experience and education to examine the theoretical foundations of psychology in the different cultural traditions of India and the West, particularly their psychologies of personality and the relation between science and religion. He stressed that "most of the psychology in India today is another edition of Western psychology" (Paranjpe, 1984, p. 3) because most of its faculties were educated in the West. However, its historical writings and current thought support that there is an indigenous Indian psychology. It provides (a) a world view, (b) a theoretical analysis of the structures and processes relating to human personality, (c) a normative account of the nature of higher and lower levels of the functioning of personality, (d) techniques designed to help the not-so-well developed individual reach more desirable levels of development, and (e) social institutions within which the growth of personality can be facilitated.

Paranjpe (1984) emphasized that the psychologies of India and the West rest on different views of the relationship between science and religion. In the Judeo–Christian tradition, God is the exclusive active agent who created people in his own image. According to the Hindu view, gods and people are part of creation and the ebb and flow of life. These cultural/religious orientations differ also in their view of people's access to knowledge about the laws of nature. Hinduism provides no prohibitions against investigating them, but the history and current traditions of Christianity do.

The goals of psychology in these different cultural traditions also differ. In the classic tradition of psychology in India, priority is assigned to self-realization and coming to terms with one's internal nature. In the empirical tradition of Western psychology, emphasis is placed on prediction and control, usually of others and particularly of nature. However, it does include a clause about adapting to aspects of nature beyond our control capacities.

In brief, these conceptual psychological systems pertaining to life are intertwined with the cultural traditions and religious belief systems in which they were developed. As Paranjpe (1984) emphasized, psychology and religion encroach upon one another, and a compelling question for the future is how they will inform each other. A scientific approach can resolve the empirical consequences of acting on beliefs; it cannot resolve the presumed ultimate validity of those beliefs.

Just as religious belief systems may suppress scientific ones, scientific belief systems may suppress cultural ones. Dachler (1998) emphasized that the dominant Western orientation in organizational psychology toward a presumed objective, value-free representation of the structure and dynamics of work organizations is based on a culturally embedded individualist belief about how we function. The use of this orientation uncritically to study how work is organized in developing cultures ignores and masks or destroys their indigenous conceptions of work organizations. It also eliminates using these alternative conceptions of work reciprocally to offset limitations of the developed world's individualist work paradigm.

In brief, scientific endeavors influence and are influenced by common sense, cultural, and religious perspectives. A culturally based scientific tradition of "objective" reporting sustains that culture's status-quo biases. One that emphasizes activist involvement to promote particular societal goals (e.g., worker mental health versus productivity) emphasizes studying quite different questions concerning how endeavors are organized, including their priorities. Humanistically oriented societies may argue that mental health is more important than short term productivity or may promote long term studies that demonstrate whether these goals are mutually supportive. This kind of interplay between science and cultural belief systems impacts both those systems as well as the people involved.

SCIENCE AND COMMON SENSE

Bronowski (1966) argued that the world of science is a new culture, a world of organized knowledge, and an agent of change. He emphasized that he was talking about the mathematical sciences which involve three ideas (order, cause, and chance). He also stressed that every living action is an act of choice and directed towards the future. Science's actions inject new ideas into the familiar culture, alter people's values, and remake the base of the culture by subjecting it to the pressures of technical modification. According to Bronowski, the message of science is that our ideas must be human and they must create their own authority; that is, they must be realistic, flexible, and unbigoted. The predictions of science serve that purpose because they are not piecemeal; they come out of science's efforts to order events and to establish a system of laws, consequently

> if any ideas have a claim to be called creative, because they have liberated that creative impulse, it is the ideas of science.... This is not only a material code. On the contrary ... I believe that science can create values; and will create them precisely as literature does, by looking into the human personality; by discovering what divides it and what cements it.... The insight of science is not different from that of the arts....
>
> It is for us to use it to broaden and to liberate our culture. These are the marks of science: that it is open for all to hear, and all are free to speak their minds in it. They are marks of the world at its best, and the human spirit at its most challenging. (Bronowski, 1966, pp. 151–154)

Bronowski's substantial contribution to an integration of common sense and science within the broad cultural framework of Western society did not provide ways to relate his conception of science to nonscientific systems of scholarship (e.g., the arts and humanities or religions). Neither did he consider how to relate Western science to other cultures and the meanings their natural languages symbolize, or to our ways of understanding ourselves and other individuals. A scientific understanding of our natures as individuals, an "unlocking of personality" in a manner of speaking, requires acknowledgment that our personalities are psychosocial and involve interrelated unaware (that is, unsymbolized) and aware knowledge of the world, ourselves, and others.

For these tasks, we must use both indirect and direct approaches to analyze our individual psychosocial constructions along with the overarching sociocultural constructions in which they are nested. Khilstrom

(1995) pointed out that in psychological research major issues arise about what the participants are doing and what our relationships to them are as investigators. His analysis and conclusions capture in a concise way the nature of the human condition and our efforts to understand it. He focused on two central ecological validity issues for understanding and using experimental situation findings to increase our knowledge of ourselves. They were the relationship between experiments and participants and between experimental and ordinary life situations.

The questions that concerned Khilstrom address what the nature of the interaction between the experimenter and the subject/participant is. Are experimenters functioning as knowers, who are active agents with intentions, choices, etc., bent on learning something about the world that can be assigned to the category of objective knowledge? If so, does that imply that subjects/participants are functioning as knowns whose behavior and thoughts are determined outside of their awareness and subjective control of their conduct? He referred to the APA *Publication Manual*'s (1994) recommendation of substituting the word "participants" for "subjects" when writing about humans and concluded that doing so "may be politically correct but it is not psychologically correct" (Khilstrom, 1995, p. 7). Khilstrom reasoned that participants understand the situation to be an experiment and their role to be that of subjects, so they act accordingly. In other words, they are making a choice as knowers to act like they are knowns, unaware beings. He argued that they are subjects, but that it is not possible to distinguish completely between the knower (the active agent) and the known (the unaware being) aspects of the conduct of either. Strictly speaking then, they are participants/subjects; that is, they are participating in the role of subjects.

Khilstrom's (1995) second issue was whether experimental arrangements are *ecologically valid*, relevant to life outside that context. He argued that situations of life and laboratory are similar in the sense that "subjects aren't just motivated to guess and confirm the experimenter's hypothesis.... They are primarily motivated to make sense of any communicative situation in which they find themselves" (Khilstrom, 1995, p. 14). Experimenter and subject are involved in contributing as knowers and knowns in advancing knowledge. The question of ecological validity is relevant and requires assessment of the comparability between these two constructed situations.

Overall then, scientists can use their belief systems to critique and evaluate their own and others' positions, study how to utilize the strengths of these different approaches to build on their respective strengths, and add to our capabilities for managing our well-being in our lifetimes. There is no way that scientists can extricate themselves from the complex milieus of their lives, communities, cultures, and belief systems. Before exploring these possibilities further, it is important to examine religious belief systems within this same metaframework.

RELIGIONS AS BELIEF SYSTEMS

It is exceedingly difficult to list the core identifying elements of religious belief systems. Although there are some issues that differentiate them from common sense and scientific belief systems and that identify them as religious, religious adherents differ among themselves about those issues. Closest to being a core requirement is the conviction of each faction that, because they consider their belief system to be a general paradigm, it cannot be defended or challenged by ordinary human procedures and must be taken on faith. Each religious system presents itself as providing the true account of the nature of naturalistic and transcendent phenomena. The latter are extranormal in nature and include beliefs about the existence of deities, about the status of humans before and beyond their earthly life, about the nature of spiritual aspects of human experience, about absolute knowledge about good and evil, and about the ability of their adherents to judge the moral status of everyone's conduct. At times, these assumptions lead to social conflict when accompanied by the belief that adherents to that religion, or their designated representatives, have an absolute basis for imposing their beliefs on others and by force, if necessary.

Although supporters of religious belief systems differ widely in their particular beliefs, those differences are not of primary concern here. Of concern are the kinds of issues that religious systems pose for common sense, scientific, and other belief systems. The following paragraphs summarize three different positions taken by Western oriented scholars on religious belief systems, along with a fourth, contrasting, Buddhist perspective.

ILLUSTRATIVE RELIGIOUS PERSPECTIVES

The Human Spiritual Heritage

Bushrui (2000) considers religious belief systems to be manifestations of the human spiritual heritage. Each is seen as an imperfect revelation of the one universal, unified God, with one universal truth given to people (*not* constructed by them). However, in different cultural settings and historical times, this truth is expressed in the way that those people are capable of understanding and acting on it. For example, one belief that is part of this universal truth found in all of the world's major religions is the golden rule. This doctrine is that we should behave towards others as we would have them behave toward us. However, in some religious belief systems it is not stated as a positive doctrine, but as a negative one of not doing anything to others you would not want them to do to you.

Bushrui (2000) describes religion as being the core to our protection and welfare because components such as fear of God are crucial in compelling us to seek and follow good and turn away from evil. It includes an orientation that goes beyond individual interpersonal behavior to address religious differences and organize a prosocial human community. Consequently, religious commitment involves not just a change in interpersonal behavior, but a transcendent change in life focus and values from material self-centeredness to a spiritual reality-centered focus on God.

Although religious diversity presupposes differences among faiths, when such differences are taken as *symbolic*, not *literal*, they tend to lead to creative conflict. Religious history is symbolic, dynamic, and transcendent; seeing it as literal and static stems from human misunderstandings and leads to destructive conflicts. Further, in Bushrui's view certain beliefs are considered evidences of misunderstandings or misinterpretations of God; for example, the belief that any one religion's manifestation at any given point in time is the *final* word on any given issue.

Religion as Temporal Power

To Smart (1981), religion is important because of its temporal power for defining the origins and natures of the world, people, society, and morality, even though we cannot establish its ultimate truth by empirical means. He attempted "to bring certain insights drawn from the history of religions to bear on the task of framing a world view which synthesizes important ingredients both from East and West and from individual experience and secular politics" (Smart, 1981, p. 12) to illuminate the nonreligious ideologies of the modern world. His thesis was that these ideologies are

> like the traditional religious symbol-systems and philosophies of action. [However,] they do not typically have that transcendental reference— that pointing to the sacred Beyond—which typifies traditional faiths. But that itself invites us to consider what the critique from the Beyond means in our world. (Smart, 1981, p. 11f.)

Smart's view was that secular ideologies, including science, have separated the spiritual and the material, denying that the individual is both. It is his belief that the modern world needs mechanisms to accommodate pluralism and individualism, authoritarianism and modern nonreligious humanism, beliefs and knowledge, the search for identity and, though not as explicitly, history.

In Smart's (1981) view, the impact of religious experience and the study of such impacts is quite independent of whether the transcendent exists in a verifiable sense and controls events. We cannot know, but have to put our hearts (beliefs) and minds (knowledge) together to form the spiritual ideology that he called transcendental pluralism. That is, we need to take account of scientific knowledge, human history, and people's sense of what lies "Beyond" in answering our existential questions about life's ultimates.

Smart (1981) attributed to religions a threefold contribution on the basis of their emphasis on empathy, organic analysis, and awareness of the symbolic. He contended that we cannot understand past religions without understanding empathically the people who lived by them—how those people made sense of their lives. We must also consider current religions as being organic wholes because people see and use them as symbolic systems that integrate and give meaning to their lives. That is, "new transformations attempt to relate old mythic functions to new forms of knowledge" (Smart, 1981, p. 68).

A valuable perspective from which to understand religions as belief systems is provided by Smart's analysis (1981). Further, his approach is compatible with science critics such as Kuhn and Sperry. Thus, his critique contributed not only to our general understanding of religions as belief systems but also to a framework for understanding how they relate to other belief systems and to people's conduct.

Transcendence, the Sacred, and Coping

Pargament (1997) had four objectives when he looked in depth at the ways U.S. religious congregations use their religious beliefs and practices in coping. His focus was on how people contend with the impact of situations and issues when they have not developed a means of managing them and the related stress. First, he sought to present a sympathetic and supportive view of religions. As a basis, he emphasized the value of religion as "illuminating perhaps the most inscrutable, deeply enigmatic aspects of life" (Pargament, 1997, p. 13) and its role in providing people with a sense of significance, sacredness, and oneness with God beyond their limited personal existence. He also stressed the importance of religion in his own life. Next, he presented his conception of personality functioning and documented how religion interrelates constructively with individual and societal functioning. His theoretical framework of how we function as knowers with a central motive to search for meaningful significance in our lives was then introduced. Pargament's next step was to use his psychological perspectives and findings to identify the circumstances that facilitate our turning to religion, the ways we use it, and the consequences of the choices we make for coping with stress and in our search for more general significance.

Pargament's (1977) efforts were directed to showing how the psychology of religion and coping can be used to achieve constructive rather than destructive human outcomes. In his view, a sense of sacredness is not just generally helpful to people in coping with life crises, but essential in that process. To test the empirical validity of that belief, he measured the relationship between religious coping approaches and the psychological criteria used to define constructive and destructive processes and outcomes. His work documented that cultural, situational, and individual forces converge to influence when people turn to their religious beliefs for help in their coping and what the empirical results of their efforts were. Findings included that people may appeal to religion for a variety of purposes that seem, from other perspectives, to vary in constructiveness and outcomes. Included were (a) assigning meaning to events not explicable within other available belief systems, (b) conserving, adjusting, or transforming an individual's sense of significance in relation to ongoing experiences, (c) providing a framework within which an individual may respond to negative events by seeking renewal and making efforts to construct or reconstruct a prosocial identity and way of life, and (d) leading people to resort to religious appeals rather than to address problems through available, empirically validated resources, e.g., using medicine to treat bacterial diseases.

Buddhism and Reality as Process

Buddhism is an almost polar opposite alternative to Christianity as well as to aspects of Hinduism from which it was derived (Smart, 1981). Examining it can broaden our understanding of the relationship of belief systems to the contexts of their origins. In his view of the human condition, Buddha emphasized the nonself rather than the soul, and the process of life and reality rather than their substantive nature. Smart suggested three main reasons for these choices. The doctrine of nonself "brought the doctrine of liberation closer to experience.... Second, in dissolving substances the doctrine also dissolved *Brahma* as a Being, and so dissolved the divine Reality of the Brahmins" (Smart, 1981, pp. 119, 120).

Buddha negated the privileged power position of the Brahmin caste in a way analogous to that used by scientists in the West to limit the power of the clergy and the royalty. Buddha challenged the reification of the person or the soul as an integrated *something in depth* (object) and emphasized that the individual is an ongoing changing process. This doctrine of impermanence provided people with a radically different way to organize meaning in their lives and guide themselves accordingly. According to Buddhist teachings, people did not need to accept and justify inequitable social conditions because of some unknown past or possible future circumstances. Instead, emphasis was placed on achieving fulfillment in this life by self-examination (perhaps through meditation) and the acquisition of self-knowledge.

PSYCHOLOGICAL CONCEPTIONS AND CORRELATES OF RELIGIOUS BELIEFS

Some psychologists have tried to avoid ultimate truth questions by focusing on the empirical correlates of religious practices. Paloutzian and Kirkpatrick (1995) edited a series of essays about the outcomes of Judeo–Christian religious practices in the United States in order to provide information about how people "process their beliefs in dealing with problems … (and) on how religious resources can contribute to progress and solutions of societal problems" (p. 5). They emphasized that they did not wish to plead for or against religions or consider the implications of research findings to advocate particular political changes. However, empirical findings and analyses do have such implications and should be part of society's ongoing public discourse. Further, they make explicit the intertwining of religious and other belief systems as is indicated in the following examples.

Dull and Skokan (1995) used a cognitive model to conceptualize the relationship between religion and physical health as one in which religions provide a basis for developing positive or negative illusions that lead people away from "logical and unbiased thinking about the course of events" (p. 52). In Dull and Skokan's judgment, whether such departures lead to constructive outcomes depends on whether they advocate using empirically validated health care practices. This approach provides a way of understanding how people form religious conceptions of life, but clings to the conviction that "logical and unbiased thinking" provides the most accurate basis for dealing with reality.

Gorsuch (1995) emphasized that religious beliefs can be of value in promoting people's attainment of well-being in this life. He cited that religious people are less likely to be substance abusers. Further, some religious people desire consideration of their beliefs during treatment. He concluded that considering those beliefs can facilitate treatment, if doing so enables individuals to shift from a restrictive, negativistic, and ritualistic religiosity to a supportive religiousness.

Donahue and Benson (1995) found that religiousness in a sample of primarily Christian adolescents in the United States was directly related to prosocial values and behavior and was negatively related to individually and socially destructive characteristics. It was also sometimes unduly constraining and religiousness declined during adolescence. They concluded that religious involvement is a prosocial force in positive adolescent developmental outcomes, and they advocated better accommodation of it by public institutions. However, they did not explore whether religious educational institutions also have mixed consequences and should accommodate pluralistic or secular educational approaches.

McFadden (1995) focused on people's reliance on religious beliefs and activities to deal with progressive debilitation and problems of loss of control, health, and companions. Older adults used religion as their most likely coping response to losses, but religious demands that could not be met had negative effects on their well-being. In his view, evaluation of religion's temporal effects must include consideration of negative and positive consequences.

IMPLICATIONS OF RELIGIOUS BELIEF SYSTEMS

Religious belief systems have substantially influenced the lives of individuals and the fates of civilizations throughout recorded history. Systems of belief range from those about the existence of ultimate truths to the idea that, although their existence can never be validated, such truths have temporal power. In spite of these differences, adherents agree that all religious beliefs have consequences for the well-being of individuals and societies in this life; they all acknowledge the value of empirical testing of the consequences of their doctrines, if not of their underlying assumptions. These positions provide a shared basis for exploring the overlaps among belief systems and the ways they can learn from and inform each other. To date, such explorations have found positive and negative consequences and raised further questions. One crucial ongoing question is what guidelines are acceptable for collaborative interactions between religious and secular belief systems that do not subjugate any of them to the general paradigms of the others?

COMMONALITIES AMONG BELIEF SYSTEMS

ISSUES TO RESOLVE

Belief systems are paradigmatic frameworks that we organize to give meaning to our lives. Understanding them and their relationships to each other and to our lives requires identifying the kinds of decisions that have necessarily been made to organize and use them. A representative few of those decisions are cited here to illustrate the nature of these choices.

The Decision to Believe

Each of us has to decide whether to make the leap to accept any belief system, including our common sense, scientific, and religious systems. In practice, we tend to rely on components from all three systems without giving much thought to the implications of doing so. However, our beliefs have profound impacts on our lives and societies. It is important to be aware of their natures so that we can build on their strengths and minimize their negative effects.

Common sense is our basic level of self-evident functioning. Throughout our lives, we use conventionally accepted patterns of discourse and evaluation to refine its criteria for belief decisions. It is also changed by any new discovery or observation that provides a more compelling account than do our previous beliefs. It eventually becomes *examined* common sense, but its scope is largely limited by our situational contexts and unsystematic criteria for evaluating ourselves and our situations. Even so, common sense remains the system we all use to evaluate and incorporate religious and scientific system explanations into our nested frameworks and patterns of discourse.

Scientific systems are based on the decision to believe that experiences can be accounted for within empirical frameworks if we follow explicit, agreed upon procedures. In practice, however, when conflicts occur over theoretical differences or paradigm shifts, contending groups often fall back on extrascientific criteria such as the beauty of a formulation or what Klineberg described as a "religious" conversion (1980, p. 40) to a new insight. Thus, scientists acknowledge that they, too, rely on tacit and untestable criteria when choosing what to believe.

Religious belief systems are alternatives to common sense and scientific belief systems. Believers assign primary importance and special meaning to experiences judged by others as lying outside the realm of the natural and as not real. These experiences are used to deal with both empirically answerable questions and aspects of life that otherwise seem incomprehensible.

All of these kinds of belief systems influence individual and collective human thoughts, feelings, and behaviors; consequently, it is important that each of us accept that they are valid psychosocial phenomena. They are important to understand if we are to understand and communicate with each other. Further, they have consequences that can be established by either common sense observation or scientific study, so identifying those effects is relevant to finding and addressing convergences, divergences, and conflicts.

Deciding Which Experiences Confirm Facts

These decisions about what is real and true rest on our prior beliefs about which experiences have significance beyond their occurrence. Some assign primacy to experiences described as transcendent, numinous, religious, or spiritual. Others prefer reference points that are observable by anyone under prescribed circumstances. In some respects, these are polarized positions, but some of their differences may be reconcilable. For example, there is a kind of transcendence (a leap) involved in assigning significance to all experiences; there is also a kind of observer agreement. Those who believe in divine or other extranatural inputs appeal to observer agreement to evaluate the claims of those who say they have received a vision or "call" to service (Pargament, 1997). In contrast, those who believe that all information is naturally produced make choices (psychosocial leaps) about which data are important.

Advocates of each of these positions distort their own positions by failing to acknowledge the limits of their positions and to resolve their inconsistencies. Paloutzian and Kirkpatrick (1995) pointed out that the psychology of religion has received little attention from psychologists and that research in this area has not been included as part of mainstream psychology. Mainstream theories and data bases are systematically distorted by excluding this information. Conversely, psychologies of religious belief systems are distorted to the extent that their adherents refuse to accept that they do rely on empirical information and that input from empirically based perspectives is relevant to sustaining their belief systems.

Decisions about Values and Their Germaneness

There may be no conflict between religious values and the scientific search for facts in Hinduism (Paranjpe, 1984), but there is in Christianity. The separation of the domains may serve important practical purposes in protecting scientists and their work from value-based sanctions of religious belief systems. However, that separation is not without costs. It has excused scientists from considering that their involvement in activities such as the development of the nuclear bomb has profound evil as well as good impacts on people's lives. All kinds of belief systems have advocated absolute, sometimes conflicting, value positions. Some belief systems advocate that any artificial means of limiting populations are unacceptable, while artificially maintaining lives is desirable. Others hold the conflicting views that it is an absolute evil for people to kill each other, but that killing is justified under certain circumstances such as war or punishment of criminals. The complexity and lack of internal consistency of such value-based beliefs is possible because of their embeddedness in circumstances, desires, and contradictory belief systems.

Ghosh (1995) wondered which so-called religious values are religious and which are secular, and he described modern-day fundamentalism as shifting from a focus on religious (spiritual) concerns to a "plethora of political, sociological, and, in the end, profane ideas" (1995, p. 31). He suggested that the emphases on territoriality and control of ideas and on political, legal, educational, and even military organizations, etc., are essentially not religious, but *supremacist*. Such beliefs are designed to provide meaning to the believers' lives and remove supposed threats through their supremacist justification for controlling real or imagined outside forces. This pattern of justification leads to the questions "why are these movements so easily pushed over the edge, why are they so violent, so destructive, and why is their thinking so filled with intolerance and hate?" (Ghosh, 1995, p. 31). He asked, is religious belief always irreversibly "cannibalized" in this way? His conclusion was that we may wish to say no, but "we must be prepared to accept that this is in fact what religion signifies in our time." Even so, he could not accept that "matters of the spirit will not, somehow, survive" (Ghosh, 1995, p. 31).

Ghosh (1995) concluded that the dichotomy of spiritual versus material characterizations of experience is a false one. Advocates of both religious and secular value systems assert values with empirical consequences of the usual secular sort and spiritual consequences of a sort scientists often call ephemeral. That is, both are secular and spiritual. Integrating a new experience affectively as well as cognitively, individually as well as socially, in a new holistic way may be what some from a common sense perspective call "mind blowing," scientists call a paradigm shift, and religionists call a revelation or a numinous experience. By making as explicit as possible that our experiences and interpretations of them are spiritual and material and embedded in values and facts, we can integrate these considerations to build on the strengths of each.

The Decision about Responsibility for Change

A consequence of endorsing any belief system is the belief system's impact on our beliefs about the forces of change and, consequently, its impact on our lives. For example, deciding that the responsibility for producing change rests within us as individuals and that we have discretionary capabilities for choosing among alternatives assigns to us the responsibility to manage our lives and situations. Conversely, choosing to believe in the deterministic nature of our lives leads to a focus on making the most of our prescribed fates, i.e., a belief that there is no point in trying to change them.

RELEVANCE OF EMPIRICAL DATA

Recent studies explored the psychosocial impact of religious belief system practices. Maton and Wells (1995) examined the preventive, healing, and empowerment resources that religion offered a U.S. community. They found that three-eighths of all volunteer activity was church related and that congregations gave more to community causes than did corporations. In addition, religious congregations help in the development of children and youth, provide support for adults, and empower the community through social action and social justice. They also noted, but paid less attention to, the negative impacts of activities such as intolerance for values and practices with which religionists do not agree. Pargament and Park (1995) proposed a shared approach in areas of convergence, emphasizing that psychologists interested in social change may find partnerships to be worthwhile with religious system representatives with whom they have shared values.

Ventis (1995) studied intrinsic, extrinsic, and quest orientations to religion and positive mental health. His findings included that quest was a particularly important, newly introduced prosocial orientation. Nonreligious approaches to mental health also provided constructive prosocial bases for positive mental health. The current limited findings provide two conflicting results. They indicate that, in contrast to the religious, the nonreligious may be among the healthiest but may also have more indications of psychological disturbance.

Bottoms, Shaver, Goodman, and Qin (1995) found compelling evidence in the United States of widespread physical abuse, withholding of medical care, and sexual abuse of children predominantly by religious authorities. Those findings led them to confront, but not resolve, a significant area of conflict between belief systems. They argued for both continued freedom of religion and its practices and for society to protect children from religion-related abuse and help religions develop better child treatment practices. In a related review, Hunsberger (1995) pointed out that the Judeo–Christian orientation to loving others could reduce prejudice, but the evidence that it does so is limited at best. Rather, a right-wing authoritarian orientation to a fundamentalist nonquesting religious approach is related to *higher* levels of prejudice. Jenkins (1995) also found evidence of religion's mixed effect on HIV infected individuals. Many retained their church ties or reported a strong spiritual outlook, but they also viewed religion negatively as a source of intolerance and punitiveness. These people use their religious beliefs to cope with loss, health problems, or added life burdens.

Pargament (1997) documented that a combination of cultural, situational, and individual forces influence when and how we decide to include religion in our coping. Also, religion and its uses fall within the ordinary realm and functions of other human activities, and they yield prosocial and constructive or antisocial and destructive outcomes. Research findings show that religion is helpful when it is life affirming and the particular stressful event or issue in question is one about which that religion is supportive. That is, there are differentially effective approaches to coping, at least with regard to definable criteria in this life, and religious coping processes can be evaluated using defined, value based ends, means, and individual-situation fit. As Pargament (1997) pointed out, "there is value to certain ways of coping, whether or not the situation turns out well.... From this perspective, the key to coping lies not in a particular act nor a particular outcome, but rather the integration among the pieces of the coping process" (p. 314). However, the issue of religious means and ends is a particularly difficult one in that religions generally emphasize the importance of total commitment as a guiding force in peoples' lives. In contrast, empirical studies support the conclusion that such single-mindedness is counterproductive in coping with stress, that "integration among the pieces" may prove more useful.

Implicit in Pargament's position is a common sense view that religion is best considered as just one of a variety of belief systems. Optimal coping is maintaining a balance with regard to factors such as ends, means, and fit. That point seems particularly applicable to judgments that do not permit of ready answers. For example, under what circumstances can sustaining one's life or that of someone else no longer be justified? Religion, science, and common sense may contribute to that decision and, in practice, often do. These kinds of choices are not subject to the same kinds of empirical evaluation as other decisions. They clarify the limits of our human capabilities and belief systems, and they also highlight the gains to be had from choosing to believe that we can gather evidence and use our judgmental capabilities to cope as effectively as possible with our life issues.

A TRANSCULTURAL ETHNIC VALIDITY MODEL APPROACH TO BELIEF SYSTEMS

Since we all must rely on personal judgments for justifying our claims about truths and values, efforts to accommodate disparate views are more likely to work if they are undertaken within a metaframework that provides equitable consideration for each perspective. A transcultural ethnic validity model (EVM) has the limitations inherent to any belief system, but its strength is based on that premise. It uses a *Resource Collaborator* (see Chapter 8) approach that involves participants in acknowledging the strengths and limitations of their positions to work out convergences, divergences, and means for containing and managing conflicts. Its assumption is that it is subject to continuing review and revision and will provide only tentative operational answers about the nature of people's realities. Thus, it is a framework for mutual exchanges among groups and individuals from similar or different "natural" cultures or belief system cultures.

THE ACCEPTABILITY OF QUESTIONS AND ANSWERS

Mutually understood exchanges among people with different belief systems resemble a form of language translation rather than the form of conversations between speakers of a common language. As with language translation, effective communication depends on relaying underlying shared meanings. It is achieved by triangulation, a process of teasing out commonalities in understanding as a basis for highlighting and addressing differences and conflicts. These commonalities are not permanent and continue changing as our lives change so that ongoing interchanges require ongoing translations.

In these discourses, we proceed by accepting these commonalities as shared criteria for determining what constitutes answerable questions and legitimate answers to those questions. That process is based on background considerations from common sense, scientific, and religious belief systems. It enables us to formulate shared agreements about values and the factual nature of events. A transcultural ethnic validity approach facilitates these processes through its framework which gives alternative perspectives legitimate status so that everyone can understand, extend their own perspective, and resolve differences. It also helps clarify understandings of ourselves and others who are involved in exchanges, the questions under consideration and answers to them, and the need to integrate changes over time.

Miller (1995) recently described how a relevant and historically significant dispute about alternative understandings of an important human event were addressed. This dispute occurred before the development of empirical science, so efforts to resolve it rested on observation and on analytic and speculative interpretations. The eighteenth-century era of

European enlightenment was a time of approaches to "competitive dying." Eminent intellectuals used their views about dying to support their positions about facing death. Some believed that people have a natural sense of morality that allowed them to face death with dignity; others, that people need religion to face death with dignity and, by implication, to behave morally throughout their lives.

The philosopher Hume, a central figure in the debate, believed in the former position and illustrated it in his personal approach to dying. Those who disagreed with him attributed his approach to death as vanity and a desire to advance his view that morality has nothing to do with religious faith. Eventually the debate was overcome, at least among the intellectuals, by "the sentimental revolution" advanced by the Scottish moral-sense theorists and Rousseau. "Man was naturally good, in the new view, and the passion of benevolence was a strong force in human beings. Morality was a function of strong feeling—a feeling that was pleasurable" (Miller, 1995, p. 39).

Miller (1995) emphasized that questions about the foundations of morality are still with us because their answers involve speculation in addition to empirical observation and analysis. Current scientific approaches can add controlled empirical studies to the earlier procedural evidence approaches to help answer such questions. However, it is no more possible now than before to establish whether people are naturally moral or require an external source, such as a deity, to enforce morality. All that we can do is identify the antecedents, correlates, and consequences of what people choose to believe.

On the Use of Empirical Findings, Scientific and Otherwise

Employing scientific approaches to identify the empirical groundings and consequences of people using belief systems has provided instructive answers, particularly about religious belief systems. However, little of that information involves intra- or interreligious system comparisons, and even less is transcultural. Most of it has focused on comparisons between religious congregants on the basis of their beliefs, not their ethnic validity frameworks. To illustrate the nature of and differences between ethnic validity and religious belief influences, I have summarized findings and implications from two sources of empirical research.

Studies by Pargament, other colleagues, and myself have compared U.S. religious practitioners and Indian Hindu pilgrims to identify the relationships between people's (a) cultural circumstances, (b) religious belief systems, (c) psychosocial competence characteristics, and (d) the psychosocial functions they tried to fulfill through religion. These studies, some of which were described in earlier chapters, yielded the following distinctive cross-sample and ethnic validity patterns.

1. Hierarchical, in contrast to horizontal, U.S. religious congregations placed more stress on the power of God and the insignificance of the person, involved members less in decision making, and restricted their individuality more. They also scored lower on trust, higher on control by powerful others and God, and were less self-critical (Pargament, Tyler, & Steele, 1979b).

2. Adaptation patterns of U.S. religious congregants show that they had found no optimal way to organize their lives. Their psychosocial competence characteristics and their congregational central–peripheral status yielded pronounced tradeoffs. The central members fit and believed more strongly than peripheral members that their lives were under the control of God and less under the control of chance and that they were more satisfied with their congregations. They also felt that their lives were less under personal control and that they were less actively engaged in their lives (Pargament, Tyler, & Steele, 1979a).

3. As reported in Chapter 6 (see Table 6.1), we found that among the U.S. congregants, it was important for them to have a sense that their lives were under the control of some stable source (Pargament, Sullivan, Tyler, & Steele, 1982).

4. There were demographic differences in relationships between the psychosocial competence characteristics and psychosocial functions (personal support, social support, social gain, and obligation) that religious participation served for U.S. college students. Women were more oriented toward personal and social support and less toward social gain than were men. African Americans were more social support oriented than were Anglo Americans. Roman Catholics were more oriented toward obligation and less toward social support than were Protestants or Jews (Echemendia & Pargament, 1982).

5. Transcultural ethnic validity differences were explored by adapting the psychosocial competence and religious function measures for a study of Hindu pilgrims. There were major differences in the respondent's life situations within their respective cultures and there also were important transcultural commonalities. Hindu pilgrims from more conservative segments of their society (high-caste Brahmins, rural residents, and the less educated) and central members of hierarchical U.S. churches were more extrinsically motivated and had fewer intrinsic concerns such as social or personal support than their respective liberal and horizontal church cohorts. Common transcultural gender differences included men

being more personal control oriented and their religious involvement more oriented to impersonal societal gains; women were more oriented to control by external forces and to seek personal and social support in religious activity (Tyler & Sinha, 1988).

The influence of ethnic validity circumstances, including religious beliefs and social and gender status, on people's psychosocial competence patterns was supported by Donahue and Benson (1995). Their survey of predominantly Christian adolescents in the United States was not transcultural, but their findings showed ethnic validity differences. The level of religiousness was higher in African Americans than whites and higher in girls than boys.

SUMMARY

This chapter explored abstract questions, such as the nature of human existence and human knowledge, and our capacities to understand and manage our lives and situations. Religious, scientific, and common sense belief systems advocate distinctive formulations of these questions and their answers. None of them is acceptable to all people, and each system in its own way ignores or rejects considerations that nonbelievers, and often some of its own adherents, consider essential. People select ideas from alternative systems to "fill in the gaps" for their own purposes. The information in this chapter expands the ways in which psychologists and others can better understand belief system perspectives to improve their own and psychology's efforts to contribute to human welfare.

Particular attention was paid to religious belief systems because of their importance in peoples' lives and because of the nature of the challenges they present to other belief systems. Religious belief systems variously assert that they are different expressions of an underlying divine reality, include special properties such as transcendence, or just provide powerful ideas that influence people. As with the belief systems of common sense or science, we can explore their temporal consequences by subjecting them to scrutiny by others.

Among Western scholars who have empirically explored the relationship between religious involvement and psychological well-being, there is agreement about the nature of temporal psychosocial well-being and the forms of religious involvement that support and enhance it. Consistent with much of Western contemporary common sense, characteristics of well-being include a coherent and positive sense of self-worth, prosocial interpersonal relationships, active life involvement, possibilities for self-fulfillment and spirituality, and a positive sense of the meaning of life. To the extent that religions or other belief systems judge their own and other perspectives by these empirical criteria, they can be considered prosocial contributors to society and the lives of those who rely on them.

Belief systems have divergent and conflicting characteristics. Choosing to guide our lives by any system involves tradeoffs that do not lead to equally benign consequences. Informing ourselves of these different consequences and acting on that information is potentially more prosocially beneficial than unquestioningly following the directives of one or several systems. The difficulty is that most belief systems are organized so that the efforts of their adherents are designed to support that system, and exploring alternatives requires evaluation of the system itself. The positivist orientation of some psychological frameworks leads to their rejecting consideration of holistic or spiritual functioning as legitimate emergent phenomena. Religious belief system adherents may resist the idea that their own and other members' conduct is a relevant criterion for challenging the system's premises. Framing prosocial solutions to such differences requires a belief that people can function as knowers and establish convergences, accept the legitimacy of certain differences, and use mutually acceptable ways to manage and resolve conflicts.

Imposing restrictive psychological, political, religious, or other belief systems on individuals or societies without attention to the consequences can be psychosocially destructive in numerous ways. For example, the belief that fearing God is necessary for people to turn to prosocial concerns such as human welfare may lead to destructive religious and societal practices. Psychological studies support that a right-wing authoritarian orientation turns people away from prosocial concerns toward interpersonal intolerance and destructiveness. They also support that life affirming, supportive orientations turn people toward prosocial concerns. Major religions' endorsement of the golden rule, i.e., that people should behave toward others as they would have others behave toward them, is evidence of a broadly applicable convergence consistent with these research findings. In other words, to determine whether people's commitments to prosocial beliefs and activities rests on fear or other grounds requires serious consideration of the idea that psychological findings have implications for the political, civil, and religious structures of societies, not just for people's psychosocial structures. It also requires substantially more attention than psychology has given to transcultural ethnic validity concerns.

A transcultural ethnic validity perspective requires us to ask a distinctive set of questions about our belief systems. For example, religions differ on whether the ultimate nature and goal of existence is stability and permanence (Western deity oriented) or process and ongoing change (Buddhism). These beliefs also differ on whether humans are created by a deity or are part of an ongoing creative process. By failing to consider such information, we may be omitting significant portions of our own and other's lives in our attempts at understanding those lives. We may also be limiting our capabilities to understand and respond to the psychosocial impacts that all belief systems, including psychologists', have on those who seek assistance. Only by exploring these kinds of questions from a transcultural ethnic validity perspective can we begin to answer how beliefs influence the quality of our individual and collective lives.

Additional areas need exploring for a more comprehensive assessment of the validity and generality of belief systems. As investigators of our own culture-defining, group conceptions of psychological well-being, we need to counteract our investment by providing for evaluation from other frameworks. We can gain from identifying shared guidelines to accommodate ethnic diversity and address societal and religion-based inequities and destructiveness. For example, reducing the authoritarianism within existing religions and other ideologies seems likely to reduce their most glaring antisocial and antihumanistic practices. The available evidence supports that psychologists can contribute to the construction of belief systems that address life's unanswerable questions in largely prosocial ways and that religious belief systems can contribute to the questions psychologists must consider for a comprehensive understanding of people.

PATHOLOGY AND COMPETENCE

INTRODUCTION

BACKGROUND

Recent literature indicates that mental health professionals see little relationship between competence, pathology, and culture. Searches of journal articles and book chapters for references between 1975 and 1995 yielded very limited results: competence and pathology, four; competence and culture, two; and pathology and culture, three. This chapter argues that psychosocial competence, pathology, and culture are interlinked and cannot be understood otherwise. These diverse perspectives are integrated because people build on their individual natures and experiences within their cultural/ethnic contexts to develop their psychosocially competent and dysfunctional characteristics. Manifestations of psychological dysfunction are indicators of problems in living, not symptoms of disease processes. A reconceptualization of how we understand psychopathology and psychosocial competence is provided to support this idea.

CHALLENGES TO REDUCTIONIST AND DICHOTOMOUS APPROACHES

As described in Chapter 3, people once believed that characteristics of abnormal behavior were evidence of demonic possession or criminality. For the past two hundred years in Western cultures, such behavior has been thought to indicate disease. Widespread acceptance of this paradigm led to research to isolate these hypothesized diseases and educate professionals to treat or cure afflicted people. Results of that research and those interventions have provided a basis for asking whether a new reconceptualization is indicated.

Sperry (1992, 1993) argued that no function of living organisms can be understood by looking for evidence of it exclusively in isolated biological processes. Rather, behavior must be understood in emergent holistic terms. His distinction somewhat parallels the one labeled knower–known. In Sperry's view, the holistic knower level can overrule the known level but is not reducible to it. It is a function of our histories, but is not totally predictable from them. For example, it may be possible to predict that creative people are more likely than others to formulate creative solutions to life situations. Neither we nor they, however, can specify just what creative solutions they will produce.

The neurologist Oliver Sacks (1995) provided a particularly useful example of the knower aspect of people's competence-related solutions to pathological events. As mentioned earlier (p. 80), he described the experiences of two elderly women with somewhat comparable cerebral vascular accidents (strokes). Each was suddenly unable to stop early childhood tunes from playing in her head. For one, the songs faded away as the blood clot dissipated; the other's disappeared with drug treatment. For one, the songs recalled a much earlier and happy time. She cherished them, and after they were gone valued having had them brought back into her life. For the other, the tunes were intrusive and recalled unpleasant memories. She disliked them and was happy to be rid of them.

Sacks (1995) did not turn to a mind–body reductionist formulation to explain these happenings. He formulated an integrated three-tiered explanatory framework: (1) a biological episode that triggered a neurological outburst; (2) the eruption of the tunes as known residues of their past experiences which he likened to a program that a computer carries out; and (3) the experiences each woman associated with the songs and included in her formulation of their meaning for her and how she used them in her life. The women's actions were discretionary with differing competence-enhancing and destructive correlates. Sacks' formulation provides a model for understanding human conduct as a function of interrelated levels of complexity. The consequences of people's psychosocial integrations or disintegrations may be destructive, but viewing them literally as disease processes is misleading.

CONCEPTUALIZING THE NATURE OF PSYCHOLOGICAL DISORDERS

As noted earlier, the conceptualization in the United States of psychological disorders as mental illnesses has faced major challenges over the past half century. Two of those challengers, Szasz and Cowen, highlighted

the issues. Szasz, a psychiatrist, argued that the concept of illness legitimately relates only to biological illness.

> The term *mental disease*, insofar as it refers to behaviors that imitate
> illness or to some other conduct regarded as undesirable—for exam-
> ple, claims of being unable to move an extremity or of being able to
> move the whole world—designates conditions that are not diseases.
> To be sure, mental illness may be thought and said to resemble bodily
> illness; but it is not such an illness. Medical disease stands in the same
> relation to mental disease as literal meaning stands to metaphorical
> meaning. (Szasz, 1978, p. xvi)

Szasz emphasized that most scientific and professional efforts are directed
toward using *talk* to understand and alter any mental deviance so that it
falls within acceptable societal and personal norms. Using language as
"the mirror of our mind" (1978, p. xvii) can be an effective way of changing
people's minds and conduct toward morally or socially acceptable behaviors, or both. Calling it *psychotherapeutic* is inappropriate; it is not therapeutic in the sense that antibiotics are.

Cowen (1973), a community psychologist, also challenged the "belief
in a structural parallelism between the onset, nature, and treatment of
psychological and physical dysfunction" (p. 429). Specifically, most disordered behavior differs from physical dysfunction in having a longer
developmental period, being influenced more by individual and social
factors, and impacting more widely on an individual's conduct. Evidential
support for the psychopathology-as-illness approach is modest at best.
However, because the mental health establishment has endorsed this medical model, others have also endorsed it and expect such problems to be
addressed (treated) and resolved (cured) in a medical fashion. He concluded that only by changing the mental health approach, making a paradigm shift, to one of reducing stress factors in people's lives and building
their positive skills can there be any realistic chance of addressing U.S.
mental health concerns. To take on that challenge, we must first understand the current paradigm's recent evolution.

EVOLUTION OF THE PATHOLOGY ORIENTED PARADIGM

Both the medical model conception of mental illness and the community mental health movement emphasized the roles of defective biogenetic
attributes and faulty socialization in contributing to people's vulnerability
to defensive socialization, mental illness, and pathology oriented therapies. Consequently, these views have almost overwhelmed other orientations. To challenge their appropriateness for improving the quality of

anyone's approach to life requires that we understand how aberrations are currently being defined.

THE DIAGNOSTIC AND STATISTICAL MANUAL (DSM) APPROACH

The medical pathology paradigmatic conceptions of psychological disorders are based on societal, medical, and legal principles, models, and rules about what constitutes mental illnesses. They have been codified and illustrated by examples (exemplars) of conduct in the *Diagnostic and Statistical Manual of Mental Disorders*, Fourth Edition (DSM-IV) (1994) whose formulation and publication is controlled by the American Psychiatric Association. A caveat in it is that "it must be admitted that no definition adequately specifies precise boundaries for the concept of 'mental disorder'" (1994, p. xxi). However, throughout the DSM-IV it is stated explicitly that there *are* mental disorders and that

> each of the mental disorders is conceptualized as a clinically significant behavioral or psychological syndrome or pattern that occurs in an individual and that is associated with present distress (e.g., a painful symptom) or disability (i.e., impairment in one or more important areas of functioning) or with a significantly increased risk of suffering death, pain, or disability, or an important loss of freedom.... Neither deviant behavior (e.g., political, religious, or sexual) nor conflicts that are primarily between the individual and society are mental disorders unless the deviance or conflict is a symptom of a dysfunction in the individual, as described above. (1994, p. xxii)

Several challenges to and limitations of a categorical approach were mentioned in the DSM-IV, but were rejected for the following reasons. The challenge that each diagnostic category is a discrete entity with absolute boundaries and that everyone placed within a category will be alike, even in important ways, was dismissed as unduly restrictive. It was agreed that using a dimensional rather than a categorical approach would increase reliability and communicate more clinical information. However, that approach was rejected because dimensional approaches had been less useful than categorical systems in clinical practice and in stimulating research, are less familiar, and there is no agreement on the optimal dimensions to be used for classification.

The categorical approach is to be used in clinical, educational, and research settings by individuals qualified through clinical training and experience in diagnosis. Caution was urged about using it for forensic purposes because of the "imperfect fit between the questions of ultimate concern to the law and the information contained in a clinical diagnosis" (1994, p. xxiii). Finally, hope was expressed that sensitivity to different cultural, ethnic, age, and gender manifestations of mental disorders would reduce the possible effects of unintended biases. These caveats do not address the issues underlying these complaints and have often been ignored.

THE DISEASE MODEL AND PSYCHOLOGICAL DISORDER

Mirowsky and Ross (1989a, 1998b) challenged the DSM-III version of the disease model as not an appropriate basis for *"research on the nature, causes, and consequences of mental, emotional, and behavioral problems"* (1989a, p. 11, italics in original). Their criticisms seem equally applicable to the DSM-IV (1994) because it rests on the same basis. They argued that categories unjustifiably impede understanding the complexities of psychological disorders and recommended that the disease model be eliminated as a basis for mental health research because

> a diagnostic system asserts that observable attributes are manifestations of unobserved categorical realities. If a diagnosis is to add information to the attributes themselves, that information must come from other research ... show[ing] that an underlying reality produces a characteristic profile of observable attributes, and that its presence or absence can be inferred from the profile with reasonable accuracy. (1989a, p. 15)

Information to support diagnostic categories is largely unobtainable because there is little of it and the available evidence is not overwhelmingly supportive. To establish the existence of diagnostic categories requires one of the following three kinds of evidence.

A *gold standard* is the presence of the phenomenon. Examples from medicine include bacteria or a broken bone. Mirowsky and Ross (1998a) stressed that many psychiatrists and epidemiologists believe that mental disease entities exist and dismiss the argument that evidence of them has not been found. The assumption is that they must be there because of the symptom picture.

The next best evidence is that of *latent biological classes*, such as a marked biochemical bimodiality correlated with a diagnostic picture. However, we also know that correlation is not the same as causation, and a correlation might occur for a variety of reasons, including that both variables are related to a third factor (e.g., environmental condition) or that the "symptom" is actually the cause of the biological state. In any case, Mirowsky and Ross (1989a) found this type of evidence also inadequate, as there were far too few correlations between biochemical variables and diagnostic categories, and even the existing ones were not strong.

The third level of evidence is *empirical syndromes*, i.e., combinations of symptoms which occur commonly enough to constitute a distinctive clinical picture and may be thought to have a single cause. Mirowsky and Ross

(1989a) pointed out that, except in relation to drug or alcohol abuse, there are no such patterns in psychopathology syndromes. There are empirical syndromes that may constitute indirect evidence of natural disorders, but even there we have reason for skepticism:

> Are there distinct clinical pictures? It depends on how you look at it. A good example comes from the factor analytic studies of Spitzer (the DSM-III chief negotiator), Endicott, and their colleagues (Endicott & Spitzer, 1972; Spitzer et al., 1967, 1970). They found that the correlations among the symptoms of psychiatric patients can be summarized in approximately a dozen factors: inappropriate or bizarre appearance or behavior, belligerence and negativism, agitation and excitement, retardation and emotional withdrawal, speech disorganization, suspicion or a sense of persecution with hallucinations, grandiosity, depression and anxiety, tendency to suicide or self-mutilation, somatic concerns, social isolation, disorientation and memory problems, antisocial impulses or acts, drug abuse, and alcohol abuse. The actual factors change somewhat from one study to another, but the factor structure across studies is quite similar. (Mirowsky & Ross, 1989a, p. 17)

Many mental health experts assume that these factors can be interpreted as evidence of categorical disorders. However, as Mirowsky and Ross (1989a, 1989b) suggested, they can also be interpreted as constellations only in that they reflect separable aspects of people's psychosocial functioning.

Mirowsky and Ross (1989a) also examined why the American Psychiatric Association and the National Institute of Mental Health made the policy decision to standardize measurement of psychological disorders as diagnostic categories rather than as configurations of multidimensional indexes. Their suggestion was that more importance was assigned to the medical and epidemiological language and traditions of psychiatry and to physicians' political desire to retain the power of diagnosis and control the sale of services, points that are discussed in greater detail in the following section. Mirowsky and Ross (1989a) stressed instead that

> scholars cannot afford to endorse and promote ideas that are ill suited to the subject, have little validity, and mislead. No one should forget that we are talking about the disturbing or disruptive thoughts, feelings, and behaviors of people, and not about unseen entities that are somehow the cause of it all. (p. 23)

THE SELLING OF THE DSM

The DSM approach had a number of origins, was the focus of considerable controversy, was sold primarily on political rather than scientific arguments, and had enormous consequences. Kirk and Kutchins (1992) reviewed those issues and arrived at conclusions similar to those of Mirowsky and Ross (1989a). However, Kirk and Kutchins placed greater emphasis on how its authors accomplished this paradigmatic shift by minimizing the inadequacy of supportive evidence and emphasizing political considerations. In the 1970s, the mental health field was growing rapidly, more public attention was given to mental health issues, and there was more public involvement in paying for mental health care. Psychiatry was a low status medical specialty and in some danger of becoming even more marginal within medicine for a number of reasons. It lacked a scientific medical base, particularly one rooted in biochemistry, and was threatened from within by the challenges of dissidents such as Szasz (1978). Further, related mental health fields, such as clinical psychology, psychiatric social work, and psychiatric nursing, were challenging psychiatry's dominance in the therapeutic treatment of psychological disorders.

Emphasizing that updating the DSM would strengthen its scientific base enabled DSM proponents to define the major terms of the subsequent debate. They shifted the responsibility for judging the efficacy of this new approach to presumed scientific experts and away from practicing clinicians. Framing the central issue as being whether disorders can be diagnosed reliably provided a way to bypass the difficult question of whether such entities exist. However, Kirk and Kuchins (1992) cited reports, including ones from the advocates of the diagnostic approach, that all of the DSM versions were adopted without any persuasive evidence of their empirical validity and that there is no such body of evidence. Most mental health personnel, primarily practicing psychiatrists, did not consider it of central importance that the DSM yielded relatively low reliabilities because their priority was to describe the patients' problems in psychodynamic terms.

DSM proponents proceeded by controlling who was chosen to form the new approach. No racial minorities were included, psychoanalytically oriented psychiatrists were kept to a minimum, prominent child psychiatrists who represented challenging views were excluded, and women were underrepresented. DSM advocates sought to win both the scientific and professional sides of the argument by stating that, in the final analysis, diagnosis must rest on professional judgment, an approach that highlighted the weakness of both the underlying disease concept and the diagnostic approach. For example, there was a highly publicized controversy over whether to consider homosexuality a pathological disorder and an embarrassing resort to a vote among psychiatrists to make that decision rather than to search for scientific evidence. Another challenge to the objectivity of diagnostic categories was Oppositional Defiant Disorder in children. Its first criterion is "often loses temper." Kirk and Kutchins (1992) pointed out that it and the other symptoms listed for this disorder each depend on a broad social context, particular circumstances, and subjective judgment. These specific diagnostic criteria contain flaws or lack precision (as do almost all of the diagnostic criteria for the disorders) and require considerable subjectivity and inference.

To highlight their point, Kirk and Kutchins (1992) cited an exchange between Spitzer and a committee of African American psychiatrists. Spitzer rejected their recommendation that racism be considered a mental disorder on the grounds that it would be associated with distress or become symptomatic only in certain environments, or both. He suggested that the same logic would apply to male chauvinism and religious fanaticism. In a quote from a letter attributed to Spitzer, he suggested the possibility "that in DSM III in the discussion of what is a mental disorder we would list racism as a good example of a condition representing a nonoptimal psychological functioning which renders a person vulnerable in certain environments to manifesting signs of disorder" (Kirk & Kutchins, 1992, p. 102). Neither this nor any related statement was subsequently included in DSM-III or DSM-IV. Spitzer's logic is similarly applicable, for example, to Paranoid Personality Disorder which also renders a person vulnerable in certain environments. The point is that deciding what was to be designated a diagnosable disorder involved decisions about how to define and control social deviance and moral conflict, not *gold standard* indices of mental illness.

Kirk and Kutchins (1992) cited other political arguments for the DSM approach, namely, (a) doctors and epidemiologists are accustomed to working with cases, (b) insurance companies and federal agencies find them valuable for public policy and budget estimate purposes, and (c) it is important to continue to use the DSM approach so that the approach in the United States will remain compatible with the *International Classification of Disease* (ICD). None of these arguments bear on whether the DSM approach is supported by a data base or is clinically relevant to the way people live. Kirk and Kutchins concluded that the supporters of the diagnostic category approach won the political battle, but not on the merits of their argument. The merits of the argument need to be pursued because they are important to the well-being of people who need services.

ONGOING CHALLENGES TO THE CURRENT PARADIGM

NAGGING ISSUES

A study by Rosenhan (1973) involved eight "pseudopatients" who gained admission to 12 hospitals by falsely reporting one particular symptom. That symptom had never been associated with a diagnosis of schizophrenia, but 11 of the 12 were so diagnosed. Once in the hospital, they stopped pretending they had the symptom and behaved normally, except they took extensive notes. Their presence or behavior never aroused the suspicion of the staff, but it was evident to other patients. When discharged, each was diagnosed as having "schizophrenia in remission."

These findings raised two serious questions about the DSM approach. One was the failure by the professional staff to identify their error. The second was the discharge diagnosis implication that the disorder can never be eliminated—an implication that should require a *gold standard* of evidence; yet, as we have just learned, there is no such evidence. The mere exhibition of similar symptoms from time to time provides no basis for deciding whether those symptoms indicate a continuation or a recurrence of a presumed disorder.

Clark, Watson, and Reynolds (1995) emphasized that many confounding considerations obscure the central question of whether the diagnostic categories represent naturally occurring disorders. If so, relevant characteristics of such individuals should be homogeneous. However, the common presence of heterogeneity within categories and mixed patterns which fall between categories also challenge the basis for the DSM system. Further, the simultaneous presence of two or more diagnosable symptom patterns in an individual (comorbidity) is widespread, difficult to identify reliably, and associated with the severity of the disorder(s), a factor that is equally or more important than the precise nature of a presumed disorder.

At present, individuals who find the DSM system lacking are turning more and more to compromises. They use the DSM-IV for economic purposes, such as reimbursement, and ignore it for purposes of their work. As these divergent patterns begin to develop, the overall situation in the mental health field begins to mimic a phase of the Copernican revolution. As Kuhn (1979) described, for some one hundred years in the Western world, ships at sea carried two sets of charts. One was required by the church and depicted its sanctioned view that the Earth is the center of the solar system. The other depicted the world according to the Copernican heliocentric theory and more accurately met the empirical criterion of arriving at one's destination. As Clark et al. (1995) noted, there are proposals to shift to other mental health approaches. Psychopathologists, in particular, advocate shifting to a dimensional system that grades symptoms by degree of severity and would reduce the three hundred plus DSM categories to a presumably more manageable set of dimensions.

CULTURE, CONTEXT, AND MENTAL DISORDER

Consideration of *culture* introduces new levels of complexity into the DSM paradigm's conception of us as separate, acontextual organisms subject to potentially debilitating disorders. Including the role of social and cultural factors in the creation of deviant behavior involves challenging the medical pathology paradigm. Durie (1994), a Maori psychiatrist in New Zealand, emphasized two important issues that contribute to a neglect of cultural factors as integral to Maori mental health. The consideration of mental disorders as being genetic or social class based automatically excludes cultural factors. Conceptualizing pathology as the primary cause and culture as only a subsidiary factor minimizes attention to cultural issues

Hughes (1993) argued that not only is the patient/psychiatrist relationship influenced at a number of levels by both parties' cultural affiliation, but that

> the practice of psychiatry—*no matter where it is practiced*—is significantly influenced by its cultural setting. Although such influence is not explicitly recognized in the Western clinical protocol, that protocol is itself an artifact of the cultural structuring of human knowledge and behavior. And the structure is not, as often assumed, the pure yield of Western biomedical science—transcendent, objective, and free from the influences of a cultural system. (p. 3)

Rather, culture is necessarily the general paradigm, and psychiatry is a limited paradigm that must be viewed within that broader context. Although human conduct is built on a substrate of biological constraints and potentials, it is culture that captures the socially transmitted system of ideas that assigns reality to selected aspects of experience by providing the exemplars needed for structuring our assumptive worlds. The very nature of our phenomenological existence, of all meaning, is embedded in the cultural context in which we are socialized.

This pervasiveness of the culturally constructed nature of meaning was also cited by the anthropologist Geertz (1995). During his field work in Indonesia and Morocco, he only gradually came to understand that Indonesian cultural reality and language were organized to convey that social status was their categorizing criterion. Similarly, he found that the categorizing criterion of Moroccan society and its people was gender. Although Geertz did not address the implications of his views for defining and understanding psychological disorder, they suggest that the more general paradigm is culture; concepts of disordered behavior are constructed within that reality.

Durie (1994) stressed the primacy of culture in the communally organized Maori whose approach to health is holistic and ecological. The four dimensions of Maori health are the spiritual, mental (thoughts and feelings), physical, and family. Like the sides of a house, they must be fitted together to complete its structure; well-being requires a balance among them. The *spiritual* is the most essential. It includes religious beliefs and practices in the Western sense and relationships with the land. It is difficult for Maori to have spiritual health without access to their tribal lands. The *mental* involves thoughts and feelings representing an integrative synthesis with wider systems, including life's current social relationships, continuity with past and future generations, and relationships to other creatures and the physical universe. The *physical* orientation to health overlaps largely with Western views. Finally, *family* health is important as the extended family is the support system providing care and nurturance across all of these domains, and family dysfunction is considered an element in individual illness. A sense of interdependence, not the independence valued in the Western world, is considered an indication of maturity (Durie, 1994).

Troubled Maori individuals display some of the symptom characteristics described in the DSM-IV, but they have different origins and cultural meanings. A major goal of Maori health perspectives has been de-medicalizing the human life cycle and "widen(ing) understandings of health, to translate health into terms which were culturally significant, and to balance physical and biological approaches with cultural and sociological views" (Durie, 1994, p. 78). Health is based on promoting well-being, not identifying and treating illness. Approaches to it include improvement "of the overall status and well being of a Maori community, tribal or family group" (Durie, 1994, p. 78).

Manson and his colleagues also emphasized cultural factors in studying the relevance of the DSM to Native American understandings of psychological dysfunction. Depression was the most frequently diagnosed problem among the Hopi, so they interviewed a previously diagnosed depressive group and a control group, asking "what are the sicknesses or things that can go wrong with people's minds or spirits?" (Manson, Shore, & Bloom, 1985, p. 336). Five categories, each with a cluster of cognitive, affective, and behavioral states were identified. Their English language labels were: *worry sickness; unhappiness; heartbroken; drunken like craziness with or without alcohol;* and *disappointment, pouting.*

There were clinical and conceptual differences between the DSM system and the Hopi's views of "things that can go wrong with the mind or spirit" (Manson et al., 1985). The associations of affective states and cognitive processes characteristic of depression in Anglos were not present among the Hopi. Auditory hallucinations were common and accepted as normative among the Hopi. Half of the Hopi clinical group members had concurrently experienced what the DSM distinguishes as chronic and major depression, and the control group members' experiences of DSM depressive symptoms were quite similar to those of the clinical group. All of the males who had experienced depression had done so secondarily to an alcoholic condition. Most indicated that there was no Hopi term equivalent to the English term "depression" although *heartbroken* showed substantial overlap, and none of the sickness forms corresponded with the DSM description of depression. *Worry sickness* was judged as the category that "most closely approximates the English equivalent of mental illness" (Manson et al., 1985, p. 337). Manson (1995) continued to build on the belief that culture at least "organizes the stimulus, manifestation, and interpretation of emotions like dysphoria" (p. 489). He and his colleagues argued that accepted psychiatric concepts and measures can be adapted for any population. However, a strong argument can be made that doing so does substantial harm to the individual and cultural phenomenology of the Hopi or any other such group.

This fundamental point, that psychological function and dysfunction are embedded in a psychosociocultural world view, has also been addressed by a husband and wife team, Duran and Duran (1995). Basing their views on his Native American heritage and their experiences with the dominant U.S. culture and health system, they emphasized that all people articulate their own ways of "being in the world" and that there are differences among Native American tribes. They believe the Western presumption that its biomedical illness model is right and all others are inferior and wrong is the height of arrogance. It is unreasonable, they argue, to expect that the DSM as "developed by non-Native American people can possibly include the life experiences of Native Americans unless a Native American world view is taken into account in the description of the diagnostic categories" (Duran & Duran, 1995, p. 206f).

Duran and Duran (1995) emphasized that Native Americans conceptualize themselves, the world, and their relationship to the world in their own ethnically valid way. The Judeo-Christian view that humans are in charge of all creation and the world exists for their exploitation contrasts with the Native American view that humans are spiritually and physically part of all creation. Native Americans think of events in process terms (a Buddhist-like concept), so "being" refers to an ongoing process, not a static identity. Further, they do not compartmentalize experience so they do not separate body from mind or soul, nor self from culture. They may think of psychological dysfunction as a "soul wound" that damages the tribe as well as the individual. Consequently, for example, the Western biomedical belief that the roots of suicide, alcoholism, etc., are in family and tribal breakdown are considered by Native Americans an affront and a denial of the institutional racism and cultural destructiveness imposed on them. A community psychology approach seems more relevant to their lives and disordered behavior because it emphasizes the shared collaborative involvement of people and providers as part of the community.

From epidemiological approaches to culture, ethnicity, and mental illness, particularly among U.S. ethnic minorities, Escobar (1993) concluded that there is enough evidence to support both common syndromes and cultural effects, including strengths and limitations. The almost exclusive concern with disadvantages associated with ethnocultural minority status has led to ignoring the cultural advantages of these NCD groups. Their strengths warrant further study to identify biological or cultural protective factors. For example, Mexicans have significantly lower suicide rates than Anglos. A new paradigmatic model is needed to provide "a clearer definition and demarcation of syndromes by using, for example, specific 'gold standards' (i.e., biological 'markers') that could be reliably identified in all countries and races" (Escobar, 1993, p. 69).

Dohrenwend and his colleagues (1992) also differentiated common and culturally specific contributions to psychological disorders. They interviewed Israeli adults of European (ethnically favored) and North African (ethnically discriminated against) descent to test the relative contribution of social selection and causation in psychological disorders. Their reasoning was that if Israelis of North African descent who are ethnically discriminated against have inherent psychopathological defects, they should continue to have high levels of pathology no matter how well they become assimilated (social selection). Conversely, if their high levels of disorder are a function of social stress, their levels of disorder should diminish with assimilation. The findings were mixed. Social selection was more significant for schizophrenia. Social causation was more significant for gender-related patterns of depression in women and for antisocial personality and substance use in men.

In Gaw's edited (1993) volume *Culture, Ethnicity and Mental Health*, there are eleven chapters by different authors. In spite of empirical challenges to the Western biomedical illness model such as those cited here, all of these authors relied on that model to address the role of culture in the clinical care of U.S. ethnocultural minorities. They said that practitioners should be sensitive and responsive to cultural beliefs and influences, but those factors were primarily described as obstacles. The underlying assumption in all cases was that treatment is to enable clients to acculturate. There were no suggestions that changing U.S. culture would improve the quality of life for any or all of us.

Military Psychiatry

During the First and Second World Wars, military psychiatrists dealt with individuals from different cultures who were facing a common set of circumstances. The relevant literature from those wars was summarized by Mandelbaum (1954), an anthropologist. He emphasized that all the variations in psychiatric incidence and symptoms that we have noted confirm the theory that psychiatric theory and therapy, in the military sphere at least, cannot well ignore considerations of culture, of society, of stage and context of military experience. In each major variation—by military situation, by branch of service, by stage of career, by social status, by general society and by culture—there are particular stresses and, often, particular psychological strengths in support.... As this concept of specific vulnerabilities, varying according to culture and social situation, becomes developed in psychiatric research and replaces the older and vaguer concept of general emotional instability, a more effective psychiatry—certainly an improved military psychiatry—should emerge. (Mandelbaum, 1954, p. 14)

Mandelbaum's conclusion was based on observations, reports of individual psychiatrists, and an organized study of how military experience influenced the medical outlook of a substantial number of senior psychiatrists. The following four findings seem particularly relevant:

1. Breakdowns varied with stage of combat career and phases of combat. They were fewer during a full retreat or during a counterattack, and they rose when opposition was first met and during periods of sustained fighting.

2. Individuals considered vulnerable to psychoneuroses in civilian life seemed to function as well or better in combat than their peers. The military "branches differ(ed) in the degree to which the social structure within a unit of a given branch support(ed) the individual" (Mandelbaum, 1954, p. 10). There were relatively low rates of breakdown in U.S. submarine crews and air crews.

3. Treating psychiatric causalities near the combat zone and quickly returning them to their units was vastly more effective than hospitalizing them. It seemed crucial to keep them in touch with their pride in their unit and their morale-sustaining ties with their comrades. Removing them from the line to distant hospitals and possibly discharging them had more adverse consequences. It confirmed the seriousness of their plight, provided the secondary gain of avoiding combat, and introduced a new primary support group in the other hospitalized soldiers whose hostility was directed not at the enemy but at the psychiatrists and the military. Further, these ill effects continued after discharge and impaired their capacity for adjusting to civilian life.

4. There were different patterns of breakdown between World War I and World War II, and different ones in different armies. For both the British and the United States, there were fewer cases of hysteria and more anxiety disorders during World War II. Among the Germans, there were substantial numbers of war neuroses in World War I, but relatively few during World War II. There were also relatively low frequencies of psycho-

neurotic behavior in heavily bombed cities. Interpretations emphasized the sustaining importance of commitment to the group as well as concern with individual survival, possibilities that are consistent with a rise in symptoms in such cities after the war ended.

Cultural differences in symptom patterns and their culturally syntonic nature was illustrated vividly by British and Indian soldiers during the India–Burma campaign of World War II (Mandelbaum, 1954). They shared the same battlefields, military discipline, and psychiatrists and were subject to the same diagnoses and treatments. However, their psychosocial realities were distinctively different. The British were more troubled by hand-to-hand fighting and guerilla warfare and expressed more guilt about killing the enemy. The Indians were more distressed at the possibility of losing face with their comrades by showing anxiety and fear. It was culturally acceptable for the British to talk about their anxieties and they did so; but they also exhibited more anxiety disorders and more often broke down *before* battle. The Indian soldiers exhibited more hysterical disorders, e.g., convulsions and functional paralyses, similar to the public displays of Indian ascetics, and were more likely to break down *after* battle. The British had a higher rate of breakdowns than did the Indians, but were more likely to recover and recovered more quickly. The Indians were less likely to recover and recovered more slowly. When British and Indian soldiers were placed together, their differences provided a basis for helping each other and they recovered faster. Irrespective of his group, each soldier "needed to be told that he was accepted and acceptable to his group, that he was useful, that any devaluation he may have suffered was a mistake" (Mandelbaum, 1954, p. 12).

We cannot understand these phenomena as simply individual differences in some intrapsychic deficit. This evidence introduces individuals as psychosocial beings who define themselves in relation to themselves, their social networks, and their relations to the others. A framework is needed that considers people's resources, resiliency, and limits in the context of overall differences in cultures and the roles of individuals in them. Such a framework can consider that many factors contribute to becoming dysfunctional. Dysfunction is not necessarily a product of a distinctive psychic defect. Dysfunctionalities can be addressed by providing social and professional support and assistance and involving the individual's resources and resilience.

THE DEBATE ON THE NATURE OF PSYCHOLOGICAL DISORDERS

Efforts to identify the nature of psychological disorders can be traced through chapters in the *Annual Review of Psychology*. In the first of those chapters, the Dohrenwends (1974) confined their review to types of disorders with no known organic basis, a restriction that limited them very little since the etiological basis of most mental disorders was unknown. They noted that expanded pathology rates after World War II seemed to be due to an expanded nomenclature, so they studied the occurrence and distribution of disorders as offering the best clues to pathology's definition and etiology. They found consistent relationships between some social and cultural factors and certain types of pathology. Their findings included (a) a higher incidence of pathology in presumably more stressful urban areas than in rural areas; (b) an inverse relation between level of pathology and social class; (c) a greater predominance of psychotic diagnoses at lower class levels and neurotic at higher ones, but equally high levels of pathology among simpler societies; and (d) gender-related findings including that newer measures were biased toward a symptomatology more characteristic of women, higher levels of symptomatology in women across urban and rural areas extending beyond North America and Europe, and women diagnosed more as neurotic and men as having personality disorders.

The Dohrewends (1974) concluded that there was not enough evidence to decide whether the patterns of pathology in Western cultures were products of social or biological factors. They did endorse that disorder patterns are universal, although their expression and distribution are subject to cultural differences. To support these conclusions, they cited that non-U.S., including non-Western, mental health professionals have little difficulty in using the Western categories expressed at that time in the DSM-II. That point could also mean that the Western medical paradigm had overwhelmed indigenous professional paradigms in other cultures.

Although King's 1978 summary largely paralleled that of the Dohrenwends, he differed in his emphasis that the paradigmatic status of the field left much to be desired. In his judgment, more attention was needed on methodology and the formulation of broader conceptions of social factors such as autonomy, mobility, and legitimate power, particularly considerations such as which "cultural reality creates conditions of vulnerability" (p. 408). He also emphasized the importance of developing base line data about what constitutes mental health. King stressed the importance of using research to offset implicit or explicit biases, concluding that "the data suggest that there is a relationship between social and cultural forces in the emergence of mental illness" (1978, p. 427), a perspective that has received little attention.

The Dohrenwends (1974) and King (1978) identified most of the major psychological questions which need answering if we are to understand psychological disorders. All three were optimistic about psychology's potential for resolving some of the substantive issues being raised. More recent reviews do not vindicate their optimism.

Strauss (1979) built on King's review, emphasizing three major themes. First, he noted that transcultural commonalities of certain general patterns of disorder need not mean that they are of biological origin and unaffected by sociocultural factors. "It is equally possible that there is a certain range of experiences that are universal to the human condition, for example, perhaps arising out of the need of all infants to be raised by older individuals" (Strauss, 1979, p. 412). Second, he pointed out the need for small and large scale studies to account for broad sociocultural patterns and for distinctive class/ethnicity/cultural ones and to assess whether hypothesized biological determinants can account for them. Third, he emphasized that the consequences of diagnosing and labeling an individual as mentally ill must be considered because such labeling has a destructive effect on people and contributes to a deteriorating pattern of functioning rather than the reverse.

Eron and Peterson (1982) rejected the term "psychopathology" in favor of "abnormal behavior" because it neither assumes nor denies the existence of an underlying disease process. They focused on how psychologically non-normative behaviors covary with social and cultural factors and how individuals learn to organize, integrate, and conduct themselves. Their results indicated that a direct, calm manner of coping based on the belief that a person is able to control events and use multiple strategies, including social skills, was likely to be an effective life strategy. They found that interrelations among social class, gender, exposure to stress, coping, and abnormal behavior generally supported the view that the roots of abnormal behavior lie in having to function in alien circumstances not permitting of effective adaptation with customary strategies or of learning appropriate new behaviors. Women, lower-class adults, and lower-class children have higher reported levels of abnormal behavior. Further, they are exposed to more stress, are less troubled by a given level of stress, and have less effective coping strategies. Lower-class children are more likely to live in conditions that do not provide adequate learning environments. In addition, women's coping strategies are less effective than men's.

The complexity of these patterns is indicated in prevalence studies that Eron and Peterson (1982) also cited. In one from India and one from Sweden, psychiatrists interviewed an entire population group and, in both cases, the upper classes had higher rates of mental illness; but, in India, the socioeconomic status differences disappeared when illness rates were related to caste and religion. Other studies that they cited indicated that even when the rate of disorders did not vary with socioeconomic status, the pattern of treatment did. In the United States, higher status individuals were more likely to receive psychotherapy and less likely to be given pharmacological treatment; nonwhites were less well served and more likely to be inappropriately served. Although prevalence rates seemed fairly constant across cultures, the symptom patterns, distribution, and prognosis of disorders varied. Symptoms most influenced were role and social behavior, and least influenced were cognition, perception, and affect. Recovery was expected in less developed cultures and was greater there. Eron and Peterson's review cited substantial support for the role of social and cultural factors in disordered behavior.

Emerging support for social causation hypotheses and a focus on stress, coping, and the process of adaptation in the development of psychological disorders was reported by Kessler, Price, and Wortman (1985). None of these three factors alone was a major determinant of clinically significant disorders, but each was related to them. Individuals from lower social classes and from minority groups, particularly African Americans, were exposed to higher than average levels of stress that seemed accounted for by social class factors. Evidence also suggested that African Americans may develop group support mechanisms that provide emotional support against the life stresses that were associated with their disadvantaged position. Women were more stressed than men by losses of people close to them. Mexican-American patients were more conflicted than were controls by incompatibilities between Mexican and American values.

Six years later, Coyne and Downey (1991) reiterated the importance of studying social factors. Investigators were now using structured interviews rather than check list measures and surveys to gather information. They had decided that to understand the complexity of disordered psychological patterns requires a narrative structure with the depth and complexity characteristic of a novel, even a multigenerational one. Research was suggesting that stress in intimate relations has a different impact than stress in more distant ones; the loss of a parent in early life may have a much less deleterious impact than prolonged family disruption during childhood. The idea was growing that an interactive life span developmental conception of the course of normal or exemplary life may be an appropriate model for how psychological disorder develops. Their focus was particularly on depressive disorders, an area of research in which another conflict had arisen. In spite of these newer findings, investigators were being advised to continue using the DSM-IIIR dichotomized diagnostic schema in their studies. The adequacy of that methodology was challenged by new research data collected with the NIMH-developed continuum indexes of disorder. They were identifying factors which differentiated severe depression from nondiagnosable depressive symptoms, suggesting that this traditional dichotomization was an unjustifiable over-simplification.

Fowles (1992) reviewed research which tested the diathesis–stress model that schizophrenia is a product of polygenetic and psychosocial factors. He emphasized that, even assuming the presence of maximal genetic contributing factors to schizophrenia, half or more of the variance must be attributable to other factors. Little evidence was found that physical factors (e.g., structural brain changes) are important. Consequently, "even though the evidence for psychosocial contributors to the onset of symptoms is often circumstantial, it is stronger than the evidence that gene-controlled biochemical changes contribute to the time of onset of symptoms" (Fowles, 1992, p. 323).

Several additional reports also contribute to understanding the role these multiple factors play in normal and disordered functioning. Lewin-sohn, Muñoz, Youngren, and Zeiss (1978) presented a social learning-based approach to depression as a syndrome (not a mental illness) involving a complex combination of learned thought, behavior, and evaluative patterns. They outlined empirically tested, step-by-step, self-help techniques for understanding and solving the real life problem of depression and related patterns.

Their findings anticipated those of Rowe (1983), a clinical psychologist in England who works with people with depressive symptoms, some of whom had not responded to medical treatment. She concluded that medical treatment is not completely effective because depression is more than an illness. Rather, "people who cope and people who get depressed see the issues of life and death in very different terms.... Depression is a prison which we build for ourselves.... So we can unlock the door and let ourselves out" (p. viii). She identified six beliefs essential to remaining depressed, including believing one is worthless, life is hopeless, and no one should be forgiven, especially oneself. Rowe elaborated on how individuals come to those beliefs, their gains from holding on to them, their fears about abandoning them, and how they can change them.

At least in the United States, mental patients sometimes lose some or all of their civil rights including, often, the right to refuse or insist on treatment. In addition, as Price and Denner (1973) and their contributors documented, these individuals are stigmatized for the remainder of their lives. They necessarily become involved in a process of redefining themselves accordingly. A vicious cycle is created as some of the situationally-induced conduct associated with being confined in a hospital context or treated as a mental patient, or both, is then interpreted as evidence of the mental illness by professionals, the patient, and others in the patient's life. That stigmatized status, they suggest, is somewhat similar to that which minority individuals must endure.

These studies support that psychosocial/ethnocultural contexts and experiences are an integral part of dysfunctional patterns. Little of this work included cultural considerations, but it suggests that people with markedly different ways of living will have somewhat distinctive, culturally syntonic ways of organizing their lives and addressing psychological disorders. The patterns called normal and those called abnormal are interwoven parts of the same whole cloth that is each person and each psychosocial context. They do not support the presence of *gold standard* natural dichotomies indicating separate normal and pathological processes or states.

Positive Mental Health

Contemporary U.S. conceptions of positive mental health (PMH) grew out of the work of the Joint Commission on Mental Illness and Health (1961). Ewalt, Director of the Commission, made it explicit that a focus on PMH involved departing from the biomedical illness model.

> We commonly use "mental health" as a term interchangeable with "mental illness," in the same euphemistic way that "public health" generally refers to the prevention or control of disease by mass methods. The behavioral scientists who have joined the mental health team and are making increasingly important contributions to the mental health movement have expressed dissatisfaction with a primary focus on "sick behavior." They argue that a new and broader perspective is needed if interest in mental health, as a positive force, is to be made conceptually clear and practically useful. They make a telling point when they propose that progress in understanding health and illness requires much research based on the study of human behavior as a natural phenomenon. (Jahoda, 1958, p. ix)

Jahoda's report on PMH provided a thoughtful review of its concepts from a psychological viewpoint with little attention to biogenetic or sociocultural factors. Concepts and criteria were assumed to apply given "a physiologic function consistent with the demands made by the society and the psychologic state of the individual" (Jahoda, 1958, p. xiii). Even though it is nearly half a century old, the report continues to provide important perspectives, including the assumptions that (a) values underlie all choices and recommendations including its own; (b) a focus on positive health is not a diversion from learning more about mental illness; (c) health is not just the absence of illness; and (d) defining PMH is a societal responsibility, not just an individual one. The Commission decided that concepts of mental illness and health applied only to individuals, although situations and societies may be more or less conducive to mental health. Finally, they assumed that the criteria for mental health and mental illness would be expected to change over time so that the relation between them was "one of the most urgent areas for future research" (Jahoda, 1958, p. 76).

The Commission's report stressed that there was an inevitable tension between personal morality and social conformity in any criteria for PMH. Resolving that tension requires that people integrate value considerations to form coherent conceptions of potentially optimal ways to live momentarily and over time. Anyone doing so must take personal responsibility for choices such as whether people should guide themselves, and require others to do the same, by fitting in to society's pressures or by following an internal compass. Finally, it requires endorsing that each of us is a responsible agent who has some freedom and responsibility about organizing and conducting our lives.

Defining an impossible PMH standard, such as an ultimate good, was rejected in favor of considering it as one goal among many, not the same for everyone, and changing over time. The following criteria continue to be cogent. PMH includes a meaningful integration of self and self–world attributes, information, and skills. It is actively and planfully achieved and based in personal psychosocial integrity and resiliency, and is characterized by an ongoing sense of self-direction, development, and use of our personal powers to enrich our own and others' lives and societies. Also included is an ability to make and follow through on choices that are more likely to serve preservation and enhancement objectives rather than destructive purposes for self and others. Embodied is a capacity and commitment to prevail over circumstances, not just fit into them.

To speak of prevailing is to assume that there is an open-ended nature to human agency, the capacity to imagine and explore unknown and untried possibilities. If we think of ourselves as human machines, we can hardly prevail; we can only try to achieve our fixed full capacity. With the possibility that we may prevail, we introduce that we are creative in open-ended ways and act as knowers as well as known. Our view of people and of PMH takes on a paradigmatic form different from that of simply preventing mental illness.

Human choice is an irreducible part of our actions, as the people of Yungay so proudly and poignantly illustrated by rebuilding their lives and their community after an avalanche (Oliver-Smith, 1986, p. ix). Even so, we cannot escape from the fact that our choices rest in part on our own heritages. Our highest values, as Jahoda (1958) noted, are irreducibly a function of our own investments in what we define as a good quality of life. Those investments include personal values and identification with a particular perspective, i.e., cultural ethnic validity, scientific, or professional.

In our roles as mental health experts, part of our commitment to research and action is dependent on and likely to shift in parallel with our own roles. For example, Jahoda and those working with her (1958) rejected the idea of a direct line between mental illness and mental health, arguing for the need to define and study mental health on its own terms. Even so, the final Joint Commission on Mental Illness and Health report recommended more research rather than immediate application of what was then known (1961). That recommendation was judged to be a cautious commitment to the status quo and its wisdom is still being questioned. As long as the mental health field is justified in terms of its efficacy for reducing explicit indicators of mental illness, a PMH perspective can never be anything more than a subset of the mental illness paradigm. Challenging that paradigm is the only way to advance consideration of other conceptions of the exemplary and problematic nature of our ways of living.

PSYCHOPATHOLOGY AND COMPETENCE/WELL-BEING: INTERRELATED ASPECTS OF HOLISTIC FUNCTIONING

A paradigmatic approach that interrelates competence and dysfunction assumes that our conduct is a complex consequence of genetic, biologic, and individual factors in conjunction with historical and contextual factors of a physical and social ethnocultural nature. It shifts our focus away from mental illness, other dysfunctions, and capabilities to the question of how we define our reality and manage our lives given our assets, limitations, and life contexts.

A half century ago, Anderson (1948) outlined a view of children using such a model. To him, children are active energy systems who respond selectively, ignoring as well as attending to stimuli as they cope with and create their world. They live in the present using memories from their previous experiences in the form of cultural values, persistent family attitudes and problems, and their more or less successful patterns of adjustment. They are actively involved in their lives, showing resiliency and a capacity for tolerating and recovering from stresses and frustrations. Current life span and competence oriented approaches also view us from infancy onward as having substantial resiliency in contending with difficulties and a capacity for managing our lives to achieve our desired outcomes. They acknowledge that events overwhelm people's capabilities for mastery so that they lose control of their lives or form dysfunctional patterns, often with self-destructive and otherwise destructive consequences. However, as Levine and Levine (1992) stressed with regard to children, the ways that less-than-successful adaptations are viewed by society vary with historical and cultural circumstances.

Glidewell (1987) provided a broader view of the relation between communities and individuals, emphasizing that communities support and enhance our psychological well-being, but also control us in ways that deplete it. Communities develop processes that lead to their inhabitants evolving mutual expectations. Usually, outcomes for everyone include both psychological ill-being and well-being although the balance is different for people in different circumstances. When the cost of the community's control becomes greater than its support, meeting its expectations becomes a source of distress and ill-being. When a community creates the belief in its citizens that meeting its demands is worth the controls it imposes, doing so becomes a source of pride and well-being.

However, community controls can far outweigh their benefits. Dumont (1992) described the pervasive societal contributions to the psychological ill-being of the U.S. urban poor. The clients in his community mental health center faced poverty, unemployment, toxic living conditions, abuse, stigmatization by professional helpers and helping agencies, and the humiliating requirements of learning to be a patient. Professionals and staff expected clients to fail and behaved accordingly, further increasing their failure expectations. Even so, clients continued their efforts to find meaning in their lives, maintain some semblance of self-respect, form relationships with others, care for their children and other loved ones, and find work or other means of sustaining themselves and contributing to their communities. Their resilience and limitations were as intertwined as the personal and societal circumstances in which they found themselves through little or no choice of their own.

From a similar perspective, Sacks (1995) described how a woman with autism managed her life. She achieved a Ph.D. in animal science, a tenured university position, substantial accomplishments in the field of animal psychology and its applications, and recognition for her work. However, she relates more comfortably to animals than to people, and she used her studies of how people manage animals to create techniques for managing her own life and circumstances. Sacks emphasized that autism is only poorly understood, but described it as involving "a radical deviation in the development of the brain and the mind" (1995, p. 246). Distinguishing between the brain and the mind provides a crucial basis for affirming that autism is more than an organic illness, and he has fruitfully explored the ways individuals develop their minds to create lives for themselves within their limitations and possibilities. In Sacks' view, this woman and other such people are more than their diagnoses—they are people who organize their lives as best they can.

Gearon (1995) found that even dysfunctional individuals diagnosed as schizophrenic are not completely prisoners of their presumed disease-related limitations or resources. She asked rehabilitation agency staffs to identify potential participants as competent or average copers. Self-ratings and reports were used to gather information about how the participants managed their lives and difficulties. The competent participants rated themselves as more intelligent, competent in more life areas, possessed of better verbal abstraction and interpersonal skills, and more competent to deal with their illness. They had a sense of their resiliency and limits and brought resourceful behaviors and learned patterns of competence to their life situations. They also reported having more external resources, including social and economic support and housing, and managing themselves and their circumstances in more constructive ways. They were more likely to seek support from others, challenge themselves to a greater extent, see experiences (even hospitalization) as opportunities, and engage in pro-active behaviors in dealing with their symptoms. Finally, although both groups saw their diagnosis as providing a framework for understanding their illness, only those in the competent group saw the stigma associated with their diagnosis as harmful, but also considered it of value in informing their approach to developing coping behaviors. Gearon suggested that attaining more competency appeared to be a developmental process, although those who were more competent had not always felt that way. Rather, particular turning points may have precipitated their decision to change the way they were approaching life and become more competent.

Strauss (1989) advanced a comprehensive psychosocial competence framework for understanding how people manage their schizophrenic and other disordered experiences. He stressed that each of us is an active agent who is centrally involved in defining, understanding, and managing our lives; a psychological disorder is not an individual's nature nor is it inflicted on an individual who has no control over it. Each person has feelings about a disorder and its course and employs regulatory mechanisms to manage those feelings and the disorder and to assert mastery over it or succumb to it. Each of us also lives within a broader context that influences all aspects of our interactions, including the history of our experiences with a disorder and our stage of dealing with it. Strauss illustrated this point by reporting that people described negotiating with their hallucinations to bring them under control. Thus, dealing with a disorder begins with understanding that we are all goal directed as are our interactions with any disordered experiences.

ETHNIC VALIDITY CONSIDERATIONS
IN UNDERSTANDING PATHOLOGY AND COMPETENCE

These ideas and findings provide a basis for a paradigmatic shift away from the assumption that some people are afflicted with psychopathological abnormalities to one that describes people as active agents working with their particular mixes of strengths and limitations to forge meaningful lives within the context of their histories and broader milieus. This paradigmatic shift places emphasis on psychosocial development within the framework of cultural and ethnic validity considerations as basic to how we experience and lead our lives. How these complex factors contribute to normative and deviant adaptations becomes our primary consideration. Even when mental health difficulties are overwhelming, they are not given primacy as defining a person. This shift places stress on attending to the quality and meaning of life for people who suffer from these difficulties. Proponents of this approach do not reject or minimize the role of biological factors and interventions. Rather, they argue that interventions based on giving more attention to psychological and sociocultural variables can "promote individual competency, increase self-esteem and self-efficacy, improve cognitive skills, enhance reasoning and problem solving, and foster insight and psychological growth" (Hunter & Marsh, 1994, p. 101).

Assuming that interactions between people are based on their common humanity builds collaborative relationships in all aspects of life. In particular, doing so provides a framework for interacting with mentally dysfunctional individuals as collaborators in their lives and in approaches to their difficulties and gives everyone involved a prosocial role in those interactions. It also eliminates a primary focus on who is to blame for the presumed pathology and, therefore, who must resolve it, who must be passive observers with nothing to add, and who must be a recipient of care with nothing to offer themselves or others.

An ethnic validity orientation takes central importance within such a model. For example, it gives the work of investigators such as Manson and his colleagues (Manson, 1995; Manson, Shore, & Bloom, 1985) a quite different meaning. It clarifies that experiences such as those of depression among some Native Americans are distinctive psychosocial phenomena that must be understood on their own terms. The psychological dysfunction has an inlying dynamic that is culturally based and is not just an overlay on a natural, universal pathological process. The previously labeled *disease process* must be reconfigured as part of an integrated, biopsychosocial process that has become dysfunctional for the individual.

Duran and Duran (1995) pointed out that Western therapists and Native American healers emphasize different, as well as parallel, symbols about what constitutes an accurate, or true, understanding of life and reality and what constitutes a healthy adaptation to it. Consequently, Native Americans often confront the choice between rejecting their heritage in order to get treatment and rejecting the services and being considered noncompliant. Treated individuals are confronted further with denying their culturally-based world view in order to be considered improved. In a parallel fashion, Durie (1994) documented the incompatibility of Maori and Anglo conceptions of psychological well-being. From these perspectives, the Anglo-dominated psychopathology approach seemed more like an effort at a religious conversion than an educational or socialization process that is sensitive to a client's culturally embedded world view.

From a broader psychosocial perspective, the situation that NCDG people face was spelled out by W. E. B. Du Bois (1940) in his description of the life situation and reality of African Americans. He wrote that the "spiritual world in which ten thousand Americans live and strive" (Du Bois, 1940, p. 1) is one of double-consciousness from being required to see themselves through the eyes of the white world that controlled their existence and again through their own eyes. In a much more recent effort to confront some of these concerns, Jenkins (1982) rejected what he saw as the mainstream psychological view that black people are deficient because the dominant white group sees them that way. Rather, he argued that it is essential to see people, all people, as active agents involved in coping with their own lives.

Perspectives such as these emphasize that NCDG people, whether in the United States or other parts of the world, develop positive views of themselves and function at adequate or superior levels. Assaults to their senses of self and self-worth associated with status may force them to form a double consciousness and contribute to their psychological dysfunctioning, but those assaults do not define them. Even their experiences of depression or the dynamics of other disorders are different from those of their CDG counterparts because of differences in their cultural and subcultural life realities. Jenkins (1982) explored the entanglement of race and class in U.S. society and documented that some of the epidemiological differences in black–white prevalence of mental health disorders disappear when class is controlled. To this we must also add that there are culturally based differences in interpreting the meaning of being lower class nonblack versus that of being lower class black, Native American, etc.

Differences in circumstances and adaptations can also be associated with gender and socioeconomic status. Werner's (1989) longitudinal study of resiliency identified a configuration of personal and contextual characteristics that differentiated between youth who transcended their impoverished and troubled childhoods and those who did not. The characteristics that distinguished those she labeled resilient included a positive sense of self, an internal locus of control, friendliness and likability, high involvement in activities, and good communication skills. They also had a belief system, such as religion, to guide their actions, a broad social support system, and some friend or member of the family who served as a source of emotional support. Both groups of youth had resources and problems, but the more favorable balance of supports and threats in the lives of the resilient ones was enough more favorable that it tipped the balance in their favor.

Similarly, Coyne and Downey concluded that

> intergenerational continuity of abuse is not inevitable. Several studies have identified a triad of factors that distinguish mothers who broke out of the cycle of abuse from those who abused their own children. The former were more likely to have received support from a nonabusive adult as a child, to have a supportive mate, and to have a reliable income. (1991, p. 417)

We need not assume that women who succumb to the rigors of their lives and environments necessarily have some fundamental internal lack because they are women. Rather, other factors may account for their difficulties. Included are their lack of the opportunities, resources, and supports needed to put together the internal confidence, positive self-regard, and skills to overcome serious hurdles.

In a focus on cross-gender differences, Nolen-Hoeksema and Girgus (1994) reviewed studies that documented the emergence of depression among females during adolescence as being two times as frequent as that among boys. There were no differences before puberty. From such relevant evidence, they concluded that "before adolescence, girls appear to develop more risk factors for depression than boys; girls also apparently face more new challenges in early adolescence than boys.... These factors combine ... to generate gender differences in depression beginning in early adolescence" (p. 424). These studies also support the conclusion that societal conceptions of gender are among the factors that are powerful contributors to disordered behaviors.

SUMMARY

The patterns that have been labeled pathology and competence are not only intertwined, they are also intermixed with issues of culture, race, class, and gender. The complexities of these interrelationships are only vaguely understood at this juncture. It no longer seems justifiable to discount them as relatively unimportant manifestations of universal processes, normal or pathological. It seems vital to challenge the prevailing view that the DSM categories based on Euro American populations accurately define the nature of dysfunctional processes. The origin and history of psychosocial dysfunctions are so different from those of biological disease processes that they lead to questions about whether that model is appropriate.

A new paradigmatic system based on broader data, including normal and dysfunctional conduct from a range of cultures, is needed to understand people in ways that are not feasible from a Western paradigmatic base. Selected studies and examples have illustrated why life circumstances must be considered centrally important in how people organize their lives and assign meaning to their experiences. They solidly support the argument that psychological dysfunction and competence are potentially better understood within a culturally based, ethnic validity context than within a biomedical disease context. They also support that societal or institutional efforts to minimize the incidence and prevalence of dysfunctional patterns will be more effective if emphasis is placed on improving social conditions and practices. Supporting and sustaining people's efforts to live meaningful lives within ethnically valid prosocial approaches is more productive for the well-being of individuals and society than is expecting everyone to conform to a dominant group's model and relying primarily on biomedical conceptions and controlling of the dysfunctional conduct of those who are judged deviant.

ELITISM, RACISM, AND PROFESSIONALISM

INTRODUCTION

Throughout this text, emphasis has been placed on how our societies define us, regulate our interpersonal relationships, allocate resources, and organize the conduct of our lives. These arrangements often become an integral part of commonly accepted beliefs and socialization practices which differentially benefit or disadvantage particular individuals or groups. The criteria on which they are based have included ascribed status by heritage, socioracial heritage, ethnicity, and gender. Other criteria have included allegiance to particular beliefs or social organizations and specialized education or experience.

To the extent that we assume that specialized roles in society should be assigned on the basis of people's capability to perform them, psychologists and other behavioral scientists can determine empirically who meets those criteria and the scope of activities and responsibilities for which their qualifications are relevant. They can also determine the special supports or benefits that are needed for the effective fulfillment of these assigned roles. Similar approaches can be used to assess whether a societal system creates significant barriers to the well-being of unjustly disadvantaged or advantaged people and their communities.

The behavioral and social sciences have contributed to the establishment of equitable grounds for such allocations through their conceptual frameworks and empirical evaluations. However, a potential limitation in having behavioral scientists perform these assessments is that they are part of these systems and have been influenced by the biases in them. They may be unaware of inequities or interpret them as justified, in part because they also benefit from them. This chapter considers how psychologists and others contribute to such biases even when they believe that such inequities are contrary to their own stated goals. It also explores potential forms that more equitable individual and societal arrangements might take.

Elitist beliefs and systems advance and maintain injustices by defining the specific characteristics (culture, sociorace, profession, gender, etc.) of some groups or individuals as being inherently superior. Those who possess these defined attributes then consider themselves uniquely qualified to define the reality of others as well as themselves. In this chapter, professionalism and racism are used as exemplars of elitist orientations. Professionals are chosen and educated by society to promote its collective and individual well-being. Professional functioning becomes professionalism when individuals adopt the belief that because of their status they are superior to others and uniquely qualified to define others' best interests, even on matters beyond their areas of expertise.

Racism becomes part of people's outlook and conduct when they adopt the elitist belief that they are superior to those with different racial characteristics. It is a pervasive exemplar of how elitism gets packaged in a presumably neutral framework. Racism perpetuates social inequities when it becomes a criterion for guiding the provision of professional and social services, access to organizations and opportunities, and grounds for interpersonal and intergroup strife. This chapter advances alternative ways of organizing our self-conceptions and interpersonal, professional, and social arrangements to minimize elitism and elitist effects.

DEFINITIONS

Prejudice is one of the most common and insidious elitist social belief patterns. At the individual level, people make judgments that some individuals or groups are of less (or more) worth or status than others. Such judgments are based on preconceptions without knowledge, thought, or reason, and often in spite of contrary evidence. The judgment is expressed through discrimination, that is, by taking actions on prejudicial grounds to grant or deny particular benefits to individuals or groups. These beliefs and the discriminations that stem from them often become institutionalized practices. The outcomes of that process are negative with respect to the common good, however defined, and often to the individuals involved. It is most difficult to detect prejudices in ourselves and our own practices, particularly those which we consider to be in the service of prosocial goals. However, as prosocially oriented psychologists and as concerned citizens, it is important that we examine our own conduct as much as we question that of others.

Racism and *ethnic bias* are widely acknowledged forms of prejudice and discrimination directed at presumed racial and ethnic groups on the basis of physical appearance, distinctive dress and conduct, or both. In both cases, evidence of being different is conspicuous and difficult to conceal. Often, when defining characteristics can be concealed, those involved reject doing so because they feel that such actions are tantamount to denying their identity and condoning unjust and unfounded elitist beliefs and conduct.

Noncultural-defining (NCD) minority, racial, or ethnic groups are often the focus of institutional discrimination. Alvarez (Zwerling et al., 1976) called such minorities the "holocaust" minorities. In the United States, they have included people of sub-Saharan African descent (blacks), Chicanos (Mexican Americans) and other Latin groups, Native Americans, Chinese, and particularly during World War II, Japanese. Discrimination has taken the form of their being "subjected to officially decreed, officially sanctioned, officially supported organized violence, paid for by public money" (Zwerling et al., 1976, p. 41). Although the term "holocaust minority" comes from Hitler's Germany, these groups exist in most societies. An understanding of how societies create and perpetuate these patterns is required before we can construct more prosocially benign societies and a better quality of life for everyone.

Professionalism is a less evident form of elitism based on the assumption that professionals are qualified by their training to decide how other people should define their realities. Responsibility for major public policies that determine social control practices is vested in professionals whose identity and judgments are grounded in the societies they are expected to serve. Modern day professionals have attained their skills and status by adopting and excelling in life patterns that emphasize delayed over immediate reward, abstract over concrete thinking, and cognitive over social, artistic, or physical skills. Those attributes may be relevant to effective professional functioning in a number of areas. However, it does not follow that they are also the most appropriate criteria for defining how fully human others are and what is best for them. Rather, presenting these judgments as necessarily being in the best interest of others leads to psychosocially destructive patterns of prejudice and discrimination.

Dumont (1992) wrote about professionalist biases within psychiatry from the perspective of his work as a community psychiatrist. He emphasized that a central concern of community psychiatry is to define and convey "what is crazy and what is not" (Dumont, 1992, p. 104) in our lives and relationships; that is, our connectedness to or disconnectedness from one another. He emphasized that contemporary psychiatry has rejected those concerns and reasserted its belief that it should use its professionalized approach to address disorders. Manifestations of disconnectedness, such as poverty, and the accompanying social and physical degradation, have been dismissed as a cause of mental health problems in favor of the argument that psychological disorders are based in biochemical or genetic flaws.

Dumont (1992) pointed out that his judgment is also based, in part, on personal and political biases. Even so, his point is relevant that professionalism can become a vehicle for maintaining prejudicial and discriminatory beliefs and practices by influencing people who are in responsible societal positions to rely on the unexamined social ethics of their privileged status as a basis for addressing individual and societal problems. For example, United States public programs to support children of impoverished families frequently specify that the family is eligible for those benefits only when no father is in the home. One result is that a father who cannot find work may move away from his wife and children to make them eligible for programs that provide food and shelter. Studies of such families report a greater percentage of broken homes among the poor. These data are then used by professionals to argue that middle class people are superior because they have intact families.

Professionalism is also found in the U.S. controversy over the requirement that community citizens be included on the policy boards of community mental health centers. Some professionals argue that community people do not have the knowledge or understanding required to help shape such policies. Alternatively, it is argued that because community people bear the brunt of these policies, they are in a unique position to point out the policies' flaws and define requirements for more desirable ones. Professionals and community people have somewhat different but equally justifiable perspectives on public policy matters. To exclude either is limiting and discriminatory.

THE GATEKEEPER ROLE

A CONCEPTION OF ALTERNATE REALITIES

Cultures are organized, total ways of life for groups of people. They rest on a definition of reality, a world view, and a conception of the nature of life and of humanity. The people in them build codes of acceptable and unacceptable beliefs, feelings, and conduct. Since some aspects of the human condition differ across cultural boundaries and the subgroups within them, people in these different groups form partially convergent, divergent, and conflicting ways of organizing their lives and interpreting their realities. Professionals function as society's gatekeepers in their role as investigators and as agents of social control and prosocial change. To the extent that they are culture and class bound or otherwise elitist, they may be prone to label divergent and conflicting patterns as psychopathological. In the words of Dumont:

> No work in this society is without its contradictions. I have always believed in "freedom" and "empowerment," and at times thought of myself as a "change agent," but much of the time my actual work has been that of social control. (1992, p. 135)

None of us, including myself, is free from these influences. Intentionally or otherwise, we control others by acting on the basis of our biases and by protecting ourselves from scrutiny by others. As has been argued throughout this book, our best approaches to freeing ourselves from their limiting and distorting effects are self-awareness, self-criticism, and subjecting ourselves and our conduct to external scrutiny. A necessary beginning point is to make our backgrounds and beliefs known at the beginning of any undertaking. How successfully I did so in the Preface and how successfully I have been following my own advice is something readers must necessarily judge from evaluating the material presented here.

As necessary as it is to transcend such personal and cultural limitations, it is also essential that both normality and pathology be defined and studied in relation to the alternate realities in which people live and their convergent views of the essential aspects of human well-being. In Chapter 6, the natures of traditional cultures and modern, urbanized, industrialized cultures were explored, and their overall differences stressed. Traditional cultures emphasize fixed roles and statuses, are resistant to change, and consider individual freedom, initiative, social mobility, and social change orientations to be maladaptive, even pathological. In modern cultures, the opposite is the case.

Judgments of well-being and even normality are outgrowths of belief systems and related behavior patterns. For example, King (1978) pointed out that Western-oriented studies report higher rates of diagnosed pathology in Muslim than in Christian countries. Mental health specialists with a Western medical-illness view of pathology consider spirit world interpretations to be superstition-based explanations and the treatment approaches of traditional healers to be placebo treatment of no scientific merit. Their cultural biases may also lead them to view Judeo–Christian religion-based interpretations and treatments of disorders as being of at least some therapeutic value. Most of these specialists also hold the contrasting belief that their psychological and psychopathological process interpretations and therapies are valid and free of cultural and metaphysical bias.

Another factor that operates primarily within cultures to influence people's well-being is their status as designated by class, caste, or societal position. There is generally an inverse relationship between societal status, control over one's life, and the prevalence of pathology. There have been a number of competing interpretations of this prevailing view of status and pathology relationships. One theory is that the ways lower class and otherwise oppressed people live are not more pathological; they are just judged so because of professional bias. A second theory is that oppressed people exhibit more pathology because of the increased stress in their lives. They are permitted fewer resources and options and then subjected to psychological and social debasement. A third theory is one of downward drift; that is, lower class people have drifted into their situations over generations because of their genetic and psychosocial inferiority. Data presently available do not permit us to judge definitively the relative merit of these theories. For that matter, studies by Hagnell and Nandi and colleagues (Eron & Peterson, 1982) found evidence of more pathology among their upper class respondents. Even limited field studies to evaluate the merits of these data and competing theories about the origins of their findings would require substantial changes in the organization of existing communities. Those changes would inevitably challenge the power and privileges of the people currently possessing them, reducing the likelihood that such research will be conducted.

Another potentially destructive consequence of oppression and privilege that has not been adequately studied is the psychosocially destructive effects of being an oppressor. Once such data are available, advantaged people may become more sensitive to the hidden costs of their life patterns. They may then be more open to exploring alternative community and cultural arrangements.

There are, however, relevant data which have been obtained in limited contexts about the types of biases that influence our interpretations of people's psychosocial conditions and conduct in ways that foster or threaten human well-being. The following sections summarize some of the evidence about the causes of ascribed cognitive defects and psychosocial pathologies. They also address current reasoning about the nature of such conditions.

IDENTIFYING AND ELIMINATING LIFE CONTEXT BIASES IN PSYCHOLOGICAL ASSESSMENT

To reduce the impact of elitist biases on people's psychological dysfunctioning, competence, and well-being, we must identify the nature of their impact on communities and individuals. We must also understand the factors involved and the steps needed to reduce patterns of discrimination if we are to improve the fairness of people's circumstances. In particular, it is crucial to identify how the personal and cultural heritages of professionals enter into their work, knowingly or unknowingly, and how these biases can be minimized.

The most direct evidence of therapists' biases, elitist and otherwise, is found in their criteria and procedures for evaluating people. At its most basic level, the right to assess others is the right to define the terms of their reality. Professionals determine which of a range of ways of living will be legitimized and valued and which declared unacceptable or devalued, a right which determines the parameters and possibilities of people's lives. In particular, the right to determine the categories and dimensions for measuring people is also the right to define hierarchical relationships. That right may include the power of admitting people to society as sane and capable beings and granting access to privileged or desired positions.

These considerations become particularly salient as issues of assessment arise with regard to people from different racial/ethnic/cultural circumstances. Professionals may unjustifiably favor people from backgrounds similar to their own and devalue people from other backgrounds. In the following sections, particular attention has been given to these issues.

THE NATURE OF HUMAN ABILITY

For more than a century, empirically-based systematic means have been used to measure people's psychological qualities in order to reduce the use of irrelevant characteristics as part of assessment judgments. Improving assessment approaches requires freeing the people who build and use the tests from their own biases and eradicating irrelevant considerations from assessment instruments and procedures. Meeting these criteria in a definitive sense is, in principle, impossible. However, it is important that we identify and reduce assessment biases as much as possible.

There is an enormous body of theory and research about how to construct unbiased psychological assessments, and a psychological testing industry has spread throughout the world. Despite enormous efforts, biases and value judgments remain. Examination of one highly publicized and instructive exemplar will help to identify the nature of some of these biases and show how value positions are often used to justify empirically unsupportable judgments which have substantial and far reaching consequences.

In psychology and related fields, no event has generated as much dialogue and controversy around these questions as the publication of *The*

Bell Curve (Herrnstein & Murray, 1994). The authors claim that their book is an unbiased analysis of the available evidence about human intelligence, and they have included a set of public policy recommendations based on their conclusions. However, some of their core premises illustrate the paradigmatic and psychosocial biases often found in assessments of human intellectual ability. Because of the widespread impact of Herrnstein and Murray's conclusions, their premises and arguments are summarized here with the cultural and elitist biases underlying them highlighted.

Herrnstein and Murray asked how U.S. society in the latter twentieth century can address people's differences in intellectual ability in order to survive and prosper without violating its historic commitment to equality. In the following paragraphs, their positions and potential alternatives are examined to determine their merits and identify sustainable justice criteria for using psychological assessments. Their recommended resolution was based on a three-faceted foundation of justice, cognitive ability, and heritability:

Justice

Herrnstein and Murray (1994) referred to the deliberations among the "Founding Fathers" of the United States who

> saw that making a stable and just government was difficult precisely *because* men were unequal in every respect except their right to advance their own interests.... The task of government was to set unequal persons into a system of laws and procedures that would, as nearly as possible, equalize their rights while allowing their differences to express themselves.... In reminding you of these views of the men who founded America, we are not appealing to their historical eminence, but to their wisdom. We think they were right. (pp. 531–532)

They acknowledged that the Founding Fathers were an elite group who believed that a meritocratic elite would inevitably arise in a free society and choose, as well as be chosen, to govern that society. Others would be relegated to a humble status within this free society as determined by the limits in their abilities "that are not their fault" (Herrnstein & Murray, 1994, p. 535). They suggested that justice and equality come together when people acknowledge that their respective roles in society and its governance are determined by their abilities. In Herrnstein and Murray's view, this ideal has been perverted and redefined as "equality of condition" (p. 532), a status which can be approximated only if the state imposes uniformity, thereby defeating the whole process.

This argument is based on assumptions about the nature of people, about what constitutes justice, and about the requirements for a stable, prosocially oriented government. Further, it is true that these are core matters which must be resolved in order to use psychological assessments in just or fair ways. However, that does not mean that the ways Herrnstein and Murray (1994) define justice and equality for everyone, their approach to the use of psychological tests, or both, are supported by existing data.

Cognitive Ability

Herrnstein and Murray (1994) sought to demonstrate (a) that cognitive ability is the core difference between who is (and should be) at the top and who is at the bottom in society and its management and (b) that people's possession of their given amounts of that ability "is not their fault." Consequently, they reasoned that the differing rewards and benefits that people receive from society are their entitlement and their responsibility. People have a reciprocal obligation to society to use their talents to pursue their own interests which, for those at the top, include investing themselves in the governing of society.

One of Herrnstein and Murray's (1994) major premises is that throughout history and across circumstances, civilizations have distinguished among people, using the same smartness–dumbness quality. That quality is the one captured in Spearman's *g*, or general factor, measured by tests that evolved from Binet's efforts in the late nineteenth century to predict which children could profit from schooling in France at that time. For that purpose, he developed a set of questions to assess level of performance on a range of cognitive tasks, not for the purpose of measuring human intelligence, anytime, anywhere. Psychometrically-inclined psychologists and others posited an underlying attribute, general intelligence, or *g*, considered to be an enduring human characteristic or trait whose amount is represented by computing an intelligence quotient.

In an era dominated by Darwinist thought, questions arose about the role of *g* in human evolution, whether it led to our supposed superiority to other species, and whether individual and group differences are evolutionary products. Specifically, people wondered whether races could be ranked according to their degree of evolutionary advancement represented by their respective relative levels of general intelligence. Those questions remain central in much of today's thought among psychologists, educators, and people throughout the world in regard to individual and group differences.

Two common examples, one from physics and one from intellectual assessment, illustrate how proposed explanations come to be viewed as established realities rather than as paradigm-based *symbolic generalizations*. In an earlier era, physicists believed that a medium was needed for the transmission of light. *Ether* was assumed to be that medium, though its qualities were unknown. When another and generally more satisfactory

theory of light transmission was accepted, ether as a symbolic generalization was no longer needed and fell into disuse. Whether the concept of
intelligence will come to suffer a similar fate remains to be seen.

In numerous countries, most students are required to take a test to
establish their intelligence quotient (IQ), their so-called "intelligence."
Many have been confronted by counselors or others in a position to evaluate their posttest performances and informed that they are overachievers
or underachievers. The implication is that, after testing, everyone should
perform at the level predicted by their earlier test scores. The empirical
evidence that tests are imperfect predictors of subsequent performances is
discounted, as is the validity of the later performances, particularly for
anyone who is deemed an overachiever. People become imperfect representations (flawed symbolic generalizations) of the test results, i.e., their
presumed *real* selves.

For Herrnstein and Murray to substantiate the claim that intelligence,
g, is the common cognitive attribute underlying differing levels of human
performance and, consequently, different life circumstances, required at
least two main strategies. They had to demonstrate that level of performance on a standard and unbiased measure of g is directly associated with
different levels of performance on criterion measures that demand a high
level of cognitive functioning. They also had to rule out other factors as
contributors to those differences.

To meet the first objective, Herrnstein and Murray lumped together a
range of intelligence, aptitude (e.g., Scholastic Aptitude Tests), and achievement tests. Their argument for doing so was that those tests are essentially
equivalent for their purposes on the grounds that all of the tests are
correlated and all have been shown, therefore, to relate to g and be measures of it. They argued further that the predictive validity of these measures verified the relation between g and performance in educational
programs, careers, and other intellectually demanding human endeavors.
They dismissed the possibility of societal biases in these measures because
their predictive validity is as high for one racial/ethnic/cultural group as
another, particularly in the mainstream institutions of the United States.
They did not dismiss the mean group differences on the tests, arguing that
those results supported the conclusion that these group differences are
inherited.

Heritability

Herrnstein and Murray (1994) acknowledged that the issue of race and
possible race differences in cognitive ability, in g, is particularly sensitive
and complex. They preferred the word *ethnic* over *race* because of the

difficulties with the latter word in the current context of the United States. Even so, they presented what, to them, was the relevant evidence about certain observed societal inequities, particularly between the average life circumstances of whites and blacks in the United States. They then addressed the issue of *race* in the following way, arguing that these differences originate in people's genes.

> How are we to classify a person whose parents hail from Panama but whose ancestry is predominantly African? Is he a Latino? A black? The rule we follow here is to classify people according to the way they classify themselves.... The studies of "blacks" or "Latinos" or "Asians" who live in America generally denote people who *say* they are black, Latino, or Asian—no more, no less. (Herrnstein & Murray, 1994, p. 271)

It must be noted that the use of such a self-selection criterion is so error ridden that it raises serious questions about whether any valid conclusions can be drawn about genetic inheritance on that basis.

Herrnstein and Murray addressed two other challenging issues, the implications of the *Flynn effect* (Flynn, 1984, 1987) and the growing convergence of mean IQ score levels of black and white students in the United States. The Flynn effect refers to a phenomenon in the United States during this century. Average scores on standard IQ tests have risen, requiring periodic renorming of the tests so that an IQ of 100 (or its equivalent) will remain the mean score for the population. Their explanation was that this pattern probably reflects a change in IQ rather than in cognitive ability—a difficult distinction for us to follow given their earlier assertion of substantial equivalence between the two.

Their argument was justified on two grounds: (a) the overall improvements in the quality of people's lives, and (b) the argument that egalitarian societies may create this effect by disproportionately improving circumstances for those at the bottom. They added that experience, at least theirs, does not support that there are more people at the upper end of the IQ scale than there were in their grandparents' time. They also sought to counter any presumed long-term consequences of the Flynn effect by pointing out that what matters is one's relative position in society, not one's overall level of cognitive ability.

Herrnstein and Murray (1994) buttressed their argument for heritability of intelligence by using an additional argument. They reasoned that in the United States the intellectually enriching level of average environments for blacks would have to be so far below and the intellectually enriching level for East Asians so far above whites' that to attribute these differences in average intelligence to environments is simply implausible. Their reasoning is faulty. They had already argued that enriching people's lives improves their IQs, and disproportionately so for those at the bottom. It is inconsistent to now argue that the presumed g levels underlying IQ differences between groups cannot be accounted for by their environments.

Further, Herrnstein and Murray (1994) pointed out that current mean IQ scores between blacks and whites in the United States are converging. However, they suggested that this effect may stem from integration and affirmative action programs, although they had also argued that environments do not influence g. Even so, they reasoned that these changes have led to enriched opportunities for the relatively small proportion of those at the upper levels of the black population and, they concluded, this convergence is unlikely to continue because the limited pool of "eligible" blacks will soon be depleted. This argument is, in principle, testable over time, but the historical record gives no evidence that the pools of those at the upper or lower levels of IQ are shrinking at all or differentially in the black, white, or East Asian groups.

A CRITIQUE OF HERRNSTEIN AND MURRAY'S ARGUMENT AND RECOMMENDATIONS

Herrnstein and Murray's arguments rest on two underlying weaknesses: (a) a combination of culturally embedded premises and unsubstantiated judgments about the nature of individuals and groups, and (b) the lack of a compelling data base to support their conclusions. However, their conclusions have important consequences for individuals and societies. One of these conclusions is that everyone generally will be better off in the kind of society that they believe was envisioned by the Founding Fathers. This kind of society is supposedly a benevolent, decentralized one in which individuals pursue their own self interest leading to a natural meritocracy that benefits everyone in a prosocial way.

Society's more favored members may find this argument persuasive and support its conclusion. Those less favored may see it as a doctrine promulgated to defend the privileges the more favored enjoy due to their current societal position. In any case, their arguments and conclusions have far reaching consequences for all of us. They warrant serious and immediate attention because of their recommendations—recommendations that any hierarchical society could adopt on similar grounds.

Herrnstein and Murray (1994) advanced several policy evaluations and recommendations as being supported by their conclusions. They proposed a reevaluation of U.S. immigration policy because of their belief that current patterns are having a dysgenic effect on the overall population's intellectual level. After comparing blacks and whites at given IQ

levels, they indicated that blacks may actually be receiving disproportionate societal rewards for their levels of merit. They did not consider that
these black respondents were at a significantly higher level with regard to
the mean IQ level of their own smaller group than were the comparison
whites. (If there is a cultural bias, the black respondents were actually
much brighter than the whites to whom they were being compared and,
using Herrnstein and Murray's reasoning, were consequently entitled to
even higher societal rewards.) Herrnstein and Murray also described U.S.
society as deteriorating and alienated by large, centralized government
programs and a combination of intellectual elitism and affluence among
the cognitively superior. They considered this situation inferior to un-
specified days gone by when there was a supposedly healthier, decentralized society and people had more of a sense of community and had
voluntary reciprocal concern for each other, although they cited no data to
support this judgment.

Rather, here are a few of the premises that they based on The Founding Fathers' self-evident beliefs which were to underlay such a healthy,
decentralized society. These beliefs, which follow, have been or can be
challenged not only by the events of history but by empirical research:
(1) People are, above all, rational beings who act in their own best interest.
(2) People necessarily know what is in their best interest. (3) People in
positions of power and leadership at the time of the Founding Fathers
were there by virtue of their qualities as members of the natural meritocratic elite. (4) The political theory the Founding Fathers espoused was in
no way influenced by their own self-interest above and beyond their
presumed rationality. (5) The Founding Fathers and their successors were
not (and could not be) corrupted by their attendant rewards and privileges, nor would they misuse them to their advantage or that of their
friends, families, fellow meritocrats, or followers.

Other premises of Herrnstein and Murray's (1994) which can be challenged include their assumption that the human qualities which distinguish this particular presumed "natural elite" are universal, inherent, and
in no way shaped or influenced by cultural, social, or individual conditions. That assumption is particularly open to challenge from an examination of their reference list. It includes approximately one thousand references, but at most one hundred (10%) of them were published outside the
United States. Also, most of the references not from U.S. sources are from
Canadian, English, and other Western sources. The content of these refer-
enced materials is primarily about racial/ethnic characteristics and cognitive ability as measured from a Western European perspective. Review of
that list suggests that little attention was paid to "natural meritocratic" or

cognitive ability as measured in other cultures using Western measures or measured anywhere from other cultural/social perspectives about the nature of meritocratic ability or of justice and equality.

In brief, there are alternative possibilities that Herrnstein and Murray did not consider. As Helms (1992) and Marks (1995) suggested, if the cultural equivalence of tests is established, black/white IQ differences might vanish. To go one step further, Helms hypothesized that if the capabilities blacks have developed to survive in their disadvantaged world were included in IQ measures, blacks might prove superior to whites. Under such circumstances, whites might be faced with developing alternative and as yet unidentified cognitive abilities.

A further critical argument against using the concept of race, however identified, for classifying people and explaining differences such as intelligence was carefully documented and presented by Marks (1995). He emphasized that, in matters of substantial public concern, it is particularly important to realize that scientists have vested interests and may justify their biases by appealing to science. By presenting their unfounded reasoning as coming from a neutral science, they may unduly sway others without scientific backgrounds. Marks' (1995) conclusions and recommendations about what he considers to be the race fallacy were based on several major points, including those that follow:

> Human races, whatever they are conceived to be, [are] to a large extent
> ... culturally rather than biologically defined.... Cultural problems
> require cultural solutions: when economic parity is attained, the differences between black and white can be expected to follow those between Irish and Italian—distinctions once thought profound and still
> often identifiable by looks, but ultimately minor.... Unlike the theorists
> of earlier generations, we now perceive that our social future lies with
> identifying talented individuals and developing them, not with assuming the innately superior or inferior abilities of large groups of
> people, based on the achievements of their ancestors or their cultures.
> (p. 275)

That is, individual talents in cognitive ability may best be considered to warrant nourishment as do others for the benefit of society and the individuals involved. Considering cognitive ability levels to be by-products of some underlying group characteristics and justifying differential treatment of people or groups on those grounds is not empirically defensible or socially just.

Herrnstein and Murray made a strong case for considering concepts of justice and equality when considering whether and how to use psychological assessments of individuals and their societies. Ironically, their work heightened attention to the possibility that culturally embedded biases of psychologists are inappropriately influencing assessment approaches and public policies. Because of the potentially far reaching consequences of this possibility, it seems particularly important to evaluate its merits and counter its unsubstantiable recommendations.

REFRAMING THE DIALOGUE

A report sponsored by the American Psychological Association Board of Scientific Affairs (BSA) was published in 1996 with an extensive italicized preamble (Neisser et al.), including the following:

> *In the fall of 1994, the publication of Herrnstein and Murray's book* The Bell Curve *sparked a new round of debate about the meaning of intelligence test scores and the nature of intelligence....* [The BSA] *concluded that there was urgent need for an authoritative report on these issues—one that all sides could use as a basis for discussion. Acting by unanimous vote, BSA established a Task Force charged with preparing such a report.... The report here has the unanimous support of the entire Task Force.* (p. 77)

The BSA report stated that these authors and many of their critics had gone beyond scientific findings in their explicit recommendations on aspects of public policy, but that the BSA's concern was not with policy. Their charge was "to make clear what has been scientifically established, what is presently in dispute, and what is still unknown. In fulfilling that charge, the only recommendations we shall make are for further research and calmer debate" (p. 78).

Despite this disclaimer, the report included implicit and explicit policy recommendations. The decision to make policy recommendations only "for further research and calmer debate" (p. 78) was a policy decision not to rebut existing, scientifically unjustifiable statements and policies. When the Task Force published their report only in the APA's major publication for policy statements, topics of general concern, and business matters, they chose to inform *only* those individuals who had access to and interest in that guild journal. In contrast, *The Bell Curve* was reported and discussed in the popular media and was widely regarded as supporting the view that there is a genetic basis for group differences in intelligence. The Task Force's public silence let that impression stand for society at large. To know that there is no scientific support for a genetic interpretation of intelligence differences, as the Task Force report indicated, has enormous policy implications and profound personal consequences for CDG and NCDG individuals. The former need to reevaluate their unjustified assumption of genetic superiority and change their related behavior. The latter have been told (and may believe) that their low status is a consequence of their genetic inferiority. They need relief from that unjustified belief and opportunities to make changes in their behavior also.

The report also included policy statements about the implication of using group means to evaluate individuals.

> The commitment to evaluate people on their own individual merit is central to a democratic society. It also makes quantitative sense.... Among other things, facts about group differences may be relevant to the need for (and the effectiveness of) affirmative action programs. But while some recent discussions of intelligence and ethnic differences (e.g., Herrnstein & Murray, 1994) have made specific policy recommendations in this area, we will not do so here. Such recommendations are necessarily based on political as well as scientific considerations, and so fall outside the scope of this report. (Neisser et al., 1996, p. 90)

The assertion that we should evaluate others on the basis of individual merit for both political and psychometric reasons is a policy statement, despite their statement that policy issues were outside the scope of the report.

Further, it is demonstrably true that we do evaluate people's individual merits on the basis of group scores. Grubb and Dozier's (1989) discussion of how Visible Racial Ethnic Groups (VREGs) are assessed is one such example. They emphasized that in our interactions with others, we knowingly and unknowingly respond to them and their conduct in relation to our expectations about them as members of a specified group. Thus, the student in Colombia who once said to me, "for a gringo, you're not so bad" was responding to me as a member of a devalued group, but also as an individual who was seen as atypical of that group. The teacher who says to African American students that they are doing well for students with their background is responding to them as members of a devalued group and also is saying that they are atypical members of that group. To not challenge unfounded conventional beliefs is to support the status quo and permit those inequities and injustices to continue, an obvious policy position.

The central figures in the early testing movement believed there was a genetic basis to racial differences in intellectual capacities (Howitt & Owosu-Bempah, 1994). A century later, the BSA Task Force's use of scientific neutrality as the rationale for not publicly challenging that position raises a question about professional ethics. There is a point at which we have a professional responsibility to challenge conventional wisdom and public statements based on erroneous or nonexistent scientific data (Kelman, 1968).

A pervasive example of selective inattention in the testing movement continues to exist with regard to the generalized use of IQ and related tests, especially given the level of their predictive validity. The Task Force report indicated that IQ can predict less than one third of the variance in academic success as that success also depends on many personal, social support, and general educational factors. IQ contributes somewhat less to job performance and even less to most negative outcomes such as juvenile delinquency. It is both a scientific and policy responsibility to be clear about the limits to the uses of test scores. For example, all scores within the standard error of measurement from a particular reference score (usually the highest score) are equivalent for predictive purposes. When using test scores in this way, called "banding," all individuals within a "band" are equally qualified. Banding may or may not serve to advantage individuals from any given racial/ethnic background, but making selection decisions in that way ensures that they are made on the basis of sound statistical reasoning (Cascio, Goldstein, Outtz, & Zedeck, 1995; Cascio, Outtz, Zedeck, & Goldstein, 1995).

The Task Force also failed to address the potential for inequities in using correlational statistics to identify common variance among test components and to construct measures such as IQ tests. This type of approach is quite limited in its ability to be responsive to cultural/ethnic differences in a heterogeneous culture. Common variance (skills) unique to a smaller group is necessarily overshadowed. Consequently, although predictions made from test scores are assumed to be equally valid for all individuals in the population, they are biased in favor of individuals from the larger group.

Two lines of reasoning lead to the conclusion that current approaches to the measurement of human cognitive abilities are biased in ways that serve to perpetuate the status quo. The first relates to the above point that neither the tests nor their conventional uses adequately consider cultural differences; the second concerns the nature of intelligence. Helms (1992) argued that there has been no serious study of the cultural equivalence of tests or of environments. Rather, the assumption has been made that there are racial differences on cognitive ability tests (CATs) and, without any demonstration of the phenomenon, it has been concluded that the Eurocentric approach to cognitive processing is universally superior. Since there are few or no VREG psychometricians and few VREG psychologists, the task of reducing Eurocentric bias is left up to white Eurocentric psychologists. The people who are in a position to challenge the Eurocentric view are the people who support it, and vice versa.

Boykin (1986, 1994) emphasized that black youth, at least in the United States, are socialized differently from white youth, and these different experiences could lead to their developing a different form of cognitive ability. Grubb and Dozier (1989) hypothesized that black youth in the

United States are "too busy to learn" the cognitive abilities valued in mainstream white society. They are engaged in other activities that have survival value in their immediate world. It would follow that blacks doing as well as whites on a test that measures what Helms (1992) has called white g are probably higher on the abilities underlying that presumed trait because they are taking a test written for another culture. To offset that imbalance would require diversification, in that

> existing tests ought to be modified to include greater cultural variety, new types of cognitive assessment must be developed and standardized, and instead of using race as a proxy for other factors (e.g., attitudes, environments), explicit principles, hypotheses, assumptions, and theoretical models for investigating these other factors must be proposed. (Helms, 1992, pp. 1097–1098)

The second and more radical challenge to the theoretical formulation of intelligence stems from its origin as a symbolic generalization that became embedded in Western culture's paradigmatic theory about human abilities. The symbolic construct and the tests are not acontextual although they are presumed to measure cognitive ability or g. They have been selected in culturally biased ways and test the respondent's skill level with the particular kind of abstract symbolizing characteristic of modern, science based societies and required for success, particularly in their schools. In cultures with different forms of education and ways of life, respondents may not have the experiences or skills to understand or perform well on these tests.

To challenge this conception of intelligence and its properties requires formulating a different paradigmatic model. That different model would define intelligence as the cognitive characteristics and skills that differentiate people on culturally valued performance dimensions. It would start with the assumption that, in biologically intact individuals whose basic nutritional requirements are met, intelligence is almost exclusively a function of ecological survival demands, socialization practices, and life experiences. For many, including African Americans and Native Americans in the United States, the intelligence characteristics they develop are those that serve well in circumstances that include being treated as if they were genetically inferior rather than products of the environments to which they are frequently relegated.

Phinney (1996) argued that ethnicity (including race) is best thought of as a "complex multidimensional construct which by itself explains little" (p. 918), rather than as a categorical variable. For psychology, the central concern is how ethnicity impacts on the individual. We can argue that, to the extent people are knowers and active agents, they can reject the influence of their labels. Even so, the effort of responding to rejection exacts a psychological cost, often an enormous one. To the extent that people are influenced as *known* and their life experiences are different because of negative attributions, the effect of these attributions is even more destructive than it would be if those affected could respond to them as active agents, as *knowers*. Phinney (1996) cited a study by Jones which showed that "interviewees who were treated in a subtly negative way actually behaved in ways that confirmed their inadequacy" (p. 924). In innumerable ways, how others define us and how we are taught to define ourselves impact on us psychologically. As Jones' research suggested, that stigmatizing can have a self-fulfilling effect that perpetuates and justifies the originally unjustified distinction.

As I emphasized in another context (F. Tyler, 1989), constructing a theory of psychology which does equal justice to individuals of more than one cultural world is different from our current approach based on Western positivism. Theories need to be developed by people with different cultural groundings and psychological traditions. Such theories are currently called indigenous psychologies, the people developing them are called indigenous psychologists, and both are assigned a secondary, pejorative status. Despite their low status, such psychologies continue to be developed and to provide us with a basis for developing culturally equivalent criteria for cognitive ability, assessment approaches, and identifying the relevance of particular aspects of cognitive abilities in different contexts. A dialogue to find the convergences, divergences, and points of conflict among these perspectives can lead to new resolutions based on contributions from all of the cultures involved.

Such an approach can sidestep the ethnocentric valuing and devaluing of people and turn the uses of assessment from deciding how superior or "human" people are in a hierarchical sense. It will not sidestep that people do differ in capabilities in a variety of ways, nor avoid the value of informing people about their skills and potential capabilities for contributing to their own well-being and to society's many differing tasks. Although each of us must come to terms with our own limitations and potentials, this alternative approach will provide other bases for doing so. We will continue, for any variety of reasons, to live with experiencing failures, accidents, or other traumas which prove devastating and shattering. It only means that people's misfortunes and blessings will not be attributed to causes which are supported by biases.

THE NATURE OF HEALTH AND PSYCHOPATHOLOGY

Dumont (1992) emphasized that there are personal and societal gains from taking an elitist CDG stance when working as a community psychiatrist who seeks to help the poor.

To be mentally ill is to feel one's membership in society up for question. It is to be marginal, deviant, outside. It has always been functional for fragmented and fluid social systems to identify and persecute deviants, who serve as the territorial markers for a false and fleeting sense of identity. We are not *them*—Jews, witches, communists, psychotics—we are *not them* (p. 141).

As nondiagnosed individuals, and especially as professionals, we must decide whether our biases contribute to the creation and sustaining of the deviant conduct we are presumably committed to alleviate. Do we actually bolster our own societal membership at others' expense by emphasizing our status-based, elitist stance in relation to people who are deviant? We cannot eliminate such biases from our thinking, our research, or our professional and personal lives until they are identified and more clearly understood. Possible sources, forms, and effects of elitist, racist, and professionalist biases are outlined in the following paragraphs.

King's (1978) review of two years of research on psychopathology is a penetrating analysis of the ways that racist and professional elitist prejudices continued to shape accepted theories and practices in diagnosis and treatment. He found that the field had changed little over two decades during which social and community contributions to disordered behavior were emphasized. The search for disease processes caused by underlying pathologies continued to be dominant. Explorations of stress-inducing psychosocial circumstances were focused primarily on how they impact patterns of pathology, not on the relationship of life status to such circumstances and breakdowns. As emphasized in Chapter 10, those emphases on the search for underlying pathologies are still predominant two decades later.

Most of the existing research on abnormal behavior is formulated within the illness model and is conducted by male members of each culture's CD groups. Most criteria and measures for diagnosing abnormal behavior embody those CDG values in a number of ways. Research and diagnostic measures often involve paper and pencil tests or verbally presented interview formats. In either case, questions emphasize CDG characteristics, so respondents must be skilled at expressing their life views and concerns in abstract verbal terms and with reference to CDG norms. Thus, professionals judge normality, in part, as conformity in values, conduct, and modes of expression with CDG world views. NCDG individuals often live in circumstances and by a conception of what constitutes a meaningful life style and world-view which are different from those of CDG individuals. Issues of whether their life circumstances are more stress inducing and their life styles more adaptive in their life contexts are not raised. Their deviations from a CDG orientation are judged as indicative of psychopathology.

However, there are studies of child rearing and of social stress that illustrate the value of knowing how specific experiences and socialization patterns influence the development of psychological disturbance. For example, there are identifiable parental attitudes and approaches to child rearing which predispose children to psychological breakdown across differences in circumstances (Baumrind, 1993). They include overprotectiveness and smothering love, harsh or authoritative domination and emotional distance, coldness or actual physical neglect, and the imposition of excessive expectations or standards. Comparisons of Mexican and U.S. children show a direct relationship between encouragement to early independence and a higher level of anxiety, irritability, and thought disorganization in the U.S. children (Albert, 1974; Laoso, Laria-Topia, & Swartz, 1974). At the very least, these findings support the conclusion that, no matter what approaches cultural CDG norms endorse, moderate levels of affection, closeness, support, and demands on children are far more benign than are extreme parental (and cultural) approaches to socializing them.

Incidence levels of abnormal psychological disturbances are also affected by the presence of social stress factors. U.S. studies found urban lower class women to be more prone to pathological disturbance and identified a cluster of stress factors that undermine a woman's capability to maintain a meaningful personal life and social role (Brown, Brokham, & Harris, 1975). That cluster included lack of emotional support early in life and, currently, present stress (young children at home), and lack of the personal status provided by work-related role expectations, and lack of the material rewards provided by a job.

Cultures, social systems, communities, and family groups can be fully understood and evaluated only if their own conceptions of reality and the nature of a meaningful life and social order are considered. Patterns of abnormality and well-being are integral parts of every culture. Similarly, the patterns of dysfunction and well-being in any NCDG or CDG are integral parts of their overarching culture. These patterns are inextricably intertwined, and all of us are carriers of them at tacit as well as explicit levels. For example, it seems highly unlikely that psychologists socialized and educated in the United States or other Western societies are going to identify themselves as racists. Yet, if we are not racists, then how can racism pervade the discipline and its scientific and professional practices?

That question has received relatively little attention, but is the central focus of *The Racism of Psychology: Time for Change* (Howitt & Owusu-

Bempah, 1994). Howitt is a native-born Briton; Owusu-Bempah is a native-born Ghanian who emigrated to England. They identified the differences between British and U.S. societies and their respective fields of psychology. They emphasized that there are many parallels and overlaps, including that the two countries' shared racism is institutional.

> Psychology, like medicine, is a social institution mirroring societal values, including racism. Besides, the professionalization of psychology was largely a phenomenon of the late nineteenth and early twentieth centuries, a period of unmitigated racism, empire building and white dominance. Institutions in this racist epoch inevitably served white society's interests—they were created to do no other, and the blueprint remains. (Howitt & Owusu-Bempah, 1994, p. 143)

Howitt and Owusu-Bempah (1994) demonstrated that psychology has many roots in the Social Darwinist and genetic approaches, including the following:

1. People's differences, particularly those between people of African and European ancestry, continue to be considered racial. It is misleading and dangerous to focus simply on the racism of a few famous psychologists such as Galton, Burt, and McDougall who were admittedly racist. Such a narrow focus permits us to ignore the racist structure of society and our discipline.

2. The "liberal" tradition in psychology continues to be characterized by the belief that black culture was so destroyed by slavery that blacks have, at best, a dysfunctional cultural fabric. Supposedly, black culture is matriarchy dominated so that it includes no basis for positive male role models or for males to have a positive image of themselves. Studies over the past twenty-five years by Hill, McAdoo, and Young (as cited in Howitt and Owusu-Bempah, 1994) used a strength/resilience approach and found that the extended black family, at least in the United States, acts to preserve itself and that black fathers are nurturant, warm, and loving to their children. Yet "notwithstanding such research evidence indicating many positive strengths of the black family structure, stereotypes about the black family abound and persist in the social science literature, *especially psychology*" (Howitt & Owusu-Bempah, 1994, p. 47; italics added).

3. "Scientific detachment" has allowed those who identify themselves as liberals to avoid directly confronting the harsh realities that racism imposes on its victims. Liberals assume that racism is perpetuated by racists. Consequently, as Howitt and Owusu-Bempah (1994) pointed out, liberals can conclude that they "need not see the locus of responsibility as much in their thinking and actions as elsewhere" (p. 61).

4. "Everyday racist psychology" (Howitt & Owusu-Bempah, 1994, p.

62) was and is an integral part of the paradigms of practicing psychologists. It contributes to biases which are accepted without question or awareness in ability testing, diagnosis, remedial education, and therapy. Goodchilds (1991) also indicated that "as to [the involvement of organized psychology in the United States with current issues], we guiltlessly acknowledge that our discipline is generally ahistorical" (p. 2). That stance is one of the reasons why the field remains racist in certain essential, if unwitting, ways; its institutional structures maintain the earlier, established patterns.

How do psychologists, even those who consider themselves antiracists, function generally to perpetuate racism? Jones (1991) summarized his understanding of the origin of current racist conceptions in psychology's approach, stating that

> blacks and other minority racial and ethnic groups share distrust of psychology as a discipline that purports to understand human behavior. This distrust of psychology stems in part from the apparent inability of traditional approaches to discern bases of strength, resilience, and capacity and competence in these racial groups. The so-called deficit model of human behavior tends to dominate the discipline and serves to alienate those psychologists and would-be psychologists from minority racial and ethnic groups from full participation in the discipline. (p. 14)

In short, psychologists contribute in many ways to a climate of distrust of their own profession, even by NCDG psychologists within the profession.

Fulani (1988) emphasized that black women in the United States are confronted both in traditional therapy and in the white (CDG) work world with having to compensate for who they are. However, they cannot because they are not middle class whites. She went further, arguing that she believes

> there is something we *can* do other than adapting people to society. We can help people adapt to history ... by facilitating the collective experience of building new social environments that meet their emotional needs, rather than adapting impotently and nondevelopmentally to existing societal environments. (p. xvii)

To help people "adapt to history" or even live with their current reality requires that we have relevant information. Yet, research about psychotherapy with African Americans has largely been marginalized in both Britain and the United States. In the 1960s and early 1970s, there was an upsurge of such articles in the United States in relation to the emphasis on social change, but they have decreased since then. There is a wide range of speculation about reasons for this limited attention including a universalist orientation, fear of socially sensitive research, current trends (e.g., social psychology has become more cognitive and less social), and an absence of ethnic minority psychologists, especially African Americans (Howitt & Owusu-Bempah, 1994; F. Tyler, Brome, & Williams, 1991). These possible explanations may have some relevance, but appealing to the absence of ethnic minority psychologists should not be used to imply that only ethnic minority psychologists are responsible for or need be concerned about sociocultural differences. Those deficiencies are the responsibility of everyone in the discipline. As Graham suggested,

> academic psychology cannot retain its integrity by continuing to allow ethnic minorities to remain so marginalized in mainstream research. In contemporary society, most of the population is not White and middle class. Neither should the subject populations in the journals of our discipline continue to be so disproportionately defined. (1992, p. 638)

Howitt and Owusu-Bempah (1994) provided a detailed and thoughtfully reasoned indictment of psychology and Western psychologists' racism. They included an account of the reasons for the continuing presence and persistence of these elements even in the face of explicit institutional policies and the efforts of many individuals directed at removing them. They also identified the changes needed to eliminate racist influences and to depict what implementing such changes would involve. Their main themes included that racism is a particularly destructive and persistent form of elitism that is manifest in the structure and practice patterns of psychology and psychologists. NCDG individuals and groups are viewed pejoratively and treated less equitably, and psychologists do not consider it their responsibility to overcome the discrimination and injustice. They believe their NCDG clients are responsible for making those changes.

Howitt and Owusu-Bempah (1994) argued that

> for some 500 years racism has been central to the activities of the European world.... Internationally and nationally, the benefits of these arrangements accrue to white people. In view of psychology's perennial complicity in this, the least today's psychology can do towards rectifying this legacy is to seek to be actively anti-racist; its theories, research and practice should arraign against racism.... Morally and ethically, the case for anti-racism is both an individual and professional matter, but nevertheless ultimately indivisible. (p. 161f)

A TRANSCULTURAL ETHNIC VALIDITY PERSPECTIVE

It has been emphasized throughout this chapter that the power to assess any part of others' realities is also the power to intervene in their lives in ways that advantage or disadvantage people and their possibilities. Howitt and Owusu-Bempah (1994) highlighted the different and parallel ways that CDG people of the United States and Great Britain have directed white racism toward NCDG black people living in those countries. When those of us with assessment power begin to make less biased judgments, we can serve the interests of people different from, as well as like, ourselves and contribute to the formation of a more benign social order. For this possibility to be realized, we must develop more supportable criteria for what constitutes less biased judgments.

The United Nations provides the most widely accepted forum for defining conceptions of desirable societies and models of individual well-being as well as desirable ways to attain these goals. Its most basic statement is that all people are equal in dignity and rights. The concepts of dignity and rights are considered psychosocial expressions of socially and individually meaningful aspects of human identity and relations. Civil and political rights characterized the initial United Nations formulations of a universal conception of human rights (Tolley, 1987). Those rights also characterized Herrnstein and Murray's conception of basic rights; however, the United Nations added to this list social, cultural, and economic rights, including the minimum requirements to sustain life.

Conceptions of desirable societies and models of individual well-being have varied on a multitude of dimensions across societies and throughout history. As noted in earlier chapters, the ways that societies and individuals organize themselves have consequences for whether and how they accomplish their objectives. All approaches provide benefits and costs, and all can be evaluated. Within the broad realm of psychological dysfunction, patterns observed in particular cultures and circumstances may be similar to those in other contexts, yet differ in their meaning. Any fixed standards about what constitutes well-being or dysfunction imposed by representatives of any group, including elitist groups, are partly a product of that group's biases, implicit or explicit, or both. Broader, transculturally valid guidelines can and should be developed for contributing to the well-being of people and their communities.

Given their institutionalized role, psychologists have a special opportunity and responsibility to help form the social requirements that must be met for individuals to define, acquire, and maintain their basic rights, including the basic economic and social rights essential to the development of cognitive and social functioning. That conclusion is particularly important because the work of psychologists, including their assessment and intervention approaches and their definitions of competence and pathology, are being widely used in most parts of today's world. Psychologists can hardly justify ignoring this responsibility.

THE HELPING PARADOX

Social and behavioral scientists justify their professional roles on the grounds that they have the professional skills and an institutionalized commitment to apply them. That commitment is to enable people to avoid or overcome debilitating and destructive conduct, live more fulfilling and productive lives, and contribute in prosocial ways to their societies. This formulation has created a paradox (F. Tyler, Pargament, & Gatz, 1983; F. Tyler, Brome, & Williams, 1991). The helper and the person(s) to be helped face the same human life span limitations and possibilities, including those associated with attaining autonomy and control over their lives and relationships. Yet, as Korchin (1976) noted, clinical psychology and related therapeutic fields have defined the role for the client as one of dependence. An overview of therapeutic models (F. Tyler, Pargament, & Gatz, 1983) showed that they emphasize unidirectionality of influence from the therapist to the client.

Therapists are expected to rely on their personal and professional resources for guidance, but not on the client (Korchin, 1976). Responsiveness to the client's view has been labeled countertransference and considered to be countertherapeutic (Greenson, 1967). The helping paradox for the client is how to become independent through acting dependent. On the other hand, therapists must learn how to impart independence to clients while treating them in a dependent fashion and expecting them to be dependent. This same dilemma is seen in more recently fashionable efforts to conceptualize the goal of therapy as that of *empowerment*. The dilemma is how to empower someone without doing so in a disempowering way.

Murrell (1973) noted that a somewhat comparable paradox arises in community psychology. The community psychologist's goal is to help communities function more effectively and more autonomously. Community psychologists provide expertise and also seek to establish a collaborative role between themselves and the communities where they are working. The paradox arises between the community's dependence on the professional's expertise and its goal to become capable of conducting its own affairs. The psychologist's paradox lies in the effort to be both a professional expert and a collaborative colleague.

As Zwerling et al. (1976) documented, community mental health policies and practitioners primarily serve elitist goals, including racism and professionalism, because the helping paradox has not been resolved at institutional or individual levels. They exclude socioracial and ethnic minorities (NCDGs) from full participation in defining their own and their communities' ways of life. Rather, the qualities of good lives and communities are defined for everyone by ethnic majority professionals (CDGs).

The available evidence supports that human well-being rests on everyone's active involvement in creating, constructing, and guiding their own lives. Individuals or groups who assume an elitist stance by defining cultural, community, or individual well-being for everyone render all of us less, not more, adequate people. The task confronting not just psychologists and other professionals, but everyone, is how to involve ourselves and others more effectively in our own lives and societies, not reduce people's involvement. Accomplishing that task requires working out a basis for interacting that does not perpetuate our power and privileged position as professionals in contrast to the position of our clients.

A Resource Collaborator Role

To resolve the helping paradox, professionals and clients must include themselves in the reciprocity of their interactions. By acknowledging the expertise of all parties and including their participation in all aspects of collective enterprises (Argyris, 1975) including community development projects (F. Tyler, Gatz, & Pargament, 1983), this paradox can be resolved. The resource–collaborator model is representative of such models in that it involves everyone in constructing more fulfilling lives and societies.

The resource collaborator model's basic assumptions are as follows: In any interaction, all of the participants are the central agents in their own lives. Each has special, unique skills and perspectives to contribute to the interaction. Each is the basic judge of her or his own perspective and can most constructively interact only when that role and perspective are understood and accepted. All interactions provide reciprocal benefits since all parties learn from them. Interaction may be initiated by either party. Thus, a resource collaborative model "involves a process of interaction in which the nature and the goals of the relationship, the nature of the problem, the problem-solving process, the point at which the relationship is terminated, and the evaluation of its success are to some degree jointly determined" (F. Tyler, Gatz, & Pargament, 1983).

The model's crucial element is its incorporation of a process that is consistent with the substance and goals of the interaction. The collaborative process integrates the role of all parties as active participants in the development of knowledge and patterns of change consistent with that process. In particular, it affirms that all of the collaborators are actively and responsibly involved in sustaining their own lives and communities and those of others.

The greater efficacy of reciprocal interactions over hierarchical and unidirectional ones has been supported in a variety of studies, including studies about work morale and productivity (Deci, 1975), the social networks of normal and disturbed people (Tolsdon, 1976; Laoso, Lara-Tapia, & Swartz, 1974), collaborative (in contrast to hierarchical) community mental health center staffs (Hurley & F. Tyler, 1976), school and community settings (Sarason & Lorentz, 1979; Sarason et al., 1977), religious congregations (Pargament, F. Tyler, & Steele, 1979), and collaborative research groups (F. Tyler, Pargament, & Gatz, 1983). Exemplars of a resource–collaborator approach have also been reported by Kagitcibasi (1996, see Chapter 6) and others from a variety of cultures. Potentially similar approaches can be productively incorporated in other aspects of individual, institutional, and societal interactions and within any ethnic validity framework.

SUMMARY

To move beyond racism, professionalism, and other forms of elitism in our individual and community lives, it is necessary to examine our unquestioned social values. Unexamined assumptions and perspectives, whether cultural, socioracial, or status based, predispose us to use the biases in them when we make judgments about ourselves and others. This is as true for professionals as for nonprofessionals.

There are many areas in which we can obtain needed information only by proceeding collaboratively with those involved. Those areas include information about the social values underlying our research approaches and the socially oriented programs we propose, implement, and evaluate. We need knowledge about the strengths and limits of diversity in communities and societies, and we need a better understanding of the role, values, and limits of self-determination and ascribed statuses in our lives and communities. The advantages and disadvantages of various patterns of intrapersonal, interpersonal, social, and cultural interactions warrant more intensive study. Finally, of course, it behooves those of us who are social or behavioral scientists or professionals, or both, to ask the individuals, communities, and cultures where they think their best interests lie and how we are hurting as well as helping them.

In summary, the data and perspectives presented in this chapter support the view that people and communities are better served if they and the professionals jointly contribute to decisions about their situations, problems, and possibilities. People and their communities are also better served when the possibilities of all humans, regardless of race, ethnic status, gender, and other characteristics are acknowledged, and their development is supported. We need to acknowledge that there are many ways of organizing human lives and societies, but none without both costs and benefits. All cultural patterns have strengths and limitations. There is much to gain if professionals and others work together to identify how people can enhance their strengths and develop mutually enriching approaches to others within their own and other cultures.

PSYCHOSOCIAL PERSPECTIVE ON VIOLENCE AND EXTREMISM

INTRODUCTION

Violence, the infliction of harm on others, and violently imposed extremist views are world wide problems. It is vital to all of us as socially responsible individuals to understand and contain violence and extremism. To seriously address this need requires a psychosocial framework because of the variety of individual, ethnic, and cultural factors that contribute to the development and expression of both. Preventing and managing violence and extremist views requires coordinated efforts to change individuals and their contexts. Unfortunately, most of the psychological material relevant to violence and extremism comes from the Western world and, in particular, from the United States. To offset that bias, emphasis in this chapter is placed on broader transcultural considerations.

The Pervasiveness of Individual Violence

The most recent nationwide survey of family violence in the United States was made in the 1970s, a particularly violent era. According to Straus and Gelles (1979), between 25 and 50 percent of spouses committed physically violent acts toward each other in 1975. One-fourth of the respondents indicated that spouse abuse is sometimes permissible. More husbands were violent toward their wives, but violent wives were more often violent. Comparable surveys revealed that over 80 percent of parents with children aged 3 to 17 used corporal punishment and nearly 3 percent of them had used a knife or gun (Segal, 1979).

Corporal punishment was pervasive in U.S. schools, and courts supported its use as a "traditional tool in Western educational systems" even though teachers and administrators are not "reliable instruments of justice" (Hentoff, 1979). The media focused on violence, and sports such as football and hockey glorified it. Crime and the use of weapons had risen, and people stoutly resisted even the control of handguns (Shields, 1981). There were also substantial amounts of rape (Brownmiller, 1975), riots, and police violence.

Through the 1990s, these patterns remain largely unchanged in the United States (*Violence*, 1996). There is also substantial evidence that domestic violence is pervasive in many cultures although its forms vary (Walker, 1999; Counts, Brown, & Campbell, 1992), including, for example, violence by children toward their parents and pervasive violence toward elders. We may protest that using violence is justified under certain circumstances. On occasion, we spank our children, slap or strike our spouses, and want a gun for protection. However, we argue that such actions do not mean that we are violent people; we see ourselves as victims, not perpetrators of violence, especially extreme acts. Unfortunately, it is not quite that simple.

Social Psychology Weighs In

The nature of violence has been an important focus of research in the United States over the past quarter century. Milgram (1974) horrified his colleagues and others with violence-related experiments demonstrating that ordinary people will inflict amazing amounts of punishment on each other in a context of being told to use punishment for teaching purposes. Even more troubling was that Milgram justified using his authority as a psychologist and experimenter to ask others to inflict pain on their fellows in his experiments. He reasoned that since the participants did not actually inflict physical harm, but only thought they had, there was no actual harm.

Although we expect a psychologist to be concerned about the possibility of psychological harm resulting from research procedures, Milgram apparently gave little consideration to it. Rather, he appealed to clinicians and sought affirmation from colleagues and the majority of the study participants (after their participation) that experimentally inciting others to be violent was justified. Of course, supporting him enabled the participants to justify their own violence. He did not consider that possibility, although it may underlie the rationales people use to defend even extreme violence.

In his epilogue, Milgram (1974) explored the broader implications of his work.

> The results, as seen and felt in the laboratory, are to this author disturbing.
> They raise the possibility that human nature, or—more specifically—

the kind of character produced in American democratic society, cannot be counted on to insulate its citizens from brutality and inhumane treatment at the direction of malevolent authority. A substantial proportion of people do what they are told to do, irrespective of the content of the act and without limitations of conscience, so long as they perceive that the command comes from a legitimate authority. (p. 189)

Left to wonder whether it is our flawed nature or our flawed society which underlies our participation in violence, Milgram concluded that flaws in our society are the more frightening possibility. I disagree. We can modify, if not completely eliminate, the more destructive aspects of our society; but if we cannot modify our own violent natures, we have little hope.

Zimbardo and his colleagues (Haney, Banks, & Zimbardo, 1973) set up a simulated prison experiment in which ordinary young adult males were randomly assigned to be either guards or prisoners. Within six days, the guards had become increasingly aggressive and sadistic; the prisoners had resisted, had tried to escape, and had become depressed, confused, and withdrawn. The effects were so strong that the study was discontinued. That study and its ramifications are still being discussed. One implication is that we seem to be creatures of context as well as captains of our own fates.

Many people and societies support the use of violence to stop other violence that is socially disapproved, and some would even destroy those who express, or act on the basis of, a viewpoint different from their own. Therein lies a counterpart to the helping paradox. That is, how can one form of violence be justified in order to curb another form of violence?

According to T. Tyler and Smith (1998), the current widespread attention to the psychology of retribution has focused attention on whether using violence to constrain disapproved behavior actually fuels more violence. The study of conceptions of distributive (fairness of outcomes) and procedural (fairness of procedures) justice has been linked to people's voluntary willingness (acting as active agents) to obey rules and accept decisions or change them or their institutions, or both. This paradigmatic approach is particularly relevant to understanding and managing the violence of people and their societies because it highlights several core points: (a) Any sense of fairness of procedures or outcomes is subjective; (b) since these judgments of fairness involve more than one person, they are social as well as individual; and (c) understanding these judgments requires understanding ourselves as individuals and as social beings and the psychosocial relationship between the two. That is, this emerging perspective has incorporated the assumption that we function as knowers who are responsible for the decisions we make to maintain and change our behavior as individuals, the nature of our societies, and the relation between the two—violence does not just happen.

SPIRALS OF VIOLENCE

A Psychosocial Competence Approach to Understanding Violence

Chapters 5 and 6 presented an individual psychosocial competence model of how people form psychosocial configurations that they use to guide their dealings with their lives and circumstances across their life spans. A number of studies have demonstrated that there are prototypic psychosocial competence patterns at the different ends of a spiral of effectiveness and dysfunction (Toch, 1992; F. Tyler, 1991; F. Tyler & Pargament, 1982). Evidence of how these kinds of spirals lead individuals and groups to adopt extremist beliefs and violent life styles is summarized below.

Exemplars of Violence as a Destructive Spiral

Toch studied violent men in prison and those who police and guard them and reported that their characteristic, violence-producing orientation rested on the premise that people's

> relationships are power-centered, one-way affairs. They involve efforts at self-assertion with a desperate, feverish quality that suggests self doubt. The violence-provoking incident typically consists of several stages: first, there is the classification of the other person as an object or a threat; second, there is some action based on this classification; third, the other person may act—if he has the chance—to protect his integrity. At this junction, the violent incident reaches its point of no return. (1969, p. 183f.)

Defending oneself against a violent attack affirms the attacker's prior belief that he will be threatened, so he escalates his attack. The cycle is now underway.

Toch explored how these men become violent and concluded that they are predisposed from their earlier experiences to behave in ways that start and accelerate these spirals:

> Self-assertiveness or defensiveness suggests that one's upbringing has been deficient in stability and emotional support, thus making it difficult for positive self-perceptions to develop.... Brittle egos spend their adult years in belated efforts to buttress themselves at the expense of other people, and these efforts become productive of violence. (1992, p. 183f.)

Uncertainty does not inevitably predict violence proneness. Contexts in which violent responses are effective are more likely to lead to spirals of violence, and they are more prevalent in oppressive environments such as urban ghettos or where there are traditions of settling personal differences violently (e.g., Sicily, Balkan countries). Yet, Toch emphasized that in the final analysis "it is these individuals, who meet the norm 'thou may be violent' much more than halfway, who best personify the sociopsychological model of subculturally induced violence" (1992, p. 191).

Gibson (1991) explored how people can be and have been taught to inflict pain, be violent, and torture others. She also examined the seemingly paradoxical issues of how countries can simultaneously train military personnel to be violent and to reduce the "institutionalized commission of pain" (p. 84). Particularly, can people be trained to disobey inappropriate orders, e.g., to torture people? She used the available evidence to construct a framework of factors that contribute to violence and to effective training of people to inflict it on others, even though doing so may be repugnant to them. Her framework integrated ways to change participants so that they (a) felt threatened and justified their own views and actions, (b) felt their future victims were evil, unworthy, or both and needed to be punished or even destroyed, and (c) believed that violence against the victims was justified. It included techniques to:

1. Teach obedience to authority, possibly as part of a "right-wing authoritarian" configuration including submissiveness, conventionalism, and aggressiveness based on fearfulness and self-righteousness.
2. Create situational characteristics that (a) emphasized approval, support, or both by the authorities for inflicting pain, and/or (b) were characterized by "circumstances that bind individuals psychologically one to another and make them comfortable, first, in situations in which they learn new obedient behaviors and, later, in situations in which they must maintain them" (Gibson, 1991, p. 76).
3. Invoke mechanisms such as the disengagement of internal controls (e.g., psychological objections to atrocities), euphemistic labeling (e.g., planning a *humane* approach to mass murder, or perhaps redefining corporal punishment, e.g., "this is going to hurt me more than you"), and dehumanizing (e.g., labeling slaves as nonhuman, religious opponents as heathen), or blaming ("you brought it on yourself") victims for the violence being inflicted on them.

Gibson emphasized that these factors are not reserved for special training of individuals being prepared for positions as torturers. The selection and training of police and military forces incorporate them. Finally, she underscored two additional points about individual differences: (a) Ordinary people can be taught to inflict pain; such behavior is not confined to people who are predisposed to inflict pain; and (b) even under extreme circumstances (e.g., military combat), some people do not inflict pain on others.

It is not necessary to seek out extreme or structured circumstances to find evidence of the dynamics of human violence. These same factors are part of people's everyday experiences, and they influence the course of patterns of violence. Grebner, Gross, Signorelli, and Morgan (1980) found that heavy television viewing of violence by adults and children not only cultivated aggressive tendencies in a minority, but also led to a generally exaggerated sense of personal risk and mistrust among the heavy viewers. Their heavier television viewing set up expectations that are likely to generate confirmation and precipitate spirals of violence.

Other studies have also linked people's previous violence-related experiences, expectations, and behaviors to their subsequent proneness to similar expectations and responses. Lewis, Shanok, Pincus, and Cilases (1979) compared more and less violent incarcerated juvenile delinquents. The more violent juveniles had experienced and witnessed more extreme physical abuse. O'Neal, Brunault, Marquis, and Carifio (1979) found that as adult males were angered, they wanted more personal space—a larger "buffer zone." Steele (as cited in Segal, 1979) confirmed that children who were abused early in life exhibited low self-esteem, a wary and watchful "hypervigilance; and inadequate skills of learning and living" (p. 587).

The interplay of people's role and relationships in overlapping contexts also contributes to patterns of violence. Parents are more abusive to their children when they are angry with each other (Aydub & Pfeifer, 1979). Hoppe (1979) found that college students were more aggressive when provoked, and that the highest level of aggression was exhibited when highly masculine males were opposed by a male. Males were less aggressive to females; females were equally aggressive to both sexes. When male social drinkers were drinking, they were not only more aggressive but could not differentiate as well between counteraggression related to their behavior and nonrelated counteraggression (Zeichner & Pihl, 1979).

THE CONSUMING NATURE OF VIOLENCE

Studies of the development of spirals of violence have led to the alarming finding that immersion in violence has a consuming character to it. Eron (1982) reported on extensive studies of the relationship between television watching and aggression in children. The studies were conducted for over 20 years and across four cultures, and results strongly supported that watching violent television leads to more aggressiveness. Further, more aggressive children watch even more television violence, and the spiral continues to expand. Huesmann and Eron (1986) emphasized that they had focused on individual violence and found that it was mainly the impact of cultural/environmental/parental norms and television that inhibited or facilitated the occurrence and expression of aggression. Personal characteristics such as self-esteem and the ability to cope with the social surroundings also contributed.

There are many additional examples of the varied aspects of violence. Obuchi (1979) and Obuchi and Oku (1980) reported experimental studies with male and female Japanese college students. In both groups, hostile subjects responded equally aggressively to aggressive and friendly opponents; nonhostile subjects differentiated between hostility and friendliness and were more friendly to friendly opponents. Dodge and Newman (1981) engaged aggressive and nonaggressive boys in the first, third, and fifth grades in a "detective game" to decide whether a peer had behaved in a hostile manner. Aggressive boys responded more quickly, were less attentive to social cues, and overly attributed violence to the suspected peer. Kelly and Stahelski's (1970) studies supported that competitive, in contrast to cooperative, subjects were more prone to see everyone as like themselves and to act accordingly. Cooperative people can employ competitive strategies, but unlike their competitive peers, they do not lose the ability to discriminate.

These studies suggest that some people are consumed by the spiral of violence. They no longer control it; it controls them. Both Shah (1978, 1981) and Toch (1969) emphasized that there are people who no longer see any other possibilities. They are controlled by the belief that they are threatened, that others are untrustworthy, and that the only way to survive is to be more menacing and watchful. Scales (1981) found a comparable perceived level of threat in extremist groups who were in opposition to sex education in the schools. They were characterized by paranoia as well as extreme fear of sexuality.

There are many factors which modulate and focus the violence in all of us, even the most extreme. Most individual violence is perpetrated on those who are close to us—spouses, family, friends (Corfman, 1979). With commitment, closeness, and continued interaction, we can build the spiral of violence enough to kill someone we love and, at times, do so. The relationship factors plus the immediate and broader sociocultural factors underlying such violence must be identified if we are to understand the overall complexities and patterns of violence and extremism.

NONPERSONAL VIOLENCE

However problematic personal violence may be, it is not usually the focus of our concern when we think of extremism and violence. Rather, we focus on psychosocial factors that are fueled by noncloseness, or at least by nonvisibility. Milgram (1974) found that people are more violent to less visible victims and are even more so if the victims can neither be seen nor heard. Ahmed (1979) confirmed that this finding also held with regard to rudeness and cheating. Further, while psychological invisibility is not the same as physical invisibility, it is an important factor in the violence of war, sexual crimes, and racial and religious violence.

Another factor contributing to violence is its justification. The *Mental Disability Law Reporter* (Oklahoma, 1980) discussed court rulings about whether involuntarily admitted mental hospital patients had the right to refuse violent treatments such as electro-shock treatment, psychosurgery, and antipsychotic drugs. The courts ruled that a state hospital and its employees "shall not forcibly treat the patient without his consent or that of his guardian except where there is a clear and present danger of extreme violence, personal injury, or attempted suicide" (p. 77). In short, if you are on the verge of violence to yourself or others, you can be dealt with violently, not just restrained.

Wicker (1975), an eminent journalist and writer, was one of the observers selected by the inmates to mediate between them and the authorities during the 1971 Attica, New York, prison riots. He wrote in a moving and thought-provoking way about those riots and how the prisoners were presumed to have brought it on themselves. He stressed that two generally believed basic assumptions were actually false; namely, that the prisoners *would be* violent and that the corrections officers *would not be*. In fact, the prisoners were amazingly controlled and nonviolent. The officers beat up the prisoners and were responsible for all of the fatalities when the riots were quelled. For the mental patients described above and the prisoners, the "you brought it on yourself" rationale was used to justify elevating violence to the level of sadism and killing.

Social psychology research supports that people who believe in a "just world" tend to devalue society's losers and unfortunates (Staub, 1989). During war, societies emphasize that their own killing is justified and even at times that the rape of the enemy's women is a just reward for victory (Brownmiller, 1975). The unfortunate losers are thought thus to deserve their fate.

An often overlooked aspect of nonpersonal violence is the indirect violence of some public policies. The people who develop the policies do not directly lay a hand on anyone or see themselves as violent. However, they rely in part on psychological studies of social problems. Many of those studies were designed to study black populations as objects responsible for their own problems and for solving them. Unsurprisingly, as Ryan (1971) and Caplan and Nelson (1973) documented, such victims are often blamed for the destructive outcomes of policies that are supported by studies designed to blame them.

Monti's (1979) studies of the 1964 Black and Puerto Rican riots in Harlem and Bedford-Stuyvesant of New York City provided such an example. These groups had few channels available for solving their problems, but first tried the conventional possibilities, then turned to nonviolent strategies. Only after those had failed, did they riot. However, the riots are mostly remembered as the fault of the rioters. The other efforts of the protesters and the indirect violence of the authorities' refusal to make needed social changes are mostly forgotten.

EXTREMIST GROUPS

Although this chapter's emphasis is on violence generally, we need to understand particularly how violent extremist groups form and sustain themselves. One example is the Ku Klux Klan, an extremist group with a long history of working to promote White and Protestant Christian superiority in the United States (Quarles, 1970; Tibbitts, 1981). Their leaders and members fit the pattern of individuals who get caught up in spirals of violence. They feel threatened, think they and their way of life are endangered by Blacks, Jews, and Catholics, and believe their only hope lies in organized resistance, including violence (Loggins & Thomas, 1981; Ezekiel, 1995).

Indirect answers to how such groups form and survive are provided by a number of studies. Kanter (1968) studied the patterns of successful and unsuccessful nineteenth century Utopian communities in the United States. Although these communities were not focused on violence, they developed a sense of cohesion through establishing certain practices. To develop a sense of belonging to the group, members were required to renounce outside influences and follow common rituals or face group threats. They were pressured to commit themselves to group control through what Kanter called mortifying—a process of being convinced that they were of no worth except through the group—and through persuasion to surrender their decision-making responsibilities to the group. Lofland and Stark (1965) described a similar process as characteristic of how individuals were recruited into a deviant religious cult. Important elements in that process included that they encountered the cult at turning points in their lives and were experiencing acutely felt tensions about their own worth and life. Ezekiel (1995) visited KKK gatherings and interviewed young men who had joined the organization. Their lives were characterized by an absence of personal support or caring, little success or encouragement in school, and few skills to gain personal, social, or economic success. The KKK offered them a rationale for their situation plus the caring and support that had been missing from their lives.

In sum, extremist groups develop from perceived social and personal threats. They thrive by offering their members special status, power, and belonging if they surrender themselves to that group and cut themselves off from competing sources of influence. Their members need not be all that different from other people, as Elms (1972) documented. These groups need not be oriented toward the violence around them; and some are not. However, they are more likely to thrive in social conditions that threaten people's worth and well-being; and they are more likely to turn violent in a society that reveres violence, particularly as an ultimate solution by the "good guys" against mysterious, nefarious "bad guys."

COLLECTIVE VIOLENCE

The most consuming forms of human violence have been wars, genocide, mass killings, and riots. Genocide and mass killings differ from war in that they ordinarily involve a more dominant group (CDG) systematically directing violence at a less dominant group (NCDG), often within their own cultures. Usually, the targets of the violence do not have the resources to retaliate or defend themselves effectively. Riots are episodic, less organized, less sustained, and kill fewer people. They ordinarily involve exploited or oppressed groups (NCDGs) acting violently toward society's presumed representatives or agents of control (e.g., police, political figures, or other CDGs or NCDGs seen as exploiters).

GENOCIDE AND MASS KILLINGS AS COLLECTIVE VIOLENCE

In Staub's studies of *The Roots of Evil* (1989), one of his themes was that the development of antisocial, destructive behavior is the mirror image of the development of prosocial behavior. He described prosocial behavior as evolving from a feeling of responsibility for others' welfare (personality factors) and a sense of personal responsibility to act accordingly (circumstantial factors). In addition, involving children in prosocial behavior leads them to be more willing to help others in future situations. He reasoned similarly that extreme destructiveness would be the last step in a continuum of destruction. In short, both prosocial and antisocial behaviors are learned in progressive steps, and their extremes are most likely outgrowths of a continuum of socialization. That logic is basic to his analysis and explanation of genocide, mass killings, and of war itself.

Staub (1989) provided empirical, historical, and conceptual support for his position that organized mistreatment of others as individuals or as members of groups arises in definable and predictable ways. The genocides throughout history were not unlike those in modern times, such as the systematic extermination of European Jews in the Holocaust and the more recent slaughters of Hutus in Rwanda and ethnic Albanians in the Yugoslavian province of Kosovo. During World War II, Germany and the Soviet Union engaged in mass slaughter of captured military and civilian groups. These instances of mass violence develop in social–political, including religious, organizations under cultural and personal preconditions that encourage the formation of psychosocial spirals of increasingly destructive antisocial violence. Faced with difficult life conditions, people often defend their physical, psychological, or social selves by striking out against their circumstances or others whom they see as responsible for their difficulties. They are also more open to giving allegiance to groups, leaders, or ideologies that offer them justifications for their plight and better lives.

Choices about using violence are influenced by the personal and cultural conditions that shape our views of ourselves and our circumstances. Aggressive cultures predispose their members to respond to difficulties in aggressive ways. The level of diversity and nature of the societal–political system contribute to how people define their circumstances and what they consider to be appropriate responses. Authoritarian systems enhance the significance of obedience to authority.

Systems that support discrimination against others over harmony among their members predispose people to engage in outwardly directed devaluation of others. Staub (1989) emphasized the role of bystanders, pointing out that their objections to outwardly directed violence restrains it. Likewise, ignoring or supporting violence facilitates it. Staub described several such patterns. In each instance, there were difficult circumstances and supportive personal and cultural patterns for outwardly directed violence. There was also a political organization using such activity for its own political and ideological reasons. For example, the evolution of the "final solution" to the Jewish problem in Nazi Germany was characterized by all of these factors.

Staub's (1989) formulation is consistent with the framework of psychosocial spirals outlined earlier. It includes a self-view as one of being threatened, a sense of the broader world as threatening, and a corollary defensive response that leads its objects to defend themselves. The victims' self-defense confirms the original perpetrators' perception of threat, and the spiral is begun. The presence of a syntonic cultural and sociopolitical context both predisposes our formation of these kinds of self, self–world, and life negotiating patterns and perpetuates and accelerates the development of these spirals. Eventually we justify mass violence and genocide.

WAR AS COLLECTIVE VIOLENCE

Wars, the epitome of organized violence, become culturally and psychologically possible because of these same kinds of factors that facilitate any violence. Wars are not incomprehensible nor beyond people's control; rather, they occur as a culmination of many events, such as those that function in psychosocial spiral forms. Using the psychosocial spiral formulation to examine war, as Staub (1989) did, requires no new basic elements. The difference is that the contending parties must be sufficiently powerful to mount and sustain massive violence toward each other. The origins of their conflict may be of a political, cultural, or ideological nature—or all three. War differs from genocide or mass killing in that everyone has the option of being part of an organized force through which they can protect themselves. However, once a war is lost, there may be a mass killing of the losers.

Further, as Staub (1989) indicated, like genocide, war may be an attempt to satisfy motivations arising from a range of difficult life conditions and cultural preconditions. It may focus on occupying territory, gaining physical dominance, or getting others to adopt one's ideals and values. Conflicts of interest—conflict over territory or beliefs or competition in trade—can give rise to hostility and war. The insecurity and fear of attack associated with any of these differences are also sources of hostility and, at times, of preventive attack. Staub emphasized that

> injured honor and the need to defend it ... are another important source of antagonism. But cultural and psychological factors determine what is insulting, what causes embarrassment or shame, and what is regarded as weakness or failure that must be balanced by the assertion of strength. (1989, p. 250)

Thus, wars are often "the outcome of steps along a continuum of antagonism. Hostile acts by one party or acts of self-defense that are perceived as hostile cause retaliation, which evokes more intense hostility" (Staub, 1989, p. 250). He called this sequence a *cycle of negative reciprocity*. Deutsch (1983) called it the *malignant social process* because of its harmful consequences. Whatever its label, the process leading to outbursts of organized violence is characterized by its reciprocal and escalating spiral nature, and it mirrors the prosocial spirals described earlier.

RIOTS AS COLLECTIVE VIOLENCE

In beginning his thoughtful analysis of riots and similar collective outbursts of destructiveness, Toch (1992) reviewed U.S. public-policy-oriented inquiries into the causes of the domestic riots of the 1960s. There were two predominant perspectives. The overly simplistic, traditional conservative view held that such collective behavior was irrational; the traditional liberal view considered it a product of frustration arising from oppression. As Toch summarized, the 1968 President's Commission on Civil Disorders suggested that the origins of these riots were more complex.

> The riot commission listed five "powerful ingredients" as "catalysts" of riots: (1) frustrated hope, generated by the civil rights struggle in the North and South; (2) a climate heavy with "approval and encouragement of violence"; (3) the frustration of feeling powerless to move the system; (4) a new mood—particularly in the young—of "self-esteem and enhanced racial pride"; and (5) the view of police as a symbol of "white power, white racism and white repression." (Toch, 1992, p. 192)

Toch emphasized that the relationship among these five factors can form a chain, i.e., a psychosocial spiral of violence, with the actual violence as its culminating link. He illustrated the relevance of his conceptualization by examining the Watts riots of 1965.

> The type of explanation offered by the Riot Commission is that of a "chain," in which unhappiness leads to unsuccessful efforts at redress, which in turn cumulates in despair, anger, and a sanctioning of violent solutions. Interviews with riot participants and sympathizers tend to confirm this view. By and large, statements at the scene of a riot are catalogues of unresolved grievances and cumulated feelings, and the riot emerges as an expression of impatience and an emotional discharge. (Toch, 1992, p. 193f.)

The list of these factors related to the origin of the Watts riots are familiar to people in the United States and other countries who have contact with public dialogues about riots. They include police brutality, retaliation against CDG exploitation, unemployment, hopelessness, anonymity, and lack of identity. Factors that facilitated rioting include a sense of common cause, a means to attract attention to shared injustices, peer pressure, revenge, and personal profit. For each person the motives were multiple and included personal histories and proclivities. In combination, they support the conclusion that accounting for such violence and creating efforts to reduce it require more than one-dimensional, simplistic explanations and approaches.

COUNTERING VIOLENCE

Many people have tried to disrupt cycles of violence; others have created prosocial cycles of interaction; some have combined these two approaches. Their differential successes have led me to believe that countering violence must include working with people's circumstances and their psychosocial configurations. Studies supporting that conclusion and approaches to develop nonviolent alternatives to conflict resolution are outlined in the following paragraphs.

Schwitzgebel (1977) and Toch (1969, 1992) found that, to understand and change violent people, it is essential to involve them in studying their own violence. Schwitzgebel found that doing so also leads them to become less violent. Toch (1992) documented the necessity of including violent people (police as well as criminals) as conceptualizers, experts, collaborators, and as targets in violence-reducing programs. The self-doubt and insecurity in the men who participated was one of the factors underlying their vulnerability to using violence. Being instructed or counseled by authorities only reinforced their sense of inferiority, creating an analogue to the helping paradox found in psychotherapy. It placed them in a hierarchical, dependent relationship with someone whose basis for influencing them rested in his or her authority and power to inflict justified violence. In contrast, when they involved them in these multiple roles, their self-doubt, insecurity, and sense of dependency were reduced. They became open to internalizing different understandings of their own behavior which they could then use to reduce their violence.

In a somewhat parallel approach, DeCharms (1976) taught middle-school children in ghetto schools that they are *origins* who create their own events and can control their lives, rather than *pawns who are* pushed around by life. He also showed them how to act like origins. Their behavior became less disruptive, more organized and planful, and their overall achievement levels improved.

T. Tyler and his colleagues (1980, 1981) established that an important variable leading people to accept judgments from authorities, such as a grade in a course, a citation for a motor vehicle violation, or an adverse public policy decision, was the level of their belief that they had been treated fairly and that the judgment had been arrived at fairly. My colleagues and I (F. Tyler & Pargament, 1981; Hodges, F. Tyler, & Brandt, 1979) found that an important factor in high school students' improvement during counseling was treating them as origins. Hurley (1975) confirmed that the professional and paraprofessional staff had a stronger sense of empowerment in more democratically run community mental health centers. People feel more involved and able to participate in nonviolent ways when they are included as participants in their situations.

Reid, Taplin, & Lorber (1981) conducted an observational study of abusive families. They found that parents may be abusive because they feel that they have lost control over their children and need to restore it. Therapeutic efforts involved not only analyzing the parents' dynamics, but also providing them with nonphysical alternatives to conflict resolution and intervention with other adult problems such as social isolation, economic deprivation, and alcoholism.

Noone, Molnar, and Hopper-Small (1979) developed a technique for preventing violence on a general psychiatric unit. It involved acceptance of the potentially violent patients, being consistent and direct with them, and enhancing their positive personality features. Their program worked by using a combination of containing the patients' violence while responding in ways that provided them with a positive sense of security and worth.

How do these findings fit together? They fit the kind of model that was successfully used during racial conflict in the United States in the 1960s (Kelman, 1968). The model is somewhat familiar to most readers because of its implementation by Martin Luther King, Jr. and his colleagues and followers and its earlier use by Gandhi in India. Singh (1979) also described it as useful in changing dacoit gangs, i.e., gangs with a long tradition and well-established role of violence in India. The model has four interlocking ingredients. First, those who are trying to disrupt the violence must behave toward the perpetrators with *firmness* accompanied by a commitment *not* to escalate the violence or retaliate violently or unjustly for current and past violence. Thus, the parties build a relationship of trust and respect. Second, all of the parties in the situation must be "re-visibilized." Martin Luther King's approach (Bryant, 1981) made him and his followers visible as individuals, but it did *not* de-individualize or de-visibilize those opposing him. Third, an alternative approach to resolving the problems at hand must be built by everyone working within a framework of shared goals or purposes—even if that sharing is limited to mutual respect. It involves creating alternative ways of working out differences. Fourth, a commitment must be made to redress grievances and, in the long run, develop more just and equitable solutions. Solutions must include changing society and people if necessary to establish genuinely equitable social arrangements.

Simply proceeding to create prosocial change by refusing to be violent and developing constructive alternatives is not enough, although such an approach is a more prosocial alternative than responding in kind and feeding the cycle of violence. However, it is risky and dangerous because, as alternative strategies begin to reduce violence, the people and the process must be protected from those who find prosocial solutions undesirable. They may be willing to attack the change agents—as was the fate of Abraham Lincoln, Mahatma Gandhi, Yitzhak Rabin, Anwar Sadat, and Martin Luther King, Jr. Others may wish to wreak violence on previous offenders, as was the case at Attica and as has been the case with the dacoits of India. To stop the spiral, earlier offenders must be protected from retribution, although justice must also be addressed.

To counter violence and create spirals of prosocial interaction, it is necessary to reestablish a sense of self-efficacy, trust, and active constructive behavior in the parties involved. In the words of Toch (1992):

> Potential participants in collective violence must come to see other means of achieving their objectives, in the same sense in which this lesson must be learned by Violent Men.... Once it becomes true that the police and other agencies remain impervious to reform ... violence cannot be remedied when there is in fact no other way to achieve dignity and status." (p. 240)

That process requires creating the conditions (e.g, benign and predictable social environments with psychosocial supports and protections from threats) for prosocial resolutions of differences. It also involves preventing opponents of these approaches from disrupting them while including those opponents in the network of prosocial solutions.

CONVERGING PROCESSES, DIVERSE PERSPECTIVES, AND CONFLICTING VALUES

Violence and other approaches to resolve people's disagreements function within broader social contexts. Consequently, there are commonalities in violence patterns across contexts and also differences that reflect culturally specific values, customs, and practices. That is, just as patterns of prosocial interactions are both similar and different, for example, in individualist and collectivist cultures, so are patterns of conflict. Societies and leaders whose goals are expansionist and who view aggression as a legitimate means to accomplish their goals will pursue organized violence within their own domains and against outsiders. In the following section, these patterns of convergence, divergence, and conflict are explored further.

CONVERGENT THEMES

Huesmann and Eron's (1986) cross-national studies of television violence and its impact on children's aggression found a correlation between cultural orientations to violence and level of violence; they also found culture-specific patterns. For example, homogeneous societies have relatively effective systems of norms that limit the occurrence of aggression and possibly minimize the differences in effect of television violence exposure on dissimilar children. In contrast,

> with its low homogeneity, its relatively high level of actual aggression and crime, and its high homogeneity of TV content, it is no surprise that the most consistent relation between TV and aggression has been found in the United States. Here, TV facilitates the adoption of aggressive habits: the actual environment is not necessarily a falsification of what is presented on the screen; the overall normative frame is no consistent inhibitor of aggression (see gun laws). The result is a reciprocal process whereby TV violence and aggression affect each other. (Huessman & Eron, 1986, p. 276)

The level of violence in the public domain influences its level in the people and vice versa. Further, as was noted earlier, those who are initially more violence prone are more attracted to television violence and become increasingly violent with greater exposure. A mutually confirming and potentially accelerating cycle of violence or nonviolence is created in the absence of contradictory messages. Television is a powerful and increasingly pervasive entertainment and communication medium. Before its advent there were other media, including wandering minstrels, secular and religious leaders, radio, and other forms of mass communications. No matter what the medium, it seems likely that it will teach and model a culture's values, including those about violence.

An emerging concern about violence has been stimulated in part by increased public attention to the interests of minority groups (ethnic/racial NCDGs throughout the world). Violence has erupted as they have confronted society to attain their rights. Consequently, social psychologists have been pressured to study intergroup relationships, including intergroup conflict. Altemeyer is a social psychologist who has adopted a social change perspective toward studying violence and its roots. He defined authoritarianism as "the covariation of authoritarian submission, authoritarian aggression, and conventionalism" (1988, p. xviii). This definition escaped being a tautology because he used the adjective "authoritarian" to mean that the action it modifies is justified solely because it is ordered by someone in authority. Based on this definition, he developed the Right Wing Authoritarianism (RWA) Scale to study the relationship between authoritarianism and the antecedents of violence in Canadian and U.S. college students, their parents, and their friends. It was his belief that there is a great potential for the acceptance of totalitarian rule in these two countries.

Although Altemeyer's (1988) findings are complex, their main themes are amazingly straightforward and directly relevant to understanding violence and how to prevent, manage, and reduce its harmful effects.

1. Personal experiences were the most substantial determinant of levels of authoritarianism, although the views of family, friends, the news, and similar factors had some effect.
2. The aggressiveness of the high-authoritarians (Highs) was linked to a sense of self-righteousness and fear that the existing order was in danger of collapse or of being overturned. A large part of the reason they "remain Highs is that, through self-selection, self-denial, and self-exclusion, they do not have the range of experiences that could have lowered their authoritarianism." (p. 89) They were also more conventional and submissive to authority, two of the tripartite bases of authoritarianism.
3. Highs had better mechanisms for denying or excusing their hostility and aggressiveness, including limiting their contacts to others like themselves so they had less basis for comparative judgment. They had more effectively learned to compartmentalize the discrepancies between their beliefs; they could comfortably believe in mercy and forgiveness and justify their aggressiveness in punishing evil doers. "Their belief system appears self-confirming, enduring, and closed.... Hostilities based on them appear highly resistant to change" (Altemeyer, 1988, p. 231).

In contrast to the closed nature of the psychosocial competence configurations of these High respondents, Altemeyer (1988) also found that

4. Higher levels of education were related to reductions in level of authoritarianism.
5. Highs and Lows who could judge nonconventional people and activities to be acceptable had (a) experienced contact with those they considered deviants, such as homosexuals, nontraditional families, etc.; (b) done nonconventional things; or (c) known someone who was nonconventional.

Thus, possibly the most important of Altemeyer's (1988) statements is that the foundation of RWA stems more from the way beliefs are held than from their content. The individuals who scored low on RWA were not "Left Wing Authoritarians" (LWAs).

Lows strike me as being fair-minded, evenhanded, tolerant, non-aggressive persons. Time and again they have indicated outrage at government injustices, regardless of the government's political stripes or the identity of its victims. They do not maintain the double standards we find among Highs.... They are not self-righteous; they do not feel superior to persons with opposing opinions. They are not mean-spirited.... They probably make awful soldiers and terrible house-wives and rebellious clergy.... But they do not remind me at all of doctrinaire Communists.... (They) strike me instead as good democratic citizens. (Altemeyer, 1988, p. 262f)

More recently, Altemeyer (1994) reported results of one approach which had limited success in reducing high RWA in Canadian college students. They were informed that they, in contrast to LWAs, (a) scored substantially higher on a scale measuring the importance of freedom (for themselves) than on one measuring the importance of equality (freedom for others), and (b) that, unbeknownst to themselves, they are unusually submissive and conventional. When they learned about themselves, they usually expressed some willingness to change and, in particular, substantially increased their support for affirmative action programs for Native Canadian college students. Also, like RWAs studied earlier, these participants were "fearful people who circumstances have kept ... in those tight circles [of people like themselves]" (p. 147). Altemeyer differentiated them from "irredeemable Nazi types" (p. 147), but was not optimistic about changing them once they had formed an RWA orientation because of the defensiveness which characterizes it.

At a broader level of analysis about individual and social change, Mennell (1989) pointed out that societies go through decivilizing (resorts to authoritarian rule and control by violence) and civilizing (democratic and nonviolent) phases. The evidence suggests that there is a seamlessness to the development and reduction of cycles of violence in people and societies. These shifts may reflect changes in the balance of power between the two orientations and lead to consequent different directions of movement along the psychosocial spirals that sustain and destroy states and the people in them. Thus, to reduce violence we must take steps to offset these spiral effects and change the balance to favor nonviolence.

Deutsch (1983) described the international situation during the Cold War as one of "insincere peace" between the superpowers of the Western and Soviet blocs. He argued that reduction in the fear of nuclear conflagration and the related violence-oriented spiral of the arms race required each side to change its conception of the other. Each had to shift from seeing itself as an adversary involved in cut-throat competition to one of a fellow contestant involved in changing the rules of the conflict. This approach bound them together in common interests (including survival). For that approach to succeed, a cooperative framework had to be developed by providing *"repeated and varied opportunities for mutually beneficial interactions"* (Deutsch, 1983, p. 28). To implement it successfully required responding to belligerent challenges with a "firm, nonbelligerent, self-confident, friendly attitude that appears to be most effective in reforming aggressive delinquents and that our research suggests is most effective in inducing cooperation" (Deutsch, 1983, p. 30). To Deutsch, the United States would have to begin with self-reform because its major barrier was its defensiveness. That conclusion converged with those of Altemeyer, Staub, and Toch. When international leaders succumb to right wing authoritarian thinking, they behave like aggressive delinquents, that is, like grown up boys for whom violence has been advantageous.

Power as a Constructive Force

Power can be a "positive drive" to accomplish prosocial individual and collective goals. It need not be based on fear as in authoritarianism. When based on participatory educational, political, or social principles, it can shift a situation's dynamics. Power can be distributed and used as a positive drive to reduce violence and accomplish other prosocially desirable goals.

As mentioned in Chapter 8, Veno and Veno worked with an Australian police unit to prevent and control violence at a motorcycle bikers rally. They focused on preventing violence by persuading all of the parties involved to commit to a peaceful event and to accommodating everyone's interests to the extent possible. The result was a successful rally with little violence, and the police gained positive regard. We can only wonder whether such a program could be so readily implemented and accepted by a society without a tradition of consensus and other culture specific characteristics. Even so, their work is an example of how to contain violence by building a constructive psychosocial spiral of interaction among disparate parties.

Universalist versus Ethnic Validity Approaches to Domestic Violence

The marginal CDG concern with ethnic validity (or cultural diversity) in the face of its demonstrable importance to understanding and ameliorating domestic violence can be seen in the contrast between two recent reports. *Violence in the Family* (1996) is a report of an American Psychological Association Presidential Task Force. The report stressed that "family violence and abuse are at epidemic proportions in the United States and in many societies worldwide" (p. 9). It also provided a detailed account of the major factors contributing to that violence, its individual and societal consequences, and approaches to ameliorating it. However, little attention was given to the cultural/ethnic circumstances or ethnic validity concerns other than to acknowledge that many factors contribute to violence and we should not overgeneralize.

In contrast, ethnic validity issues and their importance in relation to violence were highlighted in a volume edited by Javier, Herron, & Bergman (1996) and directed at clinical practitioners. For example, DiGiuseppe, Eckhardt, and Robin (1996) pointed out that cultures differ in their socially prescribed patterns of emotional experiences, what elicits them, and the appropriate social expressions and behavioral reactions in response to them. They emphasized that it is both feasible and important to distinguish between annoyance or irritation which does not lead to violence and anger and that which does and may be uncontrollable. Further, controlling violence may involve teaching people emotional distinctions and scripts for dealing with violence. They identified important cultural variations in the process of teaching therapists about such differences and found that making these distinctions was easy for therapists from Spanish speaking countries, but not for English language or Israeli (greatest difficulty) therapists. The Israeli's, in particular, said they had "few culturally accepted scripts to replace dysfunctional anger" (DiGiuseppe et al., 1996, p. 59).

Holzman (1996) found substantial cultural differences in rape proneness, the meaning of rape, and constructive psychosocial ways to deal with its aftermath. These results were consistent with those Sanday (1981) established earlier that there have been more cultures without rape than with it, although the United States is particularly rape prone. The emphasis in the United States is on individual autonomy, independence, and openness; the preferred Euro-American crisis counseling approach is "take command of your life." For women from cultures in which interdependence, external appearance, and dignity are stressed, this approach is inappropriate and unacceptable.

Holzman (1996) established that interlocking patterns of oppression based on sociorace, ethnicity, class, and sexual orientation underlie rape behavior. These patterns lead to the selective targeting of victims and influence how victims regard being raped and wish to deal with it. In the United States, African American women may be reluctant to report an African American rapist because they know of the discriminatory way African American men are stigmatized in the justice system. Religious differences may also have an impact on how women respond to rape. Buddhists are taught that everything which happens happens for a purpose, so the rape experience has something to teach for a greater purpose. Some religions offer healing rituals.

Holzman did not address how to reduce the occurrence of rape, but these examples suggest that an important factor is to change cultural

values. Euro-American cultures support male dominance. They link violence with masculinity and compliance and gentleness with femininity.
They also support the belief that women frequently say no to sexual
advances when they mean yes and that men, once aroused, cannot control
their sexuality. These two unfounded beliefs alone make it easier to understand why these cultures would be prone to and tolerant of rape.

The materials that were highlighted by Javier, Herron, and Bergman's
contributors (1996) and the American Psychological Association's Violence
Report (1996) do not contradict each other. However, they convey quite
different messages. The former stressed ethnic validity factors; the latter
minimized them. The APA recommendations focused on a universalist
orientation, emphasized comprehensive collaborative approaches among
professions, institutions, and communities, and recommended protecting
the professional status and prerogatives of psychology.

These two reports highlight how crucial it is to consider ethnic validity in efforts to understand human violence and minimize it. If therapists
or other social change agents are to provide prosocially constructive assistance to others, they must negotiate some shared understandings with
their clients. They have to identify shared ways of establishing acceptable
alternatives for coping with life issues, acceptable solutions, and feasible
ways to accomplish them. Universalist or ethnocentric professionally defined approaches cannot meet these criteria.

CONFLICT MANAGEMENT BY NEGOTIATION

Much of the psychological and social science literature conceptualizes
the issues of violence prevention, control, and reduction in social negotiation terms. That approach is different from a unidirectional professional
power orientation. As Pruitt and Carnevale (1994) emphasized, there are
both substantial cultural differences and transcultural similarities in people's approaches to conflict management. Mediation is a more prominent
approach in non-Western than in Western societies, which prefer direct
negotiations. Such ethnic-validity-based contextual and interrelationship
factors influence different kinds of negotiations. In addition, most negotiation studies have focused only on short-term outcomes. Yet, these investigators found in a community mediation study that short-term outcomes
were unrelated to long-term ones. What mattered in the long run was the
disputant's perceptions that fair procedures were used and that they were
given a chance to voice their concerns.

The potential complexity of such issues and the relevance of complex
negotiation strategies for a wide range of human conflicts was one outcome of a fascinating project involving a multidisciplinary group of medi-

ation experts. Each participant critiqued a case study account of the role of Dr. Kissinger, the United States Secretary of State, as a third party negotiator between the Israelis and their Arab neighbors from 1973 to 1975 (Rubin, 1981). The critiques highlighted an amazing variety of issues about cultural differences, negotiation approaches, disciplinary perspectives, and personal considerations which may have influenced how issues were resolved. The major value of this project may have been its demonstration of how useful social and behavioral science studies of conflict resolution activities could be to the world.

Perhaps by turning to real life issues we can better identify the opportunities and responsibilities that psychologists have to contribute to the understanding and management of individual and societal violence. An American Psychological Association (APA) subcommittee charged with preparing a report on torture as a case of human rights violations provided particularly relevant ideas for organized psychology (Suedfeld, 1990). Torture is a form of violence—intentionally induced pain with the goal of destroying the victim's will, humanity, and dignity. That is, at least one of its goals is to destroy, or at least severely debilitate, the victim's sense of self as an autonomous moral agent capable of self-directed, principled (moral) judgment and action. Because one of the basic objectives of the APA is to promote human welfare, it is explicitly opposed to activities such as torture.

Suedfeld's (1990) report also explored whether psychologists had been known to participate directly or indirectly in torture programs in societies which use such tactics and whether psychological research had been used to develop newer or more effective torture protocols or both. Neither seemed to have been the case since existing torture protocols are comprehensive and rest on centuries of experience across societies. Even so, there are many reasons for psychologists to be concerned about torture and its uses. There are psychological precursors to becoming torturers and to opting for its use. There are also debilitating psychological concomitants and consequences of being a torture victim and psychology-based approaches to facilitate recovery. Finally, although they have received less attention, there are undoubtedly psychological consequences to being a torturer.

Gibson (1990) examined the training of torturers in a military context which by nature is violent. The central concern of that context is with the nature and bounds of justified violence. Levin (1990), a philosopher, asked whether torture could be justified under sufficiently extreme social conditions. He argued that it could be justified, for example, to extract information from an apprehended terrorist about where he or she had hidden an atom bomb set to explode and destroy countless people. Levin's reasoning was that there should be a general moral prohibition against violence, even to terrorists, but that its use could be justified in the extreme case of protecting against vastly greater violent destructiveness. He asserted further that such universal prohibitions make moral sense, but also require such exceptions. That is, *even such credos* must be evaluated against common sense, otherwise they become counterproductive and unsustainable. This same issue is reflected in a controversial decision by the Supreme Court of Israel "to use force to interrogate a Palestinian believed to have information that could prevent a terrorist attack" (Cahn, 1996).

FUTURE DIRECTIONS

The ethos of each culture may have evolved because its components were either to the culture's advantage or consistent with its survival. However, no society's history justifies absolute cultural relativism or the right of some to dictate everyone else's reality. The historic violence in the subjugation of indigenous peoples or the economic exploitation of other people's resources may have been justified at one time by Social Darwinist or religious convictions, but these positions are no longer considered acceptable. Codes that glorified male control of families and violence in war may have had empirical or ideological justifications. They are difficult to sustain in the face of current, empirically-based psychological knowledge and convergent values such as those codified in the United Nations Declaration of Human Rights (Tolley, 1987).

People inevitably face conflicting basic survival demands as well as conflicts at personal, interpersonal, and even international levels. To consider how psychology and psychologists can contribute to understanding and containing human violence, we have to begin with existing paradigms and practices but not be completely constrained by them. Establishing a comprehensive framework for understanding and containing violence requires complex but coordinated approaches. For example, at a United Nations sponsored World Food Summit, U.S. representatives insisted that their country does not recognize a "right to food," although that right was recognized by 186 other states (Holmes, 1996). Whether refusing to agree that everyone has a right to enough food for survival is an act of violence may be subject to debate. However, many societies consider it to be and, in this instance, assert that changes can and should be made to minimize such violence and to take action to promote those changes. A similar set of approaches may well be applied to reducing torture and other patterns of human violence.

These findings from empirical studies and evaluations of social programs converge to provide guidelines for reducing violence and extremism, and efforts to implement them have begun. Staub, as an adolescent refugee from the Russian invasion of Hungary in 1956, completed his education in the United States. He devoted his career to studying the development of prosocial behavior (1978) and the reduction of antisocial behaviors (1989). His successful integration of personality, developmental, and social psychology led to research that provides concrete evidence of their interrelatedness and substantially advanced our understanding of how to socialize people to care about each other and work out ways of living together. People building preventive community-based programs can gain important insights from his work and promote the reduction of violence and extremism.

Other social scientists have contributed to our understanding of collective violence and the possibilities and consequences of reducing it. Monti (1979) provided a particularly instructive approach. His analyses of the Black and Puerto Rican racial controversies and culminating riots in New York City from 1960 to 1964 provided important clues about how the continued frustration of these minority groups' efforts to seek redress of their grievances led eventually to riots. Techniques similar to Monti's can provide insights about preventive interventions and efforts to defuse new or ongoing episodes of collective violence.

An anthropologist, Geertz (1977), addressed a contradiction in Gandhi's doctrine of nonviolence and compared it with therapy as a vehicle for social change. Usually, both the therapist and client want the same kind of change for the client. Gandhi wanted political/social change but was interacting with others, including British and Hindus, who did not. Gandhi could influence those who shared his goals, but not those whose goals were incompatible with his. His efforts to persuade people to change, to accept and participate in a diverse multireligious, multiethnic nonhierarchical society, became a form of coercion. His approach confronted people with making changes they were unwilling to make. Some who disagreed with him resorted to violence in opposition, killing him and setting off massive communal violence.

Containing violence requires particularly difficult choices. Gandhi's approach raised issues of incompatible goals and codes of conduct. Toch (1992) asked how to contain violence entrepreneurs, i.e., people who have learned that violence is a way to dominate or manipulate others or to obtain objectives or rewards to which they are not entitled. In Toch's words,

> We presume that a nonviolent society has no room for agencies that profit from the exercise of destructiveness, nor for persons who direct

its large-scale use. Men who press explosive buttons or who sign bloodthirsty orders are entrepreneurs of violence, and they set the stage for lone operators. The same holds for individuals who coldly plan for inconceivable contingencies, or who produce and disseminate means of destruction. When the roles exercised by such persons have been eliminated from the games societies play, we can attend to our Violent Men with a clearer conscience and a more unambiguous mandate. (1992, p. 257)

Toch put individual violence into a broader social context. Staub (1989) also addressed violence in relation to that broader context, particularly the context of nations and international relations. Societal leaders may incite violence, use violence, or both, to enhance their power or meet other goals. Nations may have formed a sense of national unity and enlisted the loyalty of their citizens and support for violence in the face of real external threats, yet maintain and enhance that violence orientation after the threats are contained. Staub pointed out that the early, great U.S. psychologist, William James, celebrated the good qualities resulting from war. In short, individuals may be as vulnerable as nations to becoming consumed in cycles of violence.

We must do more than deplore such positions. Throughout history, individuals and societies have found (at their own peril if they did not) that mechanisms to reduce escalating tensions are required. A mechanism that structures human interactions in ways that prevent or reduce cycles of violence is reciprocity, the resource collaborator model of interaction. Toch (1992) emphasized that collaboration is essential to reduce violence, and Staub (1989) stressed the importance of positive reciprocity.

Positive reciprocity is unlikely when ideologies of antagonism and a conflict mode are dominant. First, to initiate positive action requires some trust that the other will reciprocate in kind. Second, to reciprocate a positive act, the actor's intention must be judged benevolent. The greater the mistrust between parties, the less is it possible to test another's intention by unilateral positive acts.... To change a malignant mode of relating, nations must begin a process of positive reciprocity starting from the most basic level. They must move from diplomatic contact, to tourism and cultural exchanges, to cooperation in joint enterprises, to mutual help. Over time, motivations that support conflict should diminish, and the desire for cooperation and peace should increase. (1989, p. 260)

By building spirals of prosocial positive reciprocity, acrimonious past histories can be confronted and potentially neutralized. This approach also provides a way for less powerful groups, perhaps NCDGs, to influence more powerful groups in potentially positive sum ways (Staub, 1989).

SUMMARY

This chapter has emphasized our need to understand the nature of human violence, the psychosocial factors that influence it, and approaches to reduce it. Two quite disparate but necessarily interrelated sources of violence were identified. One source lies in the psychosocial orientation typified by right wing authoritarianism that justifies defining the reality of others and using force against them when they will not accept that reality. It is characterized by conformity to convention, aggressiveness on the behalf of authority, and submission to the authority embedded in religious, nationalistic, ethnic, or other psychosocially defined structures. It can justify violence ranging from controlling one's spouse to large scale social phenomena such as riots, war, and genocide. Counterviolence to such impositions arises from people's psychosocial beliefs that they have a right to survive by defending themselves from injustices. Thus, people who otherwise feel powerless and hopeless also justify violence.

Conceptions of psychosocial competence and psychosocial spirals provided a framework for understanding how people and groups progressively develop violent or nonviolent approaches to their lives. These conceptions were based in people's capacities to function as knowers and make judgments about social criteria such as justice, freedom, and equality. This psychosocial framework can be used as a basis for seeking convergences on issues such as the nature of people's basic rights and on ways to resolve their differences. In particular, this latter possibility includes when people are justified in being violent to secure or protect themselves and their rights. Finding such convergences is a vital undertaking to which psychologists can contribute useful information. However, that possibility has received little of their attention.

The material reviewed in this chapter has provided important information about the prevention, containment, and minimizing of violence. It supports that there are common factors as well as cultural, socioracial, and ethnic differences in people's understanding, uses of, and responses to violence. We know that it is difficult to temper extremist views once people have established high levels of authoritarianism. It is easier to create openness to varied experiences and new information by providing benign and predictable social environments and engaging people in collaborative approaches and activities. Thereby, we can reduce their involvement in violence and engage them in promoting nonviolent change. Once begun, opponents must be prevented from disrupting these approaches, and they must be included in the network of prosocial solutions. By building on this already validated information, psychologists can contribute to increased reciprocal power sharing and problem solving approaches at multiple levels. These steps can lead to the creation of peaceful prosocial change and the reduction of violence.

PART IV

NEW DIRECTIONS

In this part, ethnic validity and resource exchange and enhancement models serve as criteria for defining prosocial change and evaluating change approaches. The roles of commonality, diversity, coherence, and discord in any context are considered from an ethnic validity perspective. These models assume that all people, including scientists and professionals, are both interested parties and active participants in planning, implementing, and evaluating individual and collective change. It is argued that attending to that interplay will better support psychologists' contributions to the autonomy and the collective well-being of individuals and their societies. This ethnic validity based resource exchange and enhancement model can be adapted more responsively than traditional models to various contexts and different levels of societal or personal organization; it also provides a more comprehensive framework for constructing and evaluating change approaches. Finally, current efforts to implement this model, the impediments to such changes, and psychology's current change orientation are summarized.

CHAPTER 13

INTERVENTIONS: AN EVALUATIVE MATRIX

INTRODUCTION

At the beginning of the twentieth century, concerns in the United States about social injustices and inadequate provisions for people's well-being led social scientists and humanistically oriented citizens to speak out about the need for reforms. In 1903, Du Bois (1940) wrote about "the strange meaning of being black here in the dawning of the twentieth century," and emphasized that "the problem of the twentieth century is the problem of the color-line" (p. 1). Addams, a prominent U.S. social activist, worked in the settlement house movement to provide a better life for urban slum dwellers, especially women. She wrote that a new standard of social morality was needed based on a belief in "the essential dignity and equality of all" (Addams, 1902, p. 6), openness to and involvement in a wide range of social experiences, and "identification with the common lot ... [as] the essential idea of Democracy ... [and] the source and expression of social ethics" (Addams, 1902, p. 11).

At that time, U.S. psychology was being established as an empirically based, academic discipline, focused primarily on understanding people as individuals. It was not until the middle of the century that members of the American Psychological Association added the promotion of human welfare to their commitment. Today, people in many parts of the world turn to psychology for guidance in formulating social policy and taking steps to reduce human conflict and suffering and to advance human welfare.

The world continues to struggle with urban slums and poverty, "the color line," and other, often violent, dialogues (including genocide and war) about social morality, justice, and survival. Given psychology's broad social acceptance, it is timely to ask whether its efforts have largely reflected and supported societal inequalities or, on balance, made a constructive contribution to the improvement of people's lives. To seek some answers to these questions, several areas of intervention, from individually oriented psychotherapy to social change efforts, are evaluated here with particular attention to their responsiveness to ethnic validity considerations.

No worldwide overview of the rationales, practices, and impacts of psychologists on cultures other than their own has been attempted. Turtle (1987) provided a useful framework for evaluating the export and often forceful imposition of Western European paradigms on foreign cultures with traditions of their own. As she pointed out in her introduction to the papers from a conference on the movement of Western psychology to Asia and Oceania (Pakistan to Fiji), the evolution of psychology in the Far East was an example of that kind of imperialistic undertaking. Its goal was to displace existing social and political ideologies and impose Western style industrial modernization. Turtle pointed out that Western psychologists tried to impose the fundamental principles of materialism, empiricism, and determinism on

> already highly developed views of the nature of the human mind, beliefs in the power to predict future fortunes in this life and in the possibility of continuation of existence in another.... [They also sought] to offer practical solutions to problems of social planning, to advise on maximal utilization of capacities of individuals, to claim the ability to counsel, to comfort and to cure those in trouble and distress, in the face of firmly established beliefs about the proper forms of social organization and the relation of the individual thereto, and of highly valued practices of guidance, consolation and spiritual healing. (Turtle, 1987, p. 1)

Turtle emphasized that this endeavor "gives evidence either of remarkable self-confidence and/or powers of salesmanship in modern psychologists, or of extraordinary social disruption in the East, or both" (1987, p. 1). Western psychologists did impose their presumably universalist conceptions of psychology on non-Western societies. However, psychologists in Asia and Oceania developed indigenous psychologies and explored the relationships between the two (Blowers & Turtle, 1987). Further, exposure to Eastern cultures and the responses of Eastern psychologists also forced changes in their Western counterparts. Unfortunately, many Western CDG psychologists are not aware of that result.

A comprehensive evaluation of psychology-based interventions requires psychologists to ask the kinds of questions that Turtle raised. That is, what is the relationship of theories and approaches to the cultures in which they are embedded and to which they are applied? Do our knowledge and skills make a positive contribution to the world's people and not just our own society? Is psychology, in Bronowski's (1966) terms, an improvement over common sense? Are we allocating our psychological resources—time, energy, knowledge, tools, and skills—in ways which our data indicate are their optimal societal uses? Do we as psychologists participate in our field's collective role to an extent commensurate with the benefits and supports our societies provide us? If not, imbalances in personal and professional commitments indicate underutilization or misapplication of our knowledge and skills for personal or other gain.

To assess psychology's contribution to people's well-being, we must consider three aspects of its models—their values, domain, and roles. These criteria must be credible inside and outside of the field. To meet that standard, any psychological contribution must yield prosocial answers to the following kinds of questions.

1. *Values*: Criterion questions about psychology's value base include how psychologists' personal and social morality and the purposes and ethical codes of their discipline/profession guide their activities. Specifically, does the current distribution of psychological interventions serve mainly to reflect and maintain society as it is and advantage psychologists in the status quo? Or, do psychological interventions primarily inform and reform society in ways which demonstrate that psychologists are substantially involved in working to improve everyone's lives and societies?

2. *Domain*: We bear a responsibility to identify the aspects of people's conduct that can be informed and influenced in constructive ways by psychologically based approaches. Our criteria for identifying that domain need to be consistent with our evidence and our values about using psychological knowledge and skills to improve people's lives and situations. We then need to evaluate whether our focus and the impact of our psychological interventions meet those criteria.

3. *Role*: As an academic discipline and a guild, psychology in the United States has not defined any explicit responsibility for its collective involvement in, or for its members to intervene in, people's lives. In contrast, Canadian psychologists have assumed that social responsibility (Prilleltensky, 1994). Psychologists have evolved roles ranging from that of the presumably value-free scholar to the involved therapist or social change agent (F. Tyler & Speisman, 1967; F. Tyler, 1970). There is a broad consensus expressed in our institutional commitments that as scientists and professionals, we have an obligation to be involved in society's relevant policy decisions. There are social expectations that any discipline's involvement in public policy includes being responsive to societal needs. We need to ask to what extent our psychologically-based roles meet these

standards. In this chapter, individual, psychosocial, and contextual psychological interventions are evaluated on the basis of the values, models, and roles they endorse and use in their activities. Because U.S. psychology is dominant and contains the most detailed material for informing us about psychology's impact, it will be relied on most heavily in this evaluation. However, because it is culturally limited, materials from other cultures are included to provide a broader perspective.

INDIVIDUALLY FOCUSED INTERVENTIONS

Present day psychology's earliest movements into the public realm were in the fields of psychological assessment of intellectual ability and abnormal behavior. Since then, the major preoccupation of clinical and much of counseling psychology has been psychotherapy so that the importance of clinical assessment has varied in relation to its value as an adjunct to that activity. As noted earlier, these approaches to assessment and psychotherapy have been developed primarily from a universalistic framework in which the individual client is considered to be the bearer of particular properties of function or dysfunction. Little attention is paid to cultural, socioracial/ethnic, or other social determinants. The limitations of that individualist, acontextual orientation and needed changes are explored here, particularly in the area of psychotherapy.

Three reviews of the predominantly U.S. psychotherapy literature were published in the late 1980s, and their coverage complemented each other. All three included empirical, theoretical, discussion, and review articles addressing developments in research, public utilization of relevant knowledge, in-therapy behavior, therapeutic outcomes, identification of key therapeutic processes, and future research directions. The reviewers (Kazdin, 1986; Russell, 1989; Vandenbos, 1986) gave scant attention to social, socioracial/ethnic, or cultural factors in psychotherapy and did not challenge the assumed universality of the Euro-American psyche.

In addition, a U.S. conference about how people change during and apart from therapy included the facilitation of growth, change, and generativity plus the alleviation of abnormal behavior (Curtis & Stricker, 1991). Participants included clinical, family, organizational, and social psychologists. They had differences and conflicts about the nature of people, processes of change, and the role of psychologists. Once again, cultural/socioracial/ethnic factors were ignored.

Clinicians at the conference both endorsed and challenged conventional concepts such as transference, people's rationality or irrationality, and the degree to which therapeutic change is internal, external, or a function of their interaction. The role of the self, cognition, emotion, and whether therapy involves holistic or behavioral change were addressed. Also considered were how students change as they become therapists, the nature and importance of personal development during that process, and the balance between academic and experiential training.

Family, social, and organizational participants differed in that they emphasized the psychosocial nature of change. Social dynamics and social relationships were viewed as more important than intrapsychic factors in people's difficulties and their resolution. Other agencies of change outside of therapy that were considered important included those stemming from interrelationships and from involvement in the process of negotiations. Thereby, they questioned the unique role of therapy, but also, at least implicitly, reaffirmed their shared paradigmatic view that intervention by trained professionals is a primary, if not the only, vehicle for changing people's psychological natures. The need for an extraparadigmatic critique of the overall psychotherapeutic domain was not raised.

This professional orientation has been reaffirmed in the ongoing U.S. debate among psychologists about whether psychotherapies are to be based on "how-to" manuals for treating specified disorders versus approaches which are based in clinical theory, expertise, and the judgment of trained professionals. This debate was stimulated to a major extent by U.S. policy questions concerning the justification for using public funds for mental health treatments. In a recent series which explored these issues, no one argued with the judgment that existing therapeutic approaches are at best no more than modestly successful (Review and Commentaries, 1998, pp. 361–407). Major differences were aired about the relative efficacy of these approaches.

Wilson (1998) underscored that this argument raises both empirical and professional issues. There is empirical support for manual-based approaches, particularly for treating the kinds of disorders described in the DSM-IV; they establish accountability when studying the efficacy of treatments of clinical cases. Further, numerous supporters of "how to" manual approaches are skeptical of the merits of clinical judgment approaches. The data also show that social workers with master's degrees can use manuals as effectively as can doctoral level, clinical psychologists. Wilson stressed that clinical therapeutic expertise is also important in relation to the nonspecific aspects of therapy although its effects are not as readily measurable. For example, skills at establishing a therapeutic relationship and in interacting with clients in a way that acknowledges they are active agents managing their own lives may also be important to successful therapy.

Parloff (1998) deplored the research-oriented denigration of clinical judgment. He countered that manuals may be useful for training and even for practice when people's problems readily fit into category boundaries, and that even manual supporters have highlighted the importance of addressing the nonspecific factors in therapy and the professional threat stemming from their use. His conclusion was that research is needed to determine which disorders can be optimally treated using available approaches.

A scientific and professional guild dilemma arises from these findings. Psychologists currently defend their guild position that a doctor's degree is a minimum requirement to be licensed as psychotherapists. However, there is no empirical basis for this restriction unless factors such as clinical judgment are shown to contribute to treatment efficacy more than or in addition to the ability to follow treatment manuals. If not, clients can turn to other equally effective, but possibly less expensive, sources of therapeutic assistance. Thus, the assumption that doctoral level psychotherapists' advanced training entitles them to unique access to licensing and public reimbursement is subject to serious question.

Only Marques (1998) seriously critiqued the role of psychotherapy as a tool to help people acquire better ways of living and learn specific, teachable skills. She emphasized that the role of psychotherapists requires them to work at the interface of the art and science of clinical practice. They cannot simply assume that therapy is benign. Manuals may contribute to creativity and innovation, but they also contribute to standardization and the devaluation of clinical practice. In her view, the therapist's role is one of using the therapeutic process and its goal to help patients face complex psychosocial problems, and the profession must train therapists for dealing with the problems that the next generation of patients will face. Her emphasis on the psychosocial nature of mental health problems and the intermix of science and art required to address them expands our view of clients to being more than carriers of diagnosed clinical disorders. Marques pointed out that clients live in societies and bring their heritages to their current lives as do their therapists. She said that therapists need to change their conception of themselves, their clients, and the nature of therapy to be responsive to these issues.

The current acultural, ahistorical approach has faced more extensive challenges. Sarason (1981b) wrote about psychology's goal of being a value-neutral enterprise that studies individuals as if they have no social contexts. He described the consequences of this limited focus as being that psychologists have not been educated to understand the socially embedded nature of their own perspectives.

In the United States, it is primarily NCDG psychologists and clients who have challenged this universalist view of psychology as being an acontextual, value-free study of individuals. Sue and Zane (1987) underscored that after two decades of research in the United States on psychotherapy that is culturally sensitive, ethnically sensitive, or both, psychologists remained perplexed about how to proceed and ethnic minority clients were still underserved and poorly served. In addition, investigators consistently recommended that therapists need more knowledge of culture and more specific techniques based on that knowledge. A major question arises as to how twenty years of research had apparently accomplished so little.

Sue and Zane (1987) agreed that the universalist view is unsupportable, but also contended that abstract research knowledge and cultural normative approaches are too far removed from therapeutic interactions to accomplish their purpose. Both positions stereotype clients and provide a "cookbook" approach. In their view, it would be more profitable to focus on (a) establishing for each particular client the perception that the therapist is a trustworthy and effective helper (is credible), and (b) providing some indication for the client that she or he is receiving something of benefit (a gift) from the therapeutic encounters.

Those perceptions are essential to accomplishing what Sue and Zane saw as the objective of therapy, i.e., to provide clients with new learning experiences within their own ethnic cultural perspective. Their examples focused on Asian Americans, but they emphasized that the issues are the same for other NCDG clients. They did not address that even their approach supported therapy as a social conformist enterprise. It can create social change only indirectly through influencing service providers to change their own values.

Garcia and Zea's (1997) edited volume also highlighted the relevance of cultural values in therapeutic roles and domains. However, their predominant orientation was toward helping Latino clients adapt within the CDG U.S. culture, not how psychotherapists can contribute to broadening the culture's diversity tolerance. An exception was Echeverry's (1997) emphasis that "the point is not to *Americanize* Latinos, but to respect their culture and world view and to provide them with culturally sensitive services that take into consideration diversity among Latinos, their place in the acculturation continuum, and their traditional beliefs" (p. 105).

Helms and Cook (1999) focused on white–black interactions in the United States, arguing that the socioracial and cultural socialization of therapists and clients are necessarily part of any therapeutic interaction and should be addressed explicitly. They pointed out that U.S. culture is permeated by an underlying assumption that the dominant socioracial/cultural ethos is not to be questioned. All non-whites are grouped together and are expected to explain themselves. A central element in NCDG people's lives and efforts to get help is their struggle against being forced to accept the CDG's definition of them and their reality as inferior.

Helms and Cook (1999) argued that it is whites who require attention to their own cultural and socioracial histories and identities before they can function effectively as therapists or teachers of therapists. Therapists, particularly white therapists, must (a) become aware of their own socio-racial and cultural history and identity and (b) open up to an awareness of the need to learn about and accept other socioracial and cultural histories and identities as acceptable ways of being human. Presumably, these steps will lead to less oppression by therapists and potentially greater capability for being helpful—an important role change.

Even so, the implicit therapeutic goal is to enable clients to function within the dominant society. Helms and Cook (1999) addressed the need for social change and directed their remarks primarily toward therapists and those who train them. Their objective was to challenge two major white CDG beliefs. They are that white definitions of people's reality and well-being are universal and that people need treatment for CDG defined pathologies based on CDG psychological knowledge and skills. While these are important suggestions, their approach falls short of emphasizing the potential strengths of alternative NCDG belief systems and ways of dealing with life's unanswerable questions.

My colleagues and I (Tyler, Brome, & Williams, 1991) incorporated multicultural, socioracial, and ethnic values and perspectives into the do-main of psychotherapeutic interventions, emphasizing that any therapeu-tic interaction is one of resource exchange. A therapist must learn about the client's personal and contextual history, self and world view, and ways of approaching life. Clients must learn new ways of understanding and managing their lives and realities. In this process, there are both advan-tages and disadvantages when the therapist and client have similar back-grounds and when they have different ones. CDG-NCDG pairings lead to exchanges and learning that are not possible from CDG-CDG or NCDG-NCDG pairings. For example, CDG therapists can learn more from NCDG clients than they can from CDG clients about their own cultural insen-sitivities. NCDG clients are likely to learn more from CDG therapists than they can from NCDG therapists about what CDG people see as the limita-tions and possibilities of NCDG individuals.

There are therapeutic advantages to similar ethnic/racial pairings in exploring issues related to shared backgrounds; there are also limitations for learning about dealing with the world outside those backgrounds. The reverse is true for mixed therapist/client pairings. Examining therapeutic activities by focusing on the strengths and limits of different pairings keeps the focus on individual change while it is also highlights that both therapists and clients are inescapably changing socially and personally. These changed assumptions constitute the central challenges to dominant conceptions of psychotherapy. Acknowledging them emphasizes that the nature and process of psychotherapy involves resource collaboration between active agent individuals who are being altered as individuals and social change agents.

Kakar (1979), a prominent psychoanalyst in India, provided a particularly instructive example of the crucial role in psychotherapy of the participants' assumptions about underlying human values (see Chapter 9). In psychoanalysis, life is assumed to be irrational and ironic; in Hinduism, irrational and romantic. Whether life is ironic or romantic is not subject to empirical testing, though believing one rather than the other may make a difference in how we organize our lives. As Kakar stressed, a therapist approaching therapy from an acultural perspective can neither be aware of nor address that vital part of the therapeutic enterprise.

None of these examples demonstrates that psychotherapy is value free. Rather, they suggest that psychotherapeutic interventions can be powerful tools for helping people prevail over important deficits, confusions, and conflicts in their lives. Not acknowledging that cultural, socioracial, ethnic, and contextual issues are central aspects of life severely limits their potential value, especially for people from NCDG backgrounds. NCDG individuals face living in an unspoken and unexamined cultural context with substantial barriers to their full admission to the culture and full access to its benefits. For them, conventional psychotherapy is of limited value. Evaluating their improvement or the efficacy of a particular psychotherapy approach for them cannot justifiably be based on an unexamined, acontextual universalist paradigm.

Questions arise in psychotherapy about many beliefs which cannot be tested empirically. They include beliefs about the meaning of life and individual well-being. Even so, U.S. psychotherapists are committed to a generalized CDG belief system, and they unthinkingly impose it on their clients. Many psychologists support this approach to psychotherapy, its entitlement to public, social, and economic support, and the restriction allowing only doctorally trained therapists to practice psychotherapy within that framework. As Korchin (1976) declared, in this culturally sanctioned view

> psychotherapy is a professional relationship. Patently, it involves an expert offering a service to a needful person for which in return he receives a salary or fee.... As an honest professional, he sets his fee properly, sees the patient at appointed times, and otherwise keeps to the obligations of the clinical contract. (1976, p. 285)

Endorsing this fee-for-service clinical model also uncritically endorses the ethnocentric CDG economic and social values of the United States. The ethnic validity contexts in which approaches to psychotherapy are embedded and the possibility that they may have destructive and antisocial psychological correlates are not evaluated. Existing challenges to this approach have primarily been developed and implemented by professionals from NCDG backgrounds, and their work has largely been ignored within CDG contexts.

PSYCHOSOCIOCULTURALLY FOCUSED INTERVENTIONS

A number of psychologists have questioned whether individuals can change substantially if their therapist uses an acontextual individual change approach, and, therefore, whether it is justifiable to support that approach as society's primary means of addressing peoples' psychological dysfunctions. If we take the viewpoint that individual and contextual change are intertwined, we would place primary emphasis on creating better environments and psychosocial circumstances to reduce the psychologically destructive aspects of society and enhance the psychologically benign ones. However, it is an enormously complex job to identify the values that underlie a good life and a good society and define a role and domain of work for psychologists that contributes to achieving those goals. Perhaps that work could provide a basis for evaluating social and individual change approaches and their relative merits. This section reviews and evaluates some of these alternatives.

COMMUNITY APPROACHES

As was documented in Chapter 3, the U.S. community mental health movement arose in part as a response to the demonstrated impossibility of meeting the country's mental health problems through individual treatment (Joint Commission on Mental Health and Illness, 1961) and, in part to address publicly based forces which challenged societal inequities. Community psychology's formation and development has been controversial because of those origins and its challenge to psychology's individually focused paradigm. There remain questions central to community psychology's focus. For example, must individuals and their psychological problems be addressed in relation to their psychosocial contexts? Can a model focused on people's presumed pathologies provide an adequate framework for understanding and intervening with communities? Finally, and perhaps most central, what is the nature of healthy people and community life? Also, what constitutes justifiable bases (values, roles, and domains) for intervention?

Glidewell (1987) captured community psychology's vision by pointing out that most activities in a community are accomplished with no one directly in charge. People meet their expectations in the community's shared context largely because they want to and they gain satisfaction from doing so. The general task of community psychologists is to evolve a new model which enables them to constructively contribute to the way they and others live in their communities. That model must start with the notion that everyone, including the psychologists, sustains themselves and their communities and cultures through their capabilities, not in spite of their deficits.

People are the carriers of their lives, their communities, and their cultures. In communities, the emphasis is on the interconnectedness of these three facets of peoples' reality. To build on that interconnectedness, psychologists are forced to consider that the community's defining coherence or "social glue" is both individually and collectively based. For example, when asked what he saw as the anticipated benefits of his trip, a Hindu pilgrim told my colleagues and me that everyone's crops in his village would now be more bountiful. This expressed his belonging to a "coherent whole," a "unity," a community, and also his ability to act as an individual influencing that interconnectedness. Thus, a viable community psychology challenges the value base and domain of mainstream psychology's current emphasis that individuals, including themselves, are completely autonomous.

When psychologists first organized this new approach, they defined their relationships to communities in two parts: (a) as students of the institutionalized behavior of people who create habitats which in turn shape their inhabitants, and (b) as participant–conceptualizer change agents. That definition clearly indicated that psychologists are involved members of communities and also professionals "attempting to conceptualize those processes within the framework of psychological–sociological knowledge" (Bennet et al., 1966, pp. 7–8). They used that framework to create a number of significant new approaches to improve the well-being of communities and their inhabitants. These new approaches turned psychologists away from a focus on changing particular individuals to one of changing populations. To evaluate the impact of community psychology's approaches we must first understand its base in psychiatry's community mental health concepts and the preventive approaches that grew out of them.

COMMUNITY MENTAL HEALTH AND PREVENTION

The advantage of community-based preventive approaches over individually oriented treatment approaches is the greater efficiency derived by addressing both societal and other contextual factors along with individual factors. The reactive nature of individual case treatment approaches limits a therapist's ability to contribute to issues of health maintenance because problems are dealt with only after they begin to have a negative impact. At that point, therapy may be able to produce only partial restoration to pre-illness functioning and capability levels. In contrast, promoting conditions that prevent and reduce disease at a community level may allow some individuals to avoid dysfunctions and others to benefit from a more comprehensive support network to help address breakdowns and other problems. These advantages led community psychiatrists, psychologists, and other community-oriented professionals to develop preventive intervention approaches to community mental health.

Caplan (1964), a psychiatrist, used the public health model to create the most explicit formulation of community mental health concepts and programs for action. He defined individual and community mental health, specified the mental health professional's role in the community, and outlined its three-faceted schema of preventive intervention to promote community mental health. The nature and scope of his work are important to understand because it is still very influential and it raises issues for evaluating the worth of all mental health paradigms.

Despite its radical features, this community mental health approach is fundamentally a professional intervention model designed to guide the deployment of mental health resources. Professionals were to use interpersonal interaction programs to change key individuals in a community and enlist their efforts to increase the impact of preventive mental health principles. Community mental health specialists could consult with community leaders to increase the leaders' awareness of mental health problems and constructive ways to cope with them. Social action programs for community intervention could be designed to change community policies and services to be more responsive to preventive priorities. Relevant activities could include providing needed mental health supplies for the community and improving the population's ability to adjust during life crises.

Secondary prevention concepts and approaches were to reduce the prevalence of mental illness by early (in life or the onset of illness) identification of it in people at risk. They aimed to alter factors that produce new cases or, more often, to provide early diagnosis and treatment. For example, large organizations could use screening measures to identify early stage mental health problems and then provide needed services by trained mental health personnel rather than reject or exclude these individuals from their work force.

Another secondary prevention example is the development of screening approaches for early detection among children. For four decades,

Cowen and his colleagues (Cowen et. al, 1973; Cowen & Hightower, 1989) focused on elementary schools in Rochester, New York, because of the (a) socializing power of the schools, (b) geographic convenience, and (c) the school's amenability to program input. As is true of any successful community endeavor, their efforts built on a combination of conceptually and pragmatically relevant considerations. They developed and validated a brief scale for classroom teachers to record the frequency of symptom occurrences for each child. Once identified as at risk, children were referred to therapeutic and remedial education programs. The demonstrated effectiveness of Cowen's program, its continued support, and the spread of the model to other areas speak to its continued value nearly three decades later (Cowen & Hightower, 1989). The evidence showed that such an approach, though perhaps far from ideal, was demonstrably superior to traditional school mental health approaches.

Cowen's program is a model for school systems that do not have access to continued outside consultation or management. Its value was reflected in the success of a somewhat comparable approach developed by Kapur and her colleagues (Kapur & Cariapa, 1979; Kapur, Cariapa, & Parthasarathy, 1980) in Bangalore, India. First, they taught school teachers how to identify mental health problems. Next, they selected motivated and capable teachers for further training in counseling and developed an in-school referral network for these teachers to counsel children who were identified as problems. Most importantly, these schools developed effective counseling programs which were sustained after the departure of the mental health team.

The social values underlying all programs are particularly important criteria for evaluating them, as they are for community mental health. Specifically, the value base of Caplan's orientation to mental health is a traditional one that does not question existing societal structures or values. Prevention efforts are directed at reducing the occurrence and destructive impact of negative conditions on a community's residents. However, individual mental health is thought to stem primarily from individuals learning to "fit in" to an already appropriately designed community, not from the community learning to create alternative individual or social arrangements to prevent or treat specific problems. Primary prevention approaches differ radically from traditional illness treatment approaches in that they require mental health workers to extend their role and domain of activities and involve themselves in a variety of social problems, including the study of health. However, this step is undertaken for the purpose of reducing the level of illness in a community, not for reconceptualizing these problems as having a psychosocial or ecological rather than a mental illness nature. Broader social change is to be addressed only through the medium of established political channels.

Caplan's (1984) sociocultural perspective was embedded in an ethnocentric Western world view. He believed that some cultures are mentally damaging and others, primarily those with Western middle class values, are healthier. He reasoned that people who experience a richer cultural heritage will have been taught to cope with more complicated problems and be mentally healthier. Caplan ignored the context-appropriateness of disparate cultural patterns and the cultural strengths inherent in the distinctive lifestyles that are developed within different cultures. He also ignored the possibility that there may be important and unique strengths in the approaches that many impoverished and disadvantaged people in any culture use to deal with their lives.

The community mental health prevention approach included a number of important and innovative ideas. However, it was based on politically conservative medical and societal values which assumed the correctness of Social Darwinism and the inherent superiority of a Western, middle class orientation. It specified illness prevention as its domain and excluded learning or growth-oriented perspectives, so it maintained the status quo. Further, it defined the role of community mental health professionals as that of experts using an authoritative model to define and evaluate the nature and status of the community's and country's illness, health, and care. Despite its change in focus from individual to community-centered treatment, it retained the ethnocentric assumption that Euro-American, universalist values are superior. Although many of these values and approaches are inconsistent with the participative and social change characteristics of community psychology approaches, they raise questions about the nature and remediation of human dysfunction which are important to the evaluation of any psychology based conception of people's well-being.

PRIMARY PREVENTION AND PSYCHOLOGY

Some community psychologists questioned the adequacy of the illness-based community mental health model and expanded their own psychologically based prevention efforts to include a combination of competence development and illness prevention. Others constructed nonillness paradigms for understanding disordered and constructive functioning and advancing the well-being of communities and individuals. These alternative approaches rested on the assumption that all individuals have strengths and limitations, organize their lives from their own perspectives, and are entitled to be treated with dignity and respect. Related intervention programs and evaluation criteria were focused on building strengths in people and their communities.

Those programs and criteria were constructed to encourage and sustain diversity (divergences) and interconnectedness (convergences) and incorporate prosocial approaches to resolve conflicts. They conceptualized people as active agents in their own behalf and that of their families, communities, and societies. They also led to the development of psychologists' roles as collaborative and authoritative models of interaction. Perhaps the best single source of information about the nature, range, and efficacy of such efforts is the two decades of reports from The Vermont Conference on the Primary Prevention of Psychopathology (VCPPP). Included here are papers from two of those conferences spaced fifteen years apart. These papers illustrate the variety of themes that were included and questions that were raised about the criteria needed to define a paradigm which could promote and evaluate the well-being of people and their societies.

Sameroff (1977) questioned the primary prevention concept and its customary practice of using retrospective studies to establish the legitimacy of primary prevention efforts. He cited that retrospective studies of birth anoxia that begin by identifying impaired functioning in later life do find a disproportionate number of cases in which birth anoxia was reported in comparison to controls. However, when birth anoxia cases and controls are matched in prospective studies, no developmental differences are found. He concluded that it is not just initial events whose effects must be neutralized to prevent the development of disorder. Instead, a transactional model is needed which assumes that initial characteristics and environmental inputs interact continuously to shape each other and produce eventual, possibly extreme, outcomes.

Crissey (1977) conducted a 40 year follow-up study of the mental development of 49 children in the U.S. who were placed in orphanages at a time (ca. 1930) of severe economic depression and a climate of strict morality. Because there was very little acceptance of out-of-wedlock pregnancies, most of these children were put up for adoption. Children given over to state care were least likely to have come from a "good background" or least expected to have a promising future, although none of these children had neurological defects. Sophisticated psychometrics were not available, so the children's placements were based on brief impressions about them and on the match between their characteristics and the adoptive parents' requests concerning the sex, race, and religion of the child.

According to Crissey (1977), the orphanage categorized the children into four different groups: normal, dull normal, high level mentally retarded, and retarded. The twelve children judged normal at birth were never adopted and stayed in the orphanage. By age six, their average IQ had dropped out of the normal range. They became progressively less able to cope with their lives, exhibited classic patterns of mental retardation, and were transferred to a home for the mentally retarded. The children judged as dull normal were adopted into middle class or professional homes. They all graduated from high school, 70% of them went to college, and all of them had successful and fulfilling lives. Those in the high level mentally retarded group were adopted into lower middle class homes. Most completed high school, one fourth went to college, and half had good marriages and lives. Finally, the children in the group considered retarded were provided more personal stimulation on an experimental basis by their placement in a ward of older, retarded girls. They gained approximately 30 points in IQ to bring the group average up to 96 (nearly the national average), and most of them completed high school and lived independent, self-supporting lives. More than prevention was involved in the lives of these children; rather, level of stimulation was the major determinant of their intellectual and personal growth and the ongoing quality of their lives.

Fifteen years later, the VCPPP had broadened its focus to explore global perspectives on improving children's lives (Albee, Bond, & Cook-Monsey, 1992). Its range of topics included a program in Norway to reduce bullying among school children. Olweus (1992) conducted a prospective, longitudinal study designed to create a prosocial school, home, and community environment. It was characterized by warmth, positive interest, and monitoring involvement from adults, plus firm, nonhostile, nonphysical limits to unacceptable behaviors. The program reduced the occurrence of new bullying incidents (primary prevention) and the level of existing victimization problems (secondary prevention). Its impact was substantially greater than that reported from previous efforts. Olweus concluded that we know how to prevent bullying, but society's use of that knowledge depends on another criterion, i.e., its willingness to do so.

A program in Munich, Germany, with an even broader community focus was designed to foster health promotion for children and youth (Stark, 1992). The program helped people meet their needs by identifying resources inherent in themselves and their situations rather than using a traditional approach to try to meet those needs and leave the people passive. Numerous self-help groups and nonprofit organizations worked collaboratively with the city government to actively engage citizens, professionals, and city officials. Children and adults participated by researching and implementing ways to increase safe play opportunities and participate in "Futures Labs" to generate new ideas for projects. Over a five-year period, these bottom-up efforts produced significant improvement in the status of children. They encountered the most difficulties when top city officials were unsympathetic to recommendations. To Stark, the study's major lesson was that empowerment processes can be successful in creating social change only when they link community participation, neighborhood projects, and sociopolitical impact.

Sociopolitical impact was addressed even more broadly by other participants. Albee (1992) emphasized that we are exploiting human and environmental resources throughout the world, and many in irreplaceable ways. He stressed that (a) many children are born of malnourished and exploited mothers unable to provide them basic care; (b) stable loving families can socialize children in ways that develop empathy and enable them to participate in and contribute to peaceful communities and societies; (c) social conflict in the forms of exploitation of the lower social classes, male exploitation of females, and ethnocentric and racist exploitation by more powerful groups prevent their victims from using knowledge to improve their lives; and (d) professional personnel, including psychologists, do not actively contribute to changing oppressive and unjust conditions because of their commitment to scientific detachment and to one-on-one intrapsychic change approaches. From Albee's view, implementing a prevention approach necessitates undertaking a social revolution.

Wilcox and Naimark (1992) also emphasized the need for social change, focusing on the Rights of the Child document adopted by the United Nations in 1989. It provided an international, multicultural convergence on a view of children as unique individuals and as members of a family. Its definition of children's rights included not only political and civil rights, but also economic, social, and cultural ones. Thereby, the United Nations convention provided a strong moral consensus for needed social changes to which psychologists can contribute their expertise.

The values, roles, and domains of endeavor embedded in these programs took the participants beyond a status quo orientation and enabled them to reduce the incidence and prevalence of clinically defined dysfunctions. Their focus was on implementing a worldwide domain of needed societal changes, some couched in prevention terms and others in growth, coping, or social change, or some combination of those terms. Adoption of these new assumptions and criteria as a basis for the work and the world views of the participants in those programs led to changes whose effectiveness demonstrates that these views of children and of their rights must be included as criteria in evaluations of other intervention paradigms.

INDIVIDUALS IN RELATION TO CONTEXT

Twenty years ago Sarason (1981b) harshly criticized psychologists for their assumption that individuals are context free and their insistence on seeing themselves as context free, that is, their effort to be "objective." He pointed out that they had failed to address their own *weltanschauung*, their "silent background that gives shape and meaning to the figural aspects of experience" (p. 57). In his view, a new psychology was needed to enable psychologists to "see themselves and others as historical beings but not historical in a narrow, intrapsychic sense, which assigns the social structure to a very secondary status" (p. 182). Although his vision is far from being realized, there have been some changes in how psychologists view themselves, their world, and their work. As a background to considering their implications, some of the difficulties inherent in changing our weltanschauungs are illustrated in the following incident.

In 1991, I was a visiting scholar at Allahabad University in India. My wife and I were invited by our psychology department colleagues to an interdisciplinary symposium organized by the leadership of the Mahatma Gandhi Marg (conference center) and the professional and academic leaders in the city. Its topic was progress in the context of Hinduism. However, the symposium and our invitation posed a number of irreconcilable weltanschauung issues to the conference organizers.

The Director of the Marg insisted that out of respect for Gandhi (a) the discussion had to be conducted in Hindi, (b) foreigners could not attend, and (c) non-Indian products could not be sold in the Marg. The easiest issue to resolve was (c), and the non-Indian Pepsi Cola vending machine was banned. In regard to (a), the symposium topic created a true dilemma as Hindi does not have a word for progress, nor does Hinduism incorporate a belief in progress. Progress could be imagined and discussed only in another language. Finally, (b) we had been invited before the prohibition against foreigners was invoked and although we were willing to withdraw, that solution was considered unacceptable by our colleagues. A face-saving resolution was needed, so we were permitted to attend but not participate. Our friends arranged to slip an occasional word of English into the dialogue so they could discuss progress and in hopes that we could follow the general thrust of the discussion; but their efforts only highlighted the impossibility of the situation. We were all ensnarled in our different paradigms (weltanschauungs) in ways that frustrated efforts to find a constructive prosocial resolution.

More generally, we all put our lives together in ways that build on our destinies, histories, continuities, and autonomies. However, our unique efforts do not fit neatly into psychologists' theories or proclivities to professionally define our realities and plan our lives for us. For example, prosocial resource collaboration or people asking for and offering assistance to others within natural networks are activities critical to the development of relationships and communities and for each person's well-being. Thus, these natural networks grow out of people's shared history and sense of continuity as was demonstrated by Young, Giles, and Plantz (1982). They found that adult residents of rural communities in the eastern

United States were generally willing to give and seek help in relation to problems of living (e.g., anger, depression, injury, death), especially if those others were part of their networks (spouses, friends, etc.). To them, the reciprocal processes of helping and seeking help were mutually rewarding. (See Chapter 7 for more details.)

How and how effectively we relate to and use our own (autonomy) and our community's (history and continuity) resources may be related to ethnic validity and individual differences. Mitchell, Barbarin, and Hurley (1981) explored that possibility as part of a larger study (Barbarin, Tyler, & Gatz, 1979) on problem solving, resource utilization, and community involvement in neighboring black and white suburban communities in the eastern United States. Service providers and community residents were differentiated as being active or inactive in civic affairs and then were interviewed about community strengths, deficits, problem-solving alternatives, and satisfaction. In the predominantly black communities, the residents' experience of community life was related to how active they were in using influential people to solve their problems. In the predominantly white communities, it was related to their methods of handling problems and their evaluation of the available formal resources. In both, service providers and active citizens reported more strengths, deficits, alternatives, and satisfaction than did less engaged residents. Having more information was related to a more positive sense of community, especially for people with a stronger sense of internal control. The community context made a difference in what people thought they could do, what they did, and how they came to "be" as persons. Individual differences in psychosocial competence contributed to how they interacted with their situations.

In these examples, people exhibited substantial capabilities for resourceful, autonomous functioning and for forming and using networks to enhance the quality of their lives and their immediate contexts. Therein lies an important potential for our involvement as both individual and community-oriented social change agents. As psychologists who function as change agents, we can change our weltanschauungs and adopt a collaborative and supportive role to facilitate people's efforts to build on their own capabilities and self-concepts. Or we can continue to ignore, deemphasize, and refuse to assess their capacities for autonomous functioning and for developing functional networks within their life contexts.

Problem-Oriented Approaches

The best example of the interplay between people and their contexts is found in the definition of people as "problems" based on social, not individual, criteria. That is, we become a problem when our conduct is defined by others as socially destructive or merits disapproval. Werner's (1989, 1995) studies of children growing up in deprived conditions showed that the resilient ones had important personal support resources or mentors in their lives and the nonresilient (problem) ones did not; but the problems were considered to be the children—not their circumstances. Staub's (1978a,b) extensive studies on the roots of prosocial behavior found that it was more prevalent in cultures which emphasize it. He also found that in the United States schools he studied, prosocial behavior decreased between the first and the eighth grades. Again, the children, not the circumstances, were defined as prosocial or antisocial.

Ezekiel examined the roots of racism and its consequences in United States society. He tried to understand racists and their targets by studying their life situations from their points of view. From his study of inner city African Americans, he learned that the dialogue about race in the United States is conducted primarily in the face of "empty white masks"; that is, white people are not really engaged in it (Ezekiel, 1984). In his study of young white male members of extremist racist groups, Ezekiel (1995) found that they had not been cared for or supported during childhood. Consequently, they were inordinately unsure of themselves. Their leaders told them that despite their "superior nature," their security and position were threatened by NCDGs, so they became fearful and defensive.

Ezekiel (1995) concluded that research on racism will be profitable only if investigators relate to respondents as individuals whose perspectives make sense in their own contexts, however distasteful those peoples' views may seem. That process can begin only when investigators reject a detached professional role and conception that their domain of professional functioning is separate from their personal life domain. That is, our ability to respect others' views, to be concerned about what others need, and consider how people can get along, is possible only when we include our own perspectives in the matrix of factors that must be considered and evaluated.

Kelman and Hamilton (1989) focused on broad psychosocial domains in analyzing problem areas, such as crimes of obedience, and from that work formulated individual and societal guidelines for developing alternatives to such destructive behaviors. They wrote that obeying or disobeying illegal orders, such as to participate in a "sanctioned massacre," requires the person to choose between illegal obedience and principled disobedience. This choice can be adequately explained only if a combination of psychological and social forces are considered. The social conditions are important because they contribute to the origins of individuals' orientations to authority and responsibility. Kelman and Hamilton identified three types of situations and their effects: (a) Living with little power in subordinate positions predisposes people to adopt a predominant *rule* orientation and be vulnerable to crimes of obedience. (b) Living in more moderate circumstances leads to a predominant *role* orientation and the assumption of responsibility for specific behavior, but not its broader implications. (c) Living in powerful and privileged circumstances with experience in exercising decision-making predisposess people to form a *value* orientation and be less vulnerable to such crimes.

Broader social processes also influence the choice between illegal obedience and principled disobedience. Kelman and Hamilton (1989) spelled out the three socialization steps involved in this process. *Authorization* relieves people of moral responsibility and guilt, and influences them to define their choices as resting on role obligations, not moral convictions. *Routinization* reduces their opportunities for raising questions about their morality. *Dehumanization* of people's attitudes redefines their acts so that obediently doing violence to others does not raise questions about its morality.

Kelman and Hamilton's conclusion was that socializing people to exercise independent judgment in the face of authority's orders is the essence and consequence of a value orientation. They emphasized further that such value orientations are necessary for the establishment of desirable and stable societies and citizens. As a noteworthy example, they cited the small Protestant village of Chambon in southern France. Under the leadership of their pastor, the villagers organized a refuge to protect Jews during the Nazi occupation in World War II. It was their value orientation that was reflected in their independent judgment choices.

Perhaps Kelman's (1968) was the most explicit articulation in the United States of the social scientist as a participant in the stream of human existence. He wrote that the social scientist is a producer of social forces through scientific work, an experimenter and thinker, and a participant in social action. Each of these activities cuts across three value domains: human relationships, societal processes, and the scientific study of people. In Kelman's view, these roles and their value components are inescapable; that is, social science cannot be either prior to or independent of the human and social context, and all of those factors must be considered when we evaluate our undertakings.

The problem-oriented Social Therapy program of Fairweather (1980) also emphasized the importance of the interplay of psychological and social context elements in people's lives. Its approach was to provide mentally ill people a stake in their own futures. Small groups were housed in lodges and assigned responsibility for getting well and for their own and each other's well-being in their lodge home and their working life spaces. Each lodge functioned as a subsociety where the members were accorded status as fully functioning individuals whose behavior, thoughts and feelings—including their idiosyncracies—were not considered deviant.

Fairweather (1980) emphasized that internal and external changes in personal and work behaviors cannot be sustained without a societally-based social role to support them. That support is particularly important for mental patients who live in a community because part of the difficulty for them in establishing and maintaining personal changes has characteristically been community resistance to their presence. Thus, the demonstrated effectiveness of these programs could be carried over to the larger community only if the entire Lodge Society program was adopted.

Although wider adoption of the program cost less than traditional psychotherapeutic approaches, it did require public financial support for its implementation and changes in the role of professional personnel. They had to become consultants and coparticipants (possibly akin to the participant–conceptualizer role). Those changes run counter to most professionals' education and role expectations and to the beliefs of the supporting bureaucracy which is designed to maintain the status quo. In Fairweather's view, the most difficult aspect of efforts to accomplish social change is the resistance of those who have a stake in the status quo. However, these people and their issues must also be considered when assessing the worth of programs.

INTERVENTIONS AND THEIR RELATIONSHIP TO ETHNIC VALIDITY

Ethnic validity embodies the holistic integration (the ethos) of all the external characteristics that contribute to self-definitions. Those characteristics include values, definitions of reality and the meaning of life, and shared conceptions of destiny, history, continuity, autonomy, and empirical knowledge. In combination, they constitute the shared framework that people with a common tradition and identity internalize.

The existence and significance of ethnic validity becomes particularly evident when a discipline such as psychology is introduced into a different cultural or ethnic context. When psychological interventions framed within one ethnic validity paradigm are introduced into another, difficulties arise as divergent and conflicting elements are encountered. As Moghaddam (1987) documented (see Chapter 3), the domain of social psychological theorizing, research, and applications has diverged markedly in the world's so-called three stages of technological development in ways consistent with each country's different dominant ethnic validity issues. In his view, these three worlds have much to contribute to and learn from each other. To interact productively, representatives of each have to relinquish their ethnocentric orientation and retain their identity and self-reliance. They can then contribute their ethnic validity perspectives to a transcultural conception of psychology and a related framework for evaluating their respective contributions.

A particularly salient example of the importance of attending to a culture's ethnic validity patterns in psychological interventions was McClelland and Winter's (1969) effort (see also Chapter 7, p. 274). They tried to teach the need for achievement (nAch) to business entrepreneurs in India. Their objective was to establish that nAch is a crucial causal motivational factor in the economic development of countries. In that process, they imposed their value system on India's cultural patterns by designing their project using universalist individually oriented theories of psychologically based motivation (an assumed etic), entrepreneurial based economic development, and the interrelationship between the two.

Sinha (1981) and his Indian colleagues challenged the relevance of applying McClelland and Winter's reasoning about nAch to national development in India on the ethnic validity grounds that India has limited resources and the Protestant ethic is not widespread there. They tested and confirmed a counter hypothesis that high nAch will lead to maximum output only when available resources are unlimited. When they are limited, subjects with a high need for cooperation (nCoop) will produce more than will subjects with high nAch, low nCoop. After an extended cross-cultural exchange with McClelland and further studies, Sinha and Pandey (1970) concluded that "altruism distracts the nAch Ss from 'minding' their own interest" (p. 216) by introducing incongruent demands such as cooperation and helping the needy.

Whether the presumed gains from untrammeled nAch outweigh their costs to individuals and societies has far-reaching implications in today's world. Neither set of investigators explored whether their findings would generalize to other cultures. McClelland (1966) had earlier acknowledged that "concern for the common man" (as he called it) is also important for economic development, a point also underscored by Pareek (1968), an Indian psychologist. To assess the generality of these concerns within and across societies requires attention to ethnic validity perspectives.

A subsequent study in India by Sinha (1981) found that people's dependency-proneness could be changed by getting them to believe they are not dependent. That change then generalized to broader changes in functioning. Under a supervisor who took initiative and was efficient, dependency prone people worked harder and took more initiative than nondependency-prone people. These findings challenged the presumed universal superiority of the Euro-American ethnic validity value of autonomy. They also endorsed the prosocial achievement correlates of some dependency characteristics. The study did not answer how dependency-proneness would fit into the ethnic validity context of the United States or other societies.

These cross-cultural exchanges could have served as a model for cross-cultural collaboration, though there seems to be little evidence that they were used that way. McClelland apparently approached the dialogue as if it was an argument about universal principles. Sinha and Pandey, from a presumably less technologically developed society, hypothesized that nested framework factors, in this case adequacy of resources, would influence the psychosocial characteristics of individuals. The dialogue seems to have proceeded as a competitive adversarial interaction that modeled the universalist, competitive, individual-oriented first world view of science and of people.

Kagitcibasi (1996) combined the roles of transcultural investigator and social interventionist. She tested whether the divide between the individualism of some societies and the collectivism of others can be bridged, at least in the collectivist society of Turkey, by creating a model of "individual autonomy *within* relatedness" (p. 184) (see Chapter 6 for details). In an early childhood care and education project in a working class community, she combined individualist and collectivist values by introducing autonomy in child rearing while supporting traditional close-knit family values and relatedness. Her program contributed positively to the children's development, the mother's status in the home, and the sense of well-being of the mothers and children. It also enriched spousal relations and generated a self-sustaining process within the community. Thus, her work underscored the value of attending to ethnic validity differences in socialization, how they can be prosocially integrated, and the importance of considering their influence in program evaluations.

Unfortunately, psychologists can also use their knowledge to intervene across cultural and national boundaries for antisocial purposes, including the destruction of the ethnic validity of other societies. In the 1960s, U.S. agencies recruited psychologists and other social scientists and funded them to conduct a secret project in South America studying how to destabilize unfriendly governments. When this project came to light, the far reaching effects included a substantial and enduring increase in mistrust of the presumedly benign intent of social scientists, particularly cross-cultural investigators (Vallance, 1966).

The interventions of psychologists can be shaped, perhaps unwittingly, by paradigms other than their own about the nature of human affairs. A consortium of nearly 70 psychological science organizations in the United States was formed to begin using basic and applied research to solve human behavior problems of broad national interest (Human Capital Initiative, 1992). Six social problem areas from across the life span were selected on the basis of evidence that psychology and psychologists can contribute to reducing the human misery those problems produce and thereby increase the quality of many people's lives. The decision to conceptualize this effort as a "human capital" initiative fits the ethnic validity orientation of the United States, but that capitalist orientation is antithetical to other U.S. cultural values. For example, thinking of people primarily in terms of their productive capability does not fit with the belief that everyone is entitled to equal "rights and dignity."

Sullivan and Transue (1999) reviewed research on the psychological underpinnings of government as practiced in the United States and of governments from other countries, primarily in the Western world. Particular attention was paid to political tolerance, interpersonal trust, and social capital. Social capital is a more inclusive term than human capital because it emphasizes people's interconnectedness, but it also conceptualizes people in economic and political terms. Sullivan and Transue criticized the studies they reviewed for defining democracy exclusively from the U.S./British model. Within that limitation, however, they found substantial transcultural convergences in support of (a) the interlinked nature of psychological variables such as trust and active (agent) participation in voluntary associations; (b) acceptance of norms of reciprocity and tolerance of others' views and their participation in governance; and (c) the conclusion that democratically functioning societies are more likely to meet citizens' expectations, solve public and collective action problems, and provide people with a better quality of life.

Current research does not permit us to identify the lines of causality between social political arrangements and personal characteristics, nor to relate general findings to specific cultural or ethnic validity norms. However, studies can be analyzed using non-U.S./British people's conceptions of the nature of democracy. Analyzing studies using transcultural frameworks can inform us about inherent ethnocentric biases and also provide a contextually sounder basis for our efforts to advance human welfare.

Kelman's (1997) work in international conflict resolution built on his sensitivity to ethnic validity issues. It also highlighted the complexity of the issues involved in the interrelationships between the roles and conduct of individuals, the dynamics and mechanisms of group interactions, and the formation and functioning of nation states as organizations that control people's lives. To Kelman, approaches to conflict resolution converge in their shared value base which includes the importance of respect for the rights and dignity of all of the parties involved, a nonadversarial framework for conflict resolution, and an analytic approach.

Kelman (1997) formulated an approach to resolve international and ethnic conflicts, and he participated as a scholar-practitioner in facilitating a peaceful solution to the Israeli–Palestinian conflict. In his approach, participants' conflict resolution roles involve direct participation with all of the parties in the conflict. In interactive problem-solving workshops, their task is to stay focused on jointly creating a solution with the facilitation of a third party trained in conflict resolution. The workshops provide a forum where each group's internal and intersocietal ethnic validity processes (which cannot be reduced to the level of individual behavior) can be influenced by their interactions with each other as individuals and as representatives of their nations.

Combining the roles of individuals as involved citizen–participants and as involved scholar–facilitators in a problem-solving context is crucial to Kelman's approach. So is combining the participatory and detached stances of scholar–participant and participant–conceptualizer in any expert psychosocial role. The conditions, mechanisms, and informed facilitation are created by these combinations so that people can begin the psychosocial spirals of change needed for them to solve their shared problems. In sum, Kelman (1997) stressed and demonstrated that formulating an integrative conception of human functioning requires understanding how ethnic validity perspectives and psychosocial processes relate to each other.

SUMMARY

There are many and varied interrelationships among cultural and community contexts and the patterns of competence, dysfunction, and change that individuals and societies develop. Studies show the pervasiveness of social, ideological, and political impacts on people's lives when ethnic validity issues are addressed. They also show that psychological approaches can contribute to social and economic development in modernized and impoverished countries and regions and in the resolution of international conflicts.

In the past, as questions arose about psychotherapy's limited potential to help solve society's mental health problems, attention was turned to alternative ways to deal with psychological disabilities and promote psychological well-being. Included were psychosocially oriented interventions to prevent disorders and enable people to improve the quality of their lives. That shift in role and domain generated a paradigmatic conflict. This conflict concerned the appropriateness of using a medical model for psychological interventions to ameliorate dysfunctional conduct problems versus a psychosocial competence, development, community, and societally-oriented model. Today, a medical model clinical approach to psychotherapy and to the prevention of medically defined psychopathologies continues to dominate mental health policies in the United States and much of the world.

Clinical psychologists rely primarily on individually-oriented psychotherapy for intervention, even though it has been demonstrated to be of only limited effectiveness. One of its shortcomings is that it is based on a narrow acultural, acontextual model of human functioning. An additional problem is the major value conflict among psychologists about psychotherapy's nature and the appropriate criteria for evaluating it. There is agreement that changes which can be identified on standard psychometric measures and less tangible changes, such as those related to self-understanding and the ability to feel empathy for others, are both relevant to the success of therapy. However, the advocates of these respective emphases do not study both kinds of factors; instead they argue about which one should be considered important. Further, much of their research does not help determine which aspects of psychological knowledge and perspectives should be emphasized during individual psychotherapy in order to produce optimal individual and social benefits or to change destructive societal patterns.

Further, there has been little effort by psychologists to address the impact of different ethnic validity perspectives in their theoretical formulations, research investigations, programs of intervention, or evaluations. Psychologists' lives, just as those of the people they study, are embedded in different ethnic validity configurations, at times in ways they may not understand. Consequently, many psychological interventions remain ethnocentric in nature because psychologists lack an awareness of their ethnic validity biases or because of elitist biases of an ideological or professionalist nature, or both, and do not include ethnic validity criteria in evaluations.

There is also abundant evidence that, for good or ill, ethnic validity approaches have a wide range of applicability which extends from international conflict resolution to community change, to individual change, and they can contribute to improving the quality of people's lives. They do so because they place value on the role of individuals as active resourceful agents, thereby changing the psychologist's role of professional helper to that of resource collaborator. They also broaden psychology's domain of concern to include communities and societies. Unless psychology's efforts are informed by ethnic validity perspectives, they are of limited value or are even counterproductive. Incorporating ethnic validity and resource exchange and enhancement perspectives into psychological evaluation criteria will enable us to identify more effective approaches to help individuals and societies cope with and prevail over powerful conditions and circumstances that may otherwise be overwhelming. Those perspectives will also contribute to identifying approaches that are of value for enhancing the quality of peoples' lives.

CHOOSING AND EVALUATING APPROACHES TO CHANGE

INTRODUCTION

Throughout this volume, I have referred in various ways to prosocial and antisocial individual and societal changes because one aspect of the contribution psychologists make is to define and facilitate prosocial change. To make decisions about what constitutes prosocial change and how to accomplish it, we are faced with building on people's commonalities while also respecting their uniqueness and the consequent differences and conflicts between them. Another particularly salient issue for psychologists and others who act as social change agents is whether we consider ourselves separate from or part of our theories and approaches, i.e., the processes we are studying and trying to manipulate. Consequently, a final aspect of our task is to identify the special character of our expert knowledge and how to best use it.

With these ideas in mind, this chapter will distinguish between three interrelated aspects of psychology-based efforts to define and accomplish prosocial change. Specifically, *research* refers to the characteristic hypothesis-testing studies that contribute to expert knowledge. *Evaluation* refers to studies that measure the impact of an ongoing or completed activity or process, including the application of expert knowledge in regular life situations. Finally, *appraisal* refers to the judged merit of using a particular approach or paradigm such as the medical model to address loosely defined psychosocial issues such as mental health. All of these considerations (as judged from both a societal common sense and an expert point of view) determine whether actions taken on psychological grounds are considered to have accomplished prosocial changes.

DIMENSIONS IN GUIDING AND EVALUATING CHANGE

Whatever balances we strike as a basis for our work, we can best accomplish our goals if the assumptions on which we are proceeding are made explicit. Further, they must be continually revisited. The process of effecting and evaluating change is an alternating one. That is, we construct an approach and use it. We then evaluate the outcome and the approach. Depending on our appraisal of the evaluation results, we continue using our approach or change it, then proceed and repeat that process indefinitely.

There are at least four dimensions important for guiding and evaluating these steps. They are values, conceptual models, procedural guidelines, and facts, and they must be referred to at all phases of the change process. Below is a brief definition of each dimension and a summary of the role it plays.

VALUES

Values are human judgments of worth or importance arranged along a continuum of good–bad or desirable–undesirable. Although values may be based on any of a variety of standards, in the final analysis values are subjective. As stated earlier, values involve a leap of faith, a decision to accept some standard as a basis for action. Competing values cannot be tested directly, but they do have different consequences, and they determine how we act in our efforts to understand or change people (including ourselves) or social arrangements. We can and should be aware of values and take them into account, especially in relation to our decisions about other people's lives.

Value bases can be differentiated in terms of the empirically obtained information their adherents and others collect and the uses made of that information. They can be grouped into three general categories. One base rests on the assumption that there are values defined by belief systems which are not considered subject to scientific validation. Examples include the moral codes and causes of events attributed to deities and the values pertaining to what constitutes a good family and appropriate intrafamily relationships. Any deviation from those standards will be considered bad by people who hold those values. To adherents of that belief system, no empirical evidence can establish or refute these claims.

The second group of value positions rest on philosophical or moral assumptions about the natural order of the universe and what meaning life has within it. From the perspective of these positions, a family is judged good to the extent that it reflects some idealized conception of human evolution, of human nature, or of how that value serves the survival and perpetuation of the species. These types of value positions do not appeal to a hypothetical extrahuman being or force such as a deity, but rely instead on a presumed natural state of affairs.

Finally, there are value positions that assume there is no natural or ultimate meaning or worth to life; that is, all "meaning" is a subjective judgment. From this perspective, what constitutes a good family and good intrafamily relationships can be appraised only in relation to the family's life circumstances and to the empirical consequences of particular alternative arrangements. Basic to this perspective is the assumption that the meaning of human experiences and activities can be identified empirically and their merits judged accordingly.

In any case, from an empirical point of view the meaning of values can be appraised only through exploring their antecedents, correlates, and consequences. The consequences of acting on religious or other nonempirically based beliefs about the supposed nature of people and societies can be assessed as part of a general conception of life without appealing to extrahuman sources. However, the appraisal will be made according to the beliefs of the people doing the appraising. For example, the conclusions that a psychologist (or anyone) draws from any appraisal of an ongoing change process will rest on which (or which combination) of these value positions is used by the person doing the judging.

The value assumptions that I have used throughout this text include that appraisals of statements and possibilities about the human condition are to be based on empirical evidence to the extent possible. Further, the value of psychology's work must be decided in terms of how it impacts everyone affected by it, not just the select few with whom we are working. Finally, appraisals of our work as psychologists serve prosocial goals better when we include our role as part of the processes, people, and societies being studied and influenced.

MODELS

No system of values provides a complete understanding of people's choices or can serve as a guide for living. Therefore, the second dimension required for evaluating change processes is conceptual models. Models vary in comprehensiveness from untestable religious or philosophical systems about human and world order, to scientific paradigms, to individual, idiosyncratic belief systems. Within psychology, models have been constructed to encompass some or all behavior in a normative mechanical, cognitive, or biological way, a holistic way, or an ideographic way, and some have even integrated multiple facets from each of these. Each model rests on its own logic and supporting facts; however, they differ in their approaches to guiding and accounting for change, particularly prosocial change and the nature of such changes.

Currently, psychology's models represent positions across a continuum of value assumptions ranging from almost total individual to almost total system determination of the course of individual human lives. However, they often leave unanswered questions about how to identify the interrelationship between individual and system based causal factors. Civilizations cannot survive apart from the individuals in them, and individuals cannot survive without societal structures that provide some tolerance, if not support, for individual differences. The overall point is that the model one chooses for studying how people conduct their lives and how to design and evaluate change will also shape what is to be measured and evaluated, what inferences will be drawn, and what steps will then be taken. All of these factors must be considered when choosing a model to guide one's work. Excluding any of them in advance arbitrarily closes off that model's possible contribution.

To illustrate this point, consider the definition of a good family and good intrafamily relationships. In individualistic models, a good family is defined as two or more individuals, each of whom behaves in a mature way to meet her or his responsibilities to self and to the family. If the family is dysfunctional, the remedy is to identify the problem individual(s) and work with that person(s) to correct those problems. From a contrasting, holistic systems point of view, working with a dysfunctional family requires a focus on the overall properties of the family system. No family member can function in a mature way until the system is straightened out because the adequacy of each is necessarily dependent on the healthy functioning of the entire family system.

To some extent, the consequences and merits of different models can be evaluated empirically. However, the merit of any model must also be appraised in terms of the underlying values of those who make the judgments. For example, to humanistic and social ecology or community oriented change agents, the worth of a model will be determined by its distributive equity consequences for all members of a family or society (Albee, 1992). In contrast, more individually or elitist oriented change agents, e.g., Herrnstein and Murray (1994) or Caplan (1964), appraise the worth of a family or societal model in terms of whether its benefits are distributed among the involved individuals on the basis of a judged merit/rewards ratio. The point is that all models are based on underlying assumptions, and the merits of any model are judged by someone on the basis of his or her assumptions. Consequently, the merits of a model can be determined only to the extent that the effects of both sets of assumptions are taken into account in the overall appraisal.

PROCEDURAL GUIDELINES

The physical sciences laboratory research model assumes that the tasks of knowledge generation and knowledge application are separable. However, in the psychological sciences, these occur simultaneously. Human research inevitably impacts on and changes both the people being studied and the investigator as a result of their joint participation in the research. The inevitability of that impact is acknowledged in part, at least in the United States, by the publicly endorsed guidelines which require that research participants not be harmed by their participation. Those procedural guidelines, the third dimension essential to appraisal, also include that, in some circumstances, investigators must be trained in and certifiably skilled at providing interventions to protect participants from harm or at least to rectify harms that might, even unintentionally, be inflicted.

Even procedural guidelines provide only incomplete safeguards. Investigators have a limited capability to identify their own cultural and personal biases, including those associated with their scientific traditions. They can explore ways to "break out" of conventional models and approaches as one way of transcending such limits. Broader perspectives can be incorporated in research by introducing transethnic and transcultural perspectives. That is, our *normal science* approaches can be challenged as an appropriate basis for psychology's work.

Wicker provided a clear example of the impact of identifying and changing procedural guidelines. He wrote that there is a demonstrable human tendency to "think recurring thoughts" (1985, p. 1094) and that this tendency limits both theories and research. He emphasized the importance of being creative even about established approaches and concepts, not just in regard to new areas and possibilities. Deliberately not searching the existing problem-solving literature, Wicker sought alternatives for expanding conceptual frameworks and then formulated four general approaches: (a) play with ideas using processes such as applying metaphors and representing them graphically; (b) consider contexts by placing specific problems in different domains; (c) look for underlying hidden assumptions or make counter ones; and (d) clarify and systematize conceptual frameworks by scrutinizing definitions and relationships among concepts.

Toch (1979) not only articulated interactions between presumably basic and applied or intervention research, he challenged conventional wisdom even further. His argument was that the alienated within any culture are particularly culturally aware, and therefore, the most effective agents of social change.

Positivist theories take no account of the human equation. The premise that a person feels powerless because he *is* powerless, that he cannot act because he *is* circumscribed, that he cannot predict because the world *is* unpredictable, that he is a pawn because he *is* manipulated makes no allowance for the fact that a person's frame of mind can vary from his social reality and makes no provision for Man as Actor.... For the psychologist to be a change agent, he must restore Man as Perceiver and Actor into the man–environment equation. (Toch, 1979, p. 4)

Toch (1979) reasoned that people want to belong and that desire is healthy. Alienation and isolation produce both pathology and awareness of the alienating system's flaws. This awareness makes people potentially effective agents of social change. Consequently, Toch's approach to the process of change was to conduct collaborative studies with the alienated, i.e., to change the procedure. His objectives were to reinvolve them in their own lives and in changing others who are alienated along with the systems which alienated them. Implementation of his reasoning showed that individuals, systems, and attitudes about people can be changed. He demonstrated that using a nonconventional set of procedural guidelines (a different model) led to different outcomes, because it led to different facts about people and the nature of effective interventions.

FACTS

The fourth dimension of appraisal is facts, but what gets accepted as facts is limited by the value context, the model used to define facts, and the procedural guidelines used to validate them. All models necessarily emphasize searching for some particular facts while ignoring others. This process is also influenced by the extent to which the model includes strategies for transcending its own restrictions and permits the identification of complementary, supplementary, or contrary facts even though any of them can function to undermine rather than strengthen existing facts, formulations, and preferences.

For example, one form of community psychology is focused on attention to stress, contexts, and adaptation. Community psychologists who work with the model direct their efforts at "undermining the process whereby stress generates psychopathology" (Levine & Perkins, 1997, p. 157). They define adaptation as improving the fit between the individual's behavior and the specific demands of the environment. One of their foci is on understanding crises, and their work with people emphasizes coping, that is, "the cognitive and behavioral effort made to master, tolerate, or reduce demands that tax or exceed a person's resources" (Kessler, Price, & Wortman, 1985, p. 550). This approach has led to the identification of facts about stress and adaptation along with related contextual factors because an important aspect of any fact is the value matrix, model, and procedural guidelines that were used to identify and validate it. As with any model, this one has also produced facts about people's more general, active, mastery oriented style of negotiating life's events. Those facts can, in turn, challenge the adequacy of the stress and adaptation model that generated them.

PSYCHOSOCIAL CONCEPTIONS, PSYCHOLOGICAL SPECIALTIES, AND CHANGE

Change is necessarily value based and value judged. Conceptions of change, change agents, and those to be changed are necessarily influenced by the common social context that underlies them. Anyone's individual psychological meanings can be fully understood and evaluated only in that person's life contexts, and they are necessarily psychosocial in nature. Such meanings are formed both individually and psychosocially by each person and her or his social context. My colleagues and I (Tyler, Sussewell, & Williams-McCoy, 1985; Tyler, Brome, & Williams, 1991) set forth a trio of perspectives as essential to understand, manage, and evaluate the outcomes of such individual–contextual change efforts. We found that for constructive interactions to occur, people must organize a coherent matrix of convergent, divergent, and conflicting inclinations. Consideration must be given to the coherence of these autonomous and relational aspects of the context to appraise the nature of people's actions and interactions. Otherwise, any information is incomplete and limited. Sampson provided a clear way to understand this idea by describing how people's contexts and conceptions of themselves changed in Europe after feudalism.

Historically, as the European world emerged from feudalism, the community and household served less and less as the functional unit and organizing principle of society. This major transition supported the emergence of the self-contained individual. In Sampson's terms,

> a liberal individualist framework emerged.... Individuals were to be set free from all the ties and attachments that formerly defined them. Individuals, understood as self-determining, autonomous sovereigns, authors in charge of their own life's work, became the central actors on the social stage. (1989, p. 915)

This shift, therefore, allowed individuals to create their own beliefs, values, and ways of life and freed them from the pervasive constraints of tradition. It also characterized Western societies when the field of psychology was being formed and remains the basis for its practitioners and their approaches to their subject matter.

Sampson (1989) emphasized that the individualist view is inadequate for understanding human life. The case for a broader psychosocial conception of the person rests on two grounds. The first is that the individualist theory is simply not sustainable in its own terms. The only way people can define themselves separately from their contexts is to assume that they form their individual natures before they enter society—an obvious impossibility. The second reason is basically an elaboration of the first. The world context is so pervasive and intrusive that people can no longer ignore their contextual embeddedness and live as if they have complete possession of their natures and fates. To cite some highly publicized examples, people can no longer protect themselves from pollution or radioactivity. Even in principle, it is not possible for individuals to go off to the frontier or into the hills and survive apart from their surrounding society. Consequently,

> attributes (e.g., possessions, abilities, and achievements) that we currently believe are private items to be disposed of as persons wish are common goods for community consideration.... Persons become the guardians of particular assets, not their owners.... The constitutive view transforms the entire person–community relationship. The point is not simply that the community has a stake in what happens to its individual members and thus must intervene in their lives, but equally, because individuals are ... not self-contained individuals with lives apart from others ... community involvement is not experienced as an improper intrusion into their personal affairs. (Sampson, 1989, p. 919)

Carried to its extreme, Sampson's approach would lead to a complete reversal of the traditional U.S. position that the individual's rights are supreme. If a contextualist view entirely replaced that of the individualist view, then issues of autonomy and responsibility would cease to be relevant. Short of such a radical change, a satisfactory solution requires our framework to include a way to address individual agency and social embeddedness in relation to each other and to retain some of the justification for both. A model is required that defines the person and society as independent from, as well as in relation to, each other. Such a model would also define people as active agents, responsible to themselves and others, and as embedded in their destinies, histories, and senses of continuity.

One way to outline the implications of this comprehensive, integrative position is to apply it to a specific issue or approach. For example, secondary prevention is a community mental health concept for reducing the rate and destructiveness of mental illness. The potential onset of mental disorders is identified early in people's lives or early in the disorder's onset so that intervention can prevent it or diminish its effects. One approach has been for mental health personnel to use prescreening devices in large organizations (military, industry, schools) to identify "high risk" individuals and then focus their efforts on those identified.

A drawback to this approach is that organizations such as the military and industries have objectives to accomplish other than the prevention of psychological breakdown, including that they accomplish their work in a cost-effective way. Deselection of people vulnerable to such breakdowns may seem preferable to hiring or recruiting them and giving closer and expensive attention to them. Likewise, schools have the goal of educating students for the students' own benefit and that of society. Because of their limited resources, schools may also consider that nonadmission or deselection (failing the students or otherwise dismissing them) is preferable to providing closer attention.

From an individualist perspective, simply ridding these organizations of vulnerable people is an appropriate and justifiable course of action. The organization considers that its responsibilities are to its own goals and to those who contribute more than what they cost the institution. From a community mental health perspective, the organization's responsibilities do not end there. Everyone in the community is a "stakeholder," and the community bears a responsibility to them. One organization cannot simply say that the community has other organizations to take care of such responsibilities or that vulnerable individuals are responsible for their own fates. Some provision must be made to include everyone in providing for vulnerable people.

Both autonomy and relatedness are part of and necessary to the human condition. Societies acknowledge this duality as do the individuals within them. People often place the welfare of the community above themselves, such as during a war or in other types of service. Societies formalize people's responsibilities and variously honor and dishonor people and their efforts accordingly. To understand the actions of programs and of individuals and to appraise prosocial and other contributions requires that we address people's issues of autonomy and relatedness. Attention must be paid to people's commonalities, differences, and conflicts and the degree to which there is coherence among them.

It has become less tenable to justify the worth of any psychological model of intervention solely on the basis of its impact within its limited target area. Considerations of cultural, ethnic, and racial differences and of contextual and relational factors in people's lives have added dimensions and complexity to currently circumscribed frameworks. For these reasons, three major areas of psychological explorations and interventions which were considered in detail in Chapter 13 are reexamined here briefly. Clinical, community, and cross-cultural psychology will be appraised according to the extent to which they have responded to these contextual and ethnic validity challenges.

CLINICAL PSYCHOLOGY

The area of work in which the largest number of psychologists in the United States are employed is clinical practice. Depending on their values, these psychologists help people to live more fulfilling lives, overcome or live with pathologies, or both. They construct an understanding of each individual or case by using models about the nature of people and related facts about each person's conduct. Their intervention domains are primarily individual psychodiagnosis and psychotherapy as guided by the predominant DSM approach to identifying psychopathology. The DSM value base is ethnocentrically oriented to Euro-American culture; consequently, it is biased against non-Anglo socioracial/ethnic and lower class individuals and values. Most clinicians appraise their own effectiveness in psychotherapy (their major vehicle of application) in terms of the identifiable Western culture characteristics and presumed universal changes they expected of their clients.

Although individualistic theories may provide clinicians a framework for understanding and organizing their own lives, their potential value for clients and their impact on societies is limited. Approaches derived from individualistic theories are reactive, often do not deal with causes, and even when they ameliorate or "cure" dysfunctional patterns, they may not completely restore individuals to earlier levels of functioning. Extensions of individual interventions such as group or family therapy do introduce social dimensions to the therapy milieu, but they are still limited by ethnocentric constraints or biases, particularly in regard to the values accepted as desirable in mainstream U.S. society.

Limitations of individualistic models become particularly evident when cultural issues surface. U.S. publications, to highlight indigenous/ethnic minority perspectives, focus primarily on how to survive in the Anglo-dominated culture rather than advance a multicultural perspective. The model of the individualistic, "Western" woman, man, children, and family is, at least tacitly, accepted without question. Therapy may be oriented to helping clients understand and even thrive within that cultural ethos, but it is not ordinarily used as a platform to challenge that ethos.

Over twenty years ago, the point was made that Latinos may underutilize mental health services offered in U.S. community mental health centers because the model provides those services by hiring therapists from outside the immediate community. That model is alien to and un-acceptable within Latino cultures because Latinos primarily turn to professionals who are members of the community (Zwerling et al., 1976). Judging from Garcia and Zea's (1997) recent text on psychological interventions with Latino populations in the United States, that situation has not substantially changed. Even Latino therapists expect clients to adapt to the culture-defining (CDG) system rather than build on their distinctive strengths and perspectives which would broaden therapists' perspectives and enrich the host society.

Sue and Zane (1987) stressed the idea that use of cultural knowledge and cultural techniques serve to establish credibility with Asian American clients. They expect therapists to be effective and trustworthy helpers (credible) who provide something of value in therapy. Thus, by arranging therapeutic learning experiences for clients that are compatible with their cultural and personal expectations and the demands of their life situations, therapists can provide helpful therapy by using rather than challenging their clients' cultural beliefs. Unfortunately, Sue and Zane assumed a universal therapeutic process. Their evaluation guidelines were consistent with the expectation that the purpose of therapy is to assist clients in fitting into the existing cultural context.

To summarize, within clinical psychology the two major activities of psychodiagnosis and psychotherapy are primarily based on Euro-American value systems, are ethnocentric, and focus on a universalist conception of personality processes. These primary value assumptions, models, and procedural guidelines are quite limited, so the facts generated within clinical psychology and the appraisals of its contributions are equally limited. Consequently, clinical therapists restrict their capability to evaluate their work, their culture, and the implications of what they learn from their clients about the limitations and strengths of their culture and cultural views. It hardly seems justified to ask individuals who seek help from clinical psychologists, particularly those from NCDG backgrounds, to improve their own societal situations. However, until clinical psychologists evaluate and appraise the merit of their own value systems and models from a TEV perspective, their clients are forced into that role.

COMMUNITY PSYCHOLOGY

The fields of community mental health and community psychology share the purpose of proactively identifying and reducing the distress of individuals and promoting their well-being. However, they differ substantially in many of the values, psychosocial models, and evaluation guidelines that they endorse in their change efforts. Consequently, the adherents of each group seek out different facts and draw different inferences from them to accomplish their goals.

The *community mental health model* is not a learning or growth oriented model. Its perspective is that psychological dysfunctions are illnesses to be prevented or treated. It is a universalist professional model whose social change approaches and objectives are based primarily on Western middle-class ethical, cultural, and health (survival) values. Central to that belief is the assumption that the "good, superior, healthy" people and world views rise to the top and can help or be used to help the less worthy or fortunate. This Social Darwinist view includes *no* assumption that the less socially advantaged or ethnically different may have strengths of their own and should have some control over their fate and even over the forms of their communities and societies.

Community psychology is constructed as a social/psychological/behavioral science composed of a loose matrix of interrelated approaches. Included are elements of social ecology and issues of history, continuity, and autonomy in communities and individual lives. This view provides the flexibility needed to integrate different theories by combining approaches to change that build on people's strengths and others that ameliorate their limitations. It brings those approaches together in resource collaborative interaction models rather than in unidirectional, expert–client change models. Each community member's expertise is considered a contribution to the human enterprise required from a person with special skills, rather than the personal possession of an individual who is independent of and potentially superior to those who lack that expertise. Everyone, whether they are professionals or nonprofessional citizens, carries an obligation to learn about people's differences and diversity along with the interplay of their deficits and strengths. They also have an obligation to consider other cultural perspectives as potentially constructive contributions to the dominant cultural ethos, rather than as sources of deficit and dysfunction.

This more comprehensive community psychology model also incorporates procedural guidelines for professionals in particular to assess the limitations of all models, including the psychosocial competence community model, the disease model, and the individual treatment approach to mental health issues. It stresses the importance of moving beyond a focus on pathogenic agents in order to incorporate attention to people's resources. Core assumptions include that human events are of a transactional nature (Sameroff, 1977) and can best be influenced when they are understood as occurring within an integrated framework and that not everyone's environment and experiences are exemplary.

This community psychology model is an alternative framework to a pathology oriented prevention approach with an exclusive clinical focus on individuals. It provides a basis for considering how better health and improved life quality can be promoted in adequately functioning individuals and communities. Environments, systems, and people's resourcefulness are assessed to provide the information and models needed to overcome the impact on individuals of destructive societal factors. Primary emphasis is placed on utilizing the constructive and supportive characteristics of systems and environmental factors because only their impact is potentially powerful enough to produce broad societal effects.

One of the most striking differences between community psychology and community mental health approaches lies in community psychology's collaborative processes versus the hierarchical authoritative approach of community mental health. Another is that the former assumes that individuals and groups targeted for change are active participants in these change efforts, their evaluation, and their appraisals of the approach. Some of the implications of these differences can be illustrated by considering the situation of a family with a highly disruptive, violent, bullying, and generally aggressively antisocial child. From the community psychology approach, this situation might be responded to as part of an integrated community-wide endeavor to contain violence. This type of approach provides no ultimate solutions, such as the absence of "disease," but does embrace the concept that individuals and societies are interrelated with experts and ordinary citizens who are interested and concerned about everyone's well-being (Olweus, 1992).

From the alternative, community mental health perspective, early explorations might establish that this disruptive child was a victim of abuse and neglect. Consequently, he might be considered at risk for developing antisocial personality disorder (APD) and placed in a prevention program. However, in the view of Luntz and Widom (1994), this approach would be an inefficient use of resources with unknown personal and societal consequences. They found that using childhood abuse and neglect as a basis for predicting APD led to misidentifying over 50% of the slightly more than 600 participants in their study. This important but seldom considered difference in appraising the relative merits of the community psychology and community mental health models illustrates the costs of labeling people as potentially deviant or ill.

An assumption in the community psychology perspective is that although individual and system elements function somewhat autonomously, individual or community changes can occur only as the proximate surrounding conditions change. It may not require the entire country to change to solve issues of violence or other patterns of psychological dysfunction in a community, but it does require that more must be changed than just the involved individuals. While it is important to teach stress-buffering capabilities or even enriched life concepts, these skills are not enough. Changes must be tied to the overall development of more constructive life styles or social relationships, communities, and cultures which can sustain them. Different individual–context–culture frameworks must also be formulated, implemented, and evaluated when needed.

Two questions require broader consideration to provide a more comprehensive appraisal of the worth of community approaches. First, does conceptualizing psychological dysfunctions as illnesses create more problems than it solves, in contrast to simply conceptualizing them as psychosocially embedded dysfunctions? Second, how do we balance the benefits and costs of focusing on community oriented approaches rather than on individually oriented ones? Answering these two questions is important for the further growth and direction of these approaches. However, they cannot be answered unless the relative merits of both approaches are assessed empirically and somewhat independently of guild considerations.

Cross-Cultural Psychology

There is growing evidence that our cultural identities are ineradicable components of how we understand and conduct our lives and our psychological science. Identifying those components and their impact on us is in our own interests and the interests of our societies (F. Tyler, 1990). However, attention to that evidence and its implications for appraising the worth of existing psychological enterprises has been limited. A brief listing of several previously cited examples of cultural embeddedness may help underscore its importance. They include:

1. The meaning of personal control differs in diverse cultural contexts (Lefcourt, 1976; Kojima, 1984).
2. Cultural differences produced striking contrasts in soldiers' responses to common battlefield experiences and to the patterns of psychological breakdown and recovery of British and Indian soldiers in World War II (Mandelbaum, 1954).
3. Efforts to develop United States style achievement motivation in entrepreneurs in India as a way of starting a spreading circle of economic development in India proved problematic (McClelland & Winter, 1969; Sinha, 1981; Sinha & Pandey, 1968).
4. Comparisons of adolescent students in the United States and India yielded cultural differences between the CDG and NCDG students within and between these cultures (F. Tyler, Dhawan, & Sinha, 1988).

5. Differences as well as commonalities in individualism and collectivism were found with regard both to vertical (hierarchical) and horizontal (social equals) patterns of relationships among college students from an Eastern culture (Korea) ˙similar to those in a Western culture (United States). Vertical individualists tended to stress competition and hedonism; horizontals stressed self-reliance. Vertical collectivists were more authoritarian and traditional, but sociable; horizontals stressed sociability, interdependence, and hedonism (Triandis & Gelfand, 1998).

6. Masculinity/femininity was identified as a cultural distinction accounting for nearly as much variance as individualism/collectivism. However, a masculinity/femininity grouping of cultures yielded combinations quite different from the Western individualism/ Asian collectivism groupings who are already engaged in an ongoing dialogue. These studies suggested that the predominant emphasis on Individualism/Collectivism reflects cultural interests to a greater extent than is justified by the data (Hofstede & Vunderink, 1994).

In spite of the advantage of this kind of evidence, relatively few projects have involved cross-cultural components that could provide feedback on the particular strengths and limitations of different approaches in varied cultural circumstances. However, it is possible to identify some of the broad issues and outline some of the particular factors that may influence their courses and efficacy.

The 1990 Vermont Conference on Primary Prevention Programs focused on the quality of children's lives, its relationship to the nature of the societies in which they live, and efforts to improve their lives (Albee, Bond, & Monsey, 1992). Its contributors emphasized and illustrated how children are devalued, exploited, and abused for adult purposes even though they are the necessary source of any society's future survival. The three major conditions cited as responsible for this situation included (a) class conflict that keeps large segments of most societies in conditions of deprivation; (b) male-favoring sexism that keeps women and children, particularly girls, subject to violence and abuse; and (c) racism (including ethnic and religious discrimination) that also largely supports societal, class, and male-favoring sexual oppression.

Along with the identification of these transcultural commonalities, cultural differences in the status of children and in values and models of individual and social organization and conduct were also found. The point is that whatever the focus of our research, we must introduce cultural considerations. They are necessary for us to identify whether our findings and inferences are culturally specific or have broader relevance and to establish whether they are convergent, divergent, or conflicting across cultures. We can understand the nature and impact of findings from any of our studies only if we examine the results in relation to the contextual embeddedness of the questions under investigation and the people doing the studies and being studied.

TRANSCULTURAL ETHNIC VALIDITY AS A COMPREHENSIVE MODEL FOR EVALUATING CHANGE

A transcultural ethnic validity (TEV) model integrates some of the core values of individual change models (clinical psychology), holistic models (community psychology), and ethnic/racial/cultural indigenous models (cross-cultural psychology). A TEV model becomes essential once we acknowledge that, in psychology, the processes of generating knowledge and of applying it are necessarily interrelated. Because we are always producing contextually embedded change as we conduct investigations or seek to create changes, we need a TEV model to guide, evaluate, and appraise our efforts.

The shift from traditional experimental research and intervention to contextually embedded, action oriented research and evaluation is often disorienting because it challenges basic paradigmatic values. Traditional research and intervention approaches emphasize objectivity, detachment, and experimental control as essential for testing abstract principles, advancing theories, and guiding interventions. In a critique of cross-cultural psychology's traditional experimental paradigm, I stressed that in order to view psychological endeavors from a TEV perspective it is necessary to make several paradigmatic changes, including that we (a) broaden our basic exemplars of behavior to include both holistic and molecular referents from a range of cultures; (b) revise our view of human behaviors, including those of research participants, to conceptualize them as interactions rather than actions; (c) treat all research and change oriented endeavors as interventions in people's lives and thus part of ongoing change processes; (d) conceptualize cultures or other groups as being composed of heterogeneous individuals with different epistemological approaches to reality rather than as homogenous groups exhibiting normally distributed variances in characteristics; and (e) incorporate a contextually embedded conception of people's characteristics that derives from NCDG as well as CDG segments of societies and their interactions (F. Tyler, 1999). These contrasting paradigmatic characteristics make a TEV model more relevant than an experimental model for understanding and facilitating human psychosocial processes and accomplishing prosocial changes.

COMMUNITY MODELS AS EXEMPLARS OF A TEV PERSPECTIVE

The values underlying contextually embedded, action oriented psychosocial approaches are most clearly evident in community psychology. These approaches require attention to the realities of the field context in which they are implemented. Because they require assessment of existing conditions and effectiveness of program efforts, they consequently inform residents about their needs and staff about the utility of their program efforts. Their contributions to theory and to the general scientific knowledge base of action oriented approaches are equally, if not more, important than their implications for immediate actions. Unfortunately, these contributions are often deemed unimportant and ignored.

As Price and Cherniss (1977) emphasized, research and practice activities can be developed so that they facilitate each other. In their view, theories should be used to understand complex problems, respond to them, and anticipate future developments. In turn, theories, knowledge, methods, and skills are tested when they are used to solve community problems, thus both the process and outcome are evaluated and appraised. This kind of research can also have an impact on specific community needs and on advancing basic values such as social equity, distributive justice, and shared participation in program planning and decision making.

Traditionally, investigators in field settings have simply taken data and departed. Only in the more abstract sense of "contributing to human knowledge" have those studies benefitted the people in the research setting. The consideration introduced here is that, along with meeting traditional criteria, community research should also be evaluated on the basis of whether it enhances that particular setting in a direct and visible manner.

For the community-oriented psychologist, there is the ethical imperative that social action programs are introduced into communities, they build on the community's ongoing strengths (not undermine or override them), and they are appraised in ways which make them accountable to the community. When community psychologists integrate their roles in these ways, their research, theory, and programs serve as models for the kind of community functioning that they advocate. Thus, understanding and informing people about community processes and contributing to their community's level of prosocial functioning is not only of value to a community, it also contributes generalizable knowledge and theory.

The American Psychological Association's Science Directorate conferences on community psychology recommended that the contextual basis of all psychological endeavors be identified as crucial areas of research (Tolan, Keys, Chertok, & Jason, 1990). From a TEV view, each culture provides only a limited set of contexts and contextual perspectives, and investigators can transcend their culturally based paradigmatic limits about contextual possibilities and effects only if they make transcultural comparisons. Those comparisons provide the information needed to identify relevant contextual factors. That information is required to form transcultural generalizations about individual and community values and gives a basis for redefining cultural meanings concerning the ethical and moral aspects of existing social practices. Also inherent to a TEV perspective is the responsibility to identify and support people's divergent individual and community approaches to their own circumstances and their accommodation to transcendent values and perspectives. TEV comparisons can also address how to understand and manage conflicting ethnic validity views of individuality and of interpersonal and community interrelations.

The introduction and study of psychological programs in community contexts are complex and difficult undertakings. Such studies potentially benefit the individuals who have interests which are convergent with those of the program; they also threaten the well-being of individuals whose interests are divergent from or conflict with it. Consequently, community models provide a useful reference for understanding and approaching cross-cultural or cross-ethnic research and program development.

Although scholarly books on field research and program evaluation have been available for over two decades (see Campbell & Stanley, 1963; Struening & Guttentag, 1975; Guttentag & Struening, 1975), their suggested approaches were adversarial and focused on how investigators could overcome community-imposed obstacles to "good" research. In general, they emphasized conceptual and measurement problems and problems associated with entry into a community, including staff or client resistance to evaluation projects. Thereby, although their announced intent was to be helpful, they perpetuated the dichotomy between investigators and the people they are studying.

Coursey (1977) reported on a contrasting approach in a conference to develop collaborative models for community research. Emphasis was placed on bringing together professional evaluators, academics, staff from service agencies, and clients to develop program evaluation models and guidelines for their use. Evaluation approaches ranged from those focused on gaining information for exploratory or hypothesis-driven research to those designed to evaluate change. Included were useful collaborative approaches for assessing a community's needs, determining a management system's level of functioning, and establishing who a program is serving. Unfortunately, the value of all of these approaches is limited because they measure only one point in time. The information they generate becomes dated very quickly because indications of ongoing changes, those which might be expected to occur, or those which would be beneficial are missing.

TEV MODELS AND CHANGE

Most community projects have been designed to make changes within a limited context, not necessarily change the broad cultural/ethnic context where such studies are nested. This limited view creates a dilemma. As evidence from our increasingly interlinked world has made apparent, our models and approaches require a way of conceptualizing the nesting of communities and community participants in a pluralistic framework. That is, the ongoing lives of societies and people occur within these broad contexts. Our task as social and behavioral scientists becomes one of capturing the psychosocial realities of people and communities in relation to their changing, internested contexts.

Additional measures are needed because the achievement of prosocial change is the first priority of community-oriented or other social action programs. Change is a central aspect of everyone's life, and knowledge of people's concern with change is essential to hypothesis development and theory testing. While pre–post experimental designs provide a basic paradigm for measuring change, community and other field situations rarely permit of adequate experimental controls to conduct genuine experiments. Consequently, alternative designs have been developed to measure gains on preestablished goals or in ongoing activities or programs.

These alternative designs are all variants of a program development/ program evaluation (PD/PE) model that is analogous to pre–post test experimental designs. However, community projects often cannot set up control groups or randomly assign cases to different conditions, although at times another community may serve as a control or the program can be addressed to people in different life circumstances (different socioeconomic levels, etc.). Similar comparisons can also be made across cultural or ethnic boundaries to identify their respective contextual effects. PD/PE programs differ from experimental designs in that they go one step further. They provide a model for instituting community action programs and testing their efficacy. They also can be modified and repeated, and then comparisons can be made to assess the relative efficacy of the original and the revised approaches.

PD/PE approaches are quite flexible because they can be designed to take direct account of any specific program characteristics or objectives. Their advantage over controlled experiments is that the observed pro-

cesses and the obtained effects reflect the full complexity of the life situations where the studies were conducted. The comprehensive picture of the
issues that they identify is based on what those affected by them as well as
the people conducting the programs consider important. Finally, they
provide essential theoretical information about the interaction of contextual factors and psychological processes.

That capacity to study people's core values directly can be facilitated
by using *qualitative research* methods in PD/PE studies. Consequently, they
are of particular use for studying and working with the core values of
communities and thus of community psychology and a TEV approach.
Recently, Banyard and Miller (1998) summarized the emphases that were
the shared products of a symposium on community psychology's values.
They included respect for and emphasis on diversity, contextual conceptualization of topics within an ecological framework, and a focus on
research approaches that facilitate community participants' ability to empower themselves as contributors to the research and to their lives. Those
values are particularly well served by using these methods.

Qualitative research outcomes can direct attention to those values in
several ways, including laying the groundwork for the development of
contextually (culturally) anchored quantitative research methods and
measures. They also provide ways for respondents to contribute subjective
perspectives, such as personal histories and contextually-based senses of
history and continuity. Thus, qualitative research is a powerful tool for
understanding the underlying and often unquantifiable "whys" of behavior. Further, although qualitative research is not necessarily change-
oriented, it does inevitably change respondents by increasing their awareness of themselves and their circumstances and by involving them in
contributing to a broader understanding of their situation.

For example, two procedures used in qualitative research, observations and document analyses, gather information with relatively little pre-
determined structure for identifying the characteristics and patterns of
individuals and communities. They yield important information that
would otherwise not be available for generating concepts, hypotheses,
interactive interventions, and evaluations of ongoing projects. In-depth
interviews, another procedure, allow participants to present their own
experiences. The importance of each person's history is thus affirmed for
them and others. This affirmation contributes to their sense of empowerment and facilitates disseminating their communal experiences. Infor-
mally exchanging such accounts within or among groups can also help
develop greater group or contextual consciousness and collective support
patterns. These activities give more force to the views, needs, and satisfac-
tions of individuals and communities, and often-ignored information be-

comes available for the development and confirmation of hypotheses and theories.

When PD/PE and qualitative research are formulated as collaborative community-oriented models, psychologists have additional ways to obtain a broader range of information and a fuller understanding of how people function in their natural habitat, i.e., their communities. These approaches also provide opportunities and mechanisms for psychologists to place themselves in the contexts they are studying and trying to influence. Consequently, they lead to more complete answers to psychologists' questions and benefit their theories, participants, and themselves.

AN EXAMPLE OF THE POTENTIAL IMPACT OF A TEV MODEL

Perhaps the best way to understand the value of using a TEV model to understand people and societies and to effect prosocial change is through an example. A particularly pertinent and relevant one is found in the current plight of many of the world's children. The following paragraphs use a TEV model to demonstrate how children's lives are defined by their societies and to frame answers to questions about how to better help children and, by extension, others in their own contexts.

As the ongoing worldwide dialogue has made clear, there are diverging and conflicting views about the status of children. For example, Rizzini (1994) documented that in the history of Brazilian public policy, children have never been valued in their own right, only in terms of their potential societal roles as defined by adults. Unfortunately, her findings are not unique to Brazil. Children everywhere are family and community members, sources of gratification for adult desires, and contributors to their own and their family's survival and the future of their societies. Children usually live beyond their parents' life spans and may be expected to maintain the continuity of their ancestors' values, experiences, and existence, but that should hardly mean that their *only* value is to fulfill such adult purposes. They are also individuals with their own lives to live. However, as UNICEF's regular reports indicate, millions of children are exploited daily for adult purposes with little regard for their well-being (1997).

By using a TEV model, we can identify that there is an apparently convergent, if not universal, assumption that at least some labor is of socialization value for children (UNICEF, 1997). We can also analyze the contextual aspects of regulations about child labor and justifications for children's work which have taken many different, culturally defined forms. They range from its importance as a socializing experience to its value in contributing to family survival. Justifications for decisions about which children work at which tasks are also to some extent CDG sociorace and class based. As Rizzini (1994) documented, work is justified for lower class (but not upper class) children in Brazil to prevent them from becoming antisocial threats to their society. In contrast, in Peru that same pattern is justified on the grounds that lower class children are considered to be of lesser value and a different nature than their upper class peers (Ennew, 1986).

The most widespread form of justified child labor is household work. In the United States, the amount and type of children's household labor varies with their parents' beliefs about its socialization value for promoting responsibility and control, the parents' level of interaction with their children, and structural requirements such as parental work obligations that lead them to assign needed household work to their children (Blair, 1992). A national survey (Sweet & Bumpass, 1987) indicated that the most important factor leading to child labor worldwide was the *need* for it. Earlier, Anandalakshmy (1975) reported that the possibility for urban families in India to free children from working even to attend school was dependent on whether the children's labor was needed for the family's survival. Although the directness of the relationship is not clear, data also support that industrialization and foreign domination in underdeveloped societies are associated with increased involvement of children in labor, particularly outside the home (Drenovsky, 1992; Shivji, 1985).

Recently, there has been a widespread focus on the evils of child labor. The United Nations Convention on the Rights of the Child produced a statement which has been ratified by most of the countries in the world. In that document, Article 3 stated that "the best interests of the child shall be a primary consideration ... taking into account the rights and duties of his or her parents, legal guardians, or other individuals legally responsible for him or her" (LeBlanc, 1995, p. 295). That statement clearly asserts that children's rights have primacy and that the state (the embodiment of the social/community context) has a responsibility to protect those rights even in opposition to some competing rights of parents. Thus a convergent transcultural value has been advanced as overruling limited ethnic validity customs.

For reasons that are not clear, the United States is one of the few countries that has not ratified that convention. However, there is an ongoing effort in the United States to pass a law banning imports from any foreign industries that use child labor (United States Department of Labor, 1994; Child Labor Deterrence Act, 1997). While refusing to recognize the world's collective effort, the United States has sought to impose its ethnocentric perspective on other communities (states). This position is a particularly illustrative example of a culture-defining group (CDG) seeking to impose its ethnic validity views on NCDGs (other less powerful states). At the same time, the CDG will not honor the transcultural convergence (the United Nations Convention) that others ask of it.

The 1997 UNICEF report, *The State of The World's Children*, took as its focus not child labor, but abusive and exploitative labor which is widespread and requires our attention. Even so, as the report emphasized, the recent upsurge of interest in child labor has had a broader and not necessarily benign focus. Four negative myths have been advanced about child labor and persist, even though their validity has been challenged by empirical findings derived by using a TEV approach (see Table 14.1). These negative perspectives are Western CDG generated and generalized beliefs about conditions in developing countries. Because they are applied indiscriminately, any work done by a child is assumed to be bad. These beliefs confound the problems associated with abusive child labor in part because it becomes almost impossible to deal specifically with them in the ethnic validity contexts where they occur. In addition, these myths are used by CDG countries and groups to distract attention away from their own role in utilizing child labor at home while exaggerating the problem in NCD countries.

While this topic should be of substantial interest to psychologists, particularly developmental psychologists, they have paid relatively little

TABLE 14.1. Unfounded Myths About Child Labor

Myth	Data
1. Child labor is a problem of the developing world	1. Many immigrant children work in agriculture in the United States; others have summer or year-round jobs.
2. Child labor is an inevitable and natural outgrowth of poverty, so will always be present.	2. These issues can be separated, and at least some impoverished countries are doing so.
3. Most child laborers are working in sweatshops producing goods for export to the affluent developed countries.	3. Less than 5 percent are so employed.
4. There is a simple solution, such as boycotts, that will stop it now and forever.	4. Bangladesh data gathered in 1992 after the threat from the introduction of the Harkin bill in the U.S Senate found that some garment industries dismissed their child workers. Some were then working in more hazardous situations, paid less, or in prostitution. ·

Source. UNICEF, *State of the World's Children* (1997).

attention to it because it does not fit into their universalist experimental framework. Hobbs and Cornwell (1986) argued that child labor lacks an adequate psychological definition and satisfactory methods for studying it. Goodnow (1988) concluded from her transcultural literature review (mostly U.S. based studies) that there is data relevant to understanding the correlates of children's household labor, but it is scattered, poorly integrated, and has not addressed broad questions as to why children work and what its socialization correlates and impacts are. The literature contained suggestions about how to get children to work while accomplishing other adult objectives such as maintaining family harmony and justifying the work as training for the children's future. There was also attention to differentiating work and play, work for love from work for money, and work as training from work as production of a needed result. However, in all cases, work was viewed only from an adult perspective in relation to its instrumental value. Using a TEV model could have led to exploring whether children might want to do work for themselves as an instrumentally or intrinsically satisfying activity.

Possibly the most flagrant evidences of adult shortcomings with regard to children's well-being lie in the recorded experiences of homeless, runaway, and throwaway children; this is material that could be obtained only by approaching these children using a TEV model. For them, links with the presumably protective and nurturing adult society have been broken. Their survival is in their own hands for one of three major reasons: (1) their family protectors are dead or otherwise missing; (2) their family protectors have rejected and abandoned them or forced them out of the family network; (3) they have found the family network so destructive that the alternative of autonomous survival has been judged more attractive (F. Tyler, Tyler, Tommasello, & Connolly, 1992).

Often without being consulted, these out-of-place children have been defined in the professional literature and in common wisdom as the perpetrators of their own situation. Their societies appoint agencies to assume the responsibility for returning these children to a dependency status through rehabilitation and socialization. Any disagreement with this approach on the children's part is considered further proof of their immaturity or venality, despite abundant evidence that their disagreement may be related to their frequent victimization by social policies and representatives appointed to help them (F. Tyler, Brome, & Williams, 1991; F. Tyler et al., 1992).

Throughout the world, vast numbers of children work as part of family units in agricultural settings. These practices and the traditions that support them vary. Large numbers of children also work at home in cottage industries such as weaving. Little is known about these work patterns or their impact. UNICEF (1997) has documented a range of creative and successful educational programs developed to provide a blend of formal and practical education for working children in ways that enable them to fulfill their work requirements. Although careful TEV studies are desired, even informed evaluation and selective support of such creative programs offers more possibilities for improving children's situations than blanket opposition to child labor without consideration of the children's contextual circumstances and limited alternatives.

Although some public policies may be supportive and protective of children, this UNICEF (1997) report suggested that at least one reason children are exploited is that they are easier to exploit. To formulate social action policies, the psychological factors that contribute to the origins and consequences of exploiting children need to be identified. It is important to prohibit such activities and provide sanctuaries or other alternatives for children. It is even more important to introduce penalties against adult perpetrators and identify and change the factors that contribute to that adult conduct. Using a TEV perspective, ethnically valid norms and practices that provide supportive individual life and community/cultural patterns for adults and children are also needed.

As noted earlier, psychologists have paid little attention to the widespread practice of child labor, including the exploitative practices associated with it. The issue of what psychologists can do arises starkly. With their present knowledge, they could at least provide relevant information and guidelines about how children's lives can be improved and how the effects of harmful child labor can be minimized. To make this information relevant world wide, it needs to be based on a TEV approach.

Although psychologists' research can contribute to identifying and clarifying the prosocial roles that labor can have in children's lives, there are core questions that must be considered and that require a TEV model as a basis for answering them. They include:

1. What is the definition of work? Although formal and informal education presumably serve important socialization objectives, they also involve work in the sense of producing something. Apprenticeships involve acquiring work skills by performing them under supervision. Are they education or work? Can work and education be combined in prosocially constructive ways?
2. What are the socialization benefits and costs of work? What is the basis for the wide convergence on the belief that some work, in particular, household chores, is a desirable socialization activity for children? If there are any benefits from work, as most people assume, would they benefit upper as well as lower class children?

3. What constitutes hazardous and exploitative work? Who decides? We find little evidence that children's views are considered.
4. Who supports and exploits child labor? What are children's roles in gratifying or otherwise contributing to the fulfillment of adult objectives ranging from the economic and political to their exploitation for adults' personal, including sexual, gratification? Egregious examples include child slavery and indentured labor, children serving as soldiers, using children for illegal activities such as drug running and prostitution, and abusing them physically and sexually (including incest). Are adults held accountable, or just the children as Sereny (1985) documented? If so, why and how? What can be done about it?
5. What social conditions require families to involve their children in work for non-socialization reasons, even for survival? What are the costs to the children, their families, and their societies?
6. To what extent do ethnic validity beliefs and circumstances influence children's work experiences and their meaning? To the extent that they are demonstrably harmful, how can they be addressed? To the extent that they are uniquely beneficial, how can they be supported and introduced into other ethnic validity contexts?
7. Are lower class and other NCDG children different from or more threatening to society than upper class children?

There are many other questions about child labor that can and need to be asked and other steps that need to be taken to assist children in exploitive situations. The central point is that whether and how such questions are asked and answered depends on the framework of the individuals who are in a position to ask and answer them. The value of asking them from a TEV perspective is that it includes the range of the world's people and circumstances. Further, by combining a TEV framework and a community change model, our scientific, professional, cultural/ethnic, and individual perspectives, interests, and responsibilities can be included in our evaluation and appraisal of these activities.

SUMMARY

This chapter has emphasized that the values we choose, the models we rely on, the procedural guidelines we follow, and what we accept as facts are essential dimensions to manage and guide our lives and our work. To make the best use of these dimensions, we must consider how they are embedded in the concepts and tools of psychology. We must also attend to their limitations, particularly their subjective biases, as well as their strengths. The most comprehensive framework available for coping with limitations as we use the concepts and tools of psychology is the TEV model. It starts with a humanistic perspective that values everyone equally and provides for their input in (a) attempts at understanding individuals, societies, and people's circumstances, and (b) defining and providing improved circumstances and possibilities for everyone.

This chapter's central point is that when psychologists adopt a TEVM perspective as a basis for guiding and appraising their work, they are using the most comprehensive framework available. Adopting such a position creates a changed perspective that is of the magnitude of a paradigm shift which seems likely to have far-reaching prosocial consequences. Relying on it changes psychologists' role from assuming a stance of being seemingly detached and unbiased contributors of their scientific and professional skills to one of involved participants in society. They are included as subject to the same evaluation guidelines as the people traditionally called "subjects," "patients," "the needy," "indigenous," etc. The TEV perspective puts psychologists, and others working with social service roles in the position of personal and professional contributors to the ongoing enterprise of defining, developing, and enjoying a better quality of life for others and themselves.

The TEV approach proceeds on the basis that people's psychological life desires can never be completely realized because each attainment leads to others that must be addressed. Further, individuals and the social milieus in which they function are continually changing. Consequently, evaluation guidelines for appraising the merit of our efforts and accomplishments must be progressive in nature, much like the general form of program development/program evaluation approaches.

The chapter's emphasis on holistic integration perspectives does not mean that more limited models are of no value. Instead, it means that in isolation they provide an incomplete picture. As I noted in an earlier context (F. Tyler, 1996), the common phrase "all politics is local" can be modified to say "all psychology is local." That is, cultural, societal, ethnic validity, community, family, and individual psychosocial patterns are inevitably going to differ and at times conflict with each other. Consequently, psychological theories, research, and practices can most effectively be developed, evaluated, and applied from the dual perspectives of both TEVM and local ethnic validity model criteria.

Psychologists face a choice in how to direct their efforts. Conducting research, evaluation efforts, or interventions in an acontextual framework can validate hypotheses and advance general theories or even accomplish specific goals. However, that work is of limited value until its implications are exposed to broader appraisals in a TEV context and by the impact of change over time. Consequently, psychologist investigators face the question of what their responsibilities are with regard to broader appraisals of their work and its implications. Further, psychologists may consider decisions about how they direct their efforts to be a matter of individual choice, although that position is difficult to sustain. How their collective energy is invested is of broad societal concern on dimensions ranging from people's individual well-being to economic and political considerations, and their individual decisions bear on whether that concern is addressed. Even so, many psychologists assume that they bear no responsibility for the societal impact of their own or psychologists' collective endeavors. They leave society's judgments about the utility of their work to others throughout society. In contrast, a central theme of this text is that such appraisals by psychologists, individually and collectively, are essential.

CONCLUSION

Part V is an integrative summary of the central themes of this book and its conclusion. It summarizes an approach that interrelates our individual activities as mutually supporting rather than as being separate, incompatible, and unrelated to the activities of the rest of society. This orientation is not meant to imply that our lives and societies can become free of failures, differences, and conflicts. It does mean that we have the potential to use our active agent capabilities and our psychosocial resources to manage our conflicts and differences in more constructive and symbiotic ways than we have been led to believe.

This synthesizing orientation provides psychologists and others with reference behaviors for reconciling their own humanistic, scientific, and technological concerns. These behaviors include participatory involvement, resource collaboration and enhancement, networking, and other collaborative activities. As a set of possible approaches, they provide psychologists and others with a far broader pattern of interactions in professional, community, and cultural contexts than has previously been considered. As such, they have major implications for integrating our personal and professional commitments to our individual and collective well-being. They also provide guidelines for integrating our scholarship, research, professional activities, and personal lives. This complex interweaving makes up the comprehensive approach that I have sought to highlight as the major contribution of currently emerging cultural, community, and individual perspectives. It also leads to the prospects and challenges summarized in the next and final chapter.

PROSPECTS AND CHALLENGES

INTRODUCTION

This book has explored modern psychology's origins, current status, and barriers as well as potentials for future developments. In that process, changes in people's conceptions of human nature, societal organizations, the nature of scientific knowledge and knowledge systems, and justifications for guiding or remaking our lives and societies were identified. A number of psychology's earlier assumptions that still present challenges for us as we enter a new century were also highlighted. This chapter is about those challenges and potential resolutions.

One of those challenges concerns the role that choice plays in human lives. A central theme that has emerged in this book is a new understanding of human capacities to make choices, learn from experiences, solve problems, and create new possibilities. A second theme is that the abilities to abstract and make choices are emergent capacities that cannot be reduced to their basic molecular elements. These capacities function in a holistic manner to help us prevail over circumstances and misfortunes and create enriching meaning in our lives or engage in destruction of self and others. These themes are central to psychology's potential for future development.

Over the course of our individual lives and of generations, we continually change our circumstances and the meanings that we assign to our experiences. Within psychology as in other fields, the nature of our empirically based, scientific approach also changes and, consequently, so do our sciences. No scientific endeavor is completely static, internally consistent, or a complete account of reality. I have tried in this book to identify and evaluate the empirically-based personal and societal factors that have influenced psychologists' choices in building, applying, and evaluating psychology's body of knowledge and practices.

The human capacity for constructing meaning provides psychologists with an empirically testable way to guide and evaluate human conduct. However, using psychology to understand people's conduct, including their use of conceptual tools such as psychology, is a challenging task because people are complex and heterogeneous. Even so, the capacity to abstract meanings from our own psychosocial processes and our external world is what enables us to construct, appraise, and revise our understandings.

Much of this text has dealt with identifying and moving beyond some of psychology's unresolved issues and conflicting approaches. One of psychology's central, defining issues is the nature of its data. Because scientific methods were used to collect that data, it has been assumed to be acontextual and ahistorical. However, a growing body of evidence suggests that individuals contribute on an ongoing basis to defining and being defined by their experiences, contexts and histories, intentions, and desires. A psychological *investigation* is also an *intervention* in the lives of the investigators and the participants; an *intervention* is also an *investigation* into the lives of both. Therefore, psychologists need to reevaluate the adequacy of the data on which they base their search for further truths and their services.

Psychology needs a new paradigm to replace the current models that employ unidirectional, investigator controlled studies, interventions, and evaluations. It is incumbent that this new paradigm acknowledge that the production of psychological knowledge is necessarily a participatory endeavor. All participants, including the investigators, contribute according to their specialized roles and unique characteristics and experiences, and all are responsible for the impact of their participation.

One of the presumed strengths of unidirectional models is the assumption that specially trained individuals can detach themselves from their involvement in their own lives and societies and become impartial developers of objective knowledge. My argument is that impartiality cannot be achieved, leaving us to question whether our own embeddedness in our societal contexts means that our lives and our work as psychologists can only be a reflection of those particular contexts. I have also argued that all of us, including psychologists, can surmount our personal and contextual limits by using our capacities for self-awareness and self-criticism and by including the perspectives of others in our conclusions. These assumptions lead to a scientific paradigm that incorporates a less ethnocentric base of knowledge for evaluating our work and our beliefs as we seek to improve the quality of our lives and the structure and functioning of our societies.

The paradigm proposed in this text as a basis for accomplishing these objectives is called a transcultural ethnic validity (TEV) perspective. It brings a comprehensive approach to the study of the interrelations among cultures, communities, individual psychosocial competence, and individual and collective change. This approach is based on the reasoning that as all organisms become more complicated, they develop complex emergent forms of activities that function in a holistic manner and direct or override simpler activity patterns. The TEV model is presented as a framework for integrating reductionist approaches and those based on concepts of emergence. It is a holistic approach that provides a fuller account of how people overcome the supposed limits of their contexts and pasts to create new, future possibilities and make choices that enable them to go beyond those limits.

THE PSYCHOSOCIAL MATRIX OF PEOPLE'S LIVES

A psychosocial competence model was advanced in this book as an organizing framework for building and using a TEVM approach to address psychology's challenges and possibilities. The core assumptions in this model include that because we are part of nature, we are knowable through systematic study; however, we also are self-aware knowers, create meaning in our lives, have some discretion about our choices, and to some extent are inherently unpredictable. A second important assumption is that we must be responsive to contextual factors in order to manage our lives and achieve our desires. These factors are nested within increasingly comprehensive systems built on our historically based beliefs and our ongoing experiences. They range from the contexts of our individual lives, families, and communities to the contexts of our broader societies and cultures. Consequently, there are interrelationships among cultures, communities, individual psychosocial competence, and individual change.

Within these nested frameworks, we form individual psychosocial configurations. The form of each configuration is competence-oriented for particular circumstances. For example, in most societies it is ethnically valid for girls and boys to behave differently, and those who violate those relevant standards are considered incompetent or otherwise deviant. However, the specific form of gender-related behavior varies across situations requiring us to make adjustments for competent functioning when we enter new situations.

Because we live in heterogeneous societies, the frameworks we construct are complex and many of our interactions are asymmetrical in nature. In all societies, some individuals and groups are dominant and culture defining (CD); they establish the terms of their own and others' interactions. Living competently as nonculture-defining (NCD) people in a CD context requires developing individual psychosocial competence configurations that fit the context's prescribed ethnic validity norms for them. Even seeking to change social injustices in a particular context requires doing so in ways that respond to that context's socially defined ethnic validity requirements.

To guide our lives, we organize self-assigned attributes about our worth and efficacy, our relationships to the world, and our ways of behaving. That organizing takes place in psychosocial contexts which include both supports and threats and are influenced by the effectiveness of our efforts to master or adapt to those factors rather than succumb to them. Individuals who live in a benign and predictable environment tend to form a psychosocially competent way of approaching life that is characterized by a positive sense of self-efficacy, a moderately positive sense of trust, and an active, mastery-oriented planful orientation. Individuals in oppressive, malign, and unpredictable environments form psychosocial configurations that reflect these different circumstances. In all environments, circumstances and events can overwhelm anyone's capacities to find patterns of meaning and manage these patterns effectively. Even in such circumstances, individuals develop patterns of dysfunctionality that are reflective of the particular events and circumstances of their lives.

We have long, complex histories of organizing and managing individual and social change through a process of psychosocial leaps and spirals. Sensory input does not arrive in an organized way to guide our experiences. To accomplish our desires it is necessary that we function as active agents and assign meaning to our sensory input. We decide whether the input is supportive or threatening and what other meaning it might convey. Having made that leap, we build on it in a configural way by deciding what each input means for our sense of self-efficacy and worth, for the nature of our world and our relationship to it, and for what to do about it. We then act accordingly, generate new input, and continue that process throughout our lives.

We define the nature of reality for ourselves by making these leaps at all levels of meaning ranging from the individual to the cultural. Once each leap is made, we interpret and organize the meaning of subsequent experiences accordingly. Each leap can make an enormous difference in our lives. Once the decision is made that a previous leap to a particular belief is no longer credible, we face reorganizing the internal and external aspects of our lives that were built on that belief. Such shifts may be disorienting and traumatic; they may also be exhilarating and offer new possibilities. In either case, leaps are discontinuous and dislocating. In science, they are referred to as paradigm shifts.

CULTURAL DIFFERENCES

Across cultures, there are many differences in how people organize their lives and institutions. One of those differences concerns whether primacy is assigned to individual autonomy or to relatedness within a social group; other differences occur in relation to gender, ethnicity, or sociorace. The assignment of primacy has a profound impact on how we feel, what we learn, how we analyze experiences, what we believe, and what we do.

Both individual and social change require shifts in our senses of individuality and relatedness. For example, Western psychologists have developed complex and well-detailed conceptions of individuals as psychological beings, but they have given less attention to and agreed less about the nature of society or societal arrangements. Conversely, many non-Western societies assign primacy to the self as embedded-in-society. Each way of organizing a society and the role of people within it yields different strengths and limitations; however, because both emphases are ethnocentric, they create particular difficulties when people try to interact across these cultural divides. Moving beyond our culture-bound constraints requires us to make paradigm changes, something we can do only by first acknowledging our embeddedness in our contexts and our knower capabilities. We can then reformulate our senses of self, self-other relationships, and how to guide our conduct.

For example, once we understand that conduct is an internally and externally influenced and monitored sequence of interactions and not just isolated acts, it becomes important to identify the nature and consequences of interaction patterns. There is evidence that the kinds of interactions which improve the quality of people's lives and the prosocial character of their societies have elements in common. Destructive patterns of interaction also have similarities. That is, people's competent prosocial configurations contribute to sustaining and strengthening their own patterns and increase people's commitment to using them because of their mutual benefits. Conversely, their destructive patterns may be perpetuated because the failures often strengthen people's feelings of threat and ineffectiveness, leading them to increase the intensity of their destructiveness in order to be even more self-protective. To change interaction patterns, we must first learn that our identity is created and sustained both by our ways of interacting with others and our internal definitions of ourselves and the world.

INDIVIDUAL AND SOCIAL CHANGE

Individual and social change are interdependent. At the very least, changes within individuals lead them to change their contexts; changes in a context inevitably produce changes in the associated people. These processes of reconciling individual, community, and social autonomy and relatedness are occurring constantly in everyone's life, although we may not acknowledge them as we construct theories, conduct research, and seek to make changes. It takes effort at all levels to give those changes direction and realize their potential.

Most psychologists (and other change agents) lack a sophisticated understanding of communities and the psychosocial properties that sustain their interrelatedness (communality, identity, sharedness, and interlinking). They are also limited in their understanding of the interdependence of relational and autonomous processes. Although these processes are as much a part of everyone as are their individual characteristics, psychologists and lay people tend to think that relational characteristics are external in contrast to individual, presumably internal, psychological attributes. Until psychologists understand that cultures are holistic and everyone participates in them, their potential to make substantial societal contributions cannot be realized. Perhaps the most difficult part of the process is for social change agents to make these required complex changes in themselves.

Current psychological paradigms can also be challenged on the basis of their limited attention to the extent and varieties of human diversity. Psychologists need to incorporate a fuller understanding of the observation that we are not all alike and learn that the lives of those who differ from them are as valid as their own. Building new approaches within a TEV paradigm allows psychologists to use their active agent capacities to construct lives, communities, and cultures in ways that differ radically from current ones.

BELIEF SYSTEMS

In order to shift to a TEV paradigm, we are forced to reexamine our basic premises. We must address the issue that psychology's belief systems have both limitations and strengths. For example, two of psychology's particular strengths are its assumptions that (a) using systematic empirical approaches to identify the order among events is the best guide to understand and manage our futures, and (b) we must change our expectations or beliefs when experiences do not confirm them.

Although these assumptions are basic to scientific approaches and are strengths of psychology, they also have limitations that present psychologists with ongoing challenges. For example, how can important human questions be addressed scientifically if they cannot be answered empirically, and how can beliefs be evaluated whose truth cannot be tested empirically? The empirical approach suggested here is consistent with scientific assumptions and leads to resolution of these questions by study of the antecedents, correlates, and consequences of believing and acting on various answers to them. We cannot test whether there are supernatural beings, but we can study the circumstances that lead people to posit the existence of such beliefs and the consequences that result from acting on them.

People modify their common sense belief systems and their codified religious and other ideological belief systems on the basis of empirical checks, but their commitment to doing so usually involves less rigorous scrutiny than that which characterizes scientific approaches. Their commitment may also be limited by an unwillingness to reevaluate beliefs even when they are not supported by empirical evidence. The differences in approach that stem from these alternative belief systems are important because of their implications for how psychology, common sense, and ideology-based belief systems are used to inform each other and to guide our lives. For example, the relationship between religious involvement and psychological well-being has been studied. Outcomes suggest that a prosocially oriented conception of the meaning of life that includes self-fulfillment and spirituality can contribute to people's sense of well-being. However, these findings may be rejected by some who find a concept of spirituality operationally unacceptable and by others who find a goal of self-fulfillment spiritually harmful.

When psychologists exclude consideration of concepts such as spirituality on the grounds that they cannot be empirically measured, they also exclude empirical information needed for understanding the lives of those who believe in spirituality. It is psychosocially destructive to restrict the examination of beliefs without providing for dialogue at the level of common sense, providing for reciprocal exchanges, or checking on the correlates of those beliefs by empirical means. Western religions stress that the goal of existence is stability and permanence; Eastern religions stress that it is ongoing change. To the extent that psychologists ignore the consequences of such widely different beliefs, they diminish the quality and credibility of their own work and limit their potential contribution to knowledge about humans and how to help them. In contrast, examining the creation, modification, and consequences of existing belief systems, including psychological ones, provides significant opportunities for identifying their strengths and limitations; it also can guide the creation of alternative belief systems with fewer destructive consequences.

Not all belief system controversies are between scientific and nonscientific systems. There are also major belief system controversies within psychology and between it and related scientific fields. One such controversy with far reaching consequences concerns the nature of psychological disorders, particularly those characterized by people's dysfunctional ability to understand, organize, and express their feelings and thoughts in personally and socially acceptable ways. The extreme forms of such dysfunctions, i.e., mental "illnesses," have often been considered different in kind (rather than degree) from patterns of conduct considered normative, i.e., "normal."

However, relatively little attention has been given to the possible functional relationships between "pathologically" deviant patterns, competent or exemplary patterns, and cultural or other societal factors. Patterns of pathology and competence have increasingly been shown to be intertwined with psychosocial issues related to culture, race, and gender. Achieving a substantially improved understanding of such patterns and improving our ability to assist people in dealing with their dysfunctions requires constructing a new and different paradigm based on a broader range of findings about the nature and correlates of behavior.

For a paradigm to incorporate the innumerable varieties of people's experiences, it must be based on evidence from a broad range of cultures and patterns. Evidence suggests that broad-based efforts to improve social conditions are often more effective than are focused, individual approaches in reducing the occurrence of pathological psychosocial functioning in people who are identified as "at risk." Supportive social conditions and ethnically valid, prosocial treatment approaches also offer alternatives to people who want help but reject biomedical approaches that rely on drugs and require behavioral conformance to a dominant group's norms.

Using a psychosocial competence framework and adding the conception of psychosocial spirals provides a basis for understanding how people justify progressive participation in nonviolent and collaborative interactions or in increasing intensity of adversarial conflict and violent behavior. It also provides an informed basis for facilitating desired patterns and modifying undesired ones. For example, openness to new information and varied experiences yields a significant reduction in an authoritarianism that predisposes people to intolerance of differences and to the justification of violence. However, evidence indicates that it is easier to prevent closemindedness than to reverse it once it has developed. How to introduce and demonstrate the value and efficacy of such alternatives is an enormous challenge in a world regularly torn by violence at all levels.

Psychologists face alternatives with far reaching consequences and important tradeoffs in their discussions about how to direct their efforts. The alternative of a TEV perspective provides a more comprehensive framework than current approaches for guiding and appraising that work. With this perspective, psychologists follow the same guidelines as the people they study as "subjects" or treat as "patients" and assume the same responsibilities they assign to others for acting on the societal and individual implications of their lives and work. This approach asks psychologists to make a radical change, i.e., a paradigm shift in how they view themselves, others, and their work.

REPRESENTATIVE CHALLENGES IN PSYCHOLOGY AND SOCIETY

Using a comprehensive TEV framework enables us to identify questions and issues that challenge psychology's current approaches. However, to address these questions and issues, psychologists must adopt collaborative participatory processes to gather information, confirm facts, and both guide and evaluate interventions. Higher priority must be assigned to exploring significant social issues and the contextual factors that influence psychological phenomena. Meeting these requirements will start a positive psychosocial spiral because allocating a larger share of resources to these alternatives will subsequently yield benefits and costs different from those of current approaches. Topics and concerns related to these potential shifts are highlighted in the remainder of this chapter. They represent issues of societal importance which particularly need relevant psychological knowledge and expertise if we are to address them. Addressing them will not only contribute to society, it will also challenge in significant ways how psychology is currently organized.

PEOPLE'S WELL-BEING, SOCIETAL VALUE CONTROVERSIES, AND PSYCHOLOGICAL PERSPECTIVES

There are controversial issues in which psychologists' involvement is particularly subject to their own backgrounds and unquestioned beliefs. While evidence about these issues primarily involves practices in the United States, there are parallels with somewhat different details from other societies. Psychologists and psychological perspectives have contributed to these controversies as well as to the efforts to resolve them.

Such issues provide uniquely instructive examples of how psychologists and others can use psychological perspectives to better understand their own biases and the controversies. They also give direction for constructing improved psychological approaches for the resolution of such controversies and for minimizing the difficulties they present.

Child sex abuse and socioracial inequality are two social issues that arise from conflicting values about individual well-being, social justice, and societal mores. They are examples of controversies that have recently received substantial attention, particularly in the United States. Here they provide illustrations of how TEV approaches can provide more constructive use of psychological concepts, knowledge, and skills.

Child Sex Abuse (CSA)

Findings from empirical investigations about sexual abuse of children and child sex activities are controversial and need to be approached accordingly. An instructive example of the complexities involved in addressing such controversial topics occurred recently with the publication of the implications of existing research on the consequences of child sexual abuse (Rind, Tromovitch, & Bauserman, 1998). Although providing empirically grounded knowledge and guidance about patterns of children's socialization is a signally important contribution for psychology to make to society, this report initiated a widely publicized and ongoing controversy.

Rind, Tromovitch, and Bauserman (1998) emphasized that "many popular press and professional writers imply that CSA has certain basic properties or qualities irrespective of the population of interest" (p. 22). They make three basic assumptions about CSA, namely, it causes harm that is likely to be intense, is widespread among individuals with their own history of CSA, and its meaning and impact is equivalent for boys and girls. However, when these authors reviewed 59 college studies, they could not confirm these assumptions. Rather, although as a group, respondents who had been sexually abused as children were slightly less well-adjusted than controls, the effects of CSA were consistently confounded with family environment (FE). In fact, FE had a stronger effect on adjustment, and when FE was controlled, CSA effects were not significant. Self-reports indicated that "negative effects were neither pervasive nor typically intense, and that men reacted much less negatively than women" (Rind et al., p. 22). Rind and his colleagues also reported that these findings were consistent with those from national samples.

Rind, Tromovitch, and Bauserman (1998) concluded that the reason these findings did not support wide-spread, negative public opinions about CSA was because public definitions did not generally distinguish between psychological harmfulness and conceptions of moral and legal wrongfulness. In their own work, they separated the *empirical* task of identifying and addressing psychological harms and the *ideological* task of conforming to public or legal standards of morality, or to both. Existing scientific studies define CSA "as a sexual interaction involving either physical contact or no contact (e.g., exhibitionism) between either a child or adolescent and someone significantly older, or between two peers who are children or adolescents when coercion is used" (Rind et al., 1998, p. 23). Because the 59 studies used this broad definition, their examples of CSA included encounters perceived as positive by the involved adolescents and adult-adolescent sex, often considered socially acceptable and "normal" historically in the United States and in a number of cultures. In their view, if only those encounters that involve children (not adolescents), coercion, and negative reactions are labeled CSA, we will have a better basis for identifying "psychological harm" (Rind et al., 1998, p. 47) and for intervening to counter its effects.

In spite of the authors' caveats, conservative legislators and a prominent radio talk show host charged that the report sanctioned pedophilia, and by publishing it, the American Psychological Association was doing the same. A U.S. Congressional resolution was proposed to condemn the research and, by association, the APA. There were widespread and largely negative reactions from state legislatures, religious groups, family values organizations, newspaper articles, and editorial columns. At the behest of its Board of Directors, the APA's Central Office Professional Staff organized responses to clarify and defend its position that the APA is an organization that publishes scientific research and takes policy positions on the basis of scientific findings. The Board of Directors resolved to reaffirm its opposition to child abuse and its support for prevention programs and other relevant measures. In response, the U.S. Congress approved a modified resolution condemning the article, but not censuring APA (Fowler, 1999; Martin, 1999).

The controversy continued within the Association. Editorial letters included condemnation of APA's revised editorial policy as "religious dogma, immune from empirical or logical refutation" (Zuriff, 1999, p. 5) and also condemnation for publishing the article because it implied that there could possibly be a value-neutral term for adult–child sexual interactions and because it promoted a particular political agenda (Byrd, Scharman, & Larutisen, 1999, p. 5). These absolute, conflicting responses reflected the underlying beliefs their proponents were unwilling to have challenged. They permitted no middle ground and provided for no convergence in addressing this kind of taboo issue. From their positions, no policy could be developed that respected the integrity of empirical evidence and sensitivity to traditional beliefs.

The APA response missed an important opportunity to defend the importance and value of psychological research for informing psychologists and the public about the psychological consequences of acting on untested beliefs. Prohibiting relevant research and suppressing unpopular findings will not only lead to harm, in this case to children and adolescents whose experiences are denied or distorted, but more generally to basing socialization and remedial practices on inaccurate premises. Such a position also undermines psychology's scientific and public policy integrity.

This controversy highlighted many aspects of the themes mentioned throughout this text and the importance of addressing them systematically. There are many ethnic validity aspects in people's varied approaches to sexuality and vast differences in moral and legal codes. Despite psychological organizations' commitment to contribute to public policy on the basis of scientific findings, people, including psychologists, also interpret the results of studies from within their own belief systems. Scientists or scientific organizations who confine their investigations and activities to only those questions approved of by advocates of ideological belief systems are obliged to clarify their substantive and policy positions. People who reject research findings that challenge moral or legal positions have an obligation to clarify that they have become advocates for nonempirical ideological positions.

Socioracial Equality

The relationship between individual and social change is another critical issue for psychology. Social groupings, ranging from families to cultures, are becoming increasingly heterogeneous, are changing more rapidly, and are impinging on each other more directly. However, there is often a discrepancy between our individual actions and those that represent our commitment to societal norms. These discrepancies are reflected in how well or poorly social changes are accomplished. Probably the most widely studied effort to establish social equality among different ethnic or racial groups is the search for socioracial equity in the United States.

Steele (1999) demonstrated that the mere threat of discrimination is enough to have a negative impact on the performance of those who expect to be discriminated against. His findings indicated that among U.S. college students, NCDGs performed more poorly than controls on tests for which there was a stereotype predicting that outcome. Stereotype areas that were tested included African Americans versus Caucasians (re intellectual ability), women versus men (re mathematics), U.S. Caucasians versus Japanese (re mathematics), and lower class versus high class (re academic achievement) students. Additional studies indicated that these effects could be reduced by creating a supportive environment for NCDG students; that is, by creating a culturally *safe* environment. Even so, individual and societal efforts to provide such *safe* environments are constantly being challenged.

As described earlier, Howitt and Owusu-Bempan (1994) documented the structural racism built into Euro-American psychology with its predominant focus on Caucasian–African differences. They wrote that the implicit, underlying CDG assumption that people of African descent have a problem accepting their Africanness or blackness, i.e., their presumed inferiority, led to a parallel assumption that society's racial problems lie within the people of African origin, not within the CDG Caucasians. They used this reasoning to criticize a set of guidelines published by the APA's Board of Ethnic Minority Affairs for providers of services to diverse populations. To them, the guidelines represented a list of conduct rules that were completely focused on the awareness, sensitivity, and behavior of providers and practitioners. They concluded that these guidelines made the attainment of an antiracist psychology

> the responsibility of individual psychologists ... rather than of the professional body.... As such, it is a marginal statement relying on the good faith of individuals. If this is what psychologists should be like then whose responsibility must it be for ensuring that they are? (Howitt & Owusu-Bempah, 1994, pp. 173–174)

Tomes (1999) also described how organized psychology and individual psychologists have fallen short in addressing their responsibility to work in a culturally competent fashion. He emphasized that, in a multicultural society such as the United States, service providers come predominantly from the culture-defining group. Consequently, NCDG individuals who seek services, particularly persons of color or those not fluent in English, are faced with an atrocious cultural match. To remedy that situation, he recommended that organized psychology institute a requirement that all students demonstrate cultural sensitivity, all curricula teach multiculturalism, and the faculty and students become multicultural. Further, for the short term, psychologists already in the profession should retrain themselves to become at least bicultural.

An important criterion for deciding what constitutes antiracist practice was introduced by New Zealand nurses. They rejected as inadequate the criterion that CDG practitioners should be *culturally sensitive* when providing services because it is the CDG practitioners who judge what that means. They mandated instead that nurses must meet the criterion of providing *culturally safe* services as judged by the recipients (Wood & Schwarss, 1993). If psychologists adopted this approach it would introduce a radical shift in how the presence of bias in our services is assessed.

These findings and perspectives raise crucial questions about the responsibilities of organizations for forming and implementing policies, the actions of individual members of such organizations, and the discrepancies between the two. No mechanisms exist for assessing whether such objectives mandated at a policy level are actually met when their implementation is decentralized. Psychologists and their organizations face a major challenge. They must implement and evaluate policies and guidelines that they develop for reducing the biases in the structure of their field. Otherwise, their policies are empty and provide no means of remedying "the atrocious matches" (Tomes, 1999) that current practices produce and sustain.

META FRAMEWORKS

The two topics discussed above are among those which emphasize the necessity of examining the meta frameworks that underlie psychology's current paradigms. These topics were identified by examining empirical evidence, some of which was troubling and unexpected. Reactions to that evidence suggested that we cannot, as community members or scientists, continue to conduct ourselves as simply autonomous rational beings. A more appropriate model would be one in which human conduct is conceptualized as a product of the relationships of individual, social, relational, and contextual influences. In such a model, psychology would be viewed as a psychosocial science and profession based in people's capacities to observe, interpret, and guide their conduct as self-aware knowers. With this idea in mind, current efforts to improve individual models and psychology as a relationship science are discussed in this section.

Individual Models

Several new approaches have explored the nature of individual attributes. They have differed in whether these attributes are defined as bearing any relationship to broader psychosocial considerations. The following three examples have been chosen to illustrate their nature and the issues they raise for psychology.

As a central mission of his APA presidency, Seligman chose the nurturing "of a science and practice of positive psychology ... [to] measure, understand and then build the human strengths and the civic virtues … [a task that first required defining] the positive traits that transcend particular cultures and politics and approach universality" (Seligman, 1998, p. 2). He added that a taxonomy of positive psychology was needed as a guide to the "good life." The construction of that taxonomy would require that investigators determine whether there is a grouping of human strengths which are the opposite of "disorders." As salutary as Seligman's effort may be, it is limited because it does not consider diversity or relational possibilities. Rather, it characterizes psychological science and practice as primarily an undertaking of experts investigating other people as objects of study to establish and promote a universalist, central tendency of desirable human characteristics.

This approach is also illustrated by two recent reviews of studies about the nature of subjective well-being (SWB). Those studies also emphasized SWB's individualist nature and universalist character. Diener, Suh, Lucas, and Smith focused on modern theories "that stress dispositional influences, adaptation goals, and coping strategies" (1999, p. 276) as indicators of SWB. DeNeve and Cooper (1998) analyzed studies that used personality variables as predictors of SWB which they considered indicative of happiness. Most of the studies cited in both reviews were correlational and done with U.S. populations only; consequently, we do not know whether they identified any causal relations or any transcultural factors. The studies' designs indicated an almost exclusive view of SWB and its predictor variables as being internal characteristics of individuals. Although both sets of authors considered the statistical interactions among the predictors in these studies, they did not differentiate relational factors (e.g., marital status) from presumably stable individual trait factors such as personality, extroversion, economic status, or physical handicap. That is, neither happiness nor subjective well-being was conceptualized as a function of the interrelationship between the strengths and vulnerabilities of the individuals and the healthy and toxic environments in their lives.

In contrast, Neidenthal and Beike's (1997) review of self-concept research linked individualist and psychosocial paradigms. They argued that people's self-concepts range from individualist to psychosocial, depending on whether individuals form them autonomously or rely on "concepts of other people for their meaning" (p. 124). These latter were considered explicitly psychosocial because of their dependence on others' selves for their meaning. Alternatively, isolated self-concepts were seen as independent of conceptions of others, of any social linkings. From Niedenthal and Beike's view, this conceptual framework can link together existing research findings, stimulate new areas of research, and make novel predictions about a range of topics including the role of self-concepts in mental health. Their conclusion supports a universalist conception of the autonomous self, but leaves open the possibility that its nature may range from predominantly individualistic to predominantly social.

Psychology as a Relationship Science

In contrast to these preceding reviews, Berscheid (1999) stressed that psychology's conceptual frameworks need to incorporate relational variables in new and different ways. She described current experimental paradigms as being predominantly individualistic with methodological and analytical paradigms reflecting that bias. She pointed out that studies of human happiness reveal that "there is nothing people consider more meaningful and essential to their mental and physical well-being than their close relationships with other people" (Berscheid, 1999, p. 260).

Berscheid (1999) pointed out that relationships involve motivation and affect and the expectation of future interactions as central considerations. Consequently, we cannot learn about these interactions from isolated experiments that engage participants as passive beings with no motivational or affective investment nor any expectation of continuing the interactions. She urged greater emphasis on developing psychology as a multidisciplinary, relationship science and as an integrative force within the discipline and in related disciplines. To her the object of relational studies is "the oscillating rhythm of influence observed in the interactions of two people" (Berscheid, 1999, p. 261). Such an emphasis would bridge the gap between scientists and practitioners because it assumes that an individual's problems involve individual and relationship characteristics.

Berscheid (1999) stressed that relationships do not reside in a lone individual, they are not static, and they are revealed over time as the parties interact. Like the wind or gravity, relationships are invisible and can be identified only through their effects. Further, the stability and future of a relationship is a function of the members' vulnerabilities, the environmental forces (e.g., economic or psychosocial stressors) it can withstand without disintegrating, the members' strengths, and the relationship's environmental supports. Berscheid argued that in order to predict the future of marital and parental relationships, we have to first identify the characteristics of healthy and unhealthy environments as well as the strengths and vulnerabilities of the people in them. I would add to her observations that similar considerations are needed for all types of relationships ranging from intimate to antagonistic. Adopting her proposal would dramatically challenge psychology's current individualistic orientation and simplistic focus on presumably universal, acontextual human characteristics. It also seems long overdue.

Acontextual Homogeneity versus Individual and Contextual Diversity

No matter how committed we are as psychologists to concepts of diversity or contextualism, unless we design our research approaches to identify these concepts, we will not learn about them. Psychology's findings will continue to report people's shared characteristics and the range of their deviations from those commonalities. We may say that we value diversity and believe that relationships are central aspects of people's lives and well-being. However, we will not be able to identify diversity and relationship characteristics and challenge individualistic paradigms unless our methods enable us to study people as active agents who are responsive to their contexts. These points are spelled out in the following three subsections: intelligence, qualitative and quantitative research, and community approaches.

Intelligence

Sternberg argued that U.S. society needs a definition of intelligence which is broader than the current one with its limited focus on memory and analytic abilities. For him, a better definition would include "the mental abilities necessary for adaptation to, as well as shaping and selection of, any environmental context" (1997, p. 1036). For instance, his work supports that creative and practical ability also contribute to intelligence. Adding these dimensions to our criteria for measuring intelligence would create a more open system. We could identify who is talented and deserving of opportunities across a range of diverse capabilities rather than perpetuating the present self-fulfilling hierarchy.

In addition, the importance of attending to contextual considerations in intelligence testing was underlined by Greenfield (1997) who emphasized that ability tests are to some extent reflective of symbolic culture. In her view, individuals from a culture other than that where the test was constructed do not share the same built-in presuppositions about knowledge, values, and communication. I would add that this point is also relevant to tests constructed and used within a heterogeneous society. Tests are never universal instruments; they are specific and embedded in their culture of origin. To construct and equate tests for different cultures requires use of approaches such as ethnography to identify the symbols of each culture whose members are to be tested. These insider and outsider perspectives must also be included when conducting tests and when interpreting their results so that adjustments can be made for cultural or class biases.

Qualitative and Quantitative Research

The challenge of how to reconcile psychology's disparate approaches to hypothesis generation and testing is far from resolved. This point is reflected in Rosenzweig's (1999) report on the international development of psychology. He cited the preliminary results of a 1998 survey of member organizations by the International Union of Psychological Sciences. First, he reported that the good news was that over the past ten years there had been an increase in the number of psychology students and the number of psychologists doing research and there had been a growing public awareness of the value of psychology for solving problems. Further, psychology, like other sciences, was seeking to demonstrate its relevance to the social and economic well-being of societies, and was, therefore, required to be more accountable. As evidence of progress in improving the field's level of accountability, he noted the greater emphases being placed on experimental approaches and its subsequent movement away from qualitative analysis. He also pointed out that psychology is being asked with increasing frequency to contribute to the solution of ethnic conflicts. As for the bad news, Rosenzweig expressed concern about the continued perception of psychology as oriented to the provision of client services and as not to be trusted.

Rosenzweig's mixed response to the survey highlights the problems that arise from the methodological divide noted above and his response to it. That is, his sense of encouragement about psychology's greater reliance on experimental approaches runs counter to its expressed interest in contributing to people's social and economic well-being and to resolving ethnic conflicts. There is a growing body of evidence that indicates that people's subjective differences arising from their varied ethnic backgrounds and experiences provide the justification for their conflicts. We cannot study subjective differences by relying on only experimental approaches.

Psychologists have historically had little interest in culture and are not particularly equipped to contribute to resolving culture conflicts. Ethnic, class, and cultural differences are more likely to be identified if we incorporate the use of clinical, ethnographic, and other qualitative analysis approaches rather than abandoning them in favor of experimental ones. Similarly, Rosenzweig's emphasis on quantitative approaches is likely to exacerbate the other issues that concerned him, especially the field's dissension about academic/professional emphases and psychology's status as a natural versus social science.

This methodological tension was highlighted in Davidson and Trickett's (1999) editorial policy statement for the American Journal of Community Psychology. The purpose of their statement was to identify and publish the most important current contributions to normal and abnormal development. They emphasized that qualitative approaches, including ethnographic, single-case studies, and integrative work such as critical reviews and conceptual contributions, have led to major advances and have historically been among the most widely cited. Consequently, they encouraged and assigned higher priority in their journal to such contributions and rejected "traditional, variable-oriented, sample-based research strategies and data analytic techniques ... [as adequate by themselves to] reveal the complex causal processes that likely give rise to normal and abnormal behavior among different children and adolescents" (Davidson & Trickett, 1999, p. 299). While their statement did not focus directly on diversity perspectives, it offered an important balance to experimental studies which obscure the role of heterogeneous contexts and subjective perceptions.

Community Approaches

Marsella (1998) recently argued that the "fabled global community" has arrived and is imposing compelling demands on people's individual and collective psyches and senses of identity, control, and well-being. In his view, psychology can contribute to the resolution of these demands by challenging and moving beyond its paradigmatic roots in Western culture and incorporating other psychologies. Specifically, it requires the development of global-community psychology *"defined as a set of premises, methods, and practices for psychology based on multicultural, multidisciplinary, multisectoral, and multinational foundations that are global in interest, scope, relevance, and applicability"* [author's italics] (Marsella, 1988, p. 1282).

In Marsella's (1988) view, global-community is preferable to terms like international or multicultural because it shifts our attention from existing units (such as nations) to an overarching, global umbrella. This term also incorporates attention to people's embeddedness in many subgroups, and it embraces the belief that all psychologies are indigenous. Each psychology has relevance for the cultural context where it was generated, but becomes ethnocentric and oppressive when applied in other contexts. Spreading Western life styles, values, and psychologies across the world can "be considered a colonization of the mind" (Marsella, 1998, p. 1288), and maintenance of ethnocultural diversity can be as important to human survival as biological diversity. With a global-community psychology perspective, psychologists can contribute as "knowers and helpers" (Marsella, 1998, p. 1289) in the effort to create situations that enable the world's people to lead more meaningful, prosocial lives.

Bond (1999) also proposed a framework that can be used in other societies and in multicultural relations. It is based on her U.S. experiences with issues of race, gender, and social class inequities in manufacturing, educational, and community-based settings. She identified two qualities of organizational contexts that are important to the participation of diverse group members; and then she used a community perspective to create organizational settings that support their equitable participation.

The first organizational quality in Bond's (1999) framework is recognition of the presence of multiple realities and creation of a culture of connection. A CDG homogeneous work group cannot be educated about the necessity of including different (e.g., NCDG racial, gender) workers with the expectation that the work group members will automatically incorporate the new workers. The CDG workers have formed a coherent group by accumulating an implicit ethos. They may not even be aware of it, and it certainly cannot be known by others. Their CDG group provides a pattern of advantage for them, and, unless they are given explicit norms that prohibit the continuation of the behaviors and interpretations that exclude NCDG members, the context will not sustain diversity. Those who are different will be isolated and potentially excluded from participation; eventually they will be excluded from the group. A diverse setting can be sustained only through the creation of a sense of interdependence and connectedness that holds all members accountable to one another.

Bond's (1999) second organizational quality is acknowledgment and legitimation of multiple realities by understanding the forces that created them and submerged the NCDG realities. Room must then be made for NCDG participants to define and include their submerged reality. Finally, a way must be established to offset the countervailing pressure of existing concepts of equality which emphasize sameness and, therefore, conformity to CDG cultural values. Expecting or requiring sameness does not provide equality. The incorporation of diversity must be acknowledged and made explicit as the basis for equality.

To make the changes that include the participation of NCDG individuals requires what Bond called "connected disruption" [author's italics] (1999, p. 350). It involves maintaining connections to individuals while disrupting existing organizational structures. However, just as it may be essential to reassure NCDG members that there will be disruptions of existing arrangements, it may be equally essential to assure CDG members that they can remain connected to the new organizational reality being created. Further, making a new reality functional on a daily basis requires understanding the dynamics that often keep CDG individuals from recognizing their privileges and their impact on interpersonal relations and organizational functioning. Everyone must assume accountability for his or her impact on others and discount any assumption of privilege, of the correctness, or at least preferability of, his or her views.

Bond's (1999) work led her to the conclusion that organizational values which emphasize independence and sameness can create settings that prevent meaningful participation by individuals from traditionally oppressed groups. In contrast, by using a perspective that emphasizes equitable participation for diverse members, community psychologists can make important contributions to the creation of contexts in organizations that value and sustain diversity. At any of these levels, Bond's concept of connected disruption is a fundamental challenge to many existing psychological models of constructive psychological change.

CHANGE AND PSYCHOLOGICAL INTERVENTIONS

Psychological interventions are change efforts, and successful interventions necessitate change. Both Marsella (1998) and Bond (1999) emphasized that point and, in particular, that for individuals to accomplish meaningful, self-sustaining changes they must first identify a basis for those changes in their own EVMs. Further, making transcultural changes require that each person form a new TEVM based on a shared, overarching model that can sustain their diversity, control their conflicts, and incorporate their commonalities.

Betancourt and Lopez (1993) did not explicitly advocate the formation of a TEVM as an overarching model for psychology, but their critique of mainstream psychology and of psychology's cross-cultural, racial, and ethnic minority focused efforts in the United States had that effect. Specifically, they pointed out that culture, race, and ethnicity are poorly differentiated and attention is not paid to separating the role of social and psychological variables from biological or ecological ones. As a consequence, much cross-cultural, socioracial, and ethnicity-focused research is not based on a theory of the relationships between these variables and psychological characteristics. Further, most mainstream psychological research does not deal with its own cultural embeddedness or consider the cultural nature of its theoretical inferences.

Betancourt and Lopez's conclusion is in effect that the creation of a TEV model for psychology is required. This model should include the conflicting and diverging cultural and ethnic factors and the mainstream (convergent) factors being studied. We can then develop theories and knowledge that are applicable in specific homogeneous and heterogeneous situations and with specific individuals. These TEV models can also serve as nonethnocentric bases for generalizations about transcultural convergences and for developing psychological measures which are more sensitive to the diverse realities of people's heterogeneous societal groupings.

Two examples of using TEVM efforts to address such issues were mentioned earlier. They were Manson and his colleague's (1985) studies of hallucinatory patterns and conceptions of depression among Native Americans and Kagitcibasi's (1996) report on a program in Turkey to integrate patterns of individual initiative within the ethos of a collectivist culture. Both examples demonstrated that the interlacing of individual and systems variables provides a more adequate criterion for judging psychological contributions to the well-being of individuals and society.

Two initiatives to generate prosocial change illustrate the differences in conceptualization between unicultural and transcultural approaches involving psychological variables. The American Psychological Society (APS) is committed to basic and applied research, but not to professional intervention. In 1990, it convened a Behavioral Science Summit (BSS) of nearly seventy United States psychological organizations including the APA. The conferees "endorsed the development of a *national research agenda* [authors' italics] that would help policy makers in federal and other agencies set funding priorities for psychological and related sciences" (American Psychological Society, 1992, Feb., p. 7). Six priority areas were identified: productivity in the work place, schooling and literacy, the aging society, drug and alcohol abuse, health, and violence in America. The goal was not to interfere with independent research, but to define specific research initiatives and facilitate cooperation in addressing issues of common concern by producing "basic and applied research and development that strengthens America's human capital" (American Psychological Society, 1992 Feb., p. 3).

As worthy as APS's objective may be, from a TEVM perspective there are serious limitations in their approach. Defining people's worth primarily or exclusively in terms of their capacity to be productive, i.e., the lens of human capital, is quite different from the goal of the United Nations Charter to "reaffirm faith in ... the dignity and worth of the person" (United Nations, 1978, p. 3), a view that considers individuals to be more than economic production units. This divergence in focus highlights the narrow and ethnocentric APS orientation to a particular societal value.

Another limitation in the unicultural tone of the APS's initiative is that its exclusive focus on U.S. based research eliminated any possibility of gaining insights from other cultural perspectives. Not all societies define productivity in the same way, nor do the heterogeneous groups within them. Further, the various APS initiatives paid little attention to the socioracial, ethnic, and socioeconomic heterogeneity of United States society or to its social and psychological differences in relation to gender.

The APS initiative led to the publication of topical reports by its various task forces. The report on work mentioned the importance of considering the social organization of the work place (Human Capital, 1993); that on basic research identified social coordination in other groups as well as the workplace (Human Capital, 1998). Neither of these reports considered cultural, socioracial, ethnic, or gender heterogeneity. The report on reducing mental disorders (Human Capital, 1996) introduced the need to consider socioeconomic, ethnic, and gender differences as psychosocial risk factors and emphasized the need to address people from underserved groups. None of the reports mentioned race.

The *APA Monitor* published three reports (McGuire, 1998a,b,c) which provided some contrast to the Human Capital initiative. Their focus was an international conference sponsored by the American and Canadian Psychological Associations to establish a new discipline of psychology to prevent, resolve, and intervene in ethnocultural conflicts. Participants included psychologists, sociologists, political scientists, and historians identified as experienced scholars and observers of such conflicts. It was noted that anthropologists are frequently involved in such settings as observers and participants, but puzzlingly, none were included in the conference nor were there any representatives of societies caught up in interethnic conflict. The proposals of two United States psychologists who were major contributors to the conference differed markedly (McGuire, August, 1998b). Seligman emphasized the importance of taking a normative approach to identify the universal causal factors that perpetuate ethnocultural conflicts. Wessells stressed the need for sensitivity to local conditions and for evaluating the relevance of ideas from Western societies to other circumstances.

Both the APS and the International Conference initiatives hold promise for involving psychology and psychologists in a broader range of human enterprises. Despite its limitations, the scope and approach of this multicultural, multidisciplinary, ethnic conflict resolution conference came closer to a TEV model than did the Human Initiative Task force. Consequently, it seems to be better grounded for accomplishing its objectives.

INTEGRATING PERSONAL AND SOCIAL COMMITMENTS AND ACTIVITIES

This text has emphasized that the origins of psychosocially responsible and destructive conduct are related to individual and social contextual considerations. The idea that our conduct stems solely from and is directed by individual considerations is necessarily ethnocentric; it is also destructive of the social context that sustains it. Conversely, the idea that our ways of behaving originate solely from and are directed only at social contextual considerations is destructive of the individual and, consequently, also of the social context. The remaining question is how individuals and social units can balance these considerations in ways that respect and support the individuals and their nested social frameworks. As Edney (1980) pointed out, this issue has challenged people throughout history.

In recent times, this topic has been referred to as the problem of the commons and democracy. When there is a common resource (a commons such as a common grazing ground held by a community) held by a group, a balance must be established between each person's use of that resource for his or her own interests versus the group's interest in maintaining the resource for equitable distribution. The crucial need to establish a balance between individual and societal concerns is reflected in the 163 scholarly publications about the commons concept which were found in PSYCLit for the years 1966 to 1998. They reveal that efforts to address this issue have been conceptualized in biosocial and psychosocial terms. They have never been approached as a psychological concern devoid of social dimensions or as a social concern devoid of individual dimensions.

Although no solution proposed to date for reconciling individual and group differences has commanded widespread support, a TEVM approach provides a convergent solution to this problem. It does so by emphasizing that individual and societal interests must be addressed and balanced in relation to each other. It also identifies the kind of psychosocial changes required to achieve and retain a more prosocially beneficial balance for both. Needed changes include the recognition from everyone that there are multiple realities and that diversity is desirable. Further, a culture of connection is needed. Such a culture would be based on everyone's belief that their own survival and well-being necessarily rest on the survival and well-being of all others, including those who are unlike themselves. This model gives us a basis for integrating our personal and professional commitments and our relationships with others.

CLOSING REMARKS

The central theme developed throughout this text is that each person has the capability to abstract psychosocial meaning from life events and make discretionary choices about more than just biological survival. We are all socialized and live in social contexts within networks of social relationships although we also have great capabilities for guiding our lives autonomously. We develop as psychosocial beings with complex natures and capacities for symbolizing, learning from experience, and recording events; consequently, we all have personal and institutional histories. These attributes enable us to construct conceptions of ourselves and our worlds, organize styles of psychosocial competence, and even prevail over difficult circumstances to manage our lives and societies in enriching and fulfilling ways.

However, psychology has been primarily focused on understanding people as individuals and contributing to the ways they can improve their individual well-being. Its main orientation continues to be a paradigmatic view that assigns little importance to people's contexts and relationships. Emphasis is placed on a reductionist approach to explain conduct as a direct function of genetic and biological roots. Less consideration is given to trying to understand conduct as an emergent psychosocial problem-solving product of people's creative, active agent characteristics. Stress also continues to be placed on detachment from societal involvement with a primary focus of working with individuals.

As we enter a new century, our world has become much more of a global community. The heterogeneity of our contexts and relationships are growing, and it is becoming more difficult to deal with the demands of that heterogeneity. Psychology is faced with the increasingly important question of whether it will ignore this major challenge and opportunity or respond by revising its reductionist, individualistic paradigm to form an emergent multicultural paradigmatic approach.

The interrelated frameworks of the Transcultural Ethnic Validity Model and a psychosocial competence framework have been advanced to conceptualize the nature and interrelationships of the many complex factors involved in undertaking that paradigm shift. These factors include reconceptualizing individuals as being apart from and also embedded in their biogenetic natures, histories, and psychosocial contexts. This reconceptualization leads to an emphasis on the need to incorporate the diversity and connectedness in our lives and societies. It also involves redefining the science of psychology as a collaborative process in which investigations and interventions are approached by scientists, professionals, and participants as reciprocal, participatory processes rather than professionally controlled, isolated activities. Seeking to learn about or change individuals, societies, or contexts is a process of learning about how to change all three, whether or not any of those undertakings are professionally directed. Making this kind of paradigmatic shift offers exciting challenges and possibilities that are currently overlooked. These challenges offer psychology the opportunity to enrich its contributions to the well-being of individuals and societies and to their capabilities of prevailing over many of the challenges they face.

REFERENCES

Addams, J. (1902). *Democracy and social ethics*. New York: Macmillan.

Ahmed, S. M. S. (1979). Visibility of the victim and aggression, cheating and rudeness. *Journal of Social Psychology, 107,* 253–255.

Albee, G. (1992). Saving children means social revolution. In G. W. Albee, L. A. Bond, & T. V. Cook-Monsey (Eds.), *Improving children's lives: Global perspectives on prevention* (pp. 311–329). Newbury Park, CA: Sage.

Albee, G. W., Bond, L. A., & Monsey, T. V. C. (Eds.). (1992). *Improving children's lives: Global perspectives on prevention*. Newbury Park, CA: Sage.

Albee, G. W., & Joffe, J. M. (Eds.). (1977). *The issues: An overview of primary prevention*. Hanover, NH: University Press of New England.

Albert, J. S. (1974). Sociocultural determinants of personality pathology. In J. R. Lion (Ed.), *Personality disorders: Diagnosis and management*. Baltimore: Williams and Wilkins.

Altemeyer, B. (1988). *Enemies of freedom: Understanding right-wing authoritarianism*. San Francisco: Jossey-Bass.

Altemeyer, B. (1994). Reducing prejudice in right-wing authoritarianism. In M. P. Zanna & J. M. Olson (Eds.), *The psychology of prejudice: The Ontario symposium, Vol. 7* (pp. 131–148). Hillsdale, NJ: Erlbaum.

American Psychiatric Association. (1994). *Diagnostic and statistical manual of mental disorders* (4th ed.). Washington, DC: Author.

American Psychological Association. (1996). *APA presidential task force on violence and the family report*. Washington, DC: Author.

American Psychologist. (1997) 52, 684.

Anandalakshmy, S. (1975). Socialization for competence. In J. W. Berry & W. J. Lonner (Eds.), *Applied cross-cultural psychology* (pp. 202–207). Amsterdam: Swets & Zeitlinger.

Anderson, J. E. (1948). Personality organization in children. *American Psychologist, 3,* 409–416. In Reisman (Ed.), (1966). p. 270. *The development of clinical psychology*. New York: Appleton-Century-Crofts.

Antonovsky, A. (1979). *Health, stress, and coping*. San Francisco: Jossey-Bass.

Argyris, C. (1969). The incompleteness of social-psychological theory. Examples from small group, cognitive consistency, and attribution research. *American Psychologist, 24,* 893–908.

Argyris, C. (1975). Dangers in applying results from experimental social psychology. *American Psychologist, 30,* 469–485.

435

Argyris, C. (1982). How learning and reasoning processes affect organizational change. In P. S. Goodman & Associates (Eds.), *Change in organizations* (pp. 47–86). San Francisco: Jossey-Bass.

Aydub, C., & Pfeifer, D. R. (1979). Burns as a manifestation of child abuse. *Child Abuse and Neglect, 3,* 477–482.

Bakan, D. (1996). *The duality of human existence.* Boston: Beacon Press.

Banyard, V. L., & Miller, K. E. (1988). The powerful potential of qualitative research for community psychology. *American Journal of Community Psychology, 26,* 485–505.

Barbarin, O., Tyler, F. B., & Gatz, M. (January, 1979). *Individual and community competence: Developing and integrating successful coping strategies over time* (Final report: HEW #90-A-520/01 and 02). College Park, MD: University of Maryland Center on Aging and Department of Psychology.

Barker, R. G. (1964). *Ecological psychology: Concepts and methods for studying the environment of human behavior.* Stanford, CA: Stanford University Press.

Barker, R. G. (1968). *Ecological psychology.* Stanford, CA: Stanford University Press.

Barker, R., & Associates. (1978). *Habitats, environments, and human behavior.* San Francisco: Jossey-Bass.

Barker, R. G., & Gump, P. V. (1964). *Big school, small school.* Stanford, CA: Stanford University Press.

Barker, R. G., & Schoggen, P. (1973). *Qualities of community life.* San Francisco: Jossey-Bass.

Barron, F. (1973). *Creativity and psychological health.* Princeton, NJ: D. Van Nostrand.

Baumrind, D. (1993). The average expectable environment is not good enough: A response to Scarr. *Child Development, 64,* 1299–1317.

Bengston, V. L., Kaschau, P. L., & Ragan, P. K. (1977). The impact of the social structure on aging individuals. In J. E. Birren & K. W. Schaie (Eds.), *Handbook of the psychology of aging.* New York: Van Nostrand Reinhold.

Bennett, C. C., Anderson, L. S., Cooper, S., Hassol, L., Klein, D. C., & Rosenblum, G. (Eds.). (1966). *Community psychology; A report of the Boston Conference on the education of psychologists for community mental health.* Boston: Boston University Press.

Berg, J. H., & Clark, M. S. (1986). Differences in social exchange between intimate and other relationships: Gradually evolving or quickly apparent? In V. J. Derlega & B. A. Winsted (Eds.), *Friendship and social interaction.* New York: Springer-Verlag.

Berg, J. H., Piner, K. E., & Frank, S. M. (1993). Resource theory and close relationships. In U. G. Foa, J. Converse, Jr., K. Y. Tornblom, & E. B. Foa (Eds.), *Resource theory: Explanations and applications* (pp. 169–195). San Diego, CA: Academic Press.

Bernard, J. (1981). The good provider role: Its rise and fall. *American Psychologist, 36,* 1–12.

Berry, J. W. (1969). On cross-cultural comparability. *International Journal of Psychology, 4,* 119–128.

Berry, J. W. (1980a). Introduction to *Methodology*. In H. C. Triandis & R. W. Brislin (Eds.), *Handbook of cross-cultural psychology: Methodology* (Vol. 2; pp. 3–15). Boston: Allyn & Bacon.

Berry, J. W. (1980b). Social and cultural change. In H. C. Triandis & R. W. Brislin (Eds.), *Handbook of cross-cultural psychology: Social psychology* (Vol. 5; pp. 211–279). Boston: Allyn & Bacon.

Berry, J. W. (1985). Cultural psychology and ethnic psychology, a comparative analysis. In I. R. Lagunes & Y. Poortinga (Eds.), *From a different perspective: Studies of behavior across cultures* (pp. 3–15). Lisse, the Netherlands: Swets & Zeitlinger.

Berry, J. W. (1989). Imposed etics-emics-derived etics: The operationalization of a compelling idea. *International Journal of Psychology, 24,* 721–735.

Berscheid, E. (1999). The greening of relationship science. *American Psychologist, 54,* 260–266.

Betancourt, H., & Lopez, S. R. (1993). The study of culture, ethnicity, and race in American psychology. *American Psychologist, 48*(6), 629–637.

Bettelheim, B. (1990). The birthplace of psychoanalysis. *Wilson Quarterly, XIV*, No. 2, 68–77.

Birman, D. (1991). *Biculturalism, sex role attitudes, and adjustment of Latino immigrant adolescents.* Unpublished doctoral dissertation, University of Maryland, College Park.

Birman, D., & Tyler, F. B. (1994). Acculturation and alienation of Soviet Jewish refugees in the United States. *Genetic, Social, and General Psychology Monographs, 120*, 101–115.

Bishop, J. M. (1996). Enemies of promise. *Academe, 82*(1), 19–21.

Bishop, B. J., & Syme, G. J. (1992). Social change in rural settings: Lessons for community change agents. In D. Thomas & A. Veno (Eds.), *Psychology and social change* (pp. 93–111). Palmerston North, New Zealand: Dunsmore Press.

Blair, S. L. (1992). Children's participation in household labor: Child socialization versus the need for household labor. *Journal of Youth and Adolescence, 21*, 241–258.

Bleisner, R. (1993). Resource exchange in the social networks of elderly women. In U. G. Foa, J. Converse, Jr., K. Y. Tornblom, & E. B. Foa (Eds.), *Resource theory: Explanations and applications* (pp. 67–79). San Diego, CA: Academic Press.

Blowers, G. H., & Turtle, A. M. (Eds.). (1987). *Psychology moving East: The status of Western psychology in Asia and Oceania.* Boulder, CO: Westview Press.

Bond, M. (1999). Gender, race, and class in organizational contexts. *American Journal of Community Psychology, 27*, 327–355.

Bonta, B. D. (1997). Cooperation and competition in peaceful societies. *Psychological Bulletin, 121*, 299–320.

Boring, E. G. (1929). *A history of experimental psychology.* New York: Appleton-Century.

Bottoms, G. L., Shaver, P. R., Goodman, G. S., & Qin, J. (1995). In the name of God: A profile of religion-related child abuse. *Journal of Social Issues, 51*, 85–111.

Bowlby, J. (1969). *Attachment and loss* (Vol. 1), *Attachment.* London: Hogarth Press.

Bowlby, J. (1973). *Attachment and loss* (Vol. 2), *Separation.* London: Hogarth Press.

Boykin, A. W. (1986). The triple quandary and the schooling of Afro-American children. In U. Neisser (Ed.), *The school achievement of minority children* (pp. 57–92). Hillsdale, NJ: Erlbaum.

Boykin, A. W. (1994). Harvesting talent and culture: African American children and educational reform. In R. Rossi (Ed.), *Schools and students at risk* (pp. 116–138). New York: Teachers College Press.

Brewer, M. B., & Campbell, D. T. (1976). *Ethnocentrism and intergroup attitudes.* New York: Wiley.

Bronowski, J. (1966). *The common sense of science.* Cambridge, MA: Harvard University Press.

Brown, G. W., Brokham, M. N., & Harris, T. (1975). Social class and psychiatric disturbance among women in an urban population. *Sociology, 9*, 225–254.

Brown, L. M., & Gilligan, C. (1992). *Meeting at the crossroads: Women's psychology and girl's development.* Cambridge, MA: Harvard University Press.

Brown, R. W. (1980). Identity, politics, and planning: On some uses of knowledge in coping with social change. In G. V. Coelho & P. I. Ahmed (Eds.), *Uprooting and development* (pp. 41–66). New York: Plenum.

Brownmiller, S. (1975). *Against our will: Men, women and rape.* New York: Simon and Schuster.

Bryant, P. (Ed.). (1981). Stayed on freedom [special issue]. *Southern Exposure, 9*(1).

Bushrui, S. (2000). *The spiritual heritage of the human race.* Manuscript in preparation, University of Maryland, College Park.

Byrd, A. D., Scharman, S. B., & Lauritsen, E. D. (1999). Child sexual abuse article [letter to the editor]. *APA Monitor, 30*(7), 5.

Cahn, D. (1996, November 15). Israeli court allows coercion of detainee. *Washington Post*, p. A25.

Campbell, D. T., & Stanley, J. C. (1963). *Experimental and quasi-experimental designs for research.* Chicago: Rand McNally.

Caplan, G. (1964). *Principles of preventative psychiatry.* New York: Basic Books.

Caplan, N., & Nelson, S. D. (1973). On being useful: The nature and consequences of psychological research on social problems. *American Psychologist, 28,* 199–211.

Cascio, W. F., Goldstein, I. L., Outtz, J., & Zedeck, S. (1995). Twenty issues and answers about sliding bands. *Human Performance, 8,* 227–242.

Cascio, W. F., Outtz, J., Zedeck, S., & Goldstein, I. L. (1995). Statistical implications of six methods of test score use in personnel selection. *Human Performance, 4,* 233–264.

Celano, M. P., & Tyler, F. B. (1991). Behavioral acculturation among Vietnamese refugees in the United States. *The Journal of Social Psychology, 131,* 373–385.

Child Labor Deterrence Act, S. 332, 105th Cong., 1st Sess. (1997).

Churchman, C. W. (1948). *Theory of experimental inference.* New York: Macmillan.

Clark, L. A., Watson, D., & Reynolds, S. (1995). Diagnosis and classification of psychopathology: Challenges to the current system and future directions. *Annual Review of Psychology, 44,* 121–153.

Clark, M. S., & Mills, J. (1993). The difference between communal and exchange relationships. *Personality and Social Psychology Bulletin, 19,* 684–691.

Coelho, G. V., & Ahmed, P. I. (Eds.). (1980). *Uprooting and development.* New York: Plenum.

Coelho, G., Hamburg, D., & Adams, J. (Eds.). (1974). *Coping and adaptation.* New York: Basic Books.

Coelho, G. V., & Stein, J. J. (1980). Change, vulnerability, and coping: Stresses of uprooting and overcrowding. In G. V. Coelho & P. I. Ahmed (Eds.), *Uprooting and development* (pp. 19–40). New York: Plenum.

Cohn, B. S. (1983). Representing authority in Victorian India. In E. Hobsbawm & T. Ranger (Eds.), *The invention of tradition* (pp. 165–209). New York: Cambridge University Press.

Cooper, C. R. & Denner, J. (1998). Theories linking culture and psychology: Universal and community-specific processes. *Annual Review of Psychology, 49,* 559–584.

Corfman, E. G. (1979). Families today—A research sampler on families and children. (Vol. II). (NIMH Science Monographs I). Washington, DC: U.S. Government Printing Office.

Counts, D. A., Brown, J. K., & Campbell, J. C. (Eds.). (1992). *Sanctions and sanctuary: Cultural perspectives on the beating of wives.* Boulder, CO: Westview Press.

Coursey, R. D. (Ed.). (1977). *Program evaluation for mental health: Methods, strategies, and participants.* New York: Grune and Stratton.

Cowen, E. L. (1973). Social and community interventions. In P. H. Mussen & M. R. Rosenzweig (Eds.). *Annual Review of Psychology, 24,* 423–472.

Cowen, E. L., Dorr, D., Clarfield, S., Kreling, B., McWilliams, S. A., Pokracki, D., Pratt, M., Terrell, D., & Wilson, A. (1973). The AML: A quick screening device for early identification of school maladaptation. *American Journal of Community Psychology, 1,* 12–35.

Cowen, E. L., & Hightower, A. D. (1989). The primary mental health project: Thirty years after. *Prevention in Human Services, 6,* 225-257.

Coyne, J. C., & Downey, G. (1991). Social factors and psychopathology: Stress, social support, and coping processes. *Annual Review of Psychology, 42,* 401–425.

Crissey, M. S. (1977). Prevention in retrospect: Adoption follow-up studies. In G. W. Albee & J. M. Joffee (Eds.), *The issues: An overview of primary prevention* (Vol. 1; pp. 187–202). Hanover, NH: University Press of New England.

Cronbach, L. J. (1975). Beyond the two disciplines of psychology. *American Psychologist, 30,* 116–127.

Cronbach, L. J., & Meehl, P. E. (1955). Construct validity in psychological tests. *Psychological Bulletin, 52,* 281–302.

Curtis, R. C., & Stricker, G. (Eds.). (1991). *How people change: Inside and outside therapy.* New York: Plenum.

Dachler, H. P. (August 24, 1998). *Relational theorizing, power and the "ecology" of W/O psychology.* Presidential address, 24th International Congress of Applied Psychology, San Francisco, CA.

Dachler, H. P., & Wilpert, B. (1978). Conceptual dimensions and boundaries of participation in organizations: A critical evaluation. *Administrative Science Quarterly, 23,* 1–39.

Datan, N. (1971). *Women's attitudes toward the climacterium in five Israeli sub-cultures.* Unpublished doctoral dissertation, Committee on Human Development, University of Chicago. In Antonovsky, A. (Ed.), *Health, stress and coping.* San Francisco: Jossey-Bass.

Davidson, W. S., & Trickett, E. J. (Eds.). (1999). Editorial statement. *American Journal of Community Psychology, 27*(3), 299–300.

deCharms, R. (1976). *Enhancing motivation.* New York: Irvington Publishers, Inc.

Deci, E. L. (1975). *Intrinsic motivation.* New York: Plenum.

Deci, E. L., & Flaste, R. (1995). *Why we do what we do: The dynamics of personal autonomy.* New York: Putnam.

DeNeve, K. M., & Cooper, H. (1998). The happy personality: A meta-analysis of 137 personality traits and subjective well-being. *Psychological Bulletin, 124,* 197–229.

Deutsch, M. (1983). The prevention of World War III: A psychological perspective. *Political Psychology, 4,* 3–31.

Diaz-Guerrero, R. (1977). A Mexican psychology. *American Psychologist, 32,* 934–944.

Diener, E., Suh, E. M., Lucas, R. E., & Smith, H. L. (1999). Subjective well-being: Three decades of progress. *Psychological Bulletin, 125,* 276–302.

DiGiuseppe, R., Eckhardt, R. T., & Robin, M. (1996). The diagnosis and treatment of anger in a cross-cultural context. In R. A. Javier, W. G. Herron, & A. J. Bergman (Eds.), *Domestic violence: Assessment and treatment* (pp. 35–67). Northvale, NJ: Jason Aronson.

Dodge, K. A., & Newman, J. P. (1981). Biased decision-making processes in aggressive boys. *Journal of Abnormal Psychology, 90,* 375–379.

Dohrenwend, B. P., & Dohrenwend, B. S. (1974). Social and cultural influences on psychopathology. *Annual Review of Psychology, 25,* 417–452.

Dohrenwend, B. P., Levav, I., Shrout, P. E., Schwartz, S., Naveh, G., Link, B., Skodol, A. E., & Stueve, A. (1992, February 21). Socioeconomic status and psychiatric disorders: The causative—selection issues. *Science, 255.*

Donahue, M. J., & Benson, P. L. (1995). Religion and the well-being of adolescents. *Journal of Social Issues, 51,* 145–160.

Drenovsky, C. K. (1992). Children's labor force participation in the world system. *Journal of Comparative Family Studies, 23,* 183–195.

Du Bois, W. E. B. (1940). *The souls of Black folk.* New York: Gramercy Books.

Dull, V. T., & Skokan, L. A. (1995). A cognitive model of religion's influence on health. *Journal of Social Issues, 51,* 49–64.

Dumont, M. (1992). *Treating the poor: A personal sojourn through the rise and fall of community mental health.* Belmont, MA: Dymphna Press.

Duran, E., & Duran B. (1995). *Native American postcolonial psychology.* Albany, NY: State University of New York Press.

Durie, M. (1994). *Whaiora: Maori health development.* Auckland, NZ: Oxford University Press.

Echemendia, R. J., & Pargament, K. I. (1982, August). *The psychosocial functions of religion: Reconceptualization and measurement.* Paper presented at the American Psychological Association Meetings, Washington, DC.

Echeverry, J. J. (1997). Treatment barriers: Accessing and accepting professional help. In J. G. Garcia & M. C. Zea (Eds.), *Psychological research and interventions with Latino populations* (pp. 94–107). Boston: Allyn & Bacon.

Eckensberger, L. (1992, July). The social psychology of cross-cultural psychology: An introduction. In F. B. Tyler (Chair), *The social psychology of cross-cultural psychology.* Symposium conducted at the XIth Congress of the International Association of Cross-Cultural Psychology, Liege, Belgium.

Edney, J. J. (1980). The commons problem: Alternative perspectives. *American Psychologist, 35*, 131–150.

Edwards, C., Gandini, L., & Forman, G. (Eds.). *The hundred languages of children: The Reggio Emilia approach to early childhood education*. Norwood, NJ: Ablex.

Elias, M. (Ed.). (1994). Bringing together the history and future of community psychology and the SRCA. *The Community Psychologist, 28*(1).

Elms, A. C. (1972). *Social psychology and social relevance*. Boston: Little, Brown.

Ennew, J. (1986). Mujercita y Mamacita: Girls growing up in Lima. *Bulletin of Latin American Research, 5*(2), 49–66.

Erikson, E. H. (1959). Report to Vikram: Further perspectives on the life cycle. In S. Kakar (Ed.) (1979), *Identity and adulthood* (pp. 13–34). Delhi: Oxford University Press.

Erikson, E. H. (1963). *Childhood and society*. New York: Norton.

Eron, L. D. (1982). Parent–child interaction, television violence, and aggression of children. *American Psychologist, 37*, 197–211.

Eron, L. D., Gentry, J. H., & Schlegel, P. (1994). *Reason to hope: A psychosocial perspective on violence and youth*. Washington, DC: American Psychological Association.

Eron, L. D., & Peterson, R. A. (1982). Abnormal behavior: Social approaches. *Annual Review of Psychology, 32*, 231–264.

Eron, L. D., & Slaby, R. G. (1994). Introduction. In L. D. Eron, J. H. Gentry, & P. Schlegel (Eds.), *Reason to hope: A psychosocial perspective on violence and youth*. Washington, DC: American Psychological Association.

Escobar, J. I. (1993). Psychiatric epidemiology. In A. C. Gaw (Ed.), *Culture, ethnicity and mental health* (pp. 43–73). Washington, DC: American Psychiatric Press.

Ezekiel, R. S. (1984). *Voices from the corner: Poverty and racism in the inner city*. New York: Viking.

Ezekiel, R. S. (1995). *The racist mind: Portraits of American Neo-Nazis and Klansmen*. New York: Viking.

Fairweather, G. W. (1972). *Social change: The challenge to survival*. Norristown, NJ: General Learning Press.

Fairweather, G. W. (Ed.). (1980). *The Fairweather Lodge: A twenty-five year retrospective*. San Francisco: Jossey-Bass.

Fiske, A. P. (1991). *Structures of social life: The four elementary forms of human relations*. New York: Free Press.

Fletcher, G. J. O. (1984). Psychology and common sense. *American Psychologist, 39*, 203–213.

Flynn, J. R. (1984). The mean IQ of Americans: Massive gains 1932 to 1978. *Psychological Bulletin, 95*, 29–51.

Flynn, J.R. (1987). Massive IQ gains in 14 Nations: What IQ tests really measure. *Psychological Bulletin, 101*, 171–191.

Foa, U.G. (1971). Interpersonal and economic resources. *Science, 171*, 345–351. In U. G. Foa, J. Converse, Jr., K. Y. Tornblom, & E. B. Foa, *Resource theory: Explorations and applications*. New York: Academic Press.

Foa, U. G., Converse, J., Jr., Tornblom, K. Y., & Foa, E. B. (1993). *Resource theory: Explanations and applications*. San Diego, CA: Academic Press.

Foa, U. G., & Foa, E. B. (1974). *Societal structures of the mind*. Springfield, IL: Charles C. Thomas.

Forguson, L. (1989). *Common sense*. New York: Routledge.

Fowler, R. D. (1999). Battling a storm of controversy. *APA Monitor, 30*(7), 3.

Fowles, D. C. (1992). Schizophrenia: Diathesis revisited. *Annual Review of Psychology, 43*, 109–133.

Franklin, J. H., & Schweninger, L. (1999). *Runaway slaves: Rebels on the plantation.* New York: Oxford University Press.

Freeman, R. E. (1984). *Strategic management: A stakeholder approach.* Boston: Pitman.

Fulani, L. (Ed.). (1988). *The politics of race and gender in therapy.* New York: Haworth Press.

Fussell, P. (1977). *The Great War and modern memory.* New York: Oxford University Press.

Garcia, J. G., & Zea, M. C. (Eds.). (1997). *Psychological interventions and research with Latino populations.* Boston: Allyn & Bacon.

Garmezy, N. (1983). Stressors of childhood. In N. Garmezy & M. Rutter (Eds.), *Stress, coping, and development in children* (pp. 43–83). New York: McGraw-Hill.

Gartner, A., & Reissman, F. (1977). *Self-help in the human services.* San Francisco: Jossey-Bass.

Gatz, M., & Good, P. R. (1978). An analysis of the effects of the forced-choice format of Rotter's Internal–External Scale. *Journal of Clinical Psychology, 34*(2), 381–385.

Gaw, A. C. (Ed.). (1993). *Culture, ethnicity and mental health.* Washington, DC: American Psychiatric Press.

Gearon, J. S. (1995). *An exploratory study of competency and good mental health in people with schizophrenia.* Unpublished PhD. dissertation, University of Maryland, College Park.

Geertz, C. (1977). Gandhi: Non-violence as therapy. In D. Capps, W. H. Capps, & M. G. Bradford (Eds.), *Encounter with Erikson: Historical interpretation and religious biography* (pp. 113–122). Missoula, MT: Scholars Press.

Geertz, C. (1983). *Local knowledge: Further essays in interpretive anthropology.* New York: Basic Books.

Geertz, C. (1995). *After the fact: Two countries, four decades, one anthropologist.* Cambridge, MA: Harvard University Press.

Gergen, K. (1985). The social constructivist movement in modern psychology. *American Psychologist, 40*, 266–275.

Gholson, B., & Barker, P. (1985). Kuhn, Lakatos, and Laudan: Applications in the history of physics and psychology. *American Psychologist, 40*, 755–769.

Ghosh, A. (1995). Religion and the writer: The fundamentalist connection. *The Wilson Quarterly, XIX*, 19–31.

Gibson, J. T. (1990). Factors contributing to the creation of a torturer. In P. Suedfeld (Ed.), *Psychology and torture* (pp. 77–88). New York: Hemisphere.

Gibson, J. T. (1991). Training people to inflict pain: State terror and social learning. *Journal of Humanistic Psychology, 31*, 72–87.

Gilbert, D., Fiske, S. T., & Lindzey, G. (Eds.). (1998). *Handbook of Social Psychology* (4th ed., pp. 1–185). New York: Oxford University Press.

Gilligan, C. (1982). *In a different voice.* Cambridge, MA: Harvard University Press.

Gilligan, C., Lyons, N. P., & Hanmer, T. J. (Eds.). (1990). *Making connections: The relational worlds of adolescent girls at Emma Willard School.* Cambridge, MA: Harvard University Press.

Gilligan, G., Rogers, A., & Brown, L. M. (1990). Epilogue. In C. Gilligan, N. P. Lyons, & T. J. Hanmer (Eds.). (1990). *Making connections: The relational worlds of adolescent girls at Emma Willard School* (pp. 314–333). Cambridge, MA: Harvard University Press.

Glidewell, J. C. (1987). On the psychological forces in communities. *American Journal of Community Psychology, 15*, 603–611.

Goldstein, M. J. (1988). The family and psychopathology. *Annual Review of Psychology, 39*, 283–299.

Goodchilds, J. D. (Ed.). (1991). *Psychological perspectives on human diversity in America.* Washington, DC: American Psychological Association.

Goodnow, J. J. (1988). Children's household work: Its nature and functions. *Psychological Bulletin, 103*, 5–26.

Gorsuch, R. L. (1995). Religious aspects of substance abuse and recovery. *Journal of Social Issues, 51,* 65–83.

Graham, S. (1992). "Most of the subjects were white and middle class": Trends in published research on African Americans in Selected APA Journals, 1970–1989. *American Psychologist, 47,* 629–639.

Grebner, G., Gross, L., Signorelli, N., & Morgan, M. (1980). Television violence, victimization, and power. *American Behavioral Scientist, 23,* 705–716.

Greenfield, P. M. (1997). You can't take it with you: Why ability assessments don't cross cultures. *American Psychologist, 52,* 1115–1124.

Greenson, R. R. (1967). *The technique and practice of psychoanalysis* (Vol. 1). New York: International Universities Press.

Grinker, R. R., Sr., with the collaboration of Grinker, R. R., Jr., & Timberlake, J. (1962). "Mentally Healthy" young males (homoclites). *Archives of General Psychiatry, 6,* 405–453.

Groebel, J. (1986). International research on television violence: Synopsis and critique. In L. R. Huesmann & L. D. Eron (Eds.), *Television and the aggressive child: A cross-national comparison* (pp. 259–282). Hillsdale, NJ: Erlbaum.

Grubb, H. J., & Dozier, A. (1989). Too busy to learn: A "Competing Behaviors" explanation of cross-cultural differences in academic ascendancy based on the cultural distance hypothesis. *Journal of Black Psychology, 16,* 23–45.

Gurin, G., Gurin, P., Lao, R. C., & Beattie, M. (1969). Internal–external control in the motivational dynamics of Negro youth. *Journal of Social Issues, 25,* 29–53.

Guttentag, M. (1977). The prevention of sexism. In G. W. Albee & J. M. Joffe (Eds.), *The issue: An overview of primary prevention* (Vol. 1; pp. 238–253). Hanover, NH: University Press of New England.

Guttentag, M., & Struening, E. I. (1975). *Handbook of evaluation research* (Vol. 2). Beverly Hills, CA: Sage.

Guttman, D. (1977). The cross-cultural perspective: Notes toward a comparative psychology of aging. In J. E. Birren & K. M. Schaie (Eds.), *Handbook of the psychology of aging* (pp. 302–326). New York: Van Nostrand Reinhold.

Haney, C., Banks, C., & Zimbardo, P. (1973). Interpersonal dynamics in a simulated prison. *International Journal of Criminology and Penology, 1,* 69–97.

Haney, C., Banks, C., & Zimbardo, P. (September, 1973). A study of prisoners and guards in a simulated prison. *Naval Research Reviews, 26(9),* 1–17.

Helms, J. (1992). Why is there no study of cultural equivalence in standardized cognitive ability testing? *American Psychologist, 47,* 1083–1101.

Helms, J. E. (1996). The triple quandary of race, culture, and social class in standardized cognitive ability testing. In D. P. Flanaghan, J. L. Genshaft, & P. L. Harrison (Eds.), *Contemporary intellectual assessment: Theories, test, and issues* (pp. 517–532). New York: Guilford Press.

Helms, J. E. & Cook, D. A. (1999). *Using race and culture in counseling and psychotherapy: Theory and process.* Boston: Allyn & Bacon.

Herrnstein, R. J., & Murray, C. (1994). *The bell curve.* New York: The Free Press.

Highlen, P. S. (1994). Racial/ethnic diversity in doctoral programs of psychology: Challenges for the twenty-first century. *Applied and Preventive Psychology, 3(2),* 91–108.

Ho, D. Y. F. (1985). Cultural values and professional issues in clinical psychology: Implications from the Hong Kong experience. *American Psychologist, 40,* 1212–1218.

Hobbs, N. (1964). Mental health's third revolution. *American Journal of Orthopsychiatry, 34,* 822–833.

Hobbs, S., & Cornwell, D. (1986). Child labour: An underdeveloped topic in psychology. *International Journal of Psychology, 21(2),* 225–234.

Hodges, K., Tyler, F. B., & Brandt, D. (1979). Counselor's references to locus of control and therapeutic outcome. *Journal of Counseling and Psychotherapy, 1*, 95–110.

Hofstede, G. (1980). *Culture's consequences: International differences in work-related values.* Beverly Hills, CA: Sage.

Hofstede, G. (1991). *Cultures and organizations: Software of the mind.* London: McGraw-Hill.

Hofstede, G., & Vunderink, M. (1994). A case study in masculinity/feminity differences: American students in the Netherlands vs. local students. In A. Bouvy, F. J. R. van de Vijver, P. Boski, & P. Schmitz (Eds.), *Journeys into cross-cultural psychology* (pp. 329–347). Lisse: Swets and Zeitlinger.

Holahan, C. J. (1978). *Environment and behavior.* New York: Plenum Press.

Holmes, P. (November 18, 1996). At forum, U. S. rejects food "rights." *Washington Post*, p. A18.

Holzman, C. G. (1996). Multicultural perspectives on counseling survivors of rape. In R. A. Javier, W. G. Herron, & A. J. Bergman (Eds.), *Domestic violence: Assessment and treatment* (pp. 165–181). Northvale, NJ: Jason Aronson.

Hoppe, C. M. (1979). Interpersonal aggression as a function of subject's sex, subject's sex role identification, opponent's sex, and degree of provocation. *Journal of Personality, 47*, 317–329.

Horowitz, I. L. (1966). The life and death of project Camelot. *American Psychologist, 21*, 445–454.

Howitt, D., & Owusu-Bempah, J. (1994). *The racism of psychology: Time for change.* London: Harvester Wheatsheaf.

Huesmann, L. R., & Eron, L. D. (1986). The development of aggression in American children as a consequence of television violence viewing. In L. R. Huesmann & L. D. Eron (Eds.), *Television and the aggressive child: A cross-national comparison* (pp. 45–80). Hillsdale, NJ: Erlbaum.

Huesmann, L. R., & Eron, L. D. (Eds.). (1986). *Television and the aggressive child: A cross-national comparison.* Hillsdale, NJ: Erlbaum.

Hughes, C. C. (1993). Culture in clinical psychiatry. In A. C. Gaw (Ed.), *Culture, ethnicity and mental health* (pp. 3–41). Washington, DC: American Psychiatric Press.

Hui, C. H., & Triandis, H. C. (1986). Individualism-collectivism: A study of cross-cultural research. *Journal of Cross-Cultural Psychology, 17*, 225–248.

Human Capital Initiative: Report of the National Behavioral Science Research Agenda Committee. (February, 1992). [Special Issue]. *American Psychological Society Observer.*

Human Capital Initiative: The changing nature of work (Report 1) (October, 1993). [Special issue]. *American Psychological Society Observer.*

Human Capital Initiative: Reducing mental disorders. (Report 3) (February, 1996). [Special issue]. *American Psychological Society Observer.*

Human Capital Initiative: Reducing violence. (Report 5) (October, 1997). [Special issue]. *American Psychological Society Observer.*

Human Capital Initiative: Basic research in psychological science. (Report 6) (February, 1998). [Special issue]. *American Psychological Society Observer.*

Hunsberger, B. (1995). Religion and prejudice: The role of religious fundamentalism, quest, and right-wing authoritarianism. *Journal of Social Issues, 51*, 113–129.

Hunter, R. H., & Marsh, D. T. (1994). Mining giftedness: A challenge for psychologists. In D. T. Marsh (Ed.), *New directions in the psychosocial treatment of serious mental illness* (pp. 94–122). Westport, CT: Praeger.

Hurley, D. (1975). *Relationship between mental health paradigm and person-power utilization in the mental health system.* Unpublished master's thesis, The University of Maryland.

Hurley, D., & Tyler, F. B. (April, 1976). *Relationships between systems, mental health paradigm, and personpower utilization in community mental health centers.* Paper presented at the Eastern Psychological Association, New York.

Hyland, M. E. (1985). Do person variables exist in different ways? *American Psychologist, 40,* 1003–1010.

Inkeles, A., & Smith, D. (1974). *Becoming modern.* Cambridge, MA: Harvard University Press.

Iscoe, I. (1987). From Boston to Austin and points beyond: The tenacity of community psychology. *American Journal of Community Psychology, 15,* 587–590.

Iscoe, I., Bloom, B., & Spielberger, C. D. (Eds.). (1977). *Community psychology in transition.* Washington, DC: Hemisphere.

Jackson, J. J. (1972). Black Aged: in Quest of the Phoenix. In *Triple jeopardy: Myth or reality.* Washington, DC: National Council on Aging.

Jahoda, G. (1970). Supernatural beliefs and changing cognitive structures among Ghanian university students. *Journal of Cross-Cultural Psychology, 1,* 115–130.

Jahoda, M. (1958). *Current concepts of positive mental health.* New York: Basic Books.

Jahoda, M. (1977). *Freud and the dilemmas of psychology.* Lincoln, NE: University of Nebraska Press.

Javier, R. A., Herron, W. G., & Bergman, A. J. (Eds.). (1996). *Domestic violence: Assessment and treatment.* Northvale, NJ: Jason Aronson.

Jenkins, A. H. (1982). *The psychology of the Afro-American: A humanistic approach.* New York: Pergamon Press.

Jenkins, R. A. (1995). Religion and HIV: Implications for research and intervention. *Journal of Social Issues, 51,* 131–144.

Jessor, R., Graves, T. D., Hanson, R. C., & Jessor, S. (1968). *Society, personality, and deviant behavior.* New York: Holt, Rinehart and Winston.

Jin, J. (1992). *Development of a social cognitive multivariate causal model of affective depression and behavioral competence across different sociocultural contexts: Antecedents and simultaneity in path-analyses.* Unpublished doctoral dissertation, University of Maryland, College Park.

Joffe, J. M., & Albee, G. W. (Eds.). (1981). *Prevention through political action and social change.* Hanover, NH: University Press of New England.

Joint Commission on Mental Illness and Health. (1961). *Action for mental health.* New York: Basic Books.

Jones, E. E. (1964). *Ingratiation: A social psychological analysis.* New York: Appleton-Century-Crofts.

Jones, E. E., Rhodewalt, F., Berglas, S., & Skelton, J. A. (1981). Effects of strategic self-presentation on subsequent self-esteem. *Journal of Personality and Social Psychology, 41,* 407–421.

Jones, J. (1991). Psychological models of race: What have they been and what should they be? In J. Goodchilds (Ed.), *Psychological perspectives on human diversity in America* (pp. 3–46). Washington, DC: American Psychological Association.

Kagitcibasi, C. (1970). Social norms and authoritarianism. *Journal of Personality and Social Psychology, 16,* 444–451.

Kagitcibasi, C. (1996). *Family and human development across cultures.* Mahwah, NJ: Erlbaum.

Kagitcibasi, C., & Berry, J. W. (1989). Cross-cultural psychology: Current research and trends. *Annual Review of Psychology, 40,* 493–531.

Kanter, R. M. (1968). Commitment and social organization: A study of commitment mechanisms in utopian communities. *American Sociological Review, 33,* 499–517.

Kapur, M., & Cariapa, I. (1979). Training in counseling of school teachers. *International Journal of Advanced Counseling, 2,* 109–115.

Kapur, M., Cariapa, I., & Parthasarathy, R. (1980). Evaluation of an orientation course for teachers on emotional problems amongst school children. *Indian Journal of Clinical Psychology, 2,* 103–107.

Kazdin, A. E. (1986). Editor's introduction to the special issue. [Special Issue]. *Journal of Consulting and Clinical Psychology, 54,* 3.

Kelley, H. H. (1992). Common-sense psychology and scientific psychology. In M. R. Rosenzweig & L. W. Porter (Eds.). *Annual Review of Psychology, 43,* 1–24.

Kelley, H. H., & Stahelski, A. J. (1970). Social interaction basis of cooperators' and competitors' beliefs about others. *Journal of Personality and Social Psychology, 16,* 66–91.

Kelley, H. H., & Thibaut, J. W. (1978). *Interpersonal relations: A theory of interdependence.* New York: Wiley.

Kelly, A. H., Harbison, W. A., & Belz, H. (1983). *The American constitution and its origins and development.* New York: Norton.

Kelman, H. C. (1968). *A time to speak: On human values and social research.* New Haven: Yale University Press.

Kelman, H. C. (1997). Group processes in the resolution of international conflicts: Experiences from the Israeli-Palestinian case. *American Psychologist, 52,* 221–233.

Kelman, H. C., & Hamilton, V. L. (1989). *Crimes of obedience: Toward a social psychology of authority and responsibility.* New Haven, CT: Yale University Press.

Kessler, R. C., Price, R. H., & Wortman, C. B. (1985). Social factors in psychopathology: Stress, social support, and coping processes. *Annual Review of Psychology, 36,* 531–572.

Khilstrom, J. F. (1995, June). *From the subject's point of view: The experiment as conversation and collaboration between investigator and subject.* Keynote address presented at the 7th annual convention of the American Psychological Society, New York, NY.

King, E. L. (1978). Social and cultural influences on psychopathology. *Annual Review of Psychology, 29,* 405–433.

Kirk, S. A., & Kutchins, H. (1992). *The selling of DSM: The rhetoric of science in psychiatry.* Hawthorne, NY: Aldine de Gruyter.

Klineberg, O. (1980). Historical perspectives: Cross-cultural psychology before 1960. In H. C. Triandis & W. W. Lambert (Eds.), *Handbook of cross-cultural psychology: Perspectives* (Vol. 1; pp. 31–67). Boston: Allyn & Bacon.

Kluckhohn, F. R., & Strodtbeck, F. L. (1961). *Variations in value orientations.* Evanston, IL: Row, Peterson.

Kohlberg, L. (1969). *Stages in the development of moral thought and action.* New York: Holt, Rinehart and Winston.

Kojima, H. (1984). A significant stride toward the comparative study of control. *American Psychologist, 39,* 972–973.

Konopka, G. (1981). Social change, social action as prevention: The role of the professional. In J. M. Joffe & G. W. Albee (Eds.), *Prevention through political action and social change* (pp. 228–239). Hanover, NH: University Press of New England.

Kopplin, D. (1976, September). *Religious orientation of college students and related personality characteristics.* Paper presented at American Psychological Association, Washington, DC.

Korchin, S. (1976). *Modern clinical psychology: Principles of intervention in the clinic and the community.* New York: Basic Books.

Korman, N. (1974). National conference on levels and patterns of professional training in psychology: The major themes. *American Psychologist, 29,* 441–449.

Krause, D. U.S. Congress, House. Select Committee on Aging. (94th Congress, 1st session, July 8, 1975). Hearing before the subcommittee on health and long-term care (Stock No. 050-070-02903-0). Washington, DC: U.S. Government Printing Office.

Krause, D. U.S. Congress, House. Select Committee on Aging. (February 22, 1978). Hearing before the subcommittee on health and long-term care. Washington, DC: U.S. Government Printing Office.

Kuhn, T. S. (1970). *The structure of scientific revolutions* (2nd ed.). Chicago: University of Chicago Press.

Kuhn, T. S. (1979). *The Copernican revolution.* New York: Vintage Books.

L'Abate, L. L. (1994). *A theory of personality development.* New York: Wiley.

L'Abate, L. L., & Harel, T. (1993). Deriving, developing, and expanding a theory of developmental competence from resource exchange theory. In U. G. Foa, J. Converse, Jr., K. Y. Tornblom, & E. B. Foa (Eds.), *Resource theory: Explorations and applications* (pp. 233–269). New York: Academic Press.

Laoso, L. M., Lara-Tapia, L., & Swartz, J. D. (1974). Pathognomic verbalizations, anxiety, and hostility in normal Mexican and United States Anglo-American children's fantasies: A longitudinal study. *Journal of Consulting and Clinical Psychology, 72,* 73–78.

Le Blanc, L. L. (1995). *The convention on the rights of the child.* Lincoln: University of Nebraska Press.

Lefcourt, H. M. (1973). The functions of the illusions of control and freedom. *American Psychologist, 28,* 417–425.

Lefcourt, H. M. (1976). *Locus of control: Current trends in theory and research.* Hillsdale, NJ: Erlbaum.

Lefcourt, H. M. (Ed.). (1982). *Research with the locus of control construct* (Vol. 2). New York: Academic Press.

Lefcourt, H. M. (Ed.). (1984). *Research with the locus of control construct* (Vol. 3). New York: Academic Press.

Levenson, H. (1974). Activism and powerful others: Distinctions within the concept of internal-external control. *Journal of Personality Assessment, 38,* 377–383.

Levin, M. (1990). Torture and other extreme measures taken for the general good: Further reflections on a philosophical problem. In P. Suedfeld (Ed.), *Psychology and torture* (pp. 89–98). New York: Hemisphere.

Levine, M., & Levine, A. A. (1992). *Helping children: A social history.* New York: Appleton-Century-Crofts.

Levine, M., & Perkins, D. V. (1997). *Principles of community psychology: Perspectives and application.* New York: Oxford University Press.

Lewis, D. O., Shanok, S. S., Pincus, J., & Glaser, G. H. (1979). Violent juvenile delinquents: Psychiatric, neurological, psychological, and abuse factors. *Journal of the American Academy of Child Psychiatry, 18,* 307–319.

Lindemann, E. (1944). Symptomatology and management of acute grief. *American Journal of Psychiatry, 101,* 141–148.

Lofland, J., & Stark, R. (1965). Becoming a world-saver: A theory of conversion to a deviant perspective. *American Sociological Review, 30,* 862–875.

Loggins, K., & Thomas S. (1981). The new klan. Nashville, TN: The Tennessean.

Lonner, W. (1980). The search for psychological universals. In H. C. Triandis & W. W. Lambert (Eds.), *Handbook of cross-cultural psychology: Perspectives* (Vol. 1; pp. 143–204). Boston: Allyn and Bacon.

Luntz, B. K., & Widom, C. S. (1994). Antisocial personality disorder in abused and neglected children grown up. *American Journal of Psychiatry, 151,* 670–674.

MacCorquodale, K., & Meehl, P. E. (1948). On a distinction between hypothetical constructs and intervening variables. *Psychological Review, 55,* 105–122.

Mandelbaum, D. G. (1954). Psychiatry in military society I. *Human Organization, 13*(3), 5–15.

Mandelstam, N. (1970). *Hope against hope: A memoir.* New York: Atheneum.

Mannheim, K. (1936). *Ideology and utopia.* New York: Harvest Books.

Manson, S. P. (1995). Culture and major depression: Current challenges in the diagnosis of mood disorders. *Cultural Psychiatry, 18,* 487–501.

Manson, S. P., Shore, J. H., & Bloom, J. D. (1985). The depressive experience in American Indian communities: A challenge for psychiatric theory and diagnosis. In A. Kleinman & B. Good. (Eds.), *Culture and depression: Studies in the anthropology and cross-cultural psychiatry of affect and disorder* (pp. 331–368). Berkeley: University of California Press.

Marks, J. (1995). *Human biodiversity: Genes, race and history.* New York: Aldine De Gruyter.

Marris, P. (1980). The uprooting of meaning. In G. V. Coelho & P. I. Ahmed (Eds.), *Uprootedness and development* (pp. 101–116). New York: Atheneum.

Marsella, A. J. (1998). Toward a "global-community psychology." *American Psychologist, 53,* 1282–1291.

Marsh, D. T. (Ed.). (1994). *New directions in the psychosocial treatment of serious mental illness.* Westport, CT: Praeger.

Marques, C. (1998). Manual-based treatment and clinical practice. *Clinical Psychology: Science and Practice, V5N3,* 400–402.

Martin, S. (1999). APA defends stance against the sexual abuse of children. *APA Monitor, 30*(7), 47.

Maslow, A. (1962). *Toward a psychology of being.* Princeton, NJ: D. VanNostrand Co.

Maton, K. I., & Wells, E. A. (1995). Religion as a community resource for well-being: Prevention, healing and empowerment pathways. *Journal of Social Issues, 51,* 177–193.

McCarthy, C. (May, 1998). A Pro Bono life. *The Progressive, 62*(5), 30–32.

McClelland, D. C. (1966). The impulse to modernization. In M. Weiner (Ed.), *Modernization* (pp. 28–39). New York: Basic Books.

McClelland, D. C., & Winter, D. G. (1969). *Motivating economic achievement.* New York: Free Press.

McClure, G. T., & Tyler, F. B. (1967). The role of values in the study of values. *Journal of General Psychology, 77,* 217–235.

McFadden, S. H. (1995). Religion and well-being in aging persons in an aging society. *Journal of Social Issues, 51,* 161–175.

McGuire, P. A. (1998a). Experts offer theories on the roots of ethnic conflict. *APA Monitor, 29*(8), 14, 15.

McGuire, P. A. (1998b). Historic conference focuses on creating a new discipline. *APA Monitor, 29*(8), 1, 15.

McGuire, P. A. (1998c). In Northern Ireland, stories of ethnic conflict from war weary lands. *APA Monitor, 29*(8), 14, 15.

Mennell, S. (1989). *The civilization process: The development of the human self-concept.* Oxford: Oxford University Press.

Messick, D. M., & Wim, B. G. L. (1995). Individual heuristics and the dynamics of cooperation in large groups. *Psychological Review, 102,* 131–145.

Messick, S. (1995). Validity of psychological assessment. *American Psychologist, 50,* 741–749.

Milgram, S. (1974). *Obedience to authority: An experimental view.* New York: Harper and Row.

Miller, S. (1995). The death of Hume. *The Wilson Quarterly, XIX,* 30–39.

Mirowsky, J., & Ross, E. E. (1989a). Psychiatric diagnosis as reified measurement. *Journal of Health and Social Behavior, 30,* 11–25.

Mirowsky, J., & Ross, E. E. (1989b). Rejoinder—Assessing the type and severity of psychological problems: An alternative to diagnosis. *Journal of Health and Social Behavior, 30,* 38–40.

Mitchell, R., Barbarin, O., & Hurley, D. J., Jr. (1981). Problem solving, resource utilization, and community involvement in a black and white community. *American Journal of Community Psychology, 9,* 233–246.

Moffitt, T. E. (1993). Adolescence limited and life-course-persistent antisocial behavior: A developmental taxonomy. *Psychological Review, 100,* 674–701.

Moghaddam, F. M. (1987). Psychology in the three worlds: As reflected by the crisis in social psychology and the move toward indigenous third-world psychology. *American Psychologist, 42,* 912–920.

Moghni, S. M. (1987). Development of modern psychology in Pakistan. In G. H. Blowers & A. M. Turtle (Eds.), *Psychology moving east: The status of Western psychology in Asia and Oceania* (pp. 23–58). Boulder, CO: Westview Press.

Monahan, J. (1980). *The clinical prediction of violent behavior* (DHHS Publication No. (ADM) 81-921). Washington, DC: U.S. Government Printing Office.

Monti, D. J. (1979). Patterns of conflict preceding the 1964 riots: Harlem and Bedford-Stuyvesant. *Journal of Conflict Resolution, 23,* 41–69.

Moos, R. (1979). *Evaluating educational environments.* San Francisco: Jossey-Bass.

Moos, R., & Insel, P. M. (Eds.). (1974). *Issues in social ecology.* Palo Alto, CA: National Press.

Munroe, R. L., & Munroe, R. H. (1994). *Cross-cultural human development.* Monterey, CA: Waveland Press.

Murrell, S. A. (1973). *Community psychology and social systems.* New York: Behavioral Publications.

Myers, R. (1992). *The twelve who survive: Strengthening programmes of early childhood development in the Third World.* London: Routledge.

Nadler, D. A., Shaw, R. B., Walton, A. E., & Associates. (1994). *Discontinuous change: Leading organizational transformation.* San Francisco: Jossey-Bass.

Neisser, U., Boodoo, G., Bouchard, Jr., T.J., Boykin, A. W., Brody, N., Ceci, S. J., Halpern, D. F., Loehlin, J. C., Perloff, R., Sternberg, R. J., & Urbina, S. (1996). Intelligence: Knowns and unknowns. *American Psychologist, 51,* 77–101.

Niedenthal, P. M. & Beike, D. R. (1997). Interrelated and isolated self-concepts. *Personality and Social Psychology Review, 1,* 106–128.

Nolen-Hoeksema, S., & Girgus, J. S. (1994). The emergence of gender differences in depression during adolescence. *Psychological Bulletin, 115,* 424–443.

Noone, J. A., Molnar, G., & Hopper-Small, C. (1979). Dislocation of expectations management of violence on a general psychiatric unit. *Canadian Journal of Psychiatry (Ottawa), 24,* 213–217.

Obuchi, K. (1979). Hostility as unresponsiveness to friendly changes of opponent's behavior. *Japanese Journal of Psychology, 50,* 249–255.

Obuchi, K., & Oku, Y. (1980). Aggressive behavior as a function of attack pattern and hostility. *Psychologia, 23,* 146–154.

O'Gorman, N. (1981). The education of the oppressed child in a democracy. In J. M. Joffe & G. W. Albee (Eds.), *Prevention through political action and social change.* Hanover, NH: University Press of New England.

Oklahoma supreme court finds absolute right to refuse treatment in non-emergency situations; Pennsylvania approves consent order. (1979). *Mental Disability Law Reporter, 4,* 77–78.

Oliver-Smith, A. (1986). *The martyred city: Death and rebirth in the Andes* (1st ed.). Albuquerque: University of New Mexico Press.

Olweus, D. (1992). Victimization among schoolchildren: Intervention and prevention. In G. W. Albee, L. A. Bond, & T. V. C. Monsey. (Eds.), *Improving children's lives: Global perspectives on prevention* (pp. 279–295). Newbury Park, CA: Sage.

O'Neal, E. C., Brunault, M. A., Marquis, J. F., & Carifio, M. (1979). Anger and the body buffer zone. *Journal of Social Psychology, 108,* 135–136.

Otero, R. F. (1982). *The handling of stressful psychosocial life-events as a function of a hierarchical configural pattern of competence.* Unpublished doctoral dissertation, University of Maryland, College Park.

Oxford Dictionary of Quotations (3rd ed., 1979). Oxford: Oxford University Press.

Paloutzian, R. F., & Kirkpatrick, L. A. (1995). Introduction: The scope of religious influences on personal and societal well-being. *Journal of Social Issues, 51*, 1–11.

Paranjpe, A. C. (1984). *Theoretical psychology: The meeting of East and West.* New York: Plenum.

Pareek, U. (1968). A motivational paradigm of development. *Journal of Social Issues, 24,* 115–122.

Pargament, K. I. (1997). *The psychology of religion and coping.* New York: Guilford.

Pargament, K. I., & Park, L. A. (1995). Merely a defense? The variety of religious means and ends. *Journal of Social Issues, 51,* 13–32.

Pargament, K. I., Silverman, W., Johnson, S., Echenmendia, R., & Snyder, S. (1982). The psychosocial climate of religious congregations. Unpublished manuscript, 1982. (Available from Psychology Department, Bowling Green State University, Bowling Green, Ohio.)

Pargament, K. I., Steele, R. E., & Tyler, F. B. (1979). Religious participation, religious motivation, and psychosocial competence. *Journal for the Scientific Study of Religion, 18,* 412–419.

Pargament, K. I., Sullivan, M. S., Tyler, F. B., & Steele, R. E. (1982). Patterns of attribution of control and individual psychosocial competence. *Psychological Reports, 51,* 1243–1252.

Pargament, K. I., Tyler, F. B., & Steele, R. E. (1979a). Is fit it? The relationship between church/synagogue member fit and the psychosocial competence of the member. *Journal of Community Psychology, 7,* 243–252.

Pargament, K. I., Tyler, F. B., & Steele, R. (1979b). The church/synagogue and the psychosocial competence of the member: An initial inquiry into a neglected dimension. *American Journal of Community Psychology, 7,* 649–664.

Parloff, M. B. (1998). Is psychotherapy more than manual labor? *Clinical Psychology: Science and Practice, 5*(3), 376–381.

Phinney, J. S. (1996). When we talk about American ethnic groups, what do we mean? *American Psychologist, 51,* 918–927.

Pike, R. *Language in relation to a united theory of the structure of human behavior* (Pt. 1). Glendale, CA: Summer Institute of Linguistics, 1954, and The Hague: Mouton, 1966.

Polanyi, M. (1964). *Personal knowledge.* New York: Harper and Row.

Polanyi, M. (1968). Logic and psychology. *American Psychologist, 23,* 27–43.

Price, R., & Chermiss, C. (1977). Training for a new profession: Research as social action. *Professional Psychology, 8,* 222–231.

Price, R. H., & Denner, B. (Eds.). (1973). *The making of a mental patient.* New York: Holt, Rinehart and Winston.

Prilleltensky, I. (1994). *The morals and politics of psychology.* Albany, NY: State University of New York Press.

Pruitt, D. G., & Carnevale, P. J. (1994). *Negotiation in social conflict.* Buckingham, UK: Open University Press.

Pruitt, D. G., Peirce, R. S., McGillicuddy, N. B., Welton, G. L., & Castrianno, L. M. (1993). Long-term success in mediation. *Law and Social Behavior, 17,* 313–330.

Quarles, C. L. (1970). *The Ku Klux Klan in the United States: Its history, organization, and recruitment practices.* Unpublished master's thesis, University of Mississippi.

Quarrey, M., & Rosen, C. (1994). *Employee ownership and corporate performance.* Oakland, CA: National Center for Employee Ownership.

Raimy, V. C. (Ed.). (1950). *Training in clinical psychology.* Englewood Cliffs, NJ: Prentice-Hall.

Random House Webster's Dictionary. (1999). New York: Random House.

Rappaport, J. (1977). *Community psychology: Values, research, and action.* Orlando, FL: Holt, Rinehart and Winston.

Rappaport, J. (1981). In praise of paradox: A social policy of empowerment over prevention. *American Journal of Community Psychology, 9,* 1–14.

Reid, J. B., Taplin, P. S., & Lorber, R. (1981). A social interactional approach to the treatment of abusive families. In R. Stuart (Ed.), *Violent behavior*. New York: Brunner/Mazel.

Reisman, J. M. (1966). *The development of clinical psychology*. New York: Appleton-Century-Crofts.

Reissman, F. (1965). The "helper-therapy" principle. *Social Work, 10*, 27–32.

Report of the national advisory commission on civil disorders. (1968). New York: Bantam Books.

Review and Commentaries. (1998). *Clinical Psychology: Science and Practice, 5*(3), 361–407.

Ribeau, S. A., Baldwin, J. R., & Hecht, M. L. (1994). An African-American communication perspective. In L. A. Samovar & R. E. Porter (Eds.), *Intercultural communication: A reader* (pp. 140–147). Belmont, CA: Wadsworth.

Ridley, C. R. (1984). Clinical treatment of the non-disclosing black client: A therapeutic paradox. *American Psychologist, 39*, 1234–1244.

Rind, B., Tromovitch, P., & Bauserman, R. (1998). A meta-analytic examination of assumed properties of child sexual abuse using college samples. *Psychological Bulletin, 124*, 22–53.

Rizzini, I. (Ed.). (1994). *Children in Brazil today: A challenge for the third millennium*. Rio de Janeiro: Editora Universitaria Santa Ursula.

Rizzini, I. (June, 1997). *Philanthropy and repression: Children in the construction of Brazil's national identity*. Paper read at the Urban Childhood Conference. Trondheim, Norway.

Robinson, D. (1991). Text, context, and agency. *Theoretical and Philosophical Psychology, 11*(1), 1–10.

Rogers, C. R. (1961). *On becoming a person*. Boston: Houghton Mifflin.

Rosen, C., Klein, K. J., & Young, K. M. (1985). *Employee ownership in America: The equity solution*. Lexington, MA: Lexington Books.

Rosenhan, D. L. (1973, January 19). On being sane in insane places. *Science, 179*, 250–258.

Rosenzweig, M. R. (1999). Continuity and change in the development of psychology around the world. *American Psychologist, 54*, 252–259.

Rotter, J. B. (1954). *Social learning and clinical psychology*. New York: Prentice-Hall.

Rotter, J. B. (1966). Generalized expectations for internal versus external control of reinforcement. *Psychological Monographs, 80*(1), Whole No. 609.

Rotter J. B. (1975). Some problems and misconceptions related to the construct of internal versus external control of reinforcement. *Journal of Consulting and Clinical Psychology, 43*, 56–67.

Rotter, J. B. (1980). Interpersonal trust, trustworthiness and gullibility. *American Psychologist, 35*, 1–7.

Rotter, J. B., Chance, J. E., & Phares, E. J. (1972). *Applications of a social learning theory of personality*. New York: Holt, Rinehart and Winston.

Rowe, D. (1983). *Depression: The way out of your prison*. London: Routledge and Kegan Paul.

Rubin, J. Z. (1981). (Ed.). *Dynamics of third party intervention: Kissinger in the Middle East*. New York: Praeger.

Russell, R. L. (1989). Preface [Special issue]. *Clinical Psychology Review, 9*, 411.

Ryan, W. (1971). *Blaming the victim*. New York: Random House.

Sabnani, H. B., Ponterro, J. G., & Borodovksy, L. G. (1991). White racial identity development and cross-cultural counselor training: A stage model. *Counseling Psychologist, 19*(1), 76–102.

Sacks, O. (1985). *The man who mistook his wife for a hat*. New York: Summit Books.

Sacks, O. (1995). *An anthropologist on Mars*. New York: Knopf.

Sameroff, A. (1977). Concepts of humanity in primary prevention. In G. W. Albee & J. M. Joffe (Eds.), *The issue: An overview of primary prevention* (Vol. 1; pp. 42–61). Hanover, NH: University Press of New England.

Sampson, E. E. (1989). The challenge of social change for psychology: Globalization and psychology's theory of the person. *American Psychologist, 44*, 914–921.

Sampson, E. E. (1993). Identity politics: Challenges to Psychology's understanding. *American Psychologist, 48*, 1219–1230.

Sanday, P. R. (1981). The socio-cultural context of rape: A cross-cultural study. *Journal of Social Issues, 37*, 5–27.

Sansone, C., & Harackiewicz, J. M. (1996). I don't feel like it: The function of interest in self-regulation. In L. Martin & A.Tesser (Eds.), *Striving and feeling: Interactions between goals and affect* (pp. 203–228). Hillsdale, NJ: Erlbaum.

Sarason, S. B. (1981). An asocial psychology and a misdirected clinical psychology. *American Psychologist, 36*, 827–836.

Sarason, S. B. (1981). *Psychology misdirected.* New York: Free Press.

Sarason, S. B. (1993). *The case for change.* San Francisco: Jossey-Bass.

Sarason, S. B., Carroll, C. F., Maton, K., Cohen, S., & Lorentz, E. (1977). *Human services and resource networks: Rationale, possibilities, and public policy.* San Francisco: Jossey-Bass.

Sarason, S. B., & Lorentz, E. (1979). *The challenge of the resource exchange network.* San Francisco: Jossey-Bass.

Scales, P. (1981). The new opposition to sex education: A powerful threat to a democratic society. *Journal of School Health, 51*, 300–304.

Scarr, S. (1992). Developmental theories for the 1990s: Development and individual differences. *Child Development, 63*, 1–19.

Scheibe, K. E. (1985). Historical perspective on the presented self. In B. R. Schlenker (Ed.), *The self and social life* (pp. 33–64). New York: McGraw-Hill.

Schlenker, B. R. (Ed.). (1985). *The self and social life.* New York: McGraw-Hill.

Schneider, S. (1987). Meanwhile, back at the ranch … (Can community psychology save psychology?) *American Journal of Community Psychology, 15*, 591–602.

Schwitzgebel, R. K. (1977). Professional accountability in the treatment and release of dangerous persons. In B. D. Sales (Ed.), *Perspectives in law and psychology*: Vol. I. *The criminal justice system.* New York, Plenum.

Segal, J. (1979). Child abuse: A review of research. In E. Corman (Ed.), *Families today—A research sampler of families and children* (Vol. II; pp. 577–606). (NIMH Science Monographs I). Washington, DC: U.S. Government Printing Office.

Segall, M. H., Dasen, P. R., Berry, J. W., & Poortinga, Y. H. (1990). *Human behavior in global perspective: An introduction to cross-cultural psychology.* New York: Pergamon.

Segall, M. H., Doornbos, M., & Davis, C. (1976). *Political identity: A case study from Uganda.* Syracuse, NY: Maxwell Foreign and Comparative Studies/East AFRICA XXIV.

Seligman, M. E. P. (1998, October). What is the "good life"? [President's Column]. *American Psychological Association Monitor*, p. 2.

Sereny, G. (1985). *The invisible children: Child prostitution in America, West Germany and Great Britain.* New York: Knopf.

Shah, S. (1978). Dangerousness: A paradigm for exploring some issues in law and psychology. *American Psychologist, 33*, 224–237.

Shah, S. (1981). Dangerousness: Conceptual, prediction, and public policy issues. In J. Hays, T. K. Roberts, & K. S. Solvay (Eds.), *Violence and the violent individual.* New York: S. P. Medical and Scientific Books.

Sherif, M., & Sherif, C. W. (1953). *Groups in harmony and tension.* New York: Harper.

Sherif, M., & Sherif, C. W. (1956). *An Outline of Social Psychology* (2nd ed.). New York: Harper.

Shields, P. with John Grainy. (1981). *Guns don't die—People do.* New York: Arbor House.

Shinn, M. (1987). Expanding community psychology's domain. *American Journal of Community Psychology, 15*, 555–574.

Shivji, J. (1985). Law and conditions of child labour in colonial Tanganyika. *International Journal of the Sociology of Law, 13*, 221–235.

Silber, E., Hamburg, D. A., Coelho, G. V., Murphy, E. B., Rosenberg, M., & Pearlin, L. I. (1961).

Adaptive behavior in competent adolescents: Coping with the anticipation of college. *Archives of General Psychiatry, 1423*(3), 289–296.

Singh, R. G. (1979). Forms and patterns of societal resistance to dacoity: A critical overview. *Indian Journal of Social Work, 40,* 125–137.

Sinha, D. (1987). Psychology in India: A historical perspective. In G. H. Blowers & A. M. Turtle (Eds.), *Psychology moving East: The status of Western psychology in Asia and Oceania* (pp. 39–52). Boulder, CO: Westview Press.

Sinha, J. B. P., & Pandey, J. (1968). The *n*-Ach/*n*-Cooperation under limited/unlimited resource conditions. *Journal of Experimental Social Psychology, 4,* 233–246.

Sinha, J. B. P. (1981). In search of research identity In J. Pandey (Ed.), *Perspectives on experimental social psychology in India* (pp. 241–252). New Delhi: Concept Publishing.

Sinha, J. B. P., & Pandey, J. (1970). Strategies of high *n*Ach persons. *Psychologia, 13,* 60–63.

Skinner, B. F. (1971). *Beyond freedom and dignity.* New York: Knopf.

Smart, N. (1981). *Beyond ideology: Religion and the future of western civilization.* New York: Harper and Row.

Smith, M. B. (1966). Explorations in competence: A study of Peace Corps teachers in Ghana. *American Psychologist, 21,* 556–566.

Smith, M. B. (1968). Competence and socialization. In J. Clausen (Ed.), *Socialization and Society* (pp. 270–321). Boston: Little, Brown.

Smith, M. B. (1972). Normality: For an abnormal age. In D. Offer & D. X. Freedman (Eds.), *Modern psychiatry and clinical research: Essays in honor of Roy R. Grinker, Sr.* (pp. 102–119). New York: Basic Books.

Smith, M. B., & Hobbs, N. (1966). The community and the community mental health center. *American Psychologist, 15,* 113–118.

Smyer, M. A., & Gatz, M. (1979). Aging and mental health: Business as usual? *American Psychologist, 34,* 240–246.

Snowden, L. (1987). The peculiar successes of community psychology: Service delivery to ethnic minorities and the poor. *American Journal of Community Psychology, 15,* 575–586.

Snyder, C. R. (1994). *The psychology of hope: You can get there from here.* New York: Free Press.

Snyder, C. R., Higgins, R. L., & Stucky, R. J. (1983). *Excuses: Masquerades in search of grace.* New York: Wiley.

Sperry, R. (August 21, 1993). *A powerful paradigm made stronger.* Invited Address presented at the 101st American Psychological Association Convention, Toronto, Canada.

Sperry, R. W. (1992). Turnabout on consciousness: A mentalist view. *The Journal of Mind and Behavior, 13,* 259–280.

Stark, W. (1992). Empowerment and social change: Health promotion within the Healthy Cities Project of WHO—Steps toward a participative prevention program. In G. W. Albee, L. A. Bond, & T. V. Cook-Monsey (Eds.), *Improving children's lives: Global perspectives on prevention* (pp. 151–167). Newbury Park, CA: Sage.

Staub, E. (1978a). *Positive social behavior and morality: Vol. 1. Social and personal influences.* New York: Academic Press.

Staub, E. (1978b). *Positive social behavior and morality: Vol. 2. Socialization and development.* New York: Academic Press.

Staub, E. (1989). *The roots of evil.* New York: Cambridge University Press.

Staub, E., Bar-Tal, D., Karylowski, J., & Reykowski, J. (1984). *Development and maintenance of prosocial behavior: International perspectives on positive morality.* New York: Plenum.

Steele, C. M. (August, 1999). Thin Ice: "Stereotype threat" and black college students. *Atlantic Monthly, 284*(2), 44–54.

Sternberg, R. J. (1997). The concept of intelligence and its role in lifelong learning and success. *American Psychologist, 52,* 1030–1037.

Stix, G. (January, 1996). Listening to culture: Psychiatry takes a leaf from anthropology. *Scientific American*, 16, 21.

Straus, M., & Gelles, R. (1979). Physical violence in families. In E. G. Corfman, *Families today—A research sampler on families and children* (Vol. II; pp. 553–576). (NIMH Science Monographs I). Washington, DC: U.S. Government Printing Office.

Strauss, J. S. (1979). Social and cultural influences on psychopathology. *Annual Review of Psychology, 30*, 397–415.

Strauss, J. S. (1989). Subjective experiences of schizophrenia: Toward a new dynamic psychiatry—II. *Schizophrenia Bulletin, 15*(2), 179–187.

Strother, C. R. (Ed.). (1956). *Psychology and mental health*. Washington, D.C: American Psychological Association.

Struening, E. I., & Guttentag, M. (1975). *Handbook of evaluation research* (Vol. 1). Beverly Hills, CA: Sage.

Sue, S. & Zane, N. (1987). The role of culture and cultural techniques in psychotherapy: A critique and reformulation. *American Psychologist, 42*, 37–45.

Suedfeld, P. (1990). (Ed.), *Psychology and torture*. New York: Hemisphere.

Sullivan, J. L., & Transue, J. E. (1999). The psychological underpinnings of democracy: A selective review of research on political tolerance, interpersonal trust, and social capital. *Annual Review of Psychology, 50*, 625–650.

Sumner, W. G. (1906). *Folkways*. Boston: Ginn.

Sweet, J. A., & Bumpass, L. A. (1987). *American families and households*. New York: Russell Sage Foundation.

Szapocznik, J., Scopetta, M. A., Kurtines, W., & Arnalde, M. (1978). Theory and measurement of acculturation. *International Journal of Psychology, 12*, 113–130.

Szasz, T. S. (1970). *The manufacture of madness*. New York: Holt, Rinehart and Winston.

Szasz, T. S. (1978). *The myth of psychotherapy*. Garden City, NY: Doubleday.

Taylor, S., & Brown, J. D. (1988). Illusion and well-being: A social psychological perspective on mental health. *Psychological Bulletin, 103*, 193–210.

Tibbitts, F. L. (1981). *An analysis of the factors promoting middle-class, white-collar participation in the New Orleans Chapter of David Duke's Knights of the Ku Klux Klan*. Unpublished B. A. honors thesis, Harvard-Radcliffe College.

Tiryakian, E. A. (1980). Sociological dimensions of uprootedness. In G. V. Coelho & P. I. Ahmed (Eds.), *Uprooting and development* (pp. 131–152). New York: Plenum.

Toch, H. (1969). *Violent men*. Chicago: Aldine.

Toch, H. (1979). Alienation as a vehicle of change. *Journal of Community Psychology, 7*, 3–11.

Toch, H. (1992). *Violent men: An inquiry into the psychology of violence* (*revised ed.*). Washington, DC: American Psychological Association.

Tolan, P. H., Keys, C., Chertok, F., & Jason, L. (Eds.). (1990). *Researching community psychology: Integrating theories and methods*. Washington, DC: American Psychological Association.

Tolley, H., Jr. (1987). *The U.N. Commission on Human Rights*. Boulder, CO: Westview Press.

Tomes, H. (April, 1999). The need for cultural competence. *APA Monitor*, p. 31.

Tommasello, A., Tyler, F., Tyler, S., & Zhang, Y. (1992). Psychosocial correlates of drug use among Latino youth leading autonomous lives. *International Journal of Addictions, 28*, 435–450.

Tornblom, K. Y., & Nilsson, B. O. (1993). The effect of matching resource to source on their perceived importance and sufficiency. In U. G. Foa, J. Converse, Jr., K. Y. Tornblom, & E. B. Foa (Eds.), *Resource theory: Explorations and applications* (pp. 81–96). New York: Academic Press.

Triandis, H. C. (1980). Introduction to handbook of cross-cultural psychology. In H. C. Triandis & W. W. Lambert (Eds.), *Handbook of cross-cultural psychology: Perspectives* (Vol. 1; pp. 1–14). Boston: Allyn and Bacon.

Triandis, H. C. (1990). Cross-cultural studies of individualism and collectivism. In J. Berman (Ed.), *Cross-cultural perspectives* (pp. 41–133). Lincoln: University of Nebraska Press.

Triandis, H. C., & Gelfand, M. J. (1998). Converging measurement of horizontal and vertical individualism and collectivism. *Journal of Personality and Social Psychology, 74,* 118–128.

Triandis, H. C., Kashima, Y., Shimada, E., & Vallareal, M. (1986). Acculturation indices as a means of confirming cultural differences. *International Journal of Psychology, 21,* 43–70.

Triandis, H. C., & Lambert, W. W. (Eds.). (1980). *Handbook of cross-cultural psychology: Perspectives* (Vol. 1). Boston: Allyn and Bacon.

Trickett, E. J., Watts, R. J., & Birman, D. (1994). *Human diversity: Perspectives on people in context.* San Francisco: Jossey-Bass.

Turnbull, C. M. (1972). *The mountain people.* New York: Simon and Schuster.

Turtle, A. M. (1987). Introduction: A silk road for psychology. In G. H. Blowers & A. M. Turtle (Eds.), *Psychology moving East: The status of Western psychology in Asia and Oceania* (pp. 1–21). Boulder, CO: Westview Press.

Twaite, J. A., Silitsky, S., & Luchow, A. K. (1998). *Children of divorce.* Northvale, NJ: Jason Aronson.

Tyler, F. B. (1970). The shaping of the science. *American Psychologist, 25,* 219–226.

Tyler, F. B. (1978). Individual psychosocial competence: A personality configuration. *Educational and Psychological Measurement, 38,* 309–323.

Tyler, F. B. (1987). Psychosocial leaps and spirals. In J. Pandey (Ed.), *Perception and social reality* (pp. 61–79). New Delhi: Concept Publishing.

Tyler, F. B. (1989). A psychosocial perspective on cross-cultural unity in psychology. In D. M. Keats, D. Munro, & L. Mann (Eds.), *Heterogeneity in cross-cultural psychology* (pp. 54–65). Amsterdam: Swets and Zeitlinger.

Tyler, F. B. (1990). A psychosocial perspective on cross-cultural unity in psychology. In D. M. Katz, L. Munro, & L. Mann (Eds.), *Heterogeneity in cross-cultural psychology* (pp. 54–65). Berwyn, PA: Swets.

Tyler, F. B. (1991). Psychosocial competence in developing countries. *Psychology and Developing Societies, 3,* 171–192.

Tyler, F. B. (July, 1992). Resource collaboration: A model of psychology derived from cross-cultural/cross-disciplinary projects. In F. B. Tyler (Chair), *The social psychology of cross-cultural psychology.* Symposium conducted at the XIth Congress of the International Association of Cross-Cultural Psychology, Liege, Belgium.

Tyler, F. B. (1995). Community psychology in the United States: An evolving history. In A. Palmonari & B. Zani (Eds.), *Manuale di psicologia di communita* (pp. 157–204). Bologna, Italy: Societa Editrice Il Mulino.

Tyler, F. B. (1996). Psychology, social policy and social development. In C. Okorodudu (Chair, Integrated Session), *Scientific psychology and agenda-setting conferences of the United Nations.* Meeting of the XXVI International Congress of Psychology, Montreal, Canada.

Tyler, F. B. (June, 1997). *Urban settings, youth violence, and prosocial communities.* Invited paper presented at International Conference on Urban Children. Dragsvoll, Norway.

Tyler, F. B. (1999). Cross-cultural psychology: Is it time to revise the model? In W. J. Lonner, D. L. Dinnel, D. K. Forgays, & S. A. Hayes. (Eds.), *Merging past, present, and future in cross-cultural psychology: Selected proceedings of the 14th International Congress of the International Association for Cross-Cultural Psychology* (pp. 116–123). Lisse, the Netherlands: Swets and Zeitlinger.

Tyler, F. B., Brome, D. R., & Williams, J. E. (1991). *Ethnic validity, ecology, and psychotherapy.* New York: Plenum.

Tyler, F. B., Dhawan, N., & Sinha, Y. (1988). Adaptation patterns of Indian and American adolescents. *Journal of Social Psychology, 128,* 633–645.

Tyler, F. B., Dhawan, N., & Sinha, Y. (1989). Cultural contributions to constructing locus of control attributions. *Genetic, Social, and General Psychology Monographs, 115*(2), 205–220.

Tyler, F. B., & Gatz, M. A. (1976). If community psychology is so great, why don't we try it? *Professional Psychology, 7,* 185–194.

Tyler, F. B., Gatz, M. A., & Keenan, K. A. (1979). A constructivist analysis of the Rotter I-E Scale. *Journal of Personality, 47,* 11–35.

Tyler, F. B., & Pargament, K. I. (1981). Racial and personal factors and the complexities of competence-oriented changes in a high school group counseling program. *American Journal of Community Psychology, 9,* 697–714.

Tyler, F. B., & Pargament, K. I. (1982). Behavioral attributes of psychosocial competence. Unpublished manuscript.

Tyler, F. B., Paragment, K. I., & Gatz, M. (1983). The resource collaborator role: A model for interaction between change agents and community members. *American Psychologist, 38,* 388–398.

Tyler, F. B., & Sinha, Y. (1988). Psychosocial competence and belief systems among Hindus. *Genetic, Social, and General Psychology Monographs, 114,* 33–49.

Tyler, F. B., & Speisman, J. C. (1967). An emerging scientist–professional role in psychology. *American Psychologist, 22,* 839–847.

Tyler, F. B., & Tyler, S. L. (August 18, 1996). Street children and human dignity. Outcast and miscast: Street children and victims. In J. Pandey, Chair, Symposium. *Poverty and deprivation: Psychological and social consequences.* Meeting of the XXVI International Congress of Psychology, Montreal, Canada.

Tyler, F. B., Tyler, S. L., Echeverry, J. J., & Zea, M. C. (1991). Making it on the streets of Bogota: A psychosocial study of street youth. *Genetic, Social and General Psychology Monographs, 117,* 395–417.

Tyler, F. B., Tyler, S. L., Tommasello, A., & Connolly, M. R. (1992). Huckleberry Finn and street youth everywhere: An approach to primary prevention. In G. W. Albee, L. A. Bond, & T. W. Cook-Monsey (Eds.), *Improving children's lives: Global perspectives on prevention* (pp. 200–212). Newbury Park, CA: Sage.

Tyler, F. B., Tyler, S. L., Tommasello, A., & Zhang, Y. (1992). Psychosocial characteristics of marginal immigrant Latino youth. *Youth and Society, 24,* 92–115.

Tyler, F. B., & Varma, M. (1988). Help-seeking and helping behavior in children as a function of psychosocial competence. *Journal of Applied Developmental Psychology, 9,* 219–231.

Tyler, T., Boeckmann, R. J., Smith, H. J., & Huo, J. H. (1997). *Social justice in a diverse society.* Boulder, CO: Westview.

Tyler, T., & Caine, A. (1981). The influence of outcomes and procedures on satisfaction with formal leaders. *Journal of Personality and Social Psychology, 41,* 642–655.

Tyler, T., & Folger, R. (1980). Distributional and procedural aspects of satisfaction with citizen–police encounters. *Basic and Applied Social Psychology, 1,* 281–292.

Tyler, T., & Smith, H. J. (1998). Social justice and social movements. In D. Gilbert, S. T. Fiske, & G. Lindzey (Eds.), *Handbook of social psychology* (4th ed.; pp. 1–185). New York: Oxford University Press.

UNICEF (1997). *The state of the world's children.* New York: Oxford University Press.

United Nations action in the field of human rights. (1978). New York: United Nations.

United States. (1995). *The Declaration of Independence and the Constitution of the United States of America: The texts.* Washington, DC: National Defense University Press.

U.S. Department of Labor. (1994). *By the sweat and toil of children: The use of child labor in U.S. manufactured and mined imports* (Vol. 1). Washington, DC: Bureau of International Labor Affairs.

Vallance, T. R. (1966). Project Camelot: An interim postlude. *American Psychologist, 21,* 441–444.

Vance, E. T. (1973). Social disability. *American Psychologist, 28,* 839–847.

Vandenbos, G. (1986). Psychotherapy research: A special issue [Special issue]. *American Psychologist, 42,* 111–112.

Veno, A., & Veno, E. (1992). Managing public order at the Australian Motor Grand Prix. In D. Thomas & A. Veno (Eds.). *Psychology and social change* (pp. 74–92). Palmerston North, NZ: Dunmore Press.

Ventis, W. L. (1995). The relationship between religion and mental health. *Journal of Social Issues, 51,* 33–48.

Walberg, H. J., Rasher, S. P., & Singh, R. (1977). An operational test of a three-factor theory of classroom social perception. *Psychology in the Schools, 14,* 508–513.

Walker, L. E. (1999). Psychology and domestic violence around the world. *American Psychologist, 54,* 21–29.

Warner, B. S. (1991). *The effect of individual psychosocial competence and reference group pressure on the support given by young black fathers to their children.* Unpublished master's thesis, University of Maryland, College Park.

Washington Consulting Group. (1974). *Uplift: What people themselves can do.* Salt Lake City: Olympus.

Weber, S. N. (1994). The need to be: The socio-cultural significance of Black Language. In L. A. Samovar & R. E. Porter (Eds.), *Intercultural communication: A reader* (pp. 221–226). Belmont, CA: Wadsworth.

Werner, E. E. (1989). High risk children in young adulthood: A longitudinal study from birth to 32 years. *American Journal of Orthopsychiatry, 59*(1), 72–81.

Werner, E. E. (1995). Resilience in development. *Current Directions in Psychological Science, 4*(3), 81–85.

Wicker, A. W. (1985). Getting out of our conceptual ruts: Strategies for expanding conceptual frameworks. *American Psychologist, 40,* 1094–1103.

Wicker, T. (1975). *A time to die.* New York: Quadrangle/The New York Times Book Company.

Wilcox, B. L., & Naimark, H. (1992). The rights of the child: Progress toward human dignity. In G. W. Albee, L. A. Bond, & T. V. Cook-Monsey (Eds.). *Improving children's lives: Global perspectives on prevention* (pp. 357–358). Newbury Park, CA: Sage.

Wilson, G. T. (1998). Manual-based treatment and clinical practice. *Clinical psychology: Science and practice, 5*(3), 363–375.

Wolff, T. (1994). Keynote address given at the fourth biennial conference. *The Community Psychologist, 27*(3), 20–26.

Wood, N. P. (1979). *Weusi suspiciousness.* Unpublished master's thesis, University of Maryland, College Park.

Wood, P. J., & Schwass, M. (1993). Cultural safety: A framework for changing attitudes. *Nursing Praxis in New Zealand, 8*(1), 4–15.

Youmans, E. (1967). Disengagement among older rural and urban men. In E. Youmans (Ed.), *The older rural Americans.* Lexington: University of Kentucky Press.

Young, C. E., Giles, D. E., & Plantz, M. (1982). Natural networks: Help-giving and help-seeking in two rural communities. *American Journal of Community Psychology, 10,* 457–469.

Zeichner, A., & Pihl, R. O. (1979). Effects of alcohol and behavior contingencies on human aggression. *Journal of Abnormal Psychology, 88,* 153–160.

Zuriff, G. (1999). Child sexual abuse article [letter to the editor]. *APA Monitor, 30*(7), 3, 5.

Zwerdling, D. (May–June, 1979). Employee ownership: How well is it working? *Working Papers,* 15–27.

Zwerling, I., Alvarez, R., Batson, R., Carr, A., Parks, P., Peck, H., Shervington, W., & Tyler, F. B. (1976). *Racism, elitism, professionalism: Barriers to community mental health.* New York: Jason Aronson.

INDEX